Commentary on the Gospel According to Saint Luke

BY

Rev. G. A. McLaughlin, D. D.

Author of "A Living Sacrifice," "Inbred Sin," "A Clean
Heart," "Old Wine in New Bottles," "Saved and Kept,"
"The Vine and Branches," "The Promised Gift," etc.

by

SCHMUL PUBLISHERS

1974

SALEM, OHIO

PREFACE

I

An eminent ecclesiastical authority has said concerning Holiness as found in the Word of God, ''It breathes in the prophecy, thunders in the law, murmurs in the narrative, whispers in the promises, supplicates in the prayers, sparkles in the poetry, resounds in the songs, speaks in the types, glows in the imagery, voices in the language and burns in the spirit of the whole scheme, from its Alpha to Omega, from its beginning to its end. Holiness! Holiness needed! Holiness required! Holiness offered! Holiness attainable! Holiness a present duty, a present privilege, a present enjoyment, is the progress and completeness of its wondrous theme! It is the truth glowing all over, webbing all through revelation; the glorious truth which sparkles and whispers and sings and shouts in all its history and biography and poetry and prophecy and precept and promise and prayer; the great central truth of the system. The wonder is, that all do not see, that any rise up to question a truth so conspicuous, so glorious, so full of comfort.'' Another authority has written a book to show that Holiness is ''the central idea of Christianity.'' This fact, however, is not generally recognized or admitted among the commentators. Holiness seems to many to be a matter of incidental mention in the Scriptures, and many commentators succeed very well in concealing it, or in those marked passages that teach it, treat it so indefinitely as to make it intangible and misty. Hence this commentary, which attempts to reveal Holiness (either in theory or practice) in every verse, claims the right of existence. Most of the early commentaries were written from a Calvanistic standpoint, which denied the possibility of living free, either from original sin or actual transgression; asserting

iii

that Christ cannot cleanse and keep from sin, but that this
friendly work must be performed by our enemy, Death; or, if
some have admitted that Christ can perform the work, they
have denied that the Great Physician could or would cure until
we were removed from the baleful atmosphere of this sinful
world. Arminian commentators have been affected, with but few
exceptions, with this unscriptural, dogmatic taint. As we study
both Calvinistic and Arminian authorities, we many times notice
passages where, to be true to the Scripture, they unconsciously
drop their theology, and clearly and explicitly declare the possibility of being cleansed from all sin. If any reader shall say,
as we quote from these authorities, that we do not represent their
thoughts as they themselves intended, we reply, that we represent
at least Adam Clarke, John Wesley and some others correctly,
and that other writers were obliged to state their opinions as
they did or be unfaithful to Scripture, and we quote some of
them to show the inconsistency of any system that represents
Jesus Christ as a perfect Saviour, and at the same time theoret-
ically denies his power to heal the malady of sin at the very time
of the sickness. In the treatment of the miracles of Christ, commentators have been obliged to consider the healing of the body as
a type of the healing of the soul, or get no spiritual lessons from
these events. But in so doing, complete, instantaneous faith-cures
of the body have been represented as symbols of the same cures
wrought upon the souls of men. It is impossible to find a commentator who seeks to convey spiritual teaching from the cures
of lepers, who does not state the anti-type of soul-healing as
clearly and unequivocally as we could wish. We call especial
attention to the treatment of the healing of leprosy by nearly all
the commentators, who state clearly and positively that Jesus can
cleanse from the leprosy of sin. As leprosy is universally accepted
as a type of sin, its cure must therefore be accepted as a type of
the cure of sin. A large part of the cures of Christ must have a
spiritual interpretation, or none at all that shall be of any
spiritual profit to us. Happily we are not left in doubt as to this
question. Jesus interpreted to us many of his miracles, and thus
gave us the principle of interpreting miracles spiritually. (See
John 6:27-64; 9:39-41; Luke 5:1-10.) Our view of the great and

underlying thought of the Scriptures is further substantiated by
all or nearly all those grand passages which tell us the end and
aim of the Bible. (See Psalms 119:1-4, 9, 11; John 15:3; 17:17;
Eph. 5:26; 2 Tim. 3:16, 17; 2 Peter 1:4; and others.)

II

It may be objected that the author sees Holiness everywhere
in the Scriptures because he is determined to see it there. In
reply we would say that doubtless the objector may not see it
there, because he does *not* wish to see it. The scribes and Pharisees, who were certainly as well acquainted with the text of the
Old Testament as any modern divines or scholars, did not recognize the portraits of Jesus of Nazareth in those writings at all.
We would say still further that the great proof of the inspiration
of the Scriptures is in the power and privilege of proving them
true by experience, if we come candidly to Jesus seeking to know
and do his will. The doctrines of the new birth and the witness
of the Spirit, as taught in the Scriptures, have been proved true
again and again in human lives. And testimonies to this effect
are accepted in the Church today. The doctrine of the baptism
of the Holy Spirit, a work subsequent to conversion, whereby the
heart is cleansed from all sin, is just as clearly testified to by the
saints from all the denominations, men and women of sober judgment, scholarly wisdom and consistent lives.

Lastly. This commentary is not written polemically, or with
any desire to reflect on anybody or anything but sin. It is written
to assist that large and growing body of believers whose understanding, through experience of these truths, has been opened to
see these things; who have found, since their baptism of love,
that the Bible is a new book; who have the *revised version* by
the best of the revisers—the Holy Spirit.

CONCERNING THE GOSPEL BY ST. LUKE.

St. Luke was a well-trained scholar; as a physician he had
enjoyed greater educational privileges than the other evangelists.
Hence his account of the life of Jesus is the most systematic and
finished. He personally obtained his facts from those who had

seen the works and ministry of Jesus. On this account he presents a more complete biography than the other three, although they had seen him and wrote from personal knowledge. A scholarly, trained writer, who draws and combines from all sources, gives to succeeding generations a more complete picture and a better analysis of character than is possible from the testimony of any single eye-witness. The many-sided character of Christ would produce different impressions upon different individuals, according to the especial characteristics of each. Luke took the various portraits presented by different artists and blended them into one—the Christ, a complete Saviour for all men. Matthew wrote chiefly to show him as the Jewish Messiah. Mark wrote to reveal him to the power-worshipping Romans, as an omnipotent being. Mark's gospel gives chiefly displays of his divine power. John wrote especially to establish his deity. In thus exhibiting a Saviour, sufficient for all the needs of humanity, Luke dwells especially upon his humanity; as a man he saves us by his life and his death. He is the pattern man, our great example. Luke shows us how Christ exemplified Christian holiness; the manner in which we are to carry out a life of perfect love in all the emergencies and detail of everyday life. The mission of this gospel is similar to that of John the Baptist, as recorded in Chapter 1:77, ''To give knowledge of salvation unto his people by the remission of their sins.'' This gospel also illustrates, in the many cures of physical disease, the instantaneous healing of sin by faith.

CHAPTER I.

SOME PEOPLE WHO WERE MADE HOLY IN THIS LIFE.

Introduction. Vs. 1-4. A Proper Candidate for Entire Sanctification. Vs. 5-12. Holiness Is Greatness in the Sight of God. Vs. 13-17. The Faith of the Justified Lacks Completeness. Vs. 18-25. An Entirely Consecrated Woman. Vs. 26-38. Another Entirely Consecrated Woman. Vs. 39-45. Praise is the Language of Holy People. Vs. 46-56. A Spirit-Filled Man. Vs. 57-67. A Spirit-Filled Man Praises God. Vs. 68-80.

INTRODUCTION. Vs. 1-4.

1 Forasmuch as many have taken in hand to set forth in order a declaration of those things which are most surely believed among us,

2 Even as they delivered them unto us, which from the beginning were eyewitnesses, and ministers of the word;

3 It seemed good to me also, having had perrect understanding of all things from the very first, to write unto thee in order, most excellent Theophilus,

4 That thou mightest know the certainty of those things, wherein thou hast been instructed.

These four verses are St. Luke's introduction to the whole book. They are written in elegant language in the original Greek, and show that Luke was a fine scholar. They give his reason for writing ''The Gospel According to St. Luke.'' This Gospel, unlike the other three has an introduction to show why one who is a Gentile and not an eye-witness should write it.

TITLE.

The title in the original is ''According to St. Luke,'' not ''By St. Luke.'' Matthew, Mark, Luke and John were but messengers or heralds of the truth. They did not originate the Gospel. They only delivered it ''according'' to the manner and method which God enjoined. ''Saint Luke'' can just as well be translated *Holy Luke*. A saint is a holy person, hence the title means The Message of God, telling the Good News of Jesus according to the utterance and rendering of holy Luke. *The world is indebted to holy men for its best light.* The Bible was written by holy men. There have been holy men on earth in spite of the denial of the possibility of holiness by some people.

This introduction has unfortunately in some parts been inaccurately translated in the King James Version. The Revised Version has rendered it correctly thus: ''Forasmuch as many have taken in hand to draw up a narrative concerning those matters which have been fulfilled among us.'' This is somewhat different from the King James Version and shows that Luke, like Matthew, looked upon the life of Jesus as the fulfillment of prophecy although Luke does not refer to the special prophecies that Jesus fulfilled as much as Matthew.

The holy life of Jesus could not but make a stir, hence many attempts had been made in that age to write his life, by uninspired men. These biographies were so inaccurate and obscure, that Luke makes it a reason under the supervision of St. Paul, his bosom companion, for writing a full and accurate account. One great truth underlies these attempts to write the biography of Jesus by so many in all ages; and that is that holy character is the great miracle of the Gospel and it always has and always will challenge the attention of men. The biographies of holy people ought to be written as far as possible, for the benefit of the world. They ought to be written out accurately by their friends just as Luke writes the life of his Master.

''*Even as they delivered them to us which from the beginning were eye witnesses, and ministers of the word.*'' The phrase ''Which from the beginning were eye-witnesses and ministers'' does not refer to St. Luke, but to those who were actual witnesses of the events of Jesus' life. Luke of course wrote this Gospel sometime after the events occurred. There were narratives of the wonderful life of Jesus, some written and some oral, which were circulated among the Hebrew people. These narratives were not the other three Gospels, for Matthew's Gospel was not yet in circulation, and Mark wrote his in Italy. So this does not refer to them. Luke was not an eye-witness but so faithful had those, who had seen Jesus been in preaching and testifying, that he had become a believer. The world ought to know a great deal about Jesus by the testimony and lives of his friends. In these days the world ought not to have to search the scriptures to discover that there was a holy Jesus. It ought to be found out from the lives of his friends. The people of that day, who knew Jesus, had written out or told their experience with Jesus. How could anyone, who had seen Jesus keep from telling it! So Matthew, Mark, Luke and John were not the only writers about Jesus. Others had also written.

"It seemed good to me also having had perfect understanding." Here again the Revised Version gives the true rendering thus: "It seemed good to me also, having traced the course of all things accurately from the first." This implies that many of the narratives were incomplete and doubtless some of the oral narratives had become faulty from being spoken. There are very few people who can hear a story and repeat it accurately. So St. Luke under the inspiration of the Holy Spirit and the help of his dear friend Paul, carefully and laboriously collected the facts from the eye witnesses. Although he was inspired by the Holy Ghost and helped to accurately present the facts, yet this did not excuse him from the most patient and pains-taking labor. Inspiration and divine grace in the heart are no substitutes for carefulness and hard work. A holy man will not expect the Lord to bless sloth and carelessness. So Luke wrote the facts "in order." This is the scientific method.

"Most excellent Theophilus." The name Theophilus signifies in the Greek, "A lover of truth." Hence some have supposed that this name does not stand for a real person but for all lovers of truth, and is thus used symbolically. We cannot so regard it. "Most excellent" was a title given people of rank in those days. We believe this Gospel was dedicated to some person of rank by the name of Theophilus, to whom also Luke dedicates the Book of Acts (Acts 1:1). We have no other example of any book in the Bible or letter or epistle written to any symbolical character. The gospel is a direct message to people of every rank and station in society. St. Luke was a layman writing to a layman—Theophilus—hence the Roman Catholic assertion that the Bible must not be read by the laity falls to the ground. It is a palpable error. ''That thou mightest know the certainty of those things.'' The Christian church had begun to expand and multiply its converts, at the time that this Gospel was written. It was necessary therefore that the converts be trained and one of the essentials of this training was a clear and authentic account of the life and teachings of Jesus, because he had gone into the heavens. Luke was just the person qualified to do this, not only by reason of his superior scholarship, but also by reason of his intimate acquaintance with St. Paul. This friendship was warrant enough to the church for the certainty of these statements of Luke. A study of the Book of Acts shows that Luke was a constant companion of Paul.

Thank God there is an element of certainty in the Christian religion. It is more than a theory. It rests on solid facts. It has certainty for its claims. It is our privilege to be experimentally certain of these truths, of which we have *heard* since childhood. The most certain knowledge that we have is not that of the intellect, but that of the affections; not of the head but of the heart. We are more certain of what we feel and love and realize within our consciousness than of what we see or hear. God gives an experience of the inner life to those who do his will. The true method of knowing the authenticity and genuineness of the Bible is the heart proof.

A PROPER CANDIDATE FOR ENTIRE SANCTIFICATION.

Vs. 5-12.

5   There was in the days of Herod, the king of Judæa, a certain priest named Zacharias, of the course of Abia: and his wife *was* of the daughters of Aaron, and her name *was* Elisabeth.

6   And they were both righteous before God, walking in all the commandments and ordinances of the Lord blameless.

7   And they had no child, because that Elisabeth was barren, and they both were *now* well stricken in years.

8   And it came to pass, that while he executed the priest's office before God in the order of his course,

9   According to the custom of the priest's office, his lot was to burn incense when he went into the temple of the Lord.

10   And the whole multitude of the people were praying without at the time of incense.

11   And there appeared unto him an angel of the Lord standing on the right side of the altar of incense.

12   And when Zacharias saw *him,* he was troubled, and fear fell upon him.

Luke begins his account even further back than Matthew. The latter begins with the birth of Jesus but Luke goes back to the circumstances preceding the birth of John the Baptist. Both events were in the reign of Herod, the Great, an Idumean who had been made king by the Romans of all the land originally possessed by the twelve tribes together with Idumea. The father of John the Baptist was a priest by the name of Zacharias which means ''The Man of God.'' It was a fitting title. He belonged to ''the course of Abia'' or Abijah. David divided the sons of Aaron into twenty-four courses. Each of these courses or classes in turn took charge of the daily service at the temple for a week (from Sabbath to Sabbath). This would bring each priest into a service about twice a year. The courses of Abijah was the eighth (1 Chron. 24:3, 10, 19). The name of his wife was Elizabeth. The word means ''The fullness of God.''

They were both righteous before God. ''Or in other words they were both right before God.'' According to this it is not wrong for a priest to marry as the Roman Catholic Church asserts. They were married and righteous before God. No matter whether men called them righteous or wicked, they were righteous before God. He sees the motives and purposes of the heart. Luke goes still further and tells what this righteousness was, thus, ''Walking in all the commandments and ordinances of the Lord blameless.'' In every degenerate age there have been some good men in the priesthood. This couple lived without committing sin and they were under the Old Testament Dispensation. Yet some would have us believe that we can not so live under this dispensation. The New Testament definition of actual sin, (or sin as an act) is wilful transgression. These two people kept all the commandments and ordinances of God. Of course we all have such a high idea of the divine wisdom and goodness that we do not for a moment suppose that God would require anything of them beyond their ability. If they could live righteous before God under the Old Testament Dispensation, certainly we can do as well under the dispensation of the Holy Ghost, under which we live. Every truly regenerate man should so live. (1 John 3:9). This is the first step in holiness. It is initial holiness. "So perfect was their faith, and so pure their life, that God imputed *no blame* unto them. This was their *ordinary* spiritual state, yet it excluded not the *possibility* of sin." (Whedon.) Many today however plead for a so called Christian life, *below* the Old Testament standard. But Paul tells us we are expected as Christians to lead that kind of life. (Phil. 2:15.) This pious couple were good candidate for entire sanctification. Sinners are not candidates for this great blessing. Zacharias received the Fullness a few months later. See verse 67. There is not a passage in the New Testament that represents unsaved persons as either receiving or being urged to receive the fullness of the Holy Spirit. All such commands are addressed to those recognized as the people of God. No one else but the clearly justified have any hope or business to seek the Fullness.

These good people had no child. Among the Jews it was considered a great affliction to be childless. It would be a great blessing to this land if it were so considered today. Owing to their age it was along the line of human impossibilities for them to have a son at this time. But God often works along the line of human impossibilities.

Although the church was very corrupt yet it was possible for this good man and woman to live in it and be righteous before God. Fanatics have said in our day that this is impossible. The church was more corrupt then than some would have us believe that the church is today. But the record says these people were righteous before God. Zacharias went right on in the duties of the priestly office. No doubt his righteous heart was stirred at the corruption about him but he never wavered in his duty towards God. It was while in the discharge of duty that he met Gabriel and received the answer to his prayer which had been delayed for years. If we have not yet seen the answer to our prayers, we are to keep right on praying and be faithful in the discharge of duty.

Zacharias was chosen by the usual method of apportioning by lot the duties of the priests to burn incense during the week, in which his course served the temple worship. The altar of incense was in the Holy Place close to the veil which separated it from the Holy of Holies. We believe the incense of this altar symbolized the prayers of all true Christians, who seek to be admitted into the Holy of Holies—entire sanctification. Incense was burned twice a day in the temple—at 9 A. M. and 3 P. M. These occasions were called the hours of prayer. Regular hours of prayer are very helpful. Every church and every Christian today ought to have them.

As Zacharias went into the temple one day to offer sacrifice he received a remarkable answer to the prayers which he had offered for years. Let us notice the circumstances. The law required that the sacrifice be offered on the great altar in the court before the temple at the same time that the incense was offered on the golden altar in the Holy Place of the temple, and while the people were praying without. These three services were held simultaneously. The sweet odor of the incense was a symbol of prayer, for it is before God. It was this most significant time when the blood was flowing on the great altar in the outer court, the people were outside praying and Zacharias was burning incense that the latter was startled by seeing an angel standing at the right side of the altar of incense. This was the angel, Gabriel (Vs. 19), the same angel that had appeared to Daniel. This is the first angelic appearance mentioned in the New Testament. The half century that included the life of Jesus had more angelic manifestations than all the ages before or since. The dispensation of the earthly life of Jesus began with angel manifestations and concluded with them. (Acts 1:10.)

HOLINESS IS GREATNESS IN THE SIGHT OF GOD.
Vs. 13-17.

13 But the angel said unto him, Fear not, Zacharias: for thy prayer is heard; and thy wife Elisabeth shall bear thee a son, and thou shalt call his name John.
14 And thou shalt have joy and gladness; and many shall rejoice at his birth.

15 For he shall be great in the sight of the Lord, and shall drink neither wine nor strong drink; and he shall be filled with the Holy Ghost, even from his mother's womb.

16 And many of the children of Israel shall he turn to the Lord their God.

17 And he shall go before him in the spirit and power of Elias, to turn the hearts of the fathers to the children, and the disobedient to the wisdom of the just; to make ready a people prepared for the Lord.

Zacharias was frightened, as well he might be, for there had been no manifestations of angels to men for centuries. It was startling indeed. But the angel reassured him saying "Fear not." It will be noticed that the angels were constantly saying "Fear not" when they appeared to the servants of God. (See Chapt. 1:30; 2:10; Mark 16:6.) The angel was forerunner of the Gospel which says "Fear not" to the saved, under all circumstances. A better dispensation than that in which Zacharias lived was to come. The awe and dread of the old dispensation was to be exchanged for the fear-expelling Gospel.

"For thy prayer is heard." No one ought to fear, whose prayer is heard with favor. Since true prayer is always heard, he who prays sincerely and habitually ought to be freed from all fear. Zacharias must have been discouraged as time went on because his prayer was not heard. But God always hears our prayers and will answer, when the proper time comes. How few in this day like Zacharias make the obtaining of children the subject of prayer. Gabriel then assured him that he should have a son whom he should call John. The names John and Jesus were both given by divine appointment and by the same angel, Gabriel. (Vs. 31.) The name "John" means "The grace of God." It was very fitting that he, who was to open the Gospel dispensation and who was to preach "the grace of God that bringeth salvation" should be so named. Notice the names of this family— Zacharias, "The man of God," Elizabeth, "The fullness of God" and John, "The grace of God." We like the idea of scriptural and religious names. Some have derided the Puritans because of the religious names they gave their children. But they only followed the Bible usage. Gabriel added "And thou shalt have joy and gladness." Joy seems to be the inward state of the heart and gladness the outward expression of it. Certainly that is what every parent desires—children who shall bring joy and gladness to their hearts. But how many parents have been disappointed. We believe if people were as true to God as Zacharias and Elizabeth and sought children from God in prayer as they did there would be more happy homes. But this child would not only bring happiness to his own home, he would be a blessing to multitudes. "Many shall rejoice at his birth." The reason of their rejoicing would be because he would prepare them for the kingdom of heaven by his preaching. There is a peculiar bond of affection between the preacher and those whom he has helped into the kingdom of God by his preaching. Mankind rejoice in the characters of the good and great: and John was both. Their lives become the treasure of mankind. Unborn millions will yet rejoice in John the Baptist all down through the ages of the Christian church. "He shall be great in the sight of God." His parents were both *righteous* in the sight of God and he was to be *great* in the sight of God. What was the difference? It seems to us the difference was that John was to be filled with the Holy Ghost, which had not yet filled his parents. They were justified but not yet filled with the Holy Ghost. We must infer then, that to be filled with the Holy Ghost is a mark of greatness in the sight of God for Gabriel so explains it, "For he shall drink neither wine nor strong drink; and he shall be filled with the Holy Ghost from his mother's womb." He would have dominion over his animal appetites and be filled with the Spirit. Certainly the greater includes the less. It would be impossible to be filled with the Holy Spirit and not have dominion over fleshly appetites. We see then that when a soul is filled with the Holy Spirit he is great in the sight of God—not necessarily in the sight of men. "Man looketh on the outward appearance, but the Lord looketh on the heart." The Pharisee rejected this great man. (Ch. 7:30.) But even wicked Herod knew him to be a holy man. (Mark 6:20.) What a feeble, trivial thing is greatness as estimated by man. The kings and conquerors who have been called *The Great* by the world were little and unworthy the notice of heaven. We call a man great because he has killed a lot of his fellow beings or because he rules a few millions of his fellow beings or because he has large intellectual endowments, but God calls men great because they are filled with the Spirit. Most of us are willing to be called great in the eyes of men but are not so anxious to be *good* and *holy*. Holiness is cheap in this world. The world despises those who seek it. They are considered fanatics here. But yonder it will be discovered that they belong to the aristocracy of heaven. Many of them are unrecognized, uncrowned and untitled here; some of them like John have been hurried out of the world by barbarous, cruel hands but God knows who and what they are. He calls them ''My saints'' (Ps. 50:5). In that Great Day he will say ''Gather together my saints.'' If we lived in reference to that Great Day how differently we would act; what different standards we would set up for our children. How often we have ruined them by urging them to seek worldly greatness instead of the experience of holiness which is the true greatness. How often we let them get the idea that it is a small thing to be good.

It is well to note in this connection that John was a Nazarite. The Nazarites were the ''Holiness People'' of the Old Dispensation. They were also Temperance people. They abstained from all impurity. They drank no strong drink. ''He shall drink neither wine nor strong drink.'' (Vs. 15.) Does this not mean that the wine of that day was not intoxicating? He should drink neither wine *nor* strong drink. Here two kinds of drink are mentioned. According to this the wine was not strong drink. Was it not this kind that Jesus made at the wedding feast—the unfermented juice of the grape? Dr. Brown says of the Nazarites as a type of holiness ''As the leper was the living type of *sin*, so was the Nazarites as a type of holiness; nothing inflaming was to pass his lips; no razor to come on his head; no ceremonial defilement contracted. Thus was he to be holy to the Lord (ceremonially) all the days of his separation. This separation was in ordinary cases temporary and voluntary; only Samson, Samuel and John the Baptist were Nazarites from the womb. It was fitting that the utmost severity of legal consecration should be seen in Christ's forerunner. He was the *reality* and *perfection* of the Nazarite without the symbol, which perished in that living realization of it.'' It is well to note here that all holy people are uncompromisingly on the side of total abstinence; and not only in the matter of strong drink, but proper self-control in all things. It means total abstinence in that which would be a stumbling block to those who are weaker, and self control in all other things. Any one can indulge his lower nature. It takes a strong man to keep it in subjection.

Notice the connection of the parts of the fifteenth verse. He should not yield to his animal nature, but he should be filled with the Spirit. This is similar to Paul's admonition in Eph. 5:18 "Be not drunken with wine wherein is excess but be filled with the Spirit." As the world receives its stimulus which arouses its passions and animal appetites, John was to have his inspiration from the indwelling Spirt. We in this day are under obligations to be filled with the Spirit for we are so commanded. To be filled with the Spirit was only occasional under the Old Dispensation. It is now commanded to all.

The result of this indwelling of the Spirit would be to make John instrumental in turning man to the Lord. Thus we see that before Pentecost the enduement of the Spirit was held up as empowering for successful preaching. No Christian ought to rest without this great enduement. The blessing of entire sanctification is not to simply purify us but to qualify us fully for what God has for us to do. Jesus died "to purify unto himself a peculiar people zealous of good works."

John was to go before Jesus in the spirit and power of Elias or Elijah. He was not really Elijah risen from the dead as some have supposed; but in many respects, he was like Elijah. He was the Elijah of the times in his boldness and the austerity of his work of reform. He had been promised in the last chapter of the Old Testament, (Mal. 4:6). Israel had fallen far below the light of the Old Dispensation. It was necessary to bring up all willing minds to the standard of the dispensation in which they then lived, before they could be in the place proper, to receive the greater light of the new dispensation. John came to bring them up to the light they already had, before they could receive the greater light of the new dispensation. John who came to bring them up to their own standard and thus prepare them for the coming of Jesus is therefore called the forerunner of Christ. God never wastes further light on those, who are not willing to come up to their present light. Therefore Jesus spoke further in parables to the Pharisees, who did not come up to the truth that John preached. In our individual experience we are not fit for further light, except we are improving that which we now have. If we are unfaithful to our present light, further light will be but parables to us.

The object of John's ministry was three fold: I. To "turn the hearts of the fathers to the children." There have been many interpretations of this passage. We think it means that John was to be the first to take up the ministry to the Gentiles whom the Jews despised. Isaiah (Is. 29:22-23; and 63:16) recognizes the Gentiles as children whom Israel had refused to recognize as such. John preached (Luke 3:12-14) to the Gentile (Roman) soldiers, whom the Jews hated. Thus he first commenced the work of carrying the gospel to the Gentiles which was so fully entered upon by Paul about a generation later. It will be noticed that Elijah whom John resembled had also ministered to the despised Gentiles. This is what made the fellow townsmen of Jesus so angry with him, because he had reminded them of Elijah's ministry to the Gentiles (Luke 4:25, 26). The second object of John's ministry was to turn "the disobedient to the wisdom of the just." The Revised Version has it "The disobedient to walk in the wisdom of the Just." This means that another part of John's ministry was to convert obstinate sinners, and thus lead them to walk in wisdom's ways. In other words sinners were made just men, or were justified, under the ministry of John. Justification then was a fact before Pentecost. The first work of grace which we call in theological terms Justification was clearly preached by John, the Baptist about a third of a century before Pentecost. And yet there are people who seem to think that no one was justified or regenerated before Pentecost (John 3:3).

A third object of John's ministry was "to make ready a people prepared for the Lord." He was to have a people prepared for the coming of Jesus, and there were some such. The disciples of Jesus were prepared for him by the ministry of John. Jesus chose his disciples from the followers of John the Baptist, who had been justified through the teachings of John. (John 1:35-51.) By comparing Matt. 3:11 we shall see that John was a "Second

Blessing'' preacher. He preached both works of grace. Every such preacher today is preparing a people for the Second Coming of Jesus just as John was preparing a people for the First Advent. When people are persuaded to entirely consecrate themselves to God, they are prepared for the Second Coming. This is the only aim of real Gospel preaching—a prepared people. John had some success. A few did turn to God; but not the Pharisees and Scribes. John and Jesus saw very few results of their ministry.

THE FAITH OF THE JUSTIFIED LACKS COMPLETENESS. Vs. 18-25.

18 And Zacharias said unto the angel, Whereby shall I know this? for I am an old man, and my wife well stricken in years.

19 And the angel answering said unto him, I am Gabriel, that stand in the presence of God; and am sent to speak unto thee, and to shew thee these glad tidings.

20 And, behold, thou shalt be dumb, and not able to speak, until the day that these things shall be performed, because thou believest not my words, which shall be fulfilled in their season.

21 And the people waited for Zacharias, and marvelled that he tarried so long in the temple.

22 And when he came out, he could not speak unto them : and they perceived that he had seen a vision in the temple : for he beckoned unto them, and remained speechless.

23 And it came to pass, that, as soon as the days of his ministration were accomplished, he departed to his own house.

24 And after those days his wife Elisabeth conceived, and hid herself five months, saying,

25 Thus hath the Lord dealt with me in the days wherein he looked on *me,* to take away my reproach among men.

Zacharias was a man who was ''righteous before God, walking in all the commandments and ordinances of the Lord blameless.'' Yet his faith was staggered, although an angel was talking to him and telling him that his prayers were to be answered. He said to the angel ''How shall I know this?'' This is the language of unbelief. It is difficult to see how Zacharias could have had more substantial ground for faith than he had. If an angel could not inspire faith in him what could do it? This is one of the characteristics of justification. It is a mixed condition, the carnal mind within tends to the doubting of the divine promises.

This was what that splendid church at Thessalonica lacked, which led Paul to write them, that he was "night and day praying that we might see your face, and perfect that which is lacking in your faith." It requires entire sanctification to cast out the tendencies to doubt and thus make our faith perfect. Justified people today doubt God just as readily and for the same reason. Zacharias seemed to think that the day of the displays of divine power had passed. Many seem to think so now. But God gave Zacharias a holy seed—John the Baptist—and he can give us individually "fruit unto holiness." Let us be careful how we limit the power of God. Unbelief is ever asking a sign, but perfect faith relies upon the promises of God without any other evidence, for that is enough. We hear people when God promised to give spiritual fruit, even holiness of heart say, "I never will believe, until I know it." They want a sign from heaven before they will trust God. Salvation comes by faith but they want salvation first and then they expect to believe. There is no faith in such a course, at all.

"For I am an old man." Unbelief always brings up the obstacles that are in ourselves—"My age, circumstances, disposition, —all too great for the Almighty to overcome." Zacharias had no good excuse. Did he not know how wondrously God had worked in giving Abraham a son when he was very old, for Isaac was born out of due time? What excuse have any of us in doubting that God can give us fruit unto holiness when we know that he has made others holy?

The reply that the angel made was, "I am Gabriel." The word Gabriel means "the strength of God." This same angel appeared to Daniel (Daniel 8:15-18 and 9:21-23) and also to Mary. (Vs. 26.)

"Only two angels are mentioned by name in the scriptures, Gabriel and Michael. The former is the revealer of grace unto men; the latter appears rather as the executor of the divine judgments (Dan. 12:1; Jude 9; Rev. 12:7). Thus they represent the two aspects in which God is represented to us in the Bible, as Redeemer and Judge." (Abbott.) Notice that Gabriel says that he "stands in the presence of God." This seems to mean that Gabriel holds a place of special honor in the presence of God in heaven. He tells Zacharias that he is "sent to speak unto thee." This is as much as to say, It is astonishing that a man who has had a revelation of the appearance of Gabriel right from the throne of God, would not consider that a sufficient sign and proof of the truth of the promise. Unbelief often says, "If I only had a sign from heaven I would surely believe," when it has sufficient evidence already. The difficulty with unbelief is not in lack of sufficient evidence but in a heart of unbelief.

Gabriel adds "Behold thou shalt be dumb." He asked a sign and he got one that he certainly could not have relished. We had better be careful how we ask God for signs and "The Witness" before we trust him. When people are always saying "I want the witness" and "I can not believe without the Witness," it looks as if they believed in these things—signs and the witness more than in the promise of God. Dumbness was a sign of unbelief. They go well together. Faith and confessing with the mouth go together. David says "I believed and therefore have I spoken." Unbelieving talk has made many spiritually dumb. We say spiritually dumb, because they can not talk spiritual things. They can talk anything else except spiritual religion. People talk all the faith they have. When they do not talk faith it is because they have it not. Zacharias' dumbness was a prophecy and symbol of the silence that should henceforth come upon the Old Testament economy.

The people waiting and praying in the outer court of the tempel marvelled at the long tarrying of Zacharias in the temple. Doubtless they were alarmed and were fearful lest he might have done something to merit the divine displeasure and had met with death. They waited until the interview of Zacharias with Gabriel was at an end, and then they had to depart without the usual benediction, for the poor man on account of dumbness could not pronounce it. From his appearance after he came out they thought that he had seen a vision. And indeed he had, and could only express himself by signs. But it was more than an ordinary vision that he had seen. It was more substantial than a mere vision.

When he had finished his week of service, he returned home. The Hebrews looked upon children as a blessing from the Lord. And Elizabeth rejoiced that God had taken away her reproach, for not to have children was considered a mark of the divine displeasure. Modern society could learn some very salutary lessons in these particulars. As bad as the Jewish church had become, it had not descended to the depths of some sections of modern Christian society, who seem to consider it a disgrace to have children.

AN ENTIRELY CONSECRATED WOMAN. Vs. 26-38.

26   And in the sixth month the angel Gabriel was sent from God unto a city of Galilee, named Nazareth,

27   To a virgin espoused to a man whose name was Joseph, of the house of David; and the virgin's name *was* Mary.

28   And the angel came in unto her, and said, Hail, *thou that are* highly favoured, the Lord *is* with thee: blessed *art* thou among women.

29   And when she saw *him*, she was troubled at his saying, and cast in her mind what manner of salutation this should be.

30   And the angel said unto her, Fear not, Mary: for thou hast found favour with God.

31   And, behold, thou shalt conceive in thy womb, and bring forth a son, and shalt call his name JESUS.

32   He shall be great, and shall be called the Son of the Highest: and the Lord God shall give unto him the throne of his father David:

33   And he shall reign over the house of Jacob for ever; and of his kingdom there shall be no end.

34   Then said Mary unto the angel, How shall this be, seeing I know not a man?

35   And the angel answered and said unto her, The Holy Ghost shall come upon thee, and the power of the Highest shall overshadow thee: therefore also that holy thing which shall be born of thee shall be called the Son of God.

36   And, behold, thy cousin Elizabeth, she hath also conceived a son in her old age: and this is the sixth month with her, who was called barren.

37   For with God nothing shall be impossible.

38   And Mary said, Behold the handmaid of the Lord; be it unto me according to thy word. And the angel departed from her.

Six months after the annunciation to Zacharias in the temple (a month after the five months mentioned in Vs. 24) Gabriel was sent to a beautiful little village of Galilee secluded by hills and named Nazareth. His errand was to a young woman by the name of Mary who was engaged to be married to a young man of the lineage of David, whose name was Joseph. Pious Quesnel well says ''At length the moment has come which is to give a *son* to a *virgin,* a *Saviour* to the *world,* a *pattern* to *mankind,* a *sacrifice* to *sinners,* a *temple* to *divinity,* and *new principle* to the *new world.* This angel is sent from God not to the palaces of the great, but to a poor maid, the wife of a carpenter. The Son of God comes to humble the proud and to honor poverty, weakness and contempt.''

The angel, coming where she was, saluted her saying ''Hail, thou that art highly favoured, the Lord is with thee.'' The word ''Hail'' means ''Peace be with thee.'' Gabriel knew that the Lord had highly favored her in choosing her to be the mother of Jesus. He is congratulating her. The same term here translated ''highly favored'' is applied to several individuals in the Old dispensation and to all the New Testament church.

''Blessed art thou among women.'' This passage is not in the best ancient manuscripts. We do not know whether some one added it to help out the Roman Catholic idolatry of Mary or not. There is no warrant in this for the worship of Mary as the Queen of heaven, as some would have us believe. There is no basis for the monstrous doctrine that she was supernatural. There is no teaching anywhere in the scriptures that she was born without sin or is to be worshipped. Gabriel did not worship her, but congratulated her. An anonymous writer says ''The cultus or worship of the Virgin Mary is unquestionably of pagan origin. It is first mentioned by Epiphanius in the fifth century, who talks of a certain body of women, who had transferred the rites of the pagan goddess Ceres to the virgin Mary. In different parts of the Roman empire, where a like compromise was effected between paganism and Christianity, the worship formerly given to Cybele, *the mother of the gods,* according to heathen mythology, was given to the virgin Mary and the festival of the Hilaria celebrated on the 25th of March in honor of Cybele actually became ''Lady-day'' ''in honor of our Lord's mother.'' Mary was a good woman but not any higher in nature than any other holy woman.

When she saw and heard Gabriel she was ''greatly troubled.'' Contending emotions of awe, perplexity, hope and fear took control of her. Had she been supernatural as Roman Catholicism asserts she would hardly have so been disturbed. She ''cast about in her mind what manner of salutation this should be.'' If she had been supernatural she would hardly have been so ignorant of the divine plan.

The angel told her four great facts: First that there was no cause for her to fear. Every time angels appeared to mortals they were obliged to bid them not to fear. See the experience of Zacharias (Vs. 13) and of the shepherds (Chapter 2:10). "Fear not" is characteristic of the gospel of Christ which comes to cast out fear. Second she should bring forth a son. Third she was to name him Jesus. The word means Saviour. The reason for so naming him was given to Joseph (Matt. 1:21). "For he shall save his people from their sins." Let it be no more asked "What is in a name?" There is everything in this name, how slow after two thousand years even many of his professed people are to grasp this idea! He came for more than forgiveness of sins. His salvation is not a legal fiction that pardons sins and allows us to go on sinning. It means that he is a Saviour *from* sin. "This shall be his great business in the world: the great mission on which he has come, viz., to make atonement for sin; deliverance from all the power, guilt and pollution of sin, is the privilege of every believer in Christ Jesus. Less than this is not spoken of in the Gospel and less than this would be unbecoming the Gospel. The perfection of the Gospel system is, not that it makes allowance for sin, but that it makes an atonement for it; not that it tolerates sin but that it destroys it." (Adam Clarke.) Of what use for us to call him *Jesus*, if he does not save *us* from committing sin and does not destroy sin in us? The lowest idea of salvation is to escape hell—the consequence of sin. Jesus saves his people from their sins and being saved from their sins they are saved from hell which is only the consequence of sin. The New Testament abounds with passages which teach that the great object of the atonement is to save from sin. Salvation from hell is the indirect result of the larger salvation which is salvation from sin—the awful thing that sends men to hell. What folly for any one to rest satisfied until he knows that he has,

"A heart from sin set free."

The fourth part of the message of Gabriel was to declare the greatness of Jesus. "He shall be great, and shall be called the Son of the Highest." He was not great in the sight of men in his day. Those, who were supposed to correctly estimate greatness, looked upon him as a root out of dry ground" (Isa. 53:2).

But he was great in the sight of God as was John the Baptist
(Vs. 15) and he is great in the eyes of men today. This shows
that often a generation is not fit to judge of the character of those
who live in it. They are too full of prejudice. He is too near
them for them to judge of his size. Let us not expect that people
will see Jesus in us; for they could not recognize him while on
earth. True greatness is not in the estimation of the narrow
minded world but it arises from self renunciation and being filled
with the Holy Ghost. (Vs. 15.) HE was called The Son of The
Highest. All believers are by adoption called sons of God, but
only Jesus is called *The Son OF God*. We are sons. He is *The
Son*. His father David's kingdom was typical of the greater kingdom which Jesus was to sway. It was in this sense that he had come
to sit upon the throne of his father, David. There was no literal
kingdom of David, at the time of his coming and has never been
since. This spiritual kingdom is never to cease. It is a spiritual
kingdom and is set up in men's hearts.

At this most startling statement Mary asks ''How shall this
be?'' Notice the difference between her question and that of
Zacharias, when a similar announcement had been made to him.
He asked for a sign, because he did not believe. She asks for no
sign for she accepted the fact but was staggered as to how it
could be done. She simply asked how it would come to pass.
There is no doubt in her question.

She is informed that The Holy Spirit would be the agent.
Jesus and the believer are born of the same Spirit. And the same
Spirt that there and then sanctified Mary sanctifies those who are
wholly given up to him.

While, unlike Zacharias, she did not ask a sign, nevertheless
she received one, in the revelation concerning her kinswoman,
Elizabeth. God helps true faith. We need not fear that our faith
will not be strengthened and has sufficient evidence to rest upon, if
we sincerely desire to believe with the heart. The Revised Version calls Elizabeth, the *kinswoman* of Mary. There is no scriptural authority for calling her, cousin.

Speaking of the wonderful miracle in Elizabeth's case, Gabriel
says ''For with God nothing shall be impossible.'' The Revised
Version gives the true rendering thus: ''For no word from God

shall be void of power.'' Many reject the virgin birth of Jesus and also the new birth of believers because they are mysterious. But is not every natural birth mysterious? Who can fully understand it? If our holy religion is supernatural; if the miracles and words of Jesus and especially his marvellous character are more than human; if his religion is supernatural then there is no difficulty in accepting these miracles with the others. We cannot believe that the best man the world ever had was a fraud. It is easier to accept the mysteries of the birth of Jesus than not to accept them. Thank God, with him nothing is impossible, whether it be to prepare a body for the indwelling of His son on earth or to make a world; whether to create a new nature in a dead sinner or to wake the dead earth each Spring-time; whether to wholly sanctify a soul or to raise Jesus from the tomb. Jesus said, ''The words that I speak unto you, they are spirit and they are life'' and Gabriel here says ''No word from God shall be void of power.'' Thank God for these assurances from the heavenly world as to the promise of God. We can rest on them for our present salvation from all sin and our final salvation. When we hear him praying ''Sanctify them through thy truth. Thy word is truth,'' we are assured that that word is indeed truth, for it is ''not void of power.'' What he has promised he can do.

With this assurance Mary made her complete consecration. No other woman ever made a consecration to God that seemed so like throwing her womanhood away, in the eyes of mankind, as she made here. She said ''Behold the handmaid of the Lord; be it unto me according to thy word.'' She consecrated her reputation, willing to be called a bad woman in the estimation of the people and of Joseph her espoused husband. She yielded her reputation for virtue and womanly honor to God. Her affianced husband would have left her but for divine revelation. How many have staggered at the thought of yielding their reputation for the glory of God, who have not had a thousandth part of the risk to run that she had. How many are afraid of the finger of reproach because they seek to be good. Would that there were more people like Mary who could trust their reputation in the hands of God. Time has abundantly vindicated Mary and she is the most honored woman of all history, because she allowed God to take care of her reputation. How could Mary so consecrate herself? Because she had the assurance of the eternal verities of the supernatural. The angel had told her that "no word of God shall be void of power." This is one of the hardest things in the world to many—to yield up their reputation. This is usually the last thing in real consecration. If we are really persuaded of the surety of whatever God has promised, we can with Paul be assured that whatever we have committed unto Him, he will keep unto that day."

ANOTHER ENTIRELY CONSECRATED WOMAN. Vs. 39-45.

39 And Mary arose in those days, and went into the hill country with haste, into a city of Juda;

40 And entered into the house of Zacharias, and saluted Elisabeth.

41 And it came to pass, that, when Elisabeth heard the salutation of Mary, the babe leaped in her womb; and Elisabeth was filled with the Holy Ghost:

42 And she spake out with a loud voice, and said, Blessed *art* thou among women, and blessed *is* the fruit of thy womb.

43 And whence *is* this to me, that the mother of my Lord should come to me?

44 For, lo, as soon as the voice of thy salutation sounded in mine ears, the babe leaped in my womb for joy.

45 And blessed *is* she that believed: for there shall be a performance of those things which were told her from the Lord.

Mary seems to have been a woman of considerable force and determination of character, for she started in haste at once, quite a journey, to a city in the hill country of Judah. To take such a journey, in those days was quite an undertaking. With what joyful haste must she have wended her way!

"And it came to pass." With unaffected delicacy Luke narrates both the accounts of these two mothers. Maternity has become more sacred from this narration. It is possible to try our selves and know if we are pure by the manner in which this account strikes us. "To the pure all things are pure," and the contrary is equally true—to the impure all things are impure. Elizabeth was filled with the Holy Ghost," as Mary saluted her. This is very encouraging to us, for in spite of the teaching of the New Testament commanding us to "BE filled with the Spirit" there are people who deny that mortals can be filled with the Spirit. Here we have people under the Old Dispensation who were filled

with the Spirit. If God did it then, who will deny his power to
do the same today? What was the privilege of a few, selected
people in that dispensation is the birth right of all believers of
today. Notice that this filling with the Spirt was not a gradual
but an instantaneous work or act.

Notice the result, when one is filled with the Spirit. *"She spake
out."* The fullness of the Spirit always unlooses the tongue. The
reason so many say nothing as regards their religion is because
they have "so little to speak of." Jesus said "out of the abundance of the heart the mouth speaketh." Wherever in the word
we have the account of any one, being filled with the Spirit, it
always says that they *"spoke."* In these days when testimony
to the power of religion is so scarce and weak in so many places,
it is because the people have not had this blessing of being filled
with the Spirit. Those who have a hard time speaking of their
experience or of talking about their religion have not been filled
with the Spirit. The fullness drives out pride that hinders some
and cowardice that holds back others, and unties the tongue.
Elizabeth not only spake out but she spake out "with a *loud
voice.*" It is quiet in a grave yard, whether it be in the natural
or physical world. Life is always a positive force and abundance
of life is especially so. Many object to noise and demonstration.
WE do not believe in noise or demonstration for the sake of the
noise but it is impossible for the depths of human nature to be
thoroughly aroused and stirred without more or less manifestation
of the active powers of the physical man. The physical comes up
to the pace set by the spiritual. Fire makes a glow. On the day
of Pentecost there was a tremendous demonstration because the
disciples were filled with the Spirit. Men were astonished then,
and the world has not yet got over wondering about it.

Her first expression was one of love and blessing upon her kinswoman, Mary. Notice her humility. The fullness of the Spirit
never inflates with pride but always with humility. She exclaims
"Whence is this to me?" Elizabeth belonged to the aristocratic
class, being the wife of a priest. Mary was from the humblest
walks of life. Yet Elizabeth with the deepest humility acknowledges the divine favor to Mary. Holy people are lifted above the
wicked spirit of caste and free from envy. She recognized by the

divine unction upon her that Mary was to be the mother of the Messiah and calls her "The mother of my Lord." There is an unction that gives spiritual discernment to those who are filled with the Spirit. (1 John 2:20.) She pronounces a blessing on Mary because she believed, saying "Blessed is she that believed, for there shall be a fulfillment of those things which were told her from the Lord." Great is the premium that the Bible puts upon faith. Abraham, because he believed what God said to him about the birth of Isaac had it "counted to him for righteousness." That is he was justified. He was called the "Father of the Faithful" because of his great faith. Mary the mother of our Lord deserves to be called the Mother of The Faithful, because of the great and delightful example of faith which evoked this encomium from Elizabeth. Elizabeth under the inspiration of the Holy Spirit utters here a great and encouraging truth for saints of all ages to draw lessons of encouragement in the good fight of faith, to which we are all called—"Blessed is she that believeth" for God always fulfills his promises.

PRAISE IS THE LANGUAGE OF HOLY PEOPLE. Vs. 46-56.

46 And Mary said, My soul doth magnify the Lord,

47 And my spirit hath rejoiced in God my Saviour.

48 For he hath regarded the low estate of his handmaiden : for, behold, from henceforth all generations shall call me blessed.

49 For he that is mighty hath done to me great things ; and holy *is* his name.

50 And his mercy *is* on them that fear him from generation to generation.

51 He hath shewed strength with his arm ; he hath scattered the proud in the imagination of their hearts.

52 He hath put down the mighty from *their* seats, and exalted them of low degree.

53 He hath filled the hungry with good things ; and the rich he hath sent empty away.

54 He hath holpen his servant Israel, in remembrance of *his* mercy ;

55 As he spake to our fathers, to Abraham, and to his seed for ever.

56 And Mary abode with her about three months, and returned to her own house.

This entirely consecrated woman breaks forth into a most beautiful hymn of praise. This hymn is known as *The Magnificat,*

from the first word in the Latin Version which is *Magnificat* and
signifies ''doth magnify.'' Praise is as natural to a fully consecrated soul, as breath is to a healthy person. When the church is
empty of praise it is evident that it has lost the Holy Spirit.
Hannah under similar circumstances had given utterance to a lyric
of similar beauty over the gift of Samuel. (1 Sam. 2.) The hymn
is in three parts: I Thanksgiving (Vs. 46-49). II Ascription of
praise to God for his overruling providence (Vs. 49-53). III
The blessed result—redemption to Israel through Jesus (Vs.
54-55). This may well be called a faith song for she exults in
things yet to come.

''My soul doth magnify the Lord.'' To magnify means to
make large. WE use certain glasses which make things look large.
God's saints are magnifying glasses to make him great in the eyes
of the children of men. This is akin to David's exclamation, ''My
soul shall make her boast in the Lord.'' IT is the people who
know God as did Mary and David who can really magnify Him.
This was the exultation of the faith of an entirely consecrated
woman, praising God for things that had not come to pass as yet.
Are we able personally and individually to praise God for things
that our faith tells us are coming, or can we only praise him for
what we see. Those who can not believe for great things and
thank God for them in advance are usually too spiritually dull to
see much in the *present* for which to praise him.

''My spirit hath rejoiced in God my Saviour.'' This forever
destroys the doctrine that Mary was divine or sinless by nature,
and therefore worthy of worship. She puts herself on the level
with the rest of the daughters of Eve, as one who needed a
Saviour and had been saved by God, *her* Saviour. She could not
truthfully call him *her* Saviour unless he had saved her from sin.
Needing salvation herself, she could not save other people—any
more than any other saved person can save others. But notice she
calls God her personal Saviour from sin, through faith in her Son,
who was to ''save his people from their sins.'' Abbott says ''To
her he is already the one that saves from sin those that trust him.
(Matt. 1:21.)'' This entirely consecrated woman knew that God
had saved her from sin *and so does every one who makes as thorough a consecration* as she made. There are many who are seeking

to know that they are saved from sin, but who do not have the evidence because they have not made a *genuine* consecration. It is not possible to ''rejoice in God as our Saviour'' unless he has saved us.

''He hath regarded the low estate of his handmaiden.'' She considered herself the handmaiden of the Lord. This is the language of real consecration, which considers itself as being the property of the Lord. He had stooped down to her lowly condition and exalted her. Every redeemed soul can say the same and praise Him for taking them out of the pit of sin.

She then declares that all generations shall call her ''blessed.'' This was the gift of prophecy, which seemed to have been given to her. All generations should call her blessed or happy, for that is what the word means. What woman would not say that Mary had the highest happiness that woman ever had? There is no warrant from this to call Mary, The Queen of Heaven. Are not all God's saints called ''Blessed?'' Jesus said ''Blessed are the pure in heart.'' Jesus said that all can be as truly ''Blessel.'' He said ''For whosoever shall do the will of my Father, which is in heaven, the same is my brother and sister and mother.'' (Matt. 12:50.) At another time when a woman ascribed great honor to Mary for having such a son, he put Mary on a level with all who hear the word of God and keep it (Luke 11:27). Mary and the really consecrated are all on the same level.

She then goes on to praise the omnipotence and holiness of God thus ''He that is mighty . . . and holy is his name.'' ''But this omnipotence is not of a purely physical character; it is subservient to holiness. This is the second perfection which Mary, celebrates. She felt herself in this marvellous work, in immediate contact with supreme holiness, and she well knew that this perfection more than any other, constitutes the essence of God. His name is holy, the sign of an object in the mind that knows it; the *name of God* therefore denotes not only the Divine Being but the more or less adequate reflection of him in those intelligences, which are in communion with him. Hence we can see how his name can be sanctified, rendered holy. The essential nature of God may be more clearly understood by his creatures, and more completely disengaged from those clouds which have hitherto obscured it in their minds. Thus Mary had received in the experience which she had passed through, a new revelation of the holiness of the Divine.'' (Godet.) And so does every one who like her, makes the complete consecration. They receive that derived holiness which comes from God. That which he gave Mary and a few under that Dispensation he has made provision to impart to all who truly consecrate themselves to Him in this Dispensation.

Having mentioned the might and holiness of the Divine Being, she now extols his mercy. Generation after generation God had shown his mercy to the Jewish people. So she declares because they had trusted him as no other people had. She states a great principle that ''His mercy is on them that fear him in every generation. It is of no use for men to expect mercy if they do not fear God sufficiently to keep his commandments. Men do not fear God when they do not keep his commandments. It is absurd to suppose that we fear him when we go on in sin because he is so willing to forgive. His mercy is on them that fear him enough to forsake sin. His mercy is on every generation. It is the hand of God not blind chance that governs the world. Having declared his forgiving grace to those who keep his commandments, she also speaks of mercy.

A SPIRIT-FILLED MAN. Vs. 56-67.

57   Now Elizabeth's full time came that she should be delivered; and she brought forth a son.

58   And her neighbours and her cousins heard how the Lord had shewed great mercy upon her; and they rejoiced with her.

59   And it came to pass, that on the eighth day they came to circumcise the child; and they called him Zacharias, after the name of his father.

60   And his mother answered and said, Not so; but he shall be called John.

61   And they said unto her, There is none of thy kindred that is called by this name.

62   And they made signs to his father, how he would have him called.

63   And he asked for a writing table, and wrote, saying, His name is John. And they marvelled all.

64   And his mouth was opened immediately, and his tongue *loosed*, and he spake, and praised God.

65   And fear came on all that dwelt round about them: and all

these sayings were noised abroad throughout all the hill country of Judæa.

66   And all they that heard *them* laid *them* up in their hearts, saying, What manner of child shall this be! And the hand of the Lord was with him.

67   And his father Zacharias was filled with the Holy Ghost, and prophesied, saying,

In process of time Elizabeth "brought forth a son." There was a double cause for rejoicing among her neighbors and kinsfolk, for the birth of a boy always was a special cause for rejoicing among the Jews and when they heard that it was by a special manifestation of God, who had told Zacharias through an angel, it must have doubled their rejoicings and congratulations. A household to whom the entrance of a babe brings no joy is as bad as the heathen. God had especially required family religion of the Jews. He had required them to begin by circumcising all the males on the eighth day. This ordinance, which was a type of entire sanctification (Coll. 2:11) initiated the child into the Jewish church. At this time the name was given the child in remembrance of the fact that the names of Abram and Sara were changed at the time that the ordinance was instituted. (Gen. 17:5, 15). So they were about to name the child after his father, Zacharias. But Elizabeth had heard from heaven and stoutly protested declaring His name was John. When God gives names he breaks sometimes into human conventionalisms. Zacharias must during the months of his dumbness have communicated to Elizabeth what Gabriel had told him, and The Holy Spirit, who filled Elizabeth must have confirmed it. The carnal mind is often loth to use heaven-appointed names. It might have seemed strange perhaps blasphemous to the relatives to have this child named John —*The Grace of God.* It was a name imported from heaven. In these days, carnal minded people do not like God's terms and think it presumptuous to call God's people, holy. But that is the name he gives them and there is none that is better. (Ps. 50:5; Eph. 1:1; Coll. 1:2; Phil. 1:1; and 4:21.) This is the same reason that many object to the inspired words of Scripture and quarrel at the terms, Holiness, Sanctification, etc. Not to call people and things by their right names is not only childish but in these instances cowardly and wicked.

So they appealed to his father, Zacharias, who, in sign language asked for a writing tablet. This was a thin piece of wood, overlaid with a covering of wax on which people wrote with a sharp, pointed iron. On this he wrote ''His name is John.'' Gabriel had settled that long before. It was fitting that the Forerunner of Jesus should herald the *Grace of God* by his name. —John, The *Grace of God.*

This made them all marvel—not that Zacharias agreed with Elizabeth on the name but because he was so positive about it. When a man has a revelation from God and obeys it, he becomes very positive about it; so much so that it is often an astonishment to people, who perhaps have never seen anything very positive about him previously.

When he declared the heaven-originated name with such positiveness, the string of his tongue was loosed and his mouth flew open in praises to God. Faith is a mouth opener. David says ''I believed and therefore have I spoken.'' There is a worldly, unscriptural maxim much in vogue in these days that we are to ''live our religion but say nothing about it.'' But the trouble with it is that it is unscriptural and was invented as an apology for people, who have no experience worth telling. ''With the heart man believeth unto righteousness, and with the mouth confession is made unto salvation.'' The witnessing mouth can no more be dispensed with than the believing heart. Our faith will die if it does not have the proper expression of the lips. Talk your faith the best you can, or soon you will have no faith to talk. People talk all the faith they have. If Zacharias had not talked unbelief to the angel, he would not have had a dumbness of weary months. How many backslide and go into the dark because they do not confess their faith.

So ''he spake and praised the Lord.'' If silence were broken only when men praised the Lord, there would either be more silence or more praise. Human tongues were made to praise God. Instead of singing, ''O for a thousand tongues to praise the Lord,'' if we used the tongue we each have, to praise the Lord a thousand times more than we do, it would be a fair equivalent.

These wonderful events stirred the country around and had much to do doubtless in preparing the minds of the people for John's ministry and preaching.

"And his Father Zacharias was filled with the Holy Ghost." As we have seen in verse 6 he was a fully justified man and was living a justified life, and hence was a good candidate for the fullness of the Holy Spirit. Only believers received the fullness of the Spirit in Bible times, and only believers receive that blessing now. It has never yet come upon sinners. Here Zacharias, the priest of God, who was walking in all the commandments and ordinances of the Lord received the "Second blessing, properly so called" as John Wesley says.

A SPIRIT-FILLED MAN PRAISES GOD.   Vs. 68-80.

68 Blessed *be* the Lord God of Israel; for he hath visited and redeemed his people,

69 And hath raised up an horn of salvation for us in the house of his servant David;

70 As he spake by the mouth of his holy prophets, which have been since the world began:

71 That we should be saved from our enemies, and from the hand of all that hate us;

72 To perform the mercy *promised* to our fathers, and to remember his holy covenant;

73 The oath which he sware to our father Abraham,

74 That he would grant unto us, that we being delivered out of the hand of our enemies might serve him without fear,

75 In holiness and righteousness before him, all the days of our life.

76 And thou, child, shalt be called the prophet of the Highest: for thou shalt go before the face of the Lord to prepare his ways;

77 To give knowledge of salvation unto his people by the remission of their sins,

78 Through the tender mercy of our God; whereby the dayspring from on high hath visited us,

79 To give light to them that sit in darkness and *in* the shadow of death, to guide our feet into the way of peace.

80 And the child grew, and waxed strong in spirit, and was in the deserts till the day of his shewing unto Israel.

It is said that Zacharias "prophesied." Prophesying means *speaking for.* We have in our day limited it to the foretelling of future events. But this is only a partial definition. It means to speak for God as God gave utterance whether as regards the present or future. In this case it referred to both. Zacharias was fitted to declare these truths, only as he was filled and moved

by the Holy Spirit. Since Pentecost, the Spirit comes not merely
on a few (as under the Old Dispensation) but upon all who seek
and fulfill the conditions. These receive the power to tell the
great things that God reveals to them. This is the New Testament
gift of prophecy, which Paul rates next in importance to Perfect
Love. (See I Cor. 14:39 and Ch. 12:31 to Ch. 14. Also Acts
2:18 and 39.) This prophecy of Zacharias consisted of two parts.
From verse 68 to 75 he preaches the Gospel prophetically. The
remainder is a description of the work of his son, John.

His whole speech has been called his Thanksgiving Psalm and
has also been called *The Benedictus.* It is so named from the first
word, *Benedictus* in the Latin Version. The doubts of Zacharias
are now all gone and he acknowledges that ''The Lord God of
Israel'' has visited and redeemed his people'' through the dispensation which Jesus is now to open. Doubtless Zacharias speaks
better and more than he knows, as the Holy Spirit is talking
through him. To redeem means to pay a ransom price for the release of captives. The price for each of our souls was the precious
blood of Jesus, which delivers not only from the bondage of hell
but from the bondage of sin.

He declares that God had ''raised up a horn of salvation for
us in the house of his servant, David.'' We today remembering
that this was given under the inspiration of the Holy Spirit can
apply the ''for us'' to ourselves as well as to the Jews of Zacharias' day. It is *for us.* The horn being the great weapon of defence among many of the animal creation came to be used as a
figure of strength. Jesus was the *power* of salvation, which God
was now to raise up.

Zacharias adds ''As he spake by the mouth of his holy prophets.'' Here we have the statement that God has had not only
prophets, but *holy* prophets. Thank God he has had some holy
people ever since the beginning of the world. And yet some people say there never have been holy people and that it is impossible to be holy in this world of sin. Holiness in this world is
clearly taught in the word of God.

The great salvation from sin has been taught by *all* his prophets. Zacharias here teaches that salvation from sin is taught by
all God's prophets from the beginning. Is it not strange that

with the Holy Bible full of holiness so many should not see this great truth? No doubt Zacharias could see in this message of the Holy Ghost speaking through him, nothing more than a temporal victory over the Roman government. And perhaps spiritually dull people can see nothing more today, who read it; but verse 75 shows that it meant a great deal more. It meant spiritual deliverance. The promises of God in their fulfillment are grander and broader than human conception. Godet says of this verse "We find in all its purity the idea of salvation as it is described in the Old Testament, and as the son of Zacharias himself understood it to the very last. Its leading feature is the indissoluble union of the two deliverances; the religious and the political; it was a glorious theocracy founded on national holiness." Adam Clarke says "As Zacharias spoke under the inspiration of the Holy Spirit, the salvation which he mentions here must be understood in a *spiritual* sense. Satan, death and sin are the enemies from which Jesus came to deliver us. Sin is the most dangerous of all, and is properly the only enemy we have to fear. Satan is without us and can have no power over us, but what he gets through sin. Death is only in our flesh and shall finally be destroyed (as it affects us) on the morning of the resurrection. Jesus redeems us from sin; this is the grand, the glorious, the important victory. Let us get sin cast out and then we need fear neither death nor the devil. Holiness is the chief glory and deliverance of the church. "To perform the mercy." Mercy means the bestowment of unmerited favor, hence this complete salvation was not to be acquired by works but by faith.

"And to remember his holy covenant." The holy covenant was that made by God to the Israelites at mount Sinai where he promised that if they would keep his commandments he would make them a holy people. "Now therefore, if ye will obey my voice indeed, and keep my covenant, then ye shall be a peculiar treasure unto me above all people; for all the earth is mine: And ye shall be unto me a kingdom of priests and a holy nation" (Exod. 19:5-6). This was the original salvation—the original standard of religion, which the prophets were ever advocating and up to which they were continually seeking to bring the nation.

More than this, it has been so difficult to make the carnal

heart of man believe that God can make us holy in this world that God has taken his oath that he will do it. And yet there are thousands who have taken upon them the name of Christian, who do not believe it and *will not believe the Almighty under oath.* He has condescended to humor our unbelief by taking oath that he can make us holy and yet thousands of his professed followers ridicule the idea of being holy in this life. "What oath was it that he remembered? The oath made in the 22nd chapter of Genesis, at the 16th verse. Now that promise the Apostle says, was made, not unto seeds as of many; but unto one seed, as Christ; and that promise made to Abraham is realized in Christ, and in all true children of Abraham; we are children according to the flesh." (Cumming.) Jesus Christ came to fulfill the promise by making all who sincerely seek it, partakers of his holiness.

The full import then of this oath was that we being freed from sin might serve him in holiness and righteousness before him all the days of our life—not when we come to die, as some people teach. Holiness is our inward state and righteousness is our outward life. "The one represents inward purity, the other outward activity; the one the inward but negative quality, the other the outward but affirmative quality; the one, absence from stain the other positive service." (Abbott.)

Most commentators pass over in silence the words that relate to the time of this service—"All the days of our life." We wonder why? Are these words not as emphatic as the other portions of this utterance? If they do not mean what they say—that we can be holy in this life—why do not these commentators, who pass over them in silence tell us what they do mean? John Wesley who was always true to the doctrine of holiness in his "Notes" says, "Here is the substance of the great promise, that we shall be always holy, always happy; that being delivered from Satan and sin, from every uneasy and unholy temper, we shall joyfully love and serve God in every thought, word and work." We have then in this passage a declaration that the sum and substance of salvation is the experience of entire sanctification, as an obtainment in this life. Notice that this is a service (Vs. 74). We are redeemed from sin not to sit in idleness, but to enter upon a life of *service* for God. A service which is free from slavish fear, because love in us has been made perfect.

Notice again one of the seeming contradictions of the Bible—a deliverance from one service (that of sin) into another service (that of holiness). This is a service that is real freedom. We have taught here "1. That sin shall not have dominion over us nor existence in us. 2. We are to live in *holiness,* a strict conformity to the mind of Christ, and righteousness—a full outward conformity to the precepts of the Gospel. 3. This state is a state of happiness—it is without fear. Sin is all cast out. Holiness is all brought in. 4. This blessedness is to continue as long as we exist. ALL THE DAYS OF OUR LIVES, in all ages, and in all circumstances.'' (Clarke.) 5. Christ is the (horn of) power to accomplish this. He has the ability which makes it possible. 6. God will not fail to do this for all who seek to have it done, for he has given both a *promise and* an *oath* to that effect. 7. Holiness is mentioned *first,* then righteousness. A holy heart must come first. Then it manifests itself in outward *righteousness.* 8. This is to be *before God.* Men may not see or may refuse to recognize it in us. We are not to expect a certain class to see it for they failed to see it in Jesus. But we are not responsible to man for being holy but to God. If he sees it why should we care what people may say about it or us? He sees the heart and men cannot see it.

The second part of this discourse now begins where he speaks prophetically of his son, John who was to be called ''the Prophet of the Highest''—the Prophet of Jesus, foretelling his coming. Jesus is called ''The Son of the Highest''—in verse 3 and in verse 76 he is called The Highest and hence he is God as well as the Son of God and John was his prophet. John was like an ancient herald who went ahead of a king to proclaim his coming. He went before and proclaimed the coming of Jesus, The King. Verses 77 and 70 show how he was to prepare the way for the coming of Jesus.

A very important part of John's ministry was to ''Give the knowledge of salvation.'' Only God could give salvation but John could give the *Knowledge* of salvation. He could teach the *science* of salvation. He could teach them how to get saved. So we find that John preached two works of salvation—pardon and entire cleansing. (Matt. 3:11).

Jesus is compared to the Dayspring in verse 78. Dayspring

means the dawn. By the coming of Jesus a new day had come to the long night of sin that had enshrouded the world. This Dayspring had come to give light to a world sitting in the shadow of death. Notice the condition of the world without Christ as portrayed here by the Holy Spirit. And is not every man, who is unsaved in this sad state? Thank God this light of the Gospel has come to men not merely to show them their lost condition but to lead them out of it "into the way of peace." Zacharias here declares that John would lead man out of darkness into light; in other words he would have seals to his ministry. Every true preacher will have some seals to his ministry. From this time until John began his ministry we hear nothing concerning him except this statement of verse 80, "The child grew and waxed strong and was in the deserts until the day of his showing to Israel." He grew physically and waxed strong intellectually. John, a holy person, filled with the Spirit (hence with no sin in him) grew spiritually. See Chapter 2:52 where it says that Jesus grew in favor or grace. Hence growing in grace does not mean growing from one state of grace to another less sinful, and so on by degrees until sin is all grown out, for here was a holy man growing spiritually. It means always as in the case of Jesus and John, development or ripening of the grace already possessed. Let us beware of the heresy that sin may be outgrown. Only God can destroy sin.

John took up his abode "in the deserts." Alone with God he grew up. What a school for the preparation of a prophet. There was no scribe or Pharisee to corrupt him with false doctrine. Jesus and Paul were in retirement for a season before their public ministry began. (Luke 4:1, Gal. 1:17.)

If we examine the preaching of Paul (Acts 26:18) we shall see that Paul preached the same doctrine of entire cleansing and, even more fully, because he was on the other side of Pentecost. People in the degenerate day of John, the Baptist, had missed entirely the idea of salvation. They had come to look upon the Old Testament prophecies as teaching a political and not a spiritual salvation. If John had not gone before Jesus and preached a spiritual deliverance it would have been still more difficult, for the people to grasp the spirituality of the teaching of Jesus.

CHAPTER II.

HOLINESS OF TWO DISPENSATION.

Birth of the Great Exemplar of Holiness. Vs. 1-20. A Symbol of Holiness. Vs. 21-24. Two Holy People of the Old Dispensation. Vs. 25-39. Growth in Grace Is Not Growing into Holiness. Vs. 40-52.

BIRTH OF THE GREAT EXEMPLAR OF HOLINESS.
Vs. 1-20.

1. And it came to pass in those days, that there went out a decree from Cæsar Augustus, that all the world should be taxed.

2 (*And* this taxing was first made when Cyrenius was governor of Syria.)

3 And all went to be taxed, every one into his own city.

4 And Joseph also went up from Galilee, out of the city of Nazareth, into Judæa, unto the city of David, which is called Bethlehem; (because he was of the house and lineage of David:)

5 To be taxed with Mary his espoused wife, being great with child.

6 And so it was, that, while they were there, the days were accomplished that she should be delivered.

7 And she brought forth her firstborn son, and wrapped him in swaddling clothes, and laid him in a manger; because there was no room for them in the inn.

8 And there were in the same country shepherds abiding in the field, keeping watch over their flock by night.

9 And, lo, the angel of the Lord came upon them, and the glory of the Lord shone round about them: and they were sore afraid.

10 And the angel said unto them, Fear not: for, behold, I bring you good tidings of great joy, which shall be to all people.

11 For unto you is born this day in the city of David a Saviour, which is Christ the Lord.

12 And this *shall be* a sign unto you; Ye shall find the babe wrapped in swaddling clothes, lying in a. manger.

13 And suddenly there was with the angel a multitude of the heavenly host praising God, and saying,

41

14 Glory to God in the highest, and on earth peace, good will toward men.

15 And it came to pass, as the angels were gone away from them into heaven, the shepherds said one to another, Let us now go even unto Bethlehem, and see this thing which is come to pass, which the Lord hath made known unto us.

16 And they came with haste, and found Mary, and Joseph, and the babe lying in a manger.

17 And when they had seen *it*, they made known abroad the saying which was told them concerning this child.

18 And all they that heard *it* wondered at those things which were told them by the shepherds.

19 But Mary kept all these things, and pondered *them* in her heart.

20. And the shepherds returned, glorifying and praising God for all the things that they had heard and seen, as it was told unto them.

This chapter contains an account of the birth, childhood, and youth of Jesus, the great exemplar of holiness and the greeting given him by two holy people, Simeon and Anna, who were living under the Old Dispensation.

It is worthy of notice that Jesus came in the most opportune time of history—just when the world needed the exemplification of holiness. Sin had had its way long enough. The serpent had badly wounded the human race and now it was time that the world should have some conception of the nature of holiness by the revelation of a holy manhood. It was at the time when Cæsar Augustus was ruler of all the known world. All the old religions of the world had proved a failure. Pagan religions had only made men worse. Judaism had done no better, for the Jews had really, with a few exceptions, become as bad as the heathen. Such an idea as holy manhood was not only beyond the teaching of all pagan religions but was beyond the comprehension of the wise men and philosophers of the age. It was when the flowers of the world had all been blighted by sin that the Rose of Sharon bloomed in all its loveliness in the land of Judea. It is a remarkable teaching which shows how unpromising and wicked the times, and that when God gets ready to bring forth holiness no one can prevent it. He makes the powers of the world all assist in the work.

Cæsar Augustus, the first of the Roman Emperors, who, now ruled over the known world was an unconscious factor in helping on the work of God, in bringing holiness before the world.

The home of Joseph and Mary was at Nazareth, but the prophecy (Micah 5:2) had declared that Jesus should be born in Bethlehem, and God caused the Emperor, Cæsar Augustus to bring it about by his edict requiring every Jew to go to the seat of his tribe. This law required women to pay what we would call a poll tax. So Mary had to go to Bethlehem the city of the tribe of Judah and there Christ was born. When Cæsar Augustus had this enrollment made in order to get the statistics of his empire and also to raise money for its support he little knew that he was fulfilling prophecy and was helping build up a kingdom that was to outlast his throne and be flourishing when it had decayed forever.

Holiness gilds all its surroundings. The little town of Bethlehem, six miles south of Jerusalem has become one of the most renowned places on earth. Here, Rachel, the beloved wife of Jacob, died. Here David was born. It was here that Ruth the Moabitess, one of the ancestors of Jesus lived, and here that holy woman Mary gave birth to Jesus, The Holy One. What a cluster of holy names is associated with this little town!

The place was crowded, for others had come on the same errand—to have their names enrolled on the tax list. Every place of entertainment was full. ''There was no room for them in the inn.'' This was because someone else was considered of more importance. Had the Bethlehemites known who was to be born there, plenty of room could be found. How often has the world missed its greatest opportunities.

For the same reason Jesus finds no place in the hearts of the many; there is no room. Men have too much in their hearts that they do not wish to give up. Holiness is not popular because the idols, self and the world are there. Christ and his holiness must take the stable. Any inferior place will do in the estimation of many, for holiness. The humiliation of Jesus is the glory of the Gospel story. Some will not embrace holiness because the great and mighty of this world do not embrace it. Others are discouraged because it is passed by and ignored by ecclesiastics and the world in general. They forget that holiness must not expect any better treatment than Jesus received. The carnal heart does not want him. The ''Old Man'' is opposed to holy religion of any degree. Jesus had to take the manger, the cross, and the grave.

Who are we, that we will not follow holiness unless we can have a soft easy time? By his entrance into the world Jesus dignifies honorable poverty, infancy and a life of humility.

It is wonderful how many classes of people we find grouped about the birth of Jesus. Angels came from heaven to tell it and rejoiced as they told it. The holy Simeon and Anna rejoiced over it in the temple. The wise men came from far to honor Him. Herod and all Jerusalem were mightily stirred at the announcement. And Shepherds—those of the humblest walks of society, go to Bethlehem to see and then publish the glad tidings. Jesus made a stir at his very first appearing and his truth and holiness have made a stir in the world ever since. All classes have been affected by that life of thirty-three years.

The angels did not make the announcement to the high and lofty or the degenerate church men of that day, but to the shepherds. The Shepherd of Israel is first adored by shepherds who are watching their flocks by night on the same plains that his forefather, David, had watched sheep when he was a youth.

It was a startling appearance to behold the glory of the Lord shining out in the midnight darkness. God had made no such revelation for hundreds of years. It was something out of the ordinary, but the event which it announced was the most extraordinary event that the world has ever known. This great glory was undoubtedly the Shechinah, that once shone in the Holy of Holies of the temple. God thus saw fit to have his birth honored as that of none other since the world began.

If the glory of God could so startle these honest men, what will be the effect produced upon the wicked, when he shall shine forth in his glory, as he sits on his judgment throne.

But the angel spoke in tones of kindness and consolation to the terrified shepherds. ''Fear not.'' This was the first gospel message to men from angels. We may say this angel was the first Gospel preacher with his, ''Fear not.'' This is the first sentence of the Gospel message. He had come to announce a Christ who saves from fear. He proposes to save us from fear by saving us from sin, the only thing that causes slavish fear. When we are saved from sin there is nothing to fear. If angels are interested in the salvation of men so as to rejoice over it, we too certainly ought to be rejoiced over it. We certainly ought to be as much interested in our own salvation as the angels are. The angel said "I bring you good tidings." This is the definition of the word, Gospel—Good tidings—a way of escape from sin and its consequences has been found. There can be no better tidings. The angel also announced that this Gospel was bigger than simply to help the Jews. It was to be for all people—the whole world. He is the Saviour of all mankind.

The angel then went on to explain still further what he meant by the "good tidings." It was not merely a sensational expression of good will but an actual, practical matter. "Unto you." This Saviour was born not for the angels but for and to men. Angels never sinned and do not know the sweets of redeeming grace and dying love. They never had a Saviour to die for them. The assurance is doubled when the angel says "A Saviour which is Christ the Lord." We are so accustomed to these words, "Christ" and "Lord" that we fail at the first glance to note their significance. How startling these words must have sounded and how much they meant to these Jewish shepherds! "Saviour" is one who saves, "Christ" means "anointed." The word "Lord" here is the same as the Hebrew word "Jehovah," who was the Lord spoken of in the Old Testament. The full import of this wonderful message is then, "There is born to you A Saviour, who is the Anointed One, Jehovah." They would understand from this that the Messiah prophecied in the Old Testament was designated. Such a tremendous truth was too much for these men to grasp, coming upon them so suddenly, and so the angel to help them grasp and believe it, said there should be a sign given them. The sign was "a babe lying in a manger."

This is a fine illustration of the word of God by Isaiah "For my thoughts are not your thoughts, neither are your ways my ways saith the Lord." If man had given a "sign" of the approaching Messiah it would have been something majestic according to human notions. But when the Messiah, the hope of the world had come, the sign was a babe—the weakest of all the young of the animal creation. Jesus went as low down in the scale of humanity as it was possible to go.

Wonderful sign! Jehovah, the Christ lying in a manger!

What a condescension! Amazing! Holiness is like the Son of God marked by its deep humility. If we seek Christ or any degree of his salvation, we shall find the same sign—the babe. If we have reached the heights of Christian experience, we shall find a deep humility in our souls. If we have not that, we are mistaken in our supposition. Holiness does not consist in deep rapture but in the deepest humility. Jesus had to teach this great lesson to his disciples. (Matt. 18:3.) In his kingdom those, who are highest are those of the deepest humility. This is the greatest glory of our holy religion.

After this annunciation there was a sudden outburst of the angels voicing their praise. It says "Suddenly" as if the angels could hardly wait to sound forth their praises. They did not make any too much demonstration; nor can we when we remember all that this salvation means. When we get to heaven and realize as we can hardly now do, how much this salvation means, we shall wonder that we kept as quiet as we do while here below. What interest the angels took and still take in the salvation of men. Ought not we then to be more than ever interested in it as we consider this fact?

We have no desire to shatter any preconceived notions as to the singing of the angels at this time, but we can find no record of it, Verse 13 says they were "*saying* Glory to God in the Highest." Perhaps they sang too but we cannot find it although this is the way it is generally understood. There may be good reason to believe that they sang as the words are in tunable measure. Their ascription of praise was "Glory to God in the highest" heaven, because peace and good will had come to men. The good will of God to a sinful race was shown in giving Jesus. The angels were unselfish. They were praising God for our salvation. How could it be otherwise? The angels are holy and selfishness and holiness never go together, either in heaven or any other world. How shall we dwell with holy angels unless selfishness is destroyed in us? If we would join in the song in heaven with the angels we must be pure in heart. So the birth of Jesus moved heaven at the beginning and it has been moving earth ever since in greater or less degree. We are encouraged when we thus learn that heaven is interested in our salvation. Henceforth Jesus and his gospel were to be the embodiment of the praise of the angels. Glory to God and peace to men. This is the purpose of the Gospel.

And all this glory and praise was revealed to shepherds, men of toil—not belonging to the so-called higher ranks of society. How different God works from the natural accepted order of man. God hides these things from the so-called "wise and prudent." He reveals himself to the lowly. If you want to know about the deep things of spiritual life you will find them with those, who have learned from the great teacher himself and quite often he passes the high ecclesiastics and reveals himself to those in the ordinary walks of life. The Lord made no mistake in making this revelation to the shepherds, for they were candid, honest souls as may be seen in their immediate action. They said to one another "Let us now go . . . and see." Every revelation of God is but for us to test for ourselves. It is possible to prove experimentally that there is a Christ by doing as the shepherds did—putting ourselves in the way of finding out. We can have all doubts removed in our day if we are willing to go and see. If we do as the shepherds did we shall find Christ too.

And they went with haste. This shows their eagerness, and they found it as the angels had said.

When they had seen Joseph, Mary and the child, they told it abroad. No wonder. How can any one, who knows anything about the wonderful Jesus keep still about it? Those who can keep still about what they know about Jesus, do so because they know very little about him. Salvation is too big a secret to keep. It is just as natural to tell of salvation as it was for these shepherds to tell this good news.

The people, who heard the shepherds, as they told their story, "wondered." The history of Jesus always has caused wonder. It always will, because it is the wonderful story of Him whom the prophet called "Wonderful." His holy life is a wonder to the ages. But holiness, incarnate and absolute, did come to this sinful world and the fate and treatment it met are still the characteristics of the wicked human heart. We shall see as we pass along in this history that he passed through just the same kind of treatment that holiness has had to meet ever since.

While the shepherds told the story and the people wondered,

there was one person who treasured up all the sayings and doings in connection with the birth of Jesus, in her memory. It was Mary. Mothers never forget the incidents connected with the birth of their children. Mary pondered them in her heart. The word *ponder* means to weigh. She carefully went over them and sought to pierce the veil of the future and imagine what the career of her son was to be. St. Luke probably got his facts for the account of the birth of Jesus from Mary.

The shepherds returned glorifying and praising God because they had found it just as the angels had told them. They went to see and found it was true. So do real seekers of Christ find it true today. They that seek him still find him.

The prophets had foretold him. The angels had announced him and the shepherds found the message of the prophets and angels true. And living men are finding the story true today. These shepherds were good men, as their conduct in praising God indicates. The best people of the Old Dispensation were notified of the advent of Jesus. Then came John the Baptist's message and then Jesus began his public ministry. The work of preparation was all completed when Jesus began his public work.

A SYMBOL OF HOLINESS. Vs. 21-24.

21 And when eight days were accomplished for the circumcising of the child, his name was called JESUS, which was so named of the angel before he was conceived in the womb.

22 And when the days of her purification according to the law of Moses were accomplished, they brought him to Jerusalem, to present *him* to the Lord;

23 (As it is written in the law of the Lord, Every male that openeth the womb shall be called holy to the Lord;)

24 And to offer a sacrifice according to that which is said in the law of the Lord, A pair of turtledoves, or two young pigeons.

Eight days after birth, the law required every male Jewish child should be circumcised. Circumcision was the badge of membership in the church. If Jesus had not been circumcised, he would have been cast out by the Jews. This was a proof that he was of the seed of Abraham. Without it he would have been driven out of the synagogues and dwellings of the Jews as unclean. He had come to fulfill the law and by circumcision he gave proof of his mission and obedience to the law.

He was called Jesus according to the command of Gabriel. (See our notes on Matthew 1:21.) Jesus is the Greek form of the word Joshua. The word Joshua is rendered Jesus in Hebrews 4:5. When Gabriel said ''Thou shalt call his name Jesus, because he shall save his people from their sins (Matt. 1:21), he purposely gave the reason for so calling Him. The Jews would probably suppose he was to be only a temporal deliverer from the Romans, as Joshua had been a temporal deliverer into the land of Canaan, and so Gabriel wished it understood that he was Joshua (the word means deliverer) from sins—an eternal Saviour, not a political deliverer. In the circumcision of Jesus and the purification of his mother we find the great command and privilege of holiness typified. Every first born male in the original law was to be consecrated to the Lord as a holy priest. Later on, God accepted the tribe of Levi, as a substitute.

Circumcision was an act symbolical of the removal of inbred sin, by entire sanctification, as we may see by reference to Coll. 2:11. It was the type of that blessing asked in the prayer of the *Collect* in the Episcopal prayer book and rituals, ''Almighty God unto whom all hearts are open, all desires known and from whom no secrets are hid, cleanse thou the thoughts of our hearts by the inspiration of thy Holy Spirit, that we may perfectly love thee.'' This prayer is offered in all the churches that follow that ritual every time the holy communion is celebrated. Very many of those churches, that solemnly celebrate the Sacrament and offer this prayer, reject and deny that this work can be done in this life. Why then mock God with vain praying? Brown the commentator says, ''Yet in this naming of him 'Saviour' in the act of circumcising him, which was a symbolical and bloody removal of the body of sin, we have an intimation that they 'have need' as John said of his baptism, rather to be circumcised by him with the circumcision not made with hands, in the putting off of the body (of sins) of the flesh by the circumcision of Christ. Thus every Jewish male becomes a holy offering to the Lord. Verse 23.'' There are many people who have much to say about Christ being our example in water baptism, but why not in our being cleansed from all sin also. It is as much, to say the least, our duty to be circumcised in heart from all sin as to be baptized with water. Do you call Jesus, your Saviour because he has saved you from all sins?

The Jewish law was constantly teaching holiness in its symbols, not only in circumcision of males but in the purification of female children and also of the mother. Forty days was the period for the purification of a male and double that number for female children. The mother was considered unclean during the time required to purify the child. Thus God kept before them the idea of original or birth sin and by the purification of the mother, the purification of the heart from sin. At the end of forty days, the mother offered a lamb for a burnt offering, and a turtledove or young pigeon for a sin offering. If too poor to procure a lamb, she had to bring another turtledove or young pigeon. If too poor to do that, then an offering of fine flour was accepted. Verse 24 would indicate that Joseph and Mary were quite poor. Mary after presenting the babe would be sprinkled with the blood of the sacrifice by the priest. And then purification from the depravity of her nature was symbolized. ''By that babe, in due time, we were to be redeemed, 'not with corruptible things such as silver and gold, but with the precious blood of Christ,' and the consuming of the mother's burnt offering and the sprinkling of her with the blood of her sin-offering, were to find their abiding realization in the 'living sacrifice' of the Christian mother herself, in the fullness of a heart sprinkled from an evil conscience' by 'the blood which cleanseth from all sin.'' (Jamieson, Fausett, & Brown).

Thus Mary presented Jesus to the Lord (Vs. 22). God had given her the greater honor of the birth of the child, Jesus, and now she gives him back to Him. She had nothing in the world so precious, that she could give Him; nothing so precious, as an offering, as this her son. Mary set the ages an example of consecrating the *best she had* to God. She gave him of whom the lamb that she would have offered had she been rich enough, was but the type.

The Jewish priest little knew when he held up the infant Jesus before the altar just what he was doing. How short sighted is man. He was holding up the great sacrifice of the ages, whose death would make the Jewish altar and priesthood no longer necessary.

TWO HOLY PEOPLE OF THE OLD DISPENSATION.
Vs. 25-39.

25 And, behold, there was a man in Jerusalem, whose name *was* Simeon; and the same man *was* just and devout, waiting for the consolation of Israel: and the Holy Ghost was upon him.

26 And it was revealed unto him by the Holy Ghost, that he should not see death, before he had seen the Lord's Christ.

27 And he came by the Spirit into the temple: and when the parents brought in the child Jesus, to do for him after the custom of the law,

28 Then took he him up in his arms, and blessed God, and said,

29 Lord, now lettest thou thy servant depart in peace, according to thy word:

30 For mine eyes have seen thy salvation,

31 Which thou hast prepared before the face of all people;

32 A light to lighten the Gentiles, and the glory of thy people Israel.

33 And Joseph and his mother marvelled at those things which were spoken of him.

34 And Simeon blessed them, and said unto Mary his mother, Behold, this *child* is set for the fall and rising again of many in Israel; and for a sign which shall be spoken against;

35 (Yea, a sword shall pierce through thy own soul also,) that the thoughts of many hearts may be revealed.

36 And there was one Anna, a prophetess, the daughter of Phanuel, of the tribe of Aser: she was of a great age, and had lived with an husband seven years from her virginity;

37 And she *was* a widow of about fourscore and four years, which departed not from the temple, but served *God* with fastings and prayers night and day.

38 And she coming in that instant gave thanks likewise unto the Lord, and spake of him to all them that looked for redemption in Jerusalem.

39 And when they had performed all things according to the law of the Lord, they returned into Galilee, to their own city Nazareth.

God has had holy people in all dispensations since the days of Abel and Enoch and although this was a dark age yet he had a few who like the morning stars were lingering until the Sun of Righteousness should arise in the spiritual heavens. Zacharias and Elizabeth, Simeon and Anna lingered on the shores of time to bring the holiness of the Old Dispensation to lay tribute to the great Exemplar of holiness. It will be noticed that Simeon and Anna were not of the priesthood but of the laity. The truth then is that God has had holy people among the laity as well as in the priesthood in all ages. In fact when the priesthood has become very corrupt in any age, the Holy Spirit has seemed to prefer the laity. Godet says "In times of spiritual degeneracy, when an official clergy no longer cultivates anything but the form of religion, its spirit retires among the obscurer members of the religious community, and creates for itself unofficial organs, often from the lowest classes. Simeon and Anna are representatives of this spontaneous priesthood." God can raise up a new priesthood any time of the true succession of the Holy Ghost. If the officials are not fit for the work of receiving his Son, he can raise up holy laymen. What a pity that the priest that day when Jesus was presented before the altar was not spiritual enough to know the Christ as did Simeon and Anna. Let no man boast of his spirituality simply because he has clerical orders, and let him not think there is not as much piety in the pew as in the pulpit. God never sanctions the priest ridden religions in which men pride themselves, as being the true succession.

If God could make Simeon and Anna holy in that dispensation there is no excuse in this dispensation for our refusing to seek that "holiness without which no man shall see the Lord." Lyman Abbott says of Simeon, he was "Just and holy in all his dealings with his fellow men; pious in his feelings toward God, and in his observance of the ceremonial law, the two elements recognized in Micah 6:8, is all that the Lord requires for the perfection of character." Such piety was so rare in that day that verse 25 begins with the word, "BEHOLD" because it was worthy of notice. Luke says Simeon was waiting for "the Consolation of Israel." This was the term often given by the Jews to the Messiah who was to come to comfort his people.

Luke still farther states that The Holy Ghost was upon Simeon. Here was a glorious experience even before Pentecost. It became the universal privilege of all believers after Pentecost. There is no more beautiful sight on earth than an old person, filled with the Holy Ghost and ready for heaven. Their very presence is a benediction wherever they go. They have no fears, no anxiety, no worry and stand eagerly on the shore, waiting for the ferry-man to take them over to the other country. Heaven has already begun in their souls. God can reveal some things to them, that he can not communicate to other people. And so we read here that, "It was revealed to him by the Holy Ghost that he should not see death until he had seen the Lord's Christ."

Simeon "came by the Spirit into the temple" at this time. So we see that the Holy Spirit did lead some people in that day. Now he leads all truly saved souls. "As many as are led by the Spirit of God, they are the sons of God." He took the infant Jesus in his arms and blessed God. The priest was not spiritual enough to know what the import of this circumcision was. But God had this layman ready to confer upon Jesus the blessing of the holy ones of the Old Dispensation. The priesthood symbolized holiness and now that it was devoid of it, God ordained a layman to offer the praises that the priesthood should have offered. The holy old man, full of gratitude, breathes out his soul in prayer to God thus, "Lord now lettest thou thy servant depart in peace." Verses 29-32 have been called the *Nunc Dimittis*, which is the Latin for *"now lettest"* the first two words of his prayer. It was true then, and is true now, that those, who have a real vision of Jesus can die in peace. There are no terrors in death after we have once seen the Christ. God had told Simeon that he might stay on earth until Jesus came. It was "according to the word of God." The good man tells why he was ready to die. It was because "mine eyes have seen thy salvation." He had seen the Christ, through whom was to come salvation for the world. He had taken the Christ in his arms. Blessed privilege! And yet we have a greater—to have him in our hearts. If we keep his commandments he has promised with this Father to take up his abode with us. (John 14:23).

Simeon like all those who are possessed by the Spirit was lifted out of selfishness. His great heart went beyond the prejudices of the Jews against other nations. It went out to the Gentile world. He saw in Jesus more than a temporal deliverer of the Jews. He saw him as "A light to lighten the Gentiles," as well as a "glory" to Israel. The indwelling Holy Spirit saves from carnal notions of religion. How many today have only carnal, inferior notions of religion. They want earthly happiness, or spectacular display in their religion. How few have the correct idea that salvation means deliverance from sin through him who was here called Jesus because he was to save from sin. All other salvation is secondary whether it be from hell or from enemies.

All these things astonished Joseph and Mary. They did not comprehend the significance of all these things. Although Mary was a holy woman she did not have perfect judgment or wisdom. What folly then to worship her as do some!

Simeon now blessed the parents and told Mary that Jesus was set for the fall and rising again of many in Israel.'' The Revised Version translates it more accurately for ''the rising up of many in Israel.'' Jesus is still set for the testing of character and destiny. On our attitude toward him rests our eternal destiny. He is ''a savor of life unto life or of death unto death.'' See this illustrated in the experience of Pilate. Judas and the Scribes and Pharisees. Although he was God's great miracle or sign yet he was ''a sign that should be spoken against'' by those Jews, who rejected him because he did not set up a worldly kingdom. Hanna in his Life of Christ says ''No such revealer of the thoughts of men's hearts has the world ever seen as Jesus Christ. His presence, his character, his ministry brought to light the hidden things of many a human spirit. He walked abroad applying upon all sides the infallible test, which tried the temper of the soul. 'If I had not come' he said 'they had not had sin, but now they have no cloak for their sin.' In its uncloaked nakedness he made sin to appear. 'I know you' he said to the Jews, 'that ye have not the love of God in you' and the reason that he gave for this was, that they had rejected him. Coming in contact with them all in turn, he revealed the hypocrisy of the Pharisee, the worldliness of the young ruler, the faith of the Syro-Phenician woman, the malice of the Sanhedrin, the weakness of Pilate, the treachery of Judas, the rashness of Peter, the tender care and sympathy of Mary. Throughout his earthly life the description here given by Simeon was continually verified.'' Men still show what they are by the way they treat Christ and holiness. His holiness and the attitude men take towards it are constantly showing what is in men. True holiness is today the touch stone of character. The anguish of soul that Mary should feel because the nation would reject and crucify Jesus would be like a sword piercing through her soul.

Holiness is not confined to either sex. We read of ''holy women'' of the olden time (See 1 Peter 3:5). One of these women was named Anna. This is the Greek word. Hannah is the Hebrew term. She was living at Jerusalem and was a prophetess. God has had his prophets, and prophetesses in all ages. They are the irregulars, while the priests and settled clergy are the Regulars. To day the evangelist supplies almost exactly the place of the prophet. He is irregular but as truly appointed of God as the regulars. His mission like that of the prophet of old is to declare the will and messages of God. In times of great spiritual degeneracy when the Regulars have become unspiritual, God has made the most frequent use of the evangelist or prophet. There has always been an outcry against him in all ages because those to whom he is sent do not like the truth he bears. John the Baptist, Wesley, Whitefield, Finney and many others belong to the order of the prophets. A prophet means more than a predicter of future events. It means one who delivers God's messages.

We learn here in the experience of Anna that God used women as religious teachers under the Old Dispensation as well as in the New. How unscriptural is the objection to women as teachers and evangelists.

The Jewish law required the testimony of at least two witnesses to establish truth. These two witnesses, Simeon and Anna testified to what the Holy Spirit had showed them. This is the business of the holy in all ages to witness to what the Holy Spirit reveals to them. The great work of the Holy Spirit in their case was to reveal Jesus. That is his business in the world today. Jesus said in this Dispensation, in which we live, that the Holy Spirit should ''glorify me: for he shall receive of mine and shall show it unto you. All things that the Father hath are mine: therefore said I, that he shall take of mine and shall show it unto you.'' (John 16:14-15). Notice, the Holy Spirit worked in the experience of these Old Testament holy people exactly as he does in the experience of holy people—those to whom the Holy Ghost has come in this Dispensation. He ever works the same in his holy people in all ages.

This holy woman had been a widow for eighty-four years.

Her husband died seven years after their marriage. She was probably married at the age of thirteen and would at this time be about one hundred and five years old. She probably lived in one of the chambers, which were attached to the temple, which may have been assigned to her on account of her prophetic gift. ''She was dead to the outer world and only lived for the service of God.'' (Codet.) Abbott thinks that as the verb *spake* in verse 38 is in the imperfect tense which signified habitual action, it means that she, from this time on was accustomed to speak of Jesus to those who were looking for the fulfillment of the re- demption of Israel. She seemed to have the *habit* of talking about Jesus. This is a good habit for us of today, to tell of his redemption. Holy people delight in the habit of telling about redemption from all sin. So in every corrupt age God has holy people, who tell of the Great Saviour.

GROWTH IN GRACE IS NOT GROWING INTO HOLINESS.
Vs. 40-52.

40   And the child grew, and waxed strong in spirit, filled with wisdom : and the grace of God was upon him.

41   Now his parents went to Jerusalem every year at the feast of the passover.

42   And when he was twelve years old, they went up to Jerusalem after the custom of the feast.

43   And when they had fulfilled the days, as they returned, the child Jesus tarried behind in Jerusalem ; and Joseph and his mother knew not *of it*.

44   But they, supposing him to have been in the company, went a day's journey ; and they sought him among *their* kinsfolk and ac- quaintance.

45   And when they found him not, they turned back again to Je- rusalem, seeking him.

46   And it came to pass, that after three days they found him in the temple, sitting in the midst of the doctors, both hearing them, and asking them questions.

47   And all that heard him were astonished at his understanding and answers.

48   And when they saw him they were amazed : and his mother said unto him, Son, why hast thou thus dealt with us? behold, thy father and I have sought thee sorrowing.

49   And he said unto them, How is it that ye sought me? wist ye not that I must be about my Father's business?

50 And they understood not the saying which he spake unto them.
51 And he went down with them, and came to Nazareth, and was subject unto them : but his mother kept all these sayings in her heart.
52 And Jesus increased in wisdom and stature, and in favour with God and man.

Vs. 40 and 52 speak of the growth of Jesus. Of course this refers to his humanity. We can never understand the mysterious union of his two natures, and hence it is idle to speculate upon the subject. As far as that matter is concerned, we cannot understand the union of spirit and body in man and how can we understand it in Him, the Wonder of the ages. It was not growth into holiness, for he was holy already. So growth does not make us holy.

The child grew physically and waxed or increased in intellectual and spiritual development. Verse 40 is absolutely all that is said about Jesus for twelve years; and after this chapter nothing is said about him during the next eighteen years of his life. What a wonderful book of biographies the Bible! No book can say as much about a person in so few words. If uninspired men had drawn the biographical sketch of Jesus, they would have spoiled the picture. How we would like to have heard of those years of silence. But God did not give this book to satisfy curiosity, but to give us sufficient light to work out our salvation and gain an abundant entrance into heaven. ''The silence of the scriptures is often more instructive than the speech of other books so that it has been likened to 'a dial in which the shadow as well as the light informs us.' It says in verse 40 that ''the grace of God was upon him.'' The Greek word for Grace is the same as our word *Favor*. We will speak of this a little later.

All Jewish parents were obliged by the law of Moses to go up to the feast of the Passover (See Exodus 38:8). So Jesus went with his parents as boys were required to begin to go to public feasts at the age of twelve and learn a trade and also wear the phylacteries. Twelve among the Jews was considered the age of accountability. They were expected to stay in Jerusalem seven days and his parents ''having fulfilled the days'' started on their return home. As the Passover was the great national feast and everyone went from all the country, it would naturally result in great companies going together in the journey. Children would naturally run about in the slow moving caravan. Consequently Mary supposed on her journey home, that Jesus was with the rest of the company. But at the close of the first day's journey she missed him. Caravans on the Passover journey usually moved about three miles per hour. But he was not to be found in the slow moving caravan and with anxious haste they returned to Jerusalem and sought him for three days in vain. When they had sought him everywhere else to no purpose they went to the house of God and there they found him. The temple of God is the place for us to-day to find Jesus. He delighted then and now to be in the Temple. Although the Jewish church was far from being what it should be, yet he went to the temple. This building stood for the honor and glory of God. There was no other building that did. The church is the best institution on earth and it represents God to the community and we should frequent its courts and seek to make it what it should be, if it is not.

Here they found him the center of an astonished group hearing and asking questions. He was not attempting to teach them, but question and answer was the method of the day. He did not yet pretend to be a teacher. But in his modest way asked questions and answered those which were asked of him. His insight into truths and religious mysteries amazed all the hearers. He evidently went deeper than their formalities of religion. We find many traces in the record concerning Mary that show that she was far from divine or worthy of worship, as some teach. She shows here that she was far from comprehending her son. They were amazed but she began to upbraid him. If she had been divine she would not have lost him, or been worried about it; neither would she have upbraided him. How inconsistent to worship her!

She hastily and impetuously said, ''Why hast thou dealt thus with us? Behold thy father and I have sought thee sorrowing.'' If she had been divine she never would have been sorrowful about it. This is the last time that Joseph, his father, is ever mentioned in the New Testament. It is supposed that he died soon after.

His only apparent surprise was that they should have sought him anywhere else except in the temple. They should have come there at once, as he had now come to the Jewish age of accountability and they might have known where to find him had they been spiritually minded. "Wist ye not that I must be about my Father's business?" Notice she said "Thy father," referring to Joseph, but he in contrast speaks of "My Father" referring to God. He recognizes one higher than his earthly father and so should all children. They should obey their parents when their duty to God does not interfere with the commands of the parents. But it must be God first.

What an example he set for all the children of God—to make their Father's business the first thing. We are put in this world for no other purpose. We learn then that going to the house of God to get truth and to impart it is a very important part of the duty of holy people. It is a part of the business that our Father has given us. His parents did not understand what he meant. Had Mary been the Queen of Heaven and worthy of worship as we are told, she would have comprehended what her son meant.

He returned with them obediently and was subject to them. He sanctified childhood as he toiled at the carpenter's bench for the next eighteen years. (Mark 6:3). This was all the theological school he attended. Is it not wonderful when viewed from a human standpoint that without any of the education of the schools of theology of the day he introduced a system of theology that has revolutionized all the religion of the world. Where did he get it, if he was not divine?

Again as in verse 19 and 33 we are told that Mary did not know what to make of these things but kept them in her memory. Luke probably got this account, by the Spirit's help, from Mary.

During the next eighteen years, which elapsed, until the time of his baptism, we hear nothing about him. During these eighteen years he "increased in wisdom and stature, and in favor with God and man." The word Stature here is translated *Age* in the Margin. And the word *favor* is translated *Grace.*

It was a fourfold development; in wisdom, stature (age), favor with God and man. Thus his human nature grew or as the Revised Version has it "advanced." His divine nature needed no development. We have here a very important teaching, showing that growth in grace does not mean the outgrowing of sin. Jesus did not grow from one state of grace to another state less sinful as some teach growing in grace to imply, until there is no sin to outgrow. He grew all the time without any sinful nature in him. The word *favor* is the same Greek word translated in other places *grace*. Divine grace is but unmerited favor. To grow in grace is to grow in the favor of God. It has nothing to do with the destruction of sin. The Bible says that only the blood of Jesus can cleanse sin—not growth. The latter only develops what we have already. Without one single passage of scriptural proof it is strange that some religionists teach the elimination of sin by growth in grace. Adam Clarke says ''Even Christ himself who knew no sin, grew in the favor of God; and as to his human nature, increased in the graces of the Holy Spirit. From this we learn that if a man were as pure and perfect as the man Christ Jesus himself was, yet he might, nevertheless, increase in the image and consequently in the favor of God.'' Dean Alford says ''It was during this time that much of the great work of the second Adam was done. The growing up through infancy, childhood, youth, manhood, from grace to grace, holiness to holiness, in subjection, self-denial and love, without one polluting touch of sin, this it was which, consummated by the three years of active ministry, by the passion and by the cross, constituted the 'obedience of one man,' by which many were made righteous.'' So we learn here what seems very difficult to many to understand, that a perfectly holy being may grow in grace and develop, and the growth does not mean out-growing sin.

CHAPTER III.

HOLINESS OF THE TWO DISPENSATIONS.

A Holy Man Preaches the Putting Away of Sin. Vs. 1-14. Holiness of the Old Dispensation Prepares the Way for Holiness of the New Dispensation. Vs. 15-18. A Holy Preacher Never Compromises with Sin. Vs. 19-20. Jesus Symbolized the Christian Priesthood. Vs. 21-22. Holiness in Human Nature Is Possible. Vs. 23-38.

A HOLY MAN PREACHES THE PUTTING AWAY OF SIN.
Vs. 1-14.

1 Now in the fifteenth year of the reign of Tiberius Cæsar, Pontius Pilate being governor of Judæa, and Herod being tetrarch of Galilee, and his brother Philip tetrarch of Ituræa and of the region of Trachonitis, and Lysanias the tetrarch of Abilene,

2 Annas and Caiaphas being the high priests, the word of God came unto John the son of Zacharias in the wilderness.

3 And he came into all the country about Jordan, preaching the baptism of repentance for the remission of sins;

4 As it is written in the book of the words of Esaias the prophet, saying, The voice of one crying in the wilderness, Prepare ye the way of the Lord, make his paths straight.

5 Every valley shall be filled, and every mountain and hill shall be brought low; and the crooked shall be made straight, and the rough ways *shall be* made smooth:

6 And all flesh shall see the salvation of God.

7 Then said he to the multitude that came forth to be baptized of him, O generation of vipers, who hath warned you to flee from the wrath to come?

8 Bring forth therefore fruits worthy of repentance, and begin not to say within yourselves, We have Abraham to *our* father: for I say unto you, That God is able of these stones to raise up children unto Abraham.

9 And now also the axe is laid unto the root of the trees: every tree therefore which bringeth not forth good fruit is hewn down, and cast into the fire.

10   And the people asked him, saying, What shall we do then?

11   He answereth and saith unto them, He that hath two coats, let him impart to him that hath none; and he that hath meat, let him do likewise.

12   Then came also publicans to be baptized, and said unto him, Master, what shall we do?

13   And he said unto them, Exact no more than that which is appointed you.

14   And the soldiers likewise demanded of him, saying, And what shall we do? And he said unto them, Do violence to no man, neither accuse *any* falsely; and be content with your wages.

An interval of about eighteen years now passes since the events of the last lesson. We know this because Jesus was twelve years of age when he went to the temple at Jerusalem, as recorded in the last lesson and verse 23, of this chapter, tells us that he was now thirty years of age. This unwritten portion of His life was by no means unimportant, as he toiled at the carpenter's bench and went to the village school, as all Jewish children did, for there were two things that a Jewish parent was required to do. He must teach his boy a trade and give him a certain amount of education. Roman Catholic legends have depicted Jesus with a halo about his head. He did not need it. He had the halo of a holy character, that surrounded his life and made it attractive. Dean Alford says, ''We are apt to forget that it was during this time that much of the great work of the second Adam was done. The growing up through infancy childhood, youth, manhood, from grace to grace, holiness to holiness, in subjection, self-denial, and love, without one polluting touch of sin—this it was which, consummated by the three years of active ministry, by the passion, and by the Cross, constituted 'the obedience of one man whereby many were made righteous.' ''

We see here the beauty of St. Luke's literary style. He was the most systematic of all the New Testament writers except Paul. Notice how methodically he writes as to the date of the ministry of John, the Baptist. He describes the year and the place in the Roman empire and the rulers, where this ministry took place, in the most orderly way.

It was at the time when Pilate was governor of Judea, Herod Antipas was governor of Galilee, Herod Philip, ruler of Iturea in the north east, and Lysanias, governor of Abilene, a district farther still in the north east, whose exact bounds are not known. These last three rulers were called tetrarchs. The word means a governor of a fourth part of a kingdom that has been divided. The word after a time came to mean the ruler of any part of a divided kingdom. The kingdom of Herod had been divided at his death into three parts, over which were placed his children. His son, Herod Archelaus had been banished after a rule of ten years over Judea, Samaria and Idumea, and Pontius Pilate had been appointed by the Romans in his place. Luke also to make it still more accurate says, that it was when Annas and Caiaphas were the high priests. Now this may appear a little singular and apparently contradictory to fact, for but one person was made high priest at a time, according to Jewish law and he held the office until death, but Annas had been removed from the office and Caiaphas, his son-in-law had been appointed in his place. The Jews probably refused to recognize Caiaphas as the real high priest, but continued to regard Annas as the real high priest. So Luke refers to a well known fact of history.

It was at this time that John came with his ministry of preparation for the coming Messiah. We must remember that his was in the closing days of the Old Dispensation and John was the last prophet of that dispensation. John was like Elijah in his austerity and simple manner of living and rebuke of sin. He came to stir up the consciences of the dead church of the Jews and call them to repentance as a preparation for the still more advanced teaching and preaching of Jesus. John stood somewhat in the same relation to the preaching of Jesus that the Holy Spirit does in this dispensation. He came to put men under conviction for sin. All the real preachers of the Gospel have a message that appeals to slumbering consciences and uncovers sin. All holy men preach genuine repentance. They could not do otherwise, for holiness never glosses over or apologizes for sin. It takes the consecration of a real holy man to uncompromisingly rebuke and show up sin. A hireling, half-hearted ministry do not attempt it. It takes a man really consecrated to be willing to endure the opposition that is sure to come as we see in John's case. (See verses 19, 20.) Who is sufficient for these things except he is dead to the opinions of men?

So Luke says ''The word of God came to John.'' This is a frequent phrase used in the Old Testament, when God called a man for the utterance of a special line of messages. This shows that John was one of the Old Testament order of prophets. No man is fit to preach the Gospel except he feels that he has a message from God for the people to whom he ministers. If all preachers had this feeling when they preached what a different class of messages we should get! The men who have God with them today have that kind of a ministry. It is something more than to entertain or please the people when we preach the real Gospel.

John came in the wilderness country around about the river, Jordan, and the people came to hear him. John was a man filled with the Holy Ghost and such character can not be hid. No matter if it be in the back districts men will find a holy man out and be attracted by his character and his preaching. John did no miracle but his holy life was a great miracle and it drew men. There is no greater miracle. It is not so much where we are or where we live as *what* we are. If we are holy we need not sigh for a place to have our talents appreciated. Men will scent the fragrance from afar.

While emperors and magnates are attracting the attention of men, God's servants are ripening in obscurity, and when the time comes they will be known and felt. God will bring the holy out of their obscurity. John and Jesus had no ambition to shine. By his wilderness training John had learned to have few wants.

His mode of life was so simple that he did not need the patronage of the great. If we live so as to make the patronage of man a necessity we are tied up in our deliverance of the truth. When we have to depend on wealthy men to support elegant churches we will have to cater to them in the preaching of the word. John was looking for no emoluments from men. Here is where many ministers of the word fall into a snare. If we are depending on what men can do for us, then men can disappoint us and break our hearts. John was willing to wait for years until God wanted him to appear before men. A proof that a person who has the fullness of the Spirit is, that like John he seeks no honors or preferments from men.

He came now into all the region about Jordan preaching the baptism of repentance. We must keep in mind that the word baptism means cleansing. There are those who fail to distinguish between baptism and the ordinance of baptism, and hence as they think it is all an ordinance, they get nothing out of it. What a pity that people can see no difference between the sign and that which it stands for. The ordinance was with water to show that baptism meant cleansing because water is used to cleanse. We must remember too that this ordinance was not the ordinance of Christian baptism, because it was performed under the Old Dispensation and was not in the name of the Trinity. We remember that some of John's converts, who had been baptized with water had to be baptized again in order to have the ceremony of Christian baptism. (See Acts 19:1-5.) John preached the baptism of repentance that is of being baptized with water as a sign that they forsook their sins and were cleansed outwardly from their sinful acts so that they could lead a life free from sin. Repentance means such a change of mind toward sin that we no longer love it, but put it away.

He not only preached repentance but he preached it for a purpose. It was "for the remission of sins." This meant for the removal of sins, so that we can lead a clean outward life. Paul calls regeneration "the washing of regeneration" (Titus 3:5) because it makes a man's life clean before the world. "Not merely for the pardon of sins, but for the putting away of and cleansing from sin" (Abbott). The word remissions means *deliverance*. Those who in their false humility maintain, that we can not have victory over sin, are not up to the last days of the Old Dispensation, in which John was telling people they could lead a clean life.

The term "Baptism of John" means more than the ordinance of baptism. It means the ministry and teaching of John sometimes (See Chapter 11:30). Notice that the two great acts of the soul are for a definite purpose: Repentance for the remission or deliverance from sins and consecration for the entire sanctification of the nature. Paul said (Rom. 12:1-2) that we should entirely consecrate in order, that we might *prove* what is the "perfect will of God." The perfect will of God of course includes all that there is of salvation from sin.

So John came taking his stand upon the scriptures as all preachers, who are holy do. He quoted from the prophet Isaiah (40:3-5), All true preaching takes its authority from ''Thus saith the Lord.'' The metaphysical and speculative theories spun out of some pulpits are as far from preaching the word of God as they are from the understanding of the hungry people, who go away disappointed.

John quoted this passage ''The voice of one crying in the wilderness.'' John (John 1:23) told the delegation of priests and Levites, ''I am the voice of one crying.'' It is not enough that truth be put in books. God might have written it on the heavens, but he has seen fit to have it rendered by that most marvellous of all instruments, the human voice. There is no talking machine ever invented that can equal it. God wants the truth voiced by holy men. There is no power equal to this holy voicing. The great revival movements of the ages have been through the voicing of the truth by holy men. His message was the message that since that time has been given by all true preachers ''Prepare ye the way of the Lord.'' Anciently heralds went to announce the approach of a monarch and to bid the people to prepare the highways so that the roads would be smooth and easy. John came as a herald to urge the people to get ready for the coming of Jesus by having their lives right. That is what God has put the ministry of today in the world to do—not so much to argue as to herald or announce that they ought to be ready all the time for the Second Coming of Jesus, just as John urged the people of his day to be ready for the First Coming of Jesus. Preaching is not so much arguing as it is announcing—declaring the will of God.

John urged the people to make God's ''paths straight.'' His paths are in his church especially. He wanted a righteous church in that day, and he wants such a church when he comes the Second time. And he wants a righteous church before he can or will do much in convicting sinners. He wants the high mountains of pride to be levelled and the low places of doubt and failure filled up and the crookedness of our lives made straight. God wants to come through his church. That is his path—his way of coming to the world. ''The depression of ignorance and superstition, the exaltation of power and pride, crooked and corrupt ways of deviating from the straight lines of integrity, and rudeness of temper born of deficient human sympathy are all so many obstacles to the coming of the king in the soul." By comparing Chapter 1:17 we find that the great business of John was to get a righteous people ready for the coming of Jesus.

And John here adds as an encouragement (Vs. 6) that "All flesh shall see the salvation of God:" This may refer primarily to Jesus who is called the Salvation of God. (Ch. 2:30.) It also may mean in a larger sense, the salvation which Jesus brings to those who will receive it.

John was very stern and uncompromising in his preaching. The multitude had come out to him a good deal like some do to a modern popular revival, because it was the latest religious fad and were seeking to be baptized, they hardly knew why, like some today.

"O, generation of vipers." Matthew says he addressed this particularly to the Scribes and Pharisees, the leaders of the church. It was severe language to call them the offspring of vipers. Their parentage was very bad according to this. Churches that get formal usually become wicked also, and after relying for a time on the externals of religion deny the supernatural in religion and God has to raise up men who will openly rebuke their sins. When we consider that these leaders cruelly crucified Jesus, we see that John accurately described their hellish origin. They were thinking themselves, the children of Abraham, when they were the children of the Old Serpent. The church today suffers for the lack of plain speaking. Only a holy preacher has the courage to call things by their right names. These people thought themselves assured of salvation because they were members of the church, of their fathers. (Matt. 3:9.) But righteousness is not transmitted. People say sometimes why do not holy people have holy children?" Grace is not transmitted. Every man must obtain it for himself. It is a sad day when a church can tell only of the achievements of its fathers. It is a proof that God has left it.

He wanted to know who had warned them to flee from the "Wrath to come." All Gospel preachers warn men of the coming wrath. That is truly a part of the Gospel as well as to depict the joys of heaven.

Because there is a wrath to come, he exhorted this church to bring forth fruits worthy of repentance. God requires churches to repent as truly as impenitent sinners in the outside world. He does not excuse men, who sin, even if they are of his outward church. So we see it here plainly declared that church membership will not save men. Even if they did have Abraham for their founder, they must be *like* Abraham, or they would go to hell in spite of their standing in the church. These "conservative" church members rejected this message (Matt. 21:32), but the common people heard him gladly (See verse 10).

There have been and are churches that claim to have a monopoly to salvation. They announce themselves as of the Apostolic succession and claim that they are in unbroken succession from the time of the apostles. This can not be proved, but if it were true what of that? God will take away their candle from its place, as he did that of the Jews if they are not apostolic in having holiness of heart. Does not God say here that God was able to raise up another succession from the very stones that lay about the river Jordan? God wants churches that have the apostolic fire and are free from sin. Godet says "In verses 7 and 8 is a reminder of the incorruptible holiness of the judgment day."

He tells them still farther that "The axe is laid at the root of the tree." By this he meant that God was giving the Jewish church one more opportunity to redeem itself from its corruption. This figure of a tree, spared for a time is used by Jesus in two other places and every time in reference to the Jewish church. (See chapter 13:6-9 and Mark 11:13-14, 20-22.) The Jewish church was a tree at whose base God had laid the axe ready to cut it down. They could hardly believe that God would allow a church to go down, to whom he had shown so many favors in the past. Churches and individuals seem to think so now. The question is not was Abraham or Wesley or Fox or Luther our founder but are we following in the footsteps of our pious ancestry? If not God will take away our candlestick. Jesus told the Jews in another place when they said "Abraham is our father," "If ye were Abraham's children, ye would do the works of Abraham." So we may say today "If ye are the children of Wesley, or Fox or Luther you would do the works of these holy men." We learn from this, that with all the boasted improvement—new religion that proposes to set aside the teachings of the fathers that brought salvation, Jesus had no sympathy. He believed in sticking to the old faith and works of Abraham. We live in a day when men are discarding the doctrines of Wesley, especially the doctrine which he said was his chief doctrine. The principle is true, as uttered by John and Jesus that there is no real advance that does not manifest itself in the same kind of fruitage and more of it, than the fathers produced. John and Jesus were conservatives in the highest and best sense of the term. We are told that the rank and file of Wesley's church no longer preach the chief doctrine of Wesley. If they have made improvements on it, then they ought to have more and greater revivals. If not then they are recreant and may expect to have the axe not only laid at the root of the tree but also plied. The favored Jewish church was soon superseded. It means as good fruit as the fathers produced or destruction. God will put better trees in the place of these dead trees.

But the common people were more tractable and open to light and they said to John ''What shall we do then?'' As we have remarked before the common people have always been more ready to receive the Gospel and acknowledge their sins than the higher classes. So we hear them asking the same question that was asked at Pentecost and that every really convicted, penitent soul asks. (Acts 2:37; Acts 16:30.)

John in reply gives directions to three classes of people: Those, who have a surplus of the necessities of life. Those, who had two coats, were to impart one of them to those who had none. This, of course, would also apply to food. Those who had abundance of food were also to give to others. This is a good way to prove that our repentance is genuine. We are to do good to all men as far as we can and especially to the needy. There is no genuine repentance that does not have an outward manifestation. 2. He gives directions to the publicans or tax gatherers. These were a class of men who took the contract to collect the taxes, which the Jews were obliged to pay the Roman government. They were a very unpopular class with the Jews for two reasons: The Jews paid their tax with great reluctance, and often there were riots when attempts were made to collect it. 2. The publicans usually taxed them higher than they should, and there was no redress. They had to pay. John told these publicans that they must collect no more than the law allowed, and if they were true penitents God would forgive their sins. God will save even unpopular people. This was a truth that the Jews did not relish —that Publicans could be saved. Matthew tells us that those who were baptized by John, came confessing their sins. (Matt. 3:6.) 3. A third class were soldiers. We do not know who these soldiers were. But it was an age when soldiers generally looked down with contempt upon civilians, and were inclined to treat them harshly for the purpose of robbing them, and often used violence. John does not condemn their calling as soldiers but insists that they shall be honest and humane. War is a great evil and is to be shunned as much as possible. But we can hardly say that all war is wrong. We believe there have been wars that have made the world better. Wars like that of the Spanish-American conflict waged by the United States to free suffering Cuba are as much justified as an attack would be on a wild beast to rescue a child. Jesus did not condemn the Centurion (Matt. 7:9) but honored him as a man of faith.

And so we find that genuine repentance is a change of mind in people towards sin that leads them to bring forth corresponding fruits in their lives. We ought to notice that John carries out the figure of fruitage and the tree in verses 8 and 9. There must be fruits worthy of repentance or God will cut the church tree down that fails in this respect.

HOLINESS OF THE OLD DISPENSATION PREPARES THE WAY FOR HOLINESS OF THE NEW DISPENSATION.

Vs. 15-18.

15   And as the people were in expectation, and all men mused in their hearts of John, whether he were the Christ, or not;

16   John answered, saying unto *them* all, I indeed baptize you with water; but one mightier than I cometh, the latchet of whose shoes I am not worthy to unloose: he shall baptize you with the Holy Ghost and with fire:

17 Whose fan *is* in his hand, and he will thoroughly purge his floor, and will gather the wheat into his garner; but the chaff he will burn with fire unquenchable.

18 And many other things in his exhortation preached he unto the people.

In other words, the holy man John, the last prophet of the Old Dispensation is here preparing the way for Jesus, the founder of the New Dispensation, who came to preach and exemplify holiness as it had never been administered before. It is worthy of notice that Jesus and John were the two greatest men that ever walked the face of the earth. Jesus said "Among those born of women there hath not risen one greater than John the Baptist." (Matt. 11:11.) *We see then that the two greatest men that the world has ever seen were holy.* We see too that holiness is not some fad professed by the weak minded. John prepared the way of Jesus by preaching repentance and when John came he did not supersede John's doctrine but also began his preaching with repentance. (Matt. 4:17). Any advanced dispensation that is in the divine order does not discard the God honored truths of the past but honors and emphasizes them and incorporates them, no matter howsoever much it may improve upon them. This has always been the divine rule. God never disparages the truths and doctrines that he has honored in the past. We commend these facts to those who have ceased preaching the God-honored dictrine of holiness that was so successful in bringing about Methodism—the greatest revival the world has ever seen. If there is any improvement on the doctrine it does not do away with the doctrine but incorporates it in its own bosom and emphasizes it all the more and shows how it may be more fruitful. If new doctrine does not then we have gone back on what God has honored.

The people thought John was his Master, for a holy man always makes people think of God. So the people were in suspense and were debating whether he was the Messiah or not. But John at once put an end to their questioning by saying that he was not the Messiah. He only claimed to be administering a lesser baptism, while the Messiah was to come and administer the greater baptism. (John 1:20.) Here John exemplified the greatness of holiness, which is always manifest in deep humility. An ordinary man would doubtless have been upset by all this popularity and would have attempted to get some glory to himself. But real holiness is humble. He declared that he was not worthy to untie the shoe strings of the Messiah that was coming after him.　Mark 1:7.)　It take sa real holy man to exemplify humility, even in the worship and service of God.　John would not think of being a rival to Jesus. *The preacher who seeks to draw the people's love to himself rather than to Jesus has made Jesus his rival.* He who modifies his message to please the people esteems the love of the people more than the love of God.　He sets himself up as the rival of his Master.　This is really dangerous business.　It was very fitting that such a man should introduce Jesus.　It was very fitting that this holy man should bind the Old and New Testament dispensations together; for is not the great theme and purpose of all the dispensations holiness?

John now speaks of the two baptisms.　Just as there were two Dispensations, so there are two works of grace symbolized by two baptisms; on which we make a few observations to show that the baptism of John was an initial ceremony, symbolizing the experience of justification and regeneration.　(1.) The ordinance of baptism is the sign of moral purification.　It teaches that cleansing from outward sins has been effected.　The washings of the Old Testament ritual taught this.　John made these types effective and emphatic.　(2.) Those baptized confessed their sins. (Matt. 3:6.)　Confession means not only with the words of the lip but with the outward conduct.　Verses 12-14 show this.　(3.) It was an actual turning to God; for Gabriel had foretold that this was to be the result of John's preaching.　(Chapter 1:16.) (4.) This brought forgiveness of sins.　See verse 4.　Forgiveness of sins is justification and this was accomplished under the ministry of John.　(Ch. 1:16.)　(5.) All this was accompanied by a knowledge of salvation.　These happy converts of John's ministry knew that their sins were forgiven.　(Chapter 1:77.)　(6.) This produced a radical change of life as clearly defined as the change from night to day.　(Chapter 1:79.)　(7) This is not unscriptural for people were *converted* before Pentecost.　(See Isa. 55:7 and 6:10.)　(8.) This brought peace to the soul.　(See Chapter 1:79.)　(9.) John preached to bring about faith in Christ.　He told the people to believe in Jesus for salvation. (See Acts 19:4.) (10.) Those who honestly confessed and forsook their sins were regenerated. We know that some have supposed that no one was regenerated until Pentecost. But this is not true. Jesus told Nicodemus at the beginning of his ministry, ''Ye must be born again.'' This was some time before Pentecost. By a careful study of John 3:36 we shall discover that John the Baptist (not John the writer) is saying ''He that believeth on the Son hath everlasting life.'' Regeneration is eternal life begun in the soul. So we see that John the Baptist was preaching all that those preachers advance, who preach Bible conversion today.

But after he had preached and people had experienced these blessings of regeneration and peace, there was yet another baptism, another work of grace. It is called here the baptism with the Holy Ghost and with Fire. It is called in theological terms, entire sanctification. It is the second work of grace whereby the work of salvation in the soul begun in regeneration is completed.

There has been an error right here that some have fallen into, who have taught from this that there are three baptisms—one with water, another with the Holy Ghost and a third with fire. Their mistake is in not seeing that fire here is used to symbolize the work accomplished in the baptism with The Holy Ghost. The Holy Ghost and Fire is a figure of rhetoric called Hendiadys. Webster thus defines this figure. ''A figure in which the idea is expressed by two nouns connected by *and* instead of by a noun and a limiting adjective; as, we drink from *cups* and *gold* for *golden cups.*'' So John baptized with water as a symbol that the outward life was purified and Jesus on the day of Pentecost baptized with *fire* which rested upon the heads of the disciples as a symbol that they had received the baptism that purges the soul from sin as fire purges dross out of gold. Peter on the day of Pentecost declared that Jesus was the baptizer (See Acts 2:33). We notice there are two uses of fire: (1.) To separate the dross from the pure metal as we have just seen and (2.) To burn up the refuse. So John declared to this church that Jesus was to come to them as a farmer to his threshing floor and separate the good from the bad in his church. The method of winnowing in those days was to throw up into the air the grain in a shovel (called the winnowing fan) and while the wind blew away the chaff the grain fell to the floor. So the chaff fell in a pile by itself separated from the grain. We see then that Jesus makes a division in his church, and let no one object. Those who object to holiness because it makes division are really objecting to Jesus, for he did the same. Those who will not allow holy fire to purify them, will fall into hell fire. ''As to the fire of verse 17, it is expressly opposed to the fire of verse 16, by the epithet, *which is not quenched.* Whoever refuses to be baptized with the fire of holiness will be exposed to the fire of wrath.'' (Godet.) So we see it is holiness or hell. Inbred sin is hell fire in the soul. The fire of the Holy Ghost is more intense and can destroy hell fire in the soul.

We learn here that holiness is nothing new. We hear people sometimes say ''This is a new doctrine.'' It shows their ignorance of the Word of God and of the history of revealed religion. John preached holiness (the cleansing baptism with the Holy Ghost as truly as he preached forgiveness of sins. But it was not new with him. Malachi, the last of the Old Testament prophets, had foretold it saying ''He is like a refiner's fire and like a fuller's soap: and he shall sit as a refiner and purifier of silver.'' God had said through Ezekiel ''Then will I sprinkle clean water upon you and ye shall be clean, from all your filthiness and from all your idols will I cleanse you.'' We find in the prophecy of Isaiah these words ''And I will turn my hand upon thee, and purely purge away thy dross and take away all thy tin.'' David had prayed ''Create in me a clean heart.'' Jacob had declared that the angel had redeemed him from all evil at Peniel. (Gen. 48:16.) God had told Abraham to walk before Him and Be perfect. Enoch had actually walked with God for three hundred years. But way back of creation Paul says, God has ''chosen us in him before the foundation of the world that we should be holy and without blame before him in love.'' (Eph. 1:4.) John not only as a Nazarite (the Nazarites were the holiness people of the Old Dispensation) knew of it. But we are certain that the God who gave him this special dispensation of preparing the people for the coming of Jesus, gave him this commission to preach holiness. We believe that God expects preachers today to preach holiness to prepare the church for the second coming of Jesus, as truly as he gave John the message of holiness for the coming of Jesus the first time. It is the great theme of preaching in all ages.

St. Luke says ''And many other things in his exhortation preached he unto the people.'' Only the outlines of his doctrine are stated here. All his preaching clustered around the two works of grace, like all full gospel preaching today.

A HOLY PREACHER NEVER COMPROMISES WITH SIN.
Vs. 19-20.

19 But Herod the tetrarch, being reproved by him for Herodias his brother Philip's wife, and for all the evils which Herod had done,
20 Added yet this above all, that he shut up John in prison.

We have in the preaching of John the three elements that constitute real preaching—warning (vs. 9); exhortation (vs. 18) and reproof (vs. 19-20). The latter is often neglected. When practiced it is objected to and such preachers are said by the gainsaying and carnal church to be too harsh. John was faithful to his hearers. John was obliged to rebuke the adultery of the king. This was the awful sin of that day and also of this time. Paul gives it at the head of the works of the flesh. (Gal. 5:19.)

The circumstances were as follows. Herod Antipas, the king or Tetrarch of Galilee and Perea had married the wife of his brother Philip, having induced her to forsake her husband. John had not hesitated to rebuke him for his sin. It seems that he was very wicked and this seems to have been the climax as verse 20 says, he ''Added yet this above all.'' This phrase seems to voice the indignation of the writer as he depicts the infamous character of Herod. The full account of John's death is given in Matthew 14:3. Verses 19 and 20 are given here to finish up the account of John's ministry begun in the first verse of the chapter. The death of John did not occur until several months later.

JESUS SYMBOLIZED THE CHRISTIAN PRIESTHOOD.
Vs. 21-22.

21 Now when all the people were baptized, it came to pass, that Jesus also being baptized, and praying, the heaven was opened,

22 And the Holy Ghost descended in a bodily shape like a dove upon him, and a voice came from heaven, which said thou art my beloved Son; in thee I am well pleased.

It was while Jesus was praying that he received the manifestation of the opened heavens and the descending dove. If we prayed more, we should more often see opened heavens and the effusion of the Spirit. On the great occasions of his life he was praying; not only at his baptism but at his transfiguration (Chapter 9:28-29); also in Gethsemane and on the cross. There has been some perplexity, with some people, as to the nature of the baptism of Jesus. He was not baptized as our example of water baptism, for John's baptism was not Christian baptism, which is administered in the name of the Holy Trinity. He was in no sense a candidate for water baptism as we are. The ordinance of water baptism is administered to those who have sinned and have been pardoned. It is a symbol that their guilt has been washed away. The man baptized in that act confesses that he is a sinner, and has been pardoned. Jesus never sinned and that was not the significance of the act. He said he was baptized "Thus it becometh us to fulfill all righteousness." (Matt. 3:15.) He referred evidently to the outward ceremonial law. He was a priest of the order of Melchisedeck (Hebrews 5:10) and was now at the age of thirty (vs. 23) being inaugurated with the usual ceremonies, that all high priests had to pass through, from the days of Aaron. The usual ceremony of ordination for the priesthood was washing the body in pure water and anointing with oil. (See Leviticus 8:5-12.) Oil was the symbol of the anointing with the Holy Spirit. Thus he was publicly installed, being washed with water as a symbol of purity that all true priests must have and anointed with oil, as the empowerment for his life work. He has been in the priesthood ever since and has gone to heaven to intercede as a great high priest for the human race. Peter tells us about his anointing thus, "God anointed Jesus of Nazareth, with the Holy Ghost who went about doing good and healing all that were oppressed of the devil" (Acts 10:38). Jesus himself so announced it when he returned from the wilderness temptation, as he entered the synagogue in Nazareth, quoting Isaiah 61:1, "The Spirit of the Lord is upon me, because he hath anointed me to preach the Gospel to the poor; he hath sent me to heal the broken hearted, to preach deliverance to the captives, and recovering of sight to the blind, to set at liberty them that are bruised, to preach the acceptable year of the Lord.'' This teaches us that Jesus was here anointed for his life work. This ceremony of consecration—cleansing with water and anointing with oil—under the Old Dispensation represented the consecration, entire sanctification and anointing for service which God has provided for all his children who are priests of the New Dispensation. For we are priests unto God in this dispensation. Peter says, ''Ye are a chosen generation, a royal priesthood, an holy nation, a peculiar people.'' John says (Rev. 1:5-6) ''Unto him that loved us and washed us from our sins in his own blood and hath made us kings and priests unto God.'' The Revised Version translates it ''Hath made us a kingdom of priests.''

The believer is called by many names in the word of God— salt, light, a pilgrim, a witness, a friend of Jesus—but the term, priest combines them all.

There were two essentials to the priesthood: 1. Birth. The priest must be born in the family of Levi. The Christian priest must be born into the family of God, by the new birth. Unsaved people can not be members of this priesthood. 2. He must be set apart by a definite act of consecration. While all priests were Levites, all Levites were not priests because not set apart especially for that office. All Christians are not qualified for the Christian priesthood until they have set themselves apart by a complete consecration and have been cleansed from all sin and anointed with the Holy Ghost.

What is the priestly office that we are called to exercise today? It is to stand between God and man as the ancient priesthood did. We are to pray to God to save the people and we are to pray the people to be reconciled to God. Intercession for a lost world is the great business of the Christian, and who is sufficient for these things until he has been wholly sanctified?

Jesus was our file leader. He represented the experience of entire sanctification and of the anointing of the Spirit when he was baptized in Jordan and the Spirit came upon him. A careful study of the New Testament will show that his earthly life was an illustration or symbol of the spiritual experiences of the believer. For instance we are to be crucified to sin, just as he was crucified by sin. (Gal. 1:20.) We are to reckon ourselves dead to sin just as he died for it (Rom. 6:11). Just as he had a resurrection from the grave to a new life so are we to have a resurrection from sin with him (Coll. 3:1). Jesus was born of the Holy Spirit. (Luke 1:35.) So is the Christian. And so we are to set ourselves apart for the great work of praying the lost world home to God, as he illustrated it at Jordan—by an act of consecration which if done completely, will result in cleansing and empowering for our life-work of intercession.

The Spirit rested on him "like a dove." This was the outward manifestation as John doubtless saw it. It was not the inward anointing but the outward sign, for the benefit of John. On the day of Pentecost the manifestation was tongues of fire showing that the Spirit fell on the disciples, teaching that they had their hearts purified (he only typified it by the baptism) so the manifestation was of a dove. Luke says that the Spirit came in "bodily shape like a dove." The dove was the only fowl used in sacrifice. It is the gentlest of all the feathered tribe. We read that "the Spirit of God moved upon the face of the waters" (Genesis 1:2) at the creation. It may be properly translated "The Spirit of God kept fluttering after the manner of a dove upon the face of the waters." The Spirit is likened to a dove with its gentleness—not to an eagle, hawk or buzzard, birds of prey. How many have not discovered in their fancied profession of holiness that if they are filled with the Spirit they will not be like the eagle or hawk in their fierceness or the buzzard who seeks and loves carrion. They will have the gentleness of the dove.

The dove-like Spirit rested on the lamb-like Jesus; him who should "not strive nor cry, neither should his voice be heard in the street." If we have the Spirit we shall possess the dove-like nature. We will be free from the spirit of contention.

A voice came from heaven also saying "Thou art my beloved Son, in whom I am well pleased." Here we have the three persons of the Trinity clearly indicated. The Father, the first person, gives this testimony concerning the Son, the Second person.

And the Holy Spirit, the third person comes upon Jesus. Thus the three great dispensations were mingled. John represented the Dispensation of the Old Testament. Jesus represented the dispensation of the present, and the first two dispensations were all preparatory for the great dispensations of the Holy Ghost— the last of all, in which we now live. We have here an illustration of the fact that the Holy Spirit testifies to every work that he does. He testifies in conviction, in regeneration and in entire sanctification.

HOLINESS IN HUMAN NATURE IS POSSIBLE. Vs. 23-38.

23 And Jesus himself began to be about thirty years of age, being (as was supposed) the son of Joseph, which was *the son* of Heli,

24 Which was *the son* of Matthat, which was *the son* of Levi, which was *the son* of Melchi, which was *the son* of Janna, which was *the son* of Joseph,

25 Which was *the son* of Mattathias, which was *the son* of Amos, which was *the son* of Naum, which was *the son* of Esli, which was *the son* of Nagge,

26 Which was *the son* of Maath, which was *the son* of Mattathias, which was *the son* of Semei, which was *the son* of Joseph, which was *the son* of Juda,

27 Which was *the son* of Joanna, which was *the son* of Rhesa, which was *the son* of Zorobabel, which was *the son* of Salathiel, which was *the son* of Neri,

28 Which was *the son* of Melchi, which was *the son* of Addi, which was *the son* of Cosam, which was *the son* of Elmodam, which was *the son* of Er,

29 Which was *the son* of Jose, which was *the son* of Eliezer, which was *the son* of Jorim, which was *the son* of Matthat, which was *the son* of Levi,

30 Which was *the son* of Simeon, which was *the son* of Juda, which was *the son* of Joseph, which was *the son* of Jonan, which was *the son* of Eliakim,

31 Which was *the son* of Melea, which was *the son* of Menan, which was *the son* of Mattatha, which was *the son* of Nathan, which was *the son* of David,

32 Which was *the son* of Jesse, which was *the son* of Obed, which was *the son* of Booz, which was *the son* of Salmon, which was *the son* of Naasson.

33 Which was *the son* of Aminadab, which was *the son* of Aram, which was *the son* of Esrom, which was *the son* of Phares, which was *the son* of Juda,

34 Which was *the son* of Jacob, which was *the son* of Isaac, which was *the son* of Abraham, which was *the son* of Thara, which was *the son* of Nachor.

35 Which was *the son* of Saruch, which was *the son* of Ragau, which was *the son* of Phalec, which was *the son* of Heber, which was *the son* of Sala,

36 Which was *the son* of Cainan, which was *the son* of Arphaxad, which was *the son* of Sem, which was *the son* of Noe, which was *the son* of Lamech,

37 Which was *the son* of Mathusala, which was *the son* of Enoch, which was *the son* of Jared, which was *the son* of Maleleel, which was *the son* of Cainan.

38 Which was *the son* of Enos, which was *the son* of Seth, which was *the son* of Adam, which was *the son* of God.

We have now the genealogy of Jesus given. Luke and Matthew are the only two evangelists who give this. The reason that it is given is because the writers wished to show that he was really human as well as divine. John says "the word was made flesh and dwelt among us." He was not only God but sanctified human nature. It is again and again asserted that no human being can be holy. In reply we say that God made Adam holy in the beginning, and if he made one man holy he could make others holy. He made Jesus our pattern absolutely holy. His humanity was holy. It will not do to say that God can not make any one else holy unless we believe we can limit the power of Almighty God. We do not say that we can be equal to Jesus in his infinite attributes, but we may be like him in spite of our weakness, fallibility and infirmities.

It will be noticed that the two genealogies are different in Matthew and Luke. The former (Matthew) begins with David and comes down to Jesus. The latter (Luke) begins with Heli and going back to Adam, which is just the reverse from the table of Matthew. The latter was trying to show the Jews that Jesus was of the royal line of David. While the latter was writing more for the benefit of the Gentiles.

There seems a slight discrepancy between the two tables, as Jesus and Joseph are said by Luke to be descendants of Heli, while Matthew makes him son of Mary. We must remember that the Jews never allowed women's names in their genealogical tables. Women were not of much account with them. The passage will be made more clear if we translate it, as it should be, thus, "Jesus being (as was reputed) the son of Joseph (but in reality the son of Heli," or his grandson by his mother's side. Son and Grandson were used interchangeably by genealogical tables. This was the nearest they could express it because the names of women were not permitted in these tables. As Dr. Lightfoot says "Mary is not mentioned by Luke, but is only intimated or included, when the line is commenced from her father, Heli."

CHAPTER IV.

HOLINESS WILL BE TEMPTED.

The Threefold Temptation of Holy People. Vs. 1-13. Those, Who Have Received Their Pentecost, Go Forth in the Power of the Spirit. Vs. 14-15. Holiness Utters Truths Unpalatable to Carnal People. Vs. 16-30. The Power of Holy Preaching. Vs. 31-32. Holiness Can Not Tolerate Moral Uncleanness. Vs. 33-37. Holiness Delights in Good Works for Mankind. Vs. 38-44.

THE THREEFOLD TEMPTATION OF HOLY PEOPLE.
Vs. 1-13.

1 And Jesus being full of the Holy Ghost returned from Jordan, and was led by the Spirit into the wilderness,

2 Being forty days tempted of the devil. And in those days he did eat nothing: and when they were ended, he afterward hungered.

3 And the devil said unto him, If thou be the Son of God, command this stone that it be made bread.

4 And Jesus answered him, saying, It is written, That man shall not live by bread alone, but by every word of God.

5 And the devil, taking him up into an high mountain, shewed unto him all the kingdoms of the world in a moment of time.

6 And the devil said unto him, All this power will I give thee, and the glory of them: for that is delivered unto me; and to whomsoever I will I give it.

7 If thou therefore wilt worship me, all shall be thine.

8 And Jesus answered and said unto him, Get thee behind me, Satan: for it is written, Thou shalt worship the Lord thy God, and him only shalt thou serve.

9 And he brought him to Jerusalem, and set him on a pinnacle of the temple, and said unto him, If thou be the Son of God, cast thyself down from hence:

10 For it is written, He shall give his angels charge over thee, to keep thee:

11   And in *their* hands they shall bear thee up, lest at any time thou dash thy foot against a stone.

12   And Jesus answering said unto him, It is said, Thou shalt not tempt the Lord thy God.

13   And when the devil had ended all the temptation, he departed from him for a season.

Jesus, while on earth symbolized the experiences of holy people. After he had symbolized the sanctification and anointing of his saints, he was full of the Holy Spirit (Vs. 1). So will those be, who have received their Pentecost. We know this may seem too exalted a privilege to some. But we are commanded to be filled with the same Spirit that filled Jesus (Eph. 5:18). In verse 14 it says he returned in the power of the Spirit. These two experiences will be found in the experience of entirely sanctified Christians—"full of the Spirit" and "in the power of the Spirit." He now goes forth to exemplify the power of holiness and the holy way. The first thing that he met was temptation. Great blessings are usually followed by great temptations. God intends after He has given great grace to allow it to be tested and developed, just as nature develops the sturdy oak by the fierce blast of the storm, which not only proves its strength, but causes it to root deeper. It takes great temptations as well as great grace to make a great preacher or an eminent saint. "Blessed is the man that endureth temptation." Yet how few appreciate that blessedness while it is going on. Every reform in the church and every reformer has been opposed by Satan, with good reason, for true spiritual work means the subversion of the kingdom of Satan. The latter never antagonizes spurious religion. How much Satan saw in Jesus of Nazareth, or whether he realized at this time that Jesus was divine, we do not pretend to say. But he had tested all the great reformers of the past—Abraham, Moses, Elijah, David and others, and some of them had gone down under the pressure of his temptation. Now he tries his assaults upon the Son of God. How could he tempt Jesus? We do not know. How he tempts and overthrows eminent saints sometimes we do not know. There are many facts in this matter that we can never understand. They are too profound.

Did he really take Jesus to the pinnacle of the temple or to a high mountain? or did he take him there in imagination? Commentators are not agreed upon this. But of one thing we are certain, the temptations were just as real to the soul of Jesus, as if he had. There is just as surely a Satan as there is a Christ, a person. Both are mentioned in the Scriptures. Jesus came to destroy the works of Satan, which are sin and sins and here the battle begins, in the wilderness.

It is worthy of notice that Jesus was *led* into the wilderness by the Spirit. It was preparatory to his life work. The great leaders of the church went into retirement just before their great life work; for instance, Moses in Midian; Jesus and John in the wilderness and Paul in Arabia.

While in this retirement the Tempter came to Jesus. The first Adam was defeated by Satan in a garden of beauty. The second Adam defeated Satan in a howling wilderness.

Jesus was "*led* by the Spirit into the wilderness." He did not thrust himself into temptation. God never tempts us, but he suffers us to be tempted, either for our own good or for the good of others. We do not by any means think that the temptations recorded here were the only ones that Jesus encountered at this time but these were the most important. Luke says in verse 2 that he was tempted forty days. These temptations were the climax and when they were overcome, the devil left him.

These temptations are given to illustrate the nature of the threefold temptation that comes to entirely sanctified people— those who like Jesus have received their Pentecost.

These three temptations of Jesus illustrate the threefold kind of temptation that comes to those who are like Jesus (who have received their pentecost). The author of Hebrews, says of Jesus, that he was "tempted in all points like as without sin." A reference to Hebrews will show that the words in the common version, "*we are*" are italicised, showing that they are not in the original, but have been supplied by the translators to suit their notions. It means evidently that Jesus was tempted in all points like as those are tempted who are without sin. Adam was without sin when tempted, but he fell. Jesus was without sin and he was tempted and triumphed. The difference between the temptations of one who is without sin, and one who is sinful is, the temptation of the one, who is without sin is all from the outside—the devil or the world; while the temptations of the other, are from his own evil heart and from the outside also. One has both inward and outward temptations, while the other—the wholly sanctified man—has his temptations only from the outside. The former is like a nation attempting to carry on a foreign and civil war at the same time.

There is a base, current slander that holy people profess that they have arrived at a place where they are never tempted. This is not only not true but the fact is that holy people are the most tempted of any class on earth. The devil never bothers those of whom he is sure; but the further away from him we seek to get, the more he tempts us. The temptation of Jesus is a mystery. If we cannot understand how he could be tempted, it is useless to ask how can holy people be tempted. A temptation is a suggestion to do wrong, usually made to appear plausible by an attempted persuasion that wrong doing will be better for our interests.

Let us remember that it is not a mark of sin to be tempted. We note the threefold nature of the temptation peculiar to those who are entirely sanctified as illustrated by Jesus here.

1. *The temptation to fanaticism.* ''He afterward hungered.'' Satan knew just the most advantageous time to make the attack. He came when Jesus was physically weak from his long fasting. ''If thou be the son of God.'' This was a very subtle mode of attack. It was as much as to say, ''Are you after all what you claim to be, and if so make proof of it. If you are really the son of God, you would not be here alone famishing for bread. You ought to do something great to show your power. You could make bread out of these stones if you were the Son of God.'' It was an appeal to him to show off his power. Right here is where fanaticism begins. It is a glorification of self. It is an attempt to let people know what a superior being we are or what a superior experience we have. Such people have the idea that no one is sincere except themselves and that they are the favored ones of heaven. The Spirit, who led Jesus into the wilderness could supply his wants, Jesus could trust him. The fanaticism of the Pharisees was that they added to the word of God, their own traditions and thought that by keeping them they were superior to

the rest of the church. The fanatic has a superior opinion of himself. This begets a spirit of harshness towards others, who do not see as he does, and a magnifying of the non-essentials of religion, to the neglect of the chief part of religion—the love of God in the soul. The fanatic often reacts into infidelity. He is usually sincere. The devil finds that he can not hold him back so he seeks to push him ahead too far.

Jesus answers the attack by the use of the scriptures. See how the Lord himself used the Scriptures. This is a lesson for us to practice. He replied "It is written that man shall not live by bread alone, but by every word of God." He quoted from Deuteronomy 8:3. Our Lord in each of these temptations put his seal and endorsement upon the Old Testament—that much despised and much criticised book. Fanaticism puts its confidence in itself and its own opinions and impressions more than in the word of God. It seeks extraordinary manifestations—visions, tongues, etc. If we obey the plain teachings of Scripture we shall not wander into fanaticism.

2. *The temptation to compromise.* The great mission of Jesus was not merely to die for the sins of the world. He looked forward to the cross as the climax of a life of suffering, privation and persecution to the death. The devil took him up into a big mountain and showed him the kingdoms of this world and the glory of them and told him that he would give him all these if he would fall down and worship him. Alas it is too true that the devil is the king of this world—its god. Jesus could have avoided the cross and its humiliation and could have become the king of the nations with Jerusalem as his capital city. It would have been an evasion of the cross. Several times afterwards the same temptation was presented to him, when the people wanted to make him king. The devil has his worship today and his temples of worship. We have this path of compromise opened before us constantly. To walk the straight and narrow way means to bear the cross; to be stigmatized as fanatical, puritanical, etc. All sorts of excuses and apologies are made by those who tone down holiness and the work of holiness. It has always cost something to walk in the middle of the way, without turning to the right or left.

Jesus again defeats him by quoting the Scripture recorded in Deuteronomy 10:20, saying ''Get thee behind me Satan; for it is written thou shalt worship the Lord thy God and him only shalt thou serve.'' We are commanded to do the same. ''Resist the devil and he will flee from thee.'' Satan is a coward. He will flee if stoutly resisted. Here he calls him by his name, Satan, for the first time, to let him know that he recognizes, who he is. He is called here by two names—Satan (Vs. 8) and The Devil (Vs. 3, 5, 6). The word devil signifies accuser (Rev. 12:9-10). He is also called Abaddon in the Hebrew tongue, and Apollyon in the Greek. Both words mean the Destroyer (Rev. 9:11); also Belial —a good for nothing (2 Cor. 6:15); also Satan which means an adversary (Job 2:1). He is as real a person here as Jesus. To deny the personality of one is to deny the personality of the other.

3. *The temptation to presumption.* Satan now takes Jesus to a pinnacle of the temple and bids him cast himself down that the people may see the wonder of his miraculous power. This would give him favor in the eyes of the people at once and save the persecution and opposition which would come later. It was a way of escape from the cross. Satan uses Scripture saying, ''It is written, He shall give his angels charge concerning thee; and in their hands they shall bear thee up lest thou dash thy foot against a stone.'' This is a quotation from Psalms 91:11. The devil knows how to quote scripture and can quote it quite ingeni- ously when it suits him. He finds that Jesus relies on the word and so he quotes it too. Misapplied Scripture has done much mis- chief. There is not a damnable fanaticism under heaven but has sought to bring the Bible to its assistance. St. Jerome says ''If the text, which he quotes refers to Christ, he ought to have added what follows against himself—the dragon shalt thou cast under thy feet.'' (See Psalm 91:13.) It would be presumptive for Jesus to needlessly put himself into danger, expecting that angels would preserve him. Some of the saddest break-downs have been of people, who needlessly put themselves in the way of tempta- tion, relying on God to keep them, because they had a good expe- rience. They are weeping tears of bitter regret today. Faith may be pushed too far and result in presumption, for ''Evil com-

munications corrupt good manners.'' We must keep off the devil's territory, unless we have some duty to perform there.

So the devil left Jesus for a season. It suits his purpose to sometimes leave us for a season, only that his next attack may be more severe.

THOSE, WHO HAVE RECEIVED THEIR PENTECOST GO FORTH LIKE JESUS IN THE POWER OF THE SPIRIT. Vs. 14-15.

14 And Jesus returned in the power of the Spirit into Galilee: and there went out a fame of him through all the region round about.
15 And he taught in their synagogues, being glorified of all.

And Jesus returned in the power of the Spirit.'' This is a remarkable sentence. We read in verse 1 that ''Jesus being full of the Holy Ghost returned from Jordan,'' where he had symbolized entire sanctification and had been anointed by the Spirit for his life work and ministry; and being full of the Holy Ghost he was led by the Spirit into the wilderness to be tempted of the devil. And now we read that he returned from the temptation ''in the power of the Spirit.'' These two expressions are the experience of those today who have been cleansed from all sin and filled with the Holy Ghost. They have power in the time of temptation and greater power after they have triumphed. Temptation overcome is like the hardening that good soldiers receive, who have endured the exposure of a military campaign. This is so true that St. James says ''Blessed is the man that endureth temptation.''

This power brought him into public notice at once, and so we read, ''There went out a fame of him through all the region round about.'' John states that at this time he had begun to work miracles. The record is, ''Now when he was in Jerusalem at the passover, on the feast day, many believed on his name, when they saw the miracles which he did.'' This accounts for his notoriety at this time. He was beginning to fill out the work to which Peter afterwards alludes. (Acts 10:38.)

HOLINESS UTTERS TRUTHS UNPALATABLE TO
CARNAL PEOPLE. Vs. 16-30.

16   And he came to Nazareth, where he had been brought up : and as his custom was, he went into the synagogue on the sabbath day, and stood up for to read.

17   And there was delivered unto him the book of the prophet Esaias.   And when he had opened the book, he found the place where it was written,

18   The Spirit of the Lord *is* upon me, because he hath anointed me to preach the gospel to the poor; he hath sent me to heal the brokenhearted, to preach deliverance to the captives, and recovering of sight to the blind, to set at liberty them that are bruised,

19   To preach the acceptable year of the Lord.

20   And he closed the book, and he gave *it* again to the minister, and sat down.   And the eyes of all them that were in the synagogue were fastened on him.

21   And he began to say unto them, This day is this scripture fulfilled in your ears.

22   And all bare him witness, and wondered at the gracious words which proceeded out of his mouth.   And they said, Is not this Joseph's son ?

23   And he said unto them, Ye will surely say unto me this proverb, Physician, heal thyself : whatsoever we have heard done in Capernaum, do also here in thy country.

24   And he said, Verily I say unto you, No prophet is accepted in his own country.

25   But I tell you of a truth, many widows were in Israel in the days of Elias, when the heaven was shut up three years and six months, when great famine was throughout all the land ;

26   But unto none of them was Elias sent, save unto Sarepta, a *city* of Sidon, unto a woman *that was* a widow.

27   And many lepers were in Israel in the time of Eliseus the prophet ; and none of them was cleansed, saving Naaman the Syrian.

28   And all they in the synagogue, when they heard these things, were filled with wrath,

29   And rose up, and thrust him out of the city, and led him unto the brow of the hill whereon their city was built, that they might cast him down headlong.

30   But he passing through the midst of them went his way,

On their return from their sojourn in Egypt, the parents of Jesus had settled at Nazareth, a town seventy miles north of Jerusalem. (Matt. 2:32.)   Here he passed his early years.   He was a habitual church goer on the Sabbath.   The Jewish churches or ''Meeting Houses'' were built in every Jewish town.   Here the people met on the Sabbath or on feast days to worship God. This worship consisted of the reading of The Old Testament, prayer and an exposition of the passage read. Those, who were educated in the Jewish interpretation of the law usually conducted the services. Distinguished strangers were also invited to lead the service. Although the Jewish church was very corrupt and the state of religion was very low, yet Jesus went to public worship. A lesson to us to be in attendance on the house of God on the Sabbath, no matter whether those who profess to be the people of God are right or not. We are to honor God by our presence at his worship. The house of God is visible monument to the presence of God in the community and if others do not do their duty, still it is our duty to recognize God publicly by our attendance upon his house.

This was his first sermon in a synagogue and it was fitting that it should be delivered where he was brought up. The preacher's first duty is in the place where he lives. Jesus told his disciples to begin their testimony as witnesses at Jerusalem, where they then were. We have little confidence in the call of those, who profess to be led to go to the foreign missionary field, who have never said a word about personal salvation to those who live next to them or in their neighborhood.

The synagogue with its worship was established by the Jews, after their return from Babylonian captivity. It was a rectangular building. On the right were seats for males and on the left were seats for females, who sat behind a lattice work, with long veils over their faces. At one end was an ark of wood, containing the volume of the Holy Scriptures that was used in the worship, and at one side was the elevated seats for the preacher or reader. The chief seats were for the ten elders, one of whom was the chief or ruler of the synagogue, and had control of the worship.

Jesus stood up to read. The reader always stood up when he read the Scriptures, in honor of their dignity, but sat down when he began to preach or talk.

On this Sabbath there was delivered to him the book of the prophet Esaias (the word is the Greek form of Isaiah). Books at that time were written on parchment and rolled up on a cylinder.

Jesus unrolled this parchment-book to the place where his own work as a prophet had been prophesied nearly seven hundred years before. This was Isaiah 61:1-3. He did not read that part of Isaiah that prophesies his passion and death but that part, which refers to his ministry as a prophet of God, which ministry he was just now entering upon. This is a lesson to all those who are teachers of the word—to study carefully the matter of making appropriate selections of scripture. This is the second time we have had this method of using the scriptures brought to our attention. In the previous chapter he used it to defeat the devil; in the instance before us, he used it to persuade men. This passage of Isaiah was acknowledged by the Jews to be a prophecy of the work and office of the Messiah.

This passage was singularly adapted to his opening ministry. The prophet represents him as saying, ''The Spirit of the Lord is upon me.'' Jesus is called Christ, which means *anointed.* He had been anointed by the Spirit just recently at Jordan. He was the Christed or Anointed One. All true Christians are Christed or *anointed* ones. No one else except those who have had the divine anointing or are seeking it are fit to be called Christians. This is the Bible idea of the normal Christian life, instead of its being an exception or a rarity. Here we have two persons of the Trinity—Jesus, the second person is speaking of the Holy Spirit, the third person of the Trinity. The first and foremost duty for which he was anointed was to preach. There is nothing in the divine economy above or higher than preaching. It is above healing or miracle working. God has put a high premium upon preaching.

Some people get their eyes on ecclesiastical office or position, But the humble preacher of the Gospel occupies a higher place in the economy of God than popes, potentates or bishops. Any office that takes a man from preaching the word is not elevation but declination. It is coming down. The humblest, anointed preacher occupies a throne of power greater than all the humanly ordained officers of the ages. He wields a greater power. He preaches with the help of the Holy Ghost sent down from heaven and his influence is felt in three worlds.

This preaching was to the poor. Jesus commenced his first

out door sermon with a benediction upon the poor in spirit.
(Matt. 5:3.) This evidently refers to the same class of people.
Those who are humble of heart and anxious for the word of life.
They always hear the Gospel gladly and want it undiluted. They
love it in its simplicity and have no need or desire to have it
spiced up for them. This seems to be a parallel to the first beauti-
tude (Matt. 5:3). The second part of his commission was to
"heal the broken hearted." This has been promised in the Old
Testament (Psalms 147:3). Hearts break in this world of sorrow. There is nothing but the grace of God that can heal them
and God has anointed the ministry of holy preachers to bring a
Gospel that will cure the broken heart. The third part of his
commission was to preach deliverance to the captives. This
means, of course, first of all deliverance from sin which is the
greatest captivity of all. There is no greater bondage than that
of sin. But his preaching also extended to deliverance from
physical servitude. When Jesus came into the world, slavery was
a very common thing. Today it is very rare in all the world
and the great cause of this is the Gospel, which he then began
to preach and has been preached ever in his name. The fourth
part of his commission was the "recovering of sight to the
blind." How admirably he fulfilled this in healing the blind,
it is not necessary for us to state to any reader of the New
Testament. But he said he came also to relieve spiritual blindness which is worse than physical. (See John 9:39-41.) The
fifth part of his work was to "set at liberty them that are
bruised." Mankind are "bruised and mangled by the fall."
Sin has crippled the human race and Jesus has come to set at liberty them that are bruised. Man is so bruised that his awful
hurt by sin has crippled him and holds him a prisoner. Jesus
came to set at liberty, by healing the soul of all the sad results
of sin. In other words this figure means that he came to restore
the soul to perfect health—to save from all sin that we may
walk in the light and health of holiness.

In short he came to preach "the acceptable year of the
Lord." This sums up all the five-fold mission that he had just
read. This refers to the Year of Jubilee. (Leviticus 25:10.) It
occurred every fiftieth year. When it dawned it was ushered in

by the blowing of trumpets and universal rejoicing throughout the nation. Every slave was at liberty *immediately and was as free as if he had never been in bondage.*

Every ancestral estate that was encumbered by mortgage was cleared and freed. Of course such a year was hailed with delight. It meant the re-construction of society. This, Jesus tells us here, was a type of the Gospel which he preached. And just as all the slaves were set free immediately when this year began, so *the salvation of Jesus will set immediately free from all sin. The type means that or it means nothing.*

It is quite remarkable what Jesus did not read, or rather, where he stopped this reading from the prophet Isaiah. If he had read the next verse he would have read ''And the day of vengeance of our God.'' There is a day of vengeance (not a *year*) appointed in which this same Jesus is coming to judge the world. It is still in the future. He did not come the first time for vengeance but for mercy. He will come the second time for vengeance. We are between the two events. We are now in the year of jubilee. It is more than three hundred and sixty-five days in length. In this our year of jubilee we can be saved from all sin, immediately, instantly and walk with him in newness of life. Jesus was a preacher of holiness to the church.

He then closed the book and gave it to the minister, or servant who had charge of the synagogue and sat down to talk, or preach from this text. The use of a text in preaching undoubtedly arose from this example of Jesus in his preaching that day. Millions of sermons have been preached since that time after this method of taking a text from Scripture.

No wonder it says ''the eyes of all them that were in the synagogue were fastened on him.'' To hear their former village carpenter arise and utter such wonderful words filled them with astonishment. He did not say Thus and thus say the writings of the Rabbins, but he interpreted this scripture on his own authority. Where did the carpenter get this authority for such assertions, was doubtless the query that they had in their minds. They knew that he had lately been working miracles and take it all in all, they were mystified. They all acknowledged or bare witness that wonderful words of grace and beauty flowed from his lips. But they were so astonished that all they could say was, ''Is not this Joseph's son?'' If the carpenter's son was not divine, then you and I of this century are bound to be better than he for we have better opportunities. If he was divine then we are bound to accept him, obey him and seek to be like him.

As they were wondering, he read their thoughts and said, You will surely quote to me the old proverb, ''Physician heal thyself.'' They meant that he had better elevate himself and his townsmen if he was really the Messiah. He had better begin by healing his suffering fellow townsmen. It seems that he had been working miracles at Capernaum (John 4:45) and they were jealous of it.

In the same way today some people oppose foreign missions by quoting that worldly, carnal proverb, ''Charity begins at home.'' The trouble is that usually the people in communities have become Gospel hardened and refuse to receive the light. Mark (Ch. 6:5-6) says that he could do no mighty works here because of their unbelief, at which he marvelled. They refused to believe on him (although they had seen his holy life) until he worked some marvels. But he would do no miracles for such people. If he had worked miracles for such people, they would have found a way for explaining them away on some other theory. They were unspiritual and hard of heart. This was the kind of people that he was reared among. The faith that rests only on outward manifestations is not worth any thing in God's sight.

He now goes on to give some illustrations to show that people, who have become Gospel hardened and will not accept the truth, that God has brought to their doors, are left by him and the heathen are offered the Gospel that they reject. Here is one of the best arguments for foreign missions. Often times men have heard the Gospel so much at home that they have rejected their light and the more hopeful field is among the heathen. So he quotes some well known instances to show that God often passes by his professed people to save heathen. He tells them that there were many widows among the Jews in the time of Elijah but he was sent to none of them. God passed them all by and went to a heathen widow in a foreign country—outside the kingdom of Israel. And there were many lepers in Israel but they were not cured, for they were not as anxious for a cure as was Naaman, the

heathen. The Jews did not like to admit that God had any interest in the Gentiles at all, for they looked upon the Gentiles as
dogs. But God loved the Gentiles and when people get Gospel
hardened, he turns to the Gentiles with mercy. If we waited for
every body at home to be saved before we went out after the outside world, they would die in their sins, for there are many at
home who will never be saved. They have rejected their light.
Here we have still another instance of the way Jesus used Scripture. There is so much history of men and nations in the Bible
that a man, who is full of the Bible can find many illustrations to
enforce his thought.

Now their curiosity turned to wrath, for they could not endure
the mention of such a thing as the Gentiles being saved. Nor did
they like the illustration that made them no better than Gentiles
and in fact not as good. ''The avowed preference of other places
before the dwelling place of his youth; this refusal to grant to
Nazareth any share in the fame of his extraordinary works; and
the reproof so obviously given in his words and conduct, mingled
with other fanatical motives, wrought the assembly up to a pitch
of frenzy'' (Milman).

They were so angry that they forgot the sacredness of the
place and the sanctity of the Sabbath and the meeting broke up in
a mob. It is the same spirit today that thrusts him and his truth
out of the heart of those whom his truth condemns. He did not
attempt ever to go back. When people determinedly reject him he
does not try to go back to them. He met his first opposition in
his native place. Men would be just as much against Christ today
if he were on earth. Human nature is ever the same God-hating
affair, in all ages.

They thrust him out of the city and led him to the brow of the
hill that the city was built upon to cast him down. Nothing
shows more clearly the moral power of holy character. It says
that he passing through their midst escaped unharmed. His moral
grandeur cowed them as the human eye sometimes does a brute.
It was that look that cast his enemies to the ground in Gethsemane. He refused to work miracles among the people of Nazareth;
he appeared to desire to show the world that his usefulness must
be founded upon holiness as well as on his preaching and miracles.

They had known him thirty years. Of his manner of life; of his character and conversation during that period, the evangelists are silent. The appeal of our Lord to the people of Nazareth, after living among them thirty years as a man, may account for their silence. No imperfection, no taint of sin, of weakness, or of folly, could be found through that whole period, to enable those among whom he would be in the least esteem, to invalidate his lofty claim to the rank of the Divine Being whom the prophets had announced.'' (Townsend.)

THE POWER OF HOLY PREACHING. Vs. 31-32.

31 And came down to Capernaum, a city of Galilee, and taught them on the sabbath days.
32 And they were astonished at his doctrine: for his word was with power.

Being cast out of his native town, he went to Capernaum, a town north east of Nazareth on the western coast of the Sea of Galilee. We need not be discouraged if people in our own vicinity will not hear the message after we have been anointed with the Spirit. We may think now they will surely hear us. But there were people who did not even wish to hear Jesus after he was anointed with The Spirit and are we better than he? But we have this consolation that some one will receive the message, if some do reject it. It is a wide world and if a man keeps filled with the Spirit, God will have a place where he can deliver his messages.

And now we see illustrated the great fact that a Spirit filled preacher will preach with power. People were astonished as they heard his doctrine (or teaching), ''for his word was with power.'' The contrast was great between his teaching and that of the Pharisees. The latter only dealt out empty platitudes, much like that of the so called liberal preachers of today. But Jesus preached with a power such as the world had never before known. There is such a thing as power in the preaching of the Word of God. No man is ever filled with the Spirit and called to preach without preaching with power—power than can be found in no other kind of speech. The simple preaching of the story of Jesus and him crucified has accomplished, more in changing the history of this world than all the eloquence of the worldly orators of all the ages. We do not by any means say that this power is manifest in glowing eloquence, or well rounded periods, or brilliant oratorical flights. Often times no doubt much of it would not be above serious literary criticism. It has seemed foolishness in the sight of men, but God has honored it in great moral and spiritual changes in personal character and in the character of nations as has no other speech or human teaching been honored. Peter speaks of those of the preachers of Jesus who have "preached with the Holy Ghost sent down from heaven." This is as true today as ever. Thank God!

HOLINESS CAN NOT TOLERATE MORAL UNCLEANLINESS. Vs. 33-37.

33 And in the synagogue there was a man, which had a spirit of an unclean devil, and cried out with a loud voice,

34 Saying, Let *us* alone; what have we to do with thee, *thou* Jesus of Nazareth? art thou come to destroy us? I know thee who thou art; the Holy One of God.

35 And Jesus rebuked him, saying, Hold thy peace, and come out of him. And when the devil had thrown him in the midst, he came out of him, and hurt him not.

36 And they were all amazed, and spake among themselves, saying, What a word *is* this! for with authority and power he commandeth the unclean spirits, and they come out.

37 And the fame of him went out into every place of the country round about.

It was evidently on the Sabbath day as Jesus was gathered with the other people to worship, that there was a man possessed of an unclean devil, who cried out with a loud voice as he saw Jesus saying "Let us alone, what have we to do with thee, thou Jesus of Nazareth?" There was so much holy power in this Being, Jesus Christ that he was a torment to devils, as well as wicked men. His very presence stirred them. Disease often accompanied demoniacal possession. It was more than lunacy and so the sacred writers wish to be understood. In Matthew 4:24 we read that there were brought to him "those who were possessed with devils and those who were lunatic." This shows that the New Testament writers understood that there was a difference between the two. Satan was permitted for wise purposes at the time Jesus came to enter people, just as he was permitted to attack Job. As this spirit was unclean, it was of the same nature as inbred sin, which is uncleanness of soul today, and needs extirpation as truly as did the unclean spirit in this man. Only divine power can cast out either devils or the defilement and entity of sin. Jesus came to free the soul from all uncleanness. He came to destroy the works of the devil as well as to cast out devils. Satan entered into Judas. That is a plain statement of Satanic possession that no one can dispute. (See Chapter 22:3.) So the devil did possess men. The devil asked to be let alone. That is what sin always says, ''Let us alone. You are infringing on our personal liberty. If Jesus had only let the devil and sin alone he would not have been crucified. If we let the devil alone he will make no outcry. To let sin alone is to encourage it. But the devil has no rights that we are bound to respect. To ''give the devil his due,'' as we hear the expression often is to resist him. If no outcry is ever made by Satan we can safely conclude that we are an encouragement to the devil.

''What have we to do with thee?'' The devil told the truth when he said this, for Jesus and the devil have no interest in common. Strange when devils acknowledge that there is nothing but hostility between the true religion of Jesus and Satan that some professed Christians seem to think they can compromise with Satan, in their worldliness.

Nazareth was an obscure place and even the devil here throws it up to Jesus contemptuously by calling him ''Jesus of Nazareth.'' Like some one else who said ''Can anything good come out of Nazareth?'' ''Art thou come to destroy us?'' The devil knew that Jesus could destroy him. He can just as easily destroy the works of the devil today. The devil even went further than the churchmen of that time in recognizing the character of Jesus. He calls him ''The holy one of God.'' The church had become so low in spirituality that they did not recognize him. Here is a case where a professed church almost made the devil blush. The devils were an improvement on Unitarianism in this respect at least—they recognized the deity of Jesus.

Jesus rebuked the devil. He did not need the testimony of devils or any of their help. God does not need the help of bad men today to carry out his cause. If he had not rebuked the evil spirit, men might have thought that he was in league with the devil. The Pharisees did try later to make it appear so, and even accused him of it. We must beware when the devil speaks well of us. It is all for a purpose. His opposition is a thousand times better than his flattery.

Like an evicted tenant the devil, in being put out, tried to do the man all the harm that he could. He threw him down but he could not hurt him. Then he came out of him. The devils are obedient to Christ and depart at his bidding, why then can not we trust him to cast sin out of us. The casting out of this unclean spirit was a clearer proof of his deity than the testimony of devils. The congregation gave a clear and unmistakable testimony to the power of Jesus, by saying ''With authority and power he commandeth the unclean spirits and they come out.'' No wonder his fame went every where.

HOLINESS DELIGHTS IN GOOD WORKS FOR MANKIND.
Vs. 38-44.

38 And he arose out of the synagogue, and entered into Simon's house. And Simon's wife's mother was taken with a great fever ; and they besought him for her.
39 And he stood over her, and rebuked the fever ; and it left her : and immediately she arose and ministered unto them.
40 Now when the sun was setting, all they that had any sick with divers diseases brought them unto him ; and he laid his hands on every one of them, and healed them.
41 And devils also came out of many, crying out, and saying, Thou art Christ the Son of God. And he rebuking *them* suffered them not to speak : for they knew that he was Christ.
42 And when it was day, he departed and went into a desert place : and the people sought him, and came unto him, and stayed him, that he should not depart from them.
43 And he said unto them, I must preach the kingdom of God to other cities also : for therefore am I sent.
44 And he preached in the synagogues of Galilee.

We cannot help noticing how Jesus loved to go about doing good. That is a characteristic of holy people for they are like Jesus. His miracles were not merely to display his power, but to benefit mankind. We are apt to dwell wholly on the great truth that Jesus died for mankind. But we must remember that he also lived for mankind. His thirty-three years on earth were a part of his consecration for the welfare of humanity. He does not ask us to die for mankind, but he asks us to live to do them good. He tried to help the sick. And he has made it our duty to visit and help them. The awards of the last day will be administered with this as one of the tests that we shall have to meet—that we have visited his disciples, when sick, in his name. (Matt. 25:36.) Do you visit the sick brethren of Christ?

The country about Capernaum is low and marshy, and malarial fevers abound there even to this day. Here we learn that Peter's wife's mother lay sick of a fever. ''Jesus came into Peter's house and saw there a sight that would have surprised a Roman Catholic in these days, 'Simon's wife's mother' and if Peter (or Simon) had been living in these days, he must have presented a strange relation, which would have made him instantly be cast out of the church; for Peter it appears from this must have been a married man—'his wife's mother.' And therefore a bishop may be the husband of one wife; marriage may be and is honorable in all men, minister or layman; and certainly if the first pope (so assumed to be), was married, the last pope need not hesitate to imitate his example. If this was apostolic practice there seems to be a lack of apostolic succession, in the want of that practice on the part of the modern church of Rome.'' (Cumming.) We also read in 1 Cor. 9:5 that Peter's wife was accustomed to accompany him on his journeys. Jesus was asked to heal her. He immediately took her by the hand and raised her up (Mark 1:31) and immediately the fever left her. Luke says it was a great fever. Luke was a physician and hence spoke with accuracy of the severity of her sickness. Such fevers leave the victim much prostrated and it takes a long time to recover their strength, but she received strength immediately, so that she could exercise the usual duties of hospitality in taking care of her guests. This shows the completeness of the miracle.

It will be seen by verse 40 that he healed a great many others there. Mark says ''the whole city gathered about the door.'' It would have been impossible for lack of space to tell of all the miracles he wrought for men while on earth. Only those miracles are given, which illustrate spiritual truth, usually those which illustrated spiritual healing. He cured her immediately just as he does the disease of sin. She rose and ministered to him at once; just as a fully saved soul today will do—go right to work for Jesus.

In all this, he showed the fulfillment of prophecy in Isaiah. ''Himself took our infirmities and bare our sicknesses'' (Isa. 53; 4-5). Just so he took upon his heart the sins of the world—not that he took them in the sense of being a sinner—but his great heart of compassion took them as a loving burden. He did not take them in the sense of being sick on account of them, but he sympathized with suffering humanity, for sickness is the result of sin.

While on earth, he cured many of the sick. Probably not all, for he only cured when people had the faith to trust him. And we believe today that when we have the right kind—the divinely inspired faith—he still cures sickness. He bore and still bears in his sympathy the sorrows and sufferings of humanity. There is nothing that affects his people that does not command his interest and sympathy.

CHAPTER V.

SEVERAL SYMBOLS OF HOLINESS.

Holy People Are Called to Be Fishers of Men. Vs. 1-11. The Cleansing of the Heart Illustrated. Vs. 12-16. The Empowerment of the Soul by Holiness, Illustrated. Vs. 17-26. Our Holy Religion a Cure for Avarice. Vs. 27-33. Holiness Is Like the Joy of a Wedding Feast. Vs. 33-39.

HOLY PEOPLE ARE CALLED TO BE FISHERS OF MEN
Vs. 1-11.

1 And it came to pass, that, as the people pressed upon him to hear the word of God, he stood by the lake of Gennesaret,

2 And saw two ships standing by the lake: but the fishermen were gone out of them, and were washing *their* nets.

3 And he entered into one of the ships, which was Simon's, and prayed him that he would thrust out a little from the land. And he sat down, and taught the people out of the ship.

4 Now when he had left speaking, he said unto Simon, Launch out into the deep, and let down your nets for a draught.

5 And Simon answering said unto him, Master, we have toiled all the night, and have taken nothing: nevertheless at thy word I will let down the net.

6 And when they had this done, they inclosed a great multitude of fishes: and their net brake.

7 And they beckoned unto *their* partners, which were in the other ship, that they should come and help them. And they came, and filled both the ships, so that they began to sink.

8 When Simon Peter saw *it*, he fell down at Jesus' knees, saying, Depart from me; for I am a sinful man, O Lord.

9 For he was astonished, and all that were with him, at the draught of the fishes which they had taken:

10 And so *was* also James, and John, the sons of Zebedee, which were partners with Simon. And Jesus said unto Simon, Fear not; from henceforth thou shall catch men.

11 And when they had brought their ships to land, they forsook all, and followed him.

Jesus having been rejected by his fellow townsmen at Nazareth departed and made his headquarters at Capernaum, on the west coast of the Sea of Galilee, thus fulfilling the prophecy of Isaiah (Isa. 9:1-2). He immediately commenced preaching the gospel of the kingdom in dead earnest. In the previous chapter we read that his word was accompanied by great power. (Luke 4:31-32.) The result was, the people gathered from far and near to hear his wonderful words. He began to be very popular with the common people. If they had not been priest-ridden and fearful of the chief ministers of their religion and the Pharisees, his popularity would have continued, and he would not have been crucified. Salvation is so reasonable that everybody would embrace it, if they were not obliged to meet with opposition and reproach, for salvation commends itself to the common sense as well as the conscience of men. The crowd was so great that it pressed him gradually close up to the water and he was obliged to ask permission of some fishermen, who were washing their nets for the privilege of using their ship for a pulpit. Jesus could find a pulpit any where. Some preachers can not preach only under certain surroundings; with a roof over their heads or a surplice over their bodies, or where the audience is select and prepared. But Jesus was an out of doors preacher. He preached wherever he could get an opportunity. It is not necessary to have a cathedral, or a magnificent church to draw the people. There are times when we can reach them better in nature's temple. Happy the fisher of men, who can adapt himself to the preaching of the gospel anywhere, and is on the alert to take advantage of every opportunity. That ship was indeed a holy place. ''Whatever is employed in the service of Christ becomes holy by its relation to him; thus our houses, possessions, employment and even refreshments, may be sanctified to us, by being rendered subservient to his glory.'' (Scott.)

At the close of the sermon he gave a practical symbol of preaching the gospel. He commanded them to ''Launch out into the deep'' and let down their nets for a draught or haul. This seemed absurd to these tired, discouraged fishermen, who had been toiling to no purpose all night, and one of them by the name of Simon, remonstrated saying ''Master we have toiled all night and taken nothing, nevertheless at thy word I will let down the net.''

The result was a great multitude of fish were enclosed, so great that the net began to break and they had to call for help. And when they got the fish into the ships they began to sink. They had an overflowing blessing.

It is not necessary to show that this miracle was a parable of the preaching of the Gospel for Jesus so teaches. He said, ''From henceforth thou shalt catch men.'' This throws great light on the purpose of the miracles of Jesus. All of his miracles are not recorded, but *those are recorded, which were wrought to illustrate spiritual truths.* They are all parables of salvation and should be so studied. We notice first that in order to be a good fisherman, we must have a real hunger for fishing. A true fisherman has real love for his occupation. It is true also if we would be fishers of men. The man who fishes occasionally just to pass away time is not a good fisherman. There is such a thing as a real hunger to see men saved. Jesus had it and so do holy people.

The successful fisherman casts his net or hook where the fish are. The fish are not always in the very best places for the comfort of the fisherman, or the places he would choose. They are often in places hard to get at, but the tired fisherman overcomes all the difficulties in order to get at the fish. He does not mind toil or want of food if he can get the fish. Jesus fished in different places; in a ship, on the mountain side, in the highways—anywhere he could find the fish, and so will the successful seeker for souls today. If there are no fish to be caught in one place, it is our duty to try another place. They had toiled all night and caught nothing. Now he tells them to thrust out into the deep part of the lake. God intends that his fishermen should be successful, and if they have done their best and are not successful, then they may conclude that he wants them to try another fishing ground.

As in this case, so it is also true in fishing for souls that deep water is the best place usually. That is where the best fish are. Perhaps the trouble with us has been that we have been fishing in too shallow water. We had better go out where it is deeper in our experience. We have known a great many who toiled hard through many a night of discouragement, who finally launched out in their experience; went out into the deeps; got full salvation and became soul savers on a scale that they never knew before. Peter was an example of this very truth. His Pentecost made him a great soul saver. If you have honestly toiled and got little, you had better get full salvation and then after that get frequent anointings by much prayer and real abandonment to God.

It is a great encouragement that God is willing that any class of people should be fishermen for souls. He called Matthew from a business, Paul from a scholar's chair, Luke from the profession of a Physician and these fishermen of this obscure province of Galilee from their nets to be his ambassadors on the greatest and most momentous business, that ever enlisted human effort. Trench says "He, whose purpose it was by the weak things of the world to confound the strong, who meant to draw emperors to himself by fishermen, and not fishermen by emperors, lest his church should even seem to stand in the wisdom and power of men, rather than in the wisdom and power of God, saw in these unlearned fishermen of the Galileean lake the fittest instruments for his work." While God began his work with these humble instruments, he also enlisted Paul and Luke later to show that although He could get along without the culture of trained minds yet He has His place for them when their talents and culture are entirely consecrated.

This great multitude of fish was a prophecy of the souls that Peter was to catch at Pentecost after he had launched out into the deeps of salvation. He had been catching fish for death. He was now to catch souls for life eternal. And the true successors of Peter (Those who have had their Pentecost) have been catching great numbers of souls all along the ages, and the work is still going on.

Peter fell at the knees of Jesus as he saw the miracle and cried, "Depart from me for I am a sinful man, O Lord." It would be easy to show from the Scriptures that Peter was a saved man at this time as far as initial salvation is concerned. (See our notes on Chapter 3:1-16.) Peter and James and John were of the disciples of John the Baptist, who preached regeneration through repentance and faith in Jesus Christ. (See John 1:35-42.) Peter had faith enough to obey Jesus and also to see his own evil nature, as an unregenerated man could not see it. He is an illustration of a Christian, who has not been wholly sanctified, who has a conviction of inbred sin. This conviction John Wesley says is far deeper than the conviction that a sinner has for sins committed. Jacob had it when the angel asked him his name. Isaiah, the prophet had it, when he got the vision of God in the temple and cried "Woe is me." Trench says of this conviction of depravity, in a child of God "The deepest thing in man's heart under the law, is a sense of God's holiness, as something bringing death and destruction in the unholy creature. Below this is the utterly profane state, in which there is no contradiction felt between God and the sinner. Above this is a state of grace, in which all the contradiction is felt; God is still a consuming fire, yet not any more for the sinner, but only for the sin." Regeneration gives us wonderful light on the nature of inbred sin and the spirituality of God's law, thus intelligently preparing us for that circumcision of heart that removes depravity and enables us thus circumcised to love the Lord God with all the heart. (Deut. 30:6.)

We can not understand how those, who call themselves Christians can dismiss the subject of inbred depravity in a flippant way or make excuse for keeping in that condition or feel anything but an earnest desire to be free from it. A man who has grace at all we believe, like Peter will grieve over the depravity of his nature.

If one like Peter who loved Jesus could feel his sinfulness when he saw the display of Almighty power, how will men feel their sinfulness when they stand in the presence of the Judge, at his coming!

James and John, the sons of Zebedee, who were partners of Peter were as much astonished as Peter at the wonderful draught of fish. Jesus to reassure them said "Fear not; from henceforth thou shalt catch men." In the original it meant not only to catch but to "catch alive."

These three men bade their occupation of fishing farewell, from that hour. It was a crisis in their lives as they now forsook all and followed Jesus. They had followed him to some extent previously (John 1:42-43), but now they left all and made it their one business to follow him, for life.

THE CLEANSING OF THE HEART ILLUSTRATED.
Vs. 12-16.

12   And it came to pass, when he was in a certain city, behold a man full of leprosy: who seeing Jesus fell on *his* face, and besought him, saying, Lord, if thou wilt, thou canst make me clean.

13   And he put forth *his* hand, and touched him, saying, I will: be thou clean. And immediately the leprosy departed from him.

14   And he charged them to tell no man: but go, and shew thyself to the priest, and offer for thy cleansing, according as Moses commanded, for a testimony unto them.

15   But so much the more went there a fame abroad of him: and great multitudes came together to hear, and to be healed by him of their infirmities.

16   And he withdrew himself into the wilderness, and prayed.

As Jesus was passing through a city a leper came and threw himself at his feet and besought him to cure him. This was the first case of leprosy that Jesus cured in this his first missionary tour through Galilee. It was a very bad case of leprosy. The awful and unnatural whiteness of the face showed the man to be "full of leprosy."

Leprosy was the scriptural type of sin. We know this to be true because no other disease had a religious ceremony required whenever it was cured. See Leviticus (Ch. 14). In the first chapter of Isaiah the sinful condition of Israel is compared to leprosy thus, "The whole head is sick and the whole heart faint. From the sole of the foot even to the head there is no soundness in it; but wounds and bruises and putrefying sores: they have not been closed neither bound up, neither mollified with ointment." Note the points of analogy between leprosy and sin.

1.   They are loathesome diseases. "Leprosy in its worst form, was one of the most terrible of diseases. It began with red spots upon the body, grouped in circles, and covered with a shiny scale or scab. It became generally incurable, and so corrupted the system that it became hereditary for generations. The body crumbled, the limbs fell apart, and the man literally went to pieces." If we could see the soul of a sinner as God sees it, we should see something equally as bad. God uses this figure to show how offensive sin is to him. Unless men get rid of it it will corrupt the soul completely.

2. Both were hereditary. The child born into the leper's family had in him leprous tendencies which sooner or later manifested themselves. All children born into this world have in them the tendencies to sin which sooner or later manifest themselves. Our children are innocent but not pure. We find in them a tendency to go wrong. This is seen in the fact that we never have to teach them to be bad, it comes natural. But we do have to teach them to be good. This is the doctrine of every evangelical church.

3. Leprosy and sin are constitutional diseases, that have their outward manifestation. Leprosy has outward eruptions in the scale or scab. Sin his its eruptions in the wicked word, the act of sin, the evil thought and the evil look. Sin and leprosy are therefore diseases of the outward and inward man.

4. Nothing but a cure of the inward disease can meet the requirements of the case. It is so with sin. Do all you please to reform men and culture them, if you stop there, the cause of the world's evils has not been touched, and sin will manifest itself sooner or later. Outside treatment will not cure it. It would have been useless to doctor the outside eruptions of the leper. It is as useless to try to save men by anything except the Gospel cure, that Jesus came to provide, which reaches the seat of the disease—the heart—and destroys the disease.

5. Lepers and sinners must be banished from the presence of those, who were well and sound. The law required it. The leper must be separated from society. He could dwell with no one but lepers. Unless we are set free from sin we too must be forever banished from the presence of god and holy angels. It is holiness or hell.

6. All classes are subject to these diseases. The king on his throne might have it as well as the beggar in the hovel. Sin is among all classes. We are apt to think that because a man dresses well or has a good deal of money or is refined or cultured after the fashion of this world that he is not so wretched in the sight of God as those who dwell in squalid surroundings. But God does not care for class distinctions, for broadcolth or money.

7. A leper on a throne is as bad in his sight as a wretched beggar. Sin is sin with God. We need to insist on this, as many do not seem to think so.

8. There is no earthly cure for sin or leprosy. Men have been trying their cures for sin for thousands of years but it baffles human skill.

9. God sometimes cured leprosy, and he sometimes (whenever men are willing to fulfill the conditions) cures sin. Power divine is more than a match for sin. ''For this purpose the son of God was manifested, that he might destroy the works of the devil.'' Jesus is a physician as well as an Advocate. Some have only looked upon him as an Advocate, who gets men free from the demands of the law. But the Bible calls him a physician. It is not right to neglect this part of his office and invite and urge men to seek pardon for their sinful acts and not tell them that he is also ready to cleanse from the disease.

10. When these diseases (leprosy and sin) are cured they are not merely suppressed but they are gone entirely. There is a class of religionists who assert that the best we can have in this life is a salvation that keeps sin suppressed or held down. But when the leper was cured of leprosy it was not suppressed. It was cured. And the cleansing of leprosy is a type of the cleansing of sin. Therefore it means that we may be free from sin. When Jesus said, ''Blessed are the pure in heart,'' he was not talking about suppression of sin in the heart for that is not purity. Purity means the absence—not the suppression—of impurity. Let us then see how this man was cured of his leprosy and thereby see how we may be cured of sin.

1. He became a seeker. He was in earnest to be cured. Many would like full salvation but they do not want it enough to single themselves out from the crowd and make a business of seeking. All many do is to indulge in a few gentle desires for cleansing, but the man who gets it, must make a business of seeking, and be as much in earnest about it as was this leper. It makes us weary to hear people say they want a sanctified heart, who will make no definite, pronounced effort to obtain it. The man who will not be willing to do anything that will help him to get to Jesus. whether it be to pray, go to an altar, confess his need, or anything else, prefers sin to holiness, and is simply getting what he wants most. We have that which we most prefer.

It cost this man something to break over the law that required lepers to keep away from the people, who were well. It meant that the people would condemn him. Society today will condemn us, if we get very much in earnest in seeking for salvation. If we care more for the good opinions of men than for soul health, we shall not be cured.

2. He asked for the cure. He made it a matter of prayer. Full salvation from all sin ought to be made a matter of prayer. We protest against and object to reasoning people into the experience of holiness; taking a passage of scripture and forming an argument from it and calling it done. To be sure there is no virtue in prayer itself; faith is the requisite, but prayer is a great help to the exercise of that genuine faith that brings the blessing. It does not seem to us that if a soul has a real conviction of the nature of the corruption of his heart, he can be any more passive in the matter, than the Apostle, who cried out of the depths of his heart, ''O wretched man that I am, who shall deliver me from the body of this death.'' Anything that is worth having is worth asking for. IT is the son that *asks* bread, who is not turned away with a stone. We are to ask that we may receive. We love to see such a realization of the horrible nature of inbred sin as begets a tremendous earnestness in seeking deliverance from it.

3. He asked in faith. He said ''Lord if thou wilt thou canst make me clean.'' He believed that the Lord could do it. His faith measured up to what light he had. He did not have the light we have today. God has given us greater assurance that he can cure leprosy of sin than this man had. *Then*, it was sovereignly bestowed. Now the cure of sin is graciously bestowed. We have so many promises that are unqualified that assure us that we may be cleansed from all sin, that we would mock God, if we said ''Lord if thou wilt,'' for we know he wants to do it. Notice the reply of Jesus is almost identical with the words of the leper, with the exception of the word ''if.'' He said, ''Lord, if thou wilt.'' Jesus took out the ''if'' and replied, ''I will; be thou clean.'' Let us under the greater light of the Gospel dispensation say, ''Lord thou canst, thou wilt make me clean.'' Let us take him at his word. Even this man was ahead of some today. He believed the Lord had the power to cleanse him. There are those, who seem to doubt the ability of the Lord to cleanse their hearts. They

think they are too hard cases for Him. Others believe the Lord can do it but believe He is not willing. If He is not willing, then it is a reflection on Him, which we can not for a moment believe. He is too compassionate to let men go on crippled and handicapped with sin who really are anxious, at any cost, to get rid of it. It is a libel on his great heart of compassion to say that He can but will not cure.

Notice the time it took to effect the cure. "Immediately his leprosy was cleansed." It was instantaneous. There are those, who seem to doubt that the same One who instantly cured leprosy can instantly cure sin. But as sure as lep: osy is the type of sin and its cure is the type of the cure of sin, so sure immediateness of the cure of leprosy means immediateness of the cure of sin.

Jesus "touched him" because he was "moved with compassion" (Mark 1:41). The touch was a touch of pity more wonderful because not only a universal prejudice, but also the Levitical law forbade touching any unclean thing (Lev. 5:3). "Yet even this act of Christ exemplifies the truth that he had come to fulfill the law, though he seemed to violate it and did not observe its letter. For the object of the law was the preservation of purity; but Christ did better than preserve himself from impurity; by his touch he communicated purity to the impure. It is never wrong to come in contact with impurity for the purpose of curing it, if we are strong in God to accomplish our beneficent purpose." (Abbott.) He then commanded him to show himself to the priest in accordance with the law. (See Lev. Ch. 14 which tells what the sacrifices or "gift" required were.) This requiring God's priest to pronounce him clean, after certain sacrifices kept before the Jews the fact that leprosy typified sin. He also commanded him to tell no man. This in no sense militates against the idea that we are not to tell of the cure of sin. In this case Jesus charged him not to tell, lest the priest should deny that he had been cured, if the news got ahead of him, before he reached the temple. After the priest had seen him and pronounced the cure then there could be no reason for his keeping still about it. Jesus did not release people from the duty of confession as we see, when he required the woman who was cured of the issue of blood to come forward and confess it publicly. (Mark 5:33.) Mark gives another reason for his not wishing it announced. The man did not obey him but went out and told it everywhere insomuch that Jesus could no more enter the city but had to go into desert places (see Mark 1:45). The crowds became so great that he had to withdraw. Let those who seek to find encouragement from this in withholding their testimony remember that they have no excuse unless they are going to attract so great crowds that it will hinder others from getting salvation, which is an improbable case today. He told the man who was freed from the devils to go home and tell it (Mark 5:19). So we cannot lay down a general principle from this case before us.

Because of the cure of the leper, his fame spread abroad everywhere. Great multitudes came from afar to be healed by him. But he instead of being elated withdrew into the wilderness to pray. It is a good thing for a preacher if he gets popular to do a good deal of praying. Jesus prayed a great deal. He who does much for God should pray a great deal. Much prayer and much activity should go together. We learn here of a good employment for ministers in their vacation—much prayer.

THE EMPOWERMENT OF THE SOUL, BY HOLINESS, ILLUSTRATED. Vs. 17-26.

17 And it came to pass on a certain day, as he was teaching, that there were Pharisees and doctors of the law sitting by, which were come out of every town of Galilee, and Judæa, and Jerusalem: and the power of the Lord was *present* to heal them.

18 And, behold, men brought in a bed a man which was taken with a palsy: and they sought *means* to bring him in, and to lay *him* before him.

19 And when they could not find by what *way* they might bring him in because of the multitude, they went upon the housetop, and let him down through the tiling with *his* couch into the midst before Jesus.

20 And when he saw their faith, he said unto him, Man, thy sins are forgiven thee.

21 And the scribes and the Pharisees began to reason, saying, Who is this which speaketh blasphemies? Who can forgive sins, but God alone?

22 But when Jesus perceived their thoughts, he answering said unto them, What reason ye in your hearts?

23 Whether is easier, to say, Thy sins be forgiven thee; or to say, Rise up and walk?

24 But that ye may know that the Son of man hath power upon earth to forgive sins, (he said unto the sick of the palsy,) I say unto thee, Arise, and take up thy couch, and go into thine house.

25 And immediately he rose up before them, and took up that whereon he lay, and departed to his own house, glorifying God.

26 And they were all amazed, and they glorified God, and were filled with fear, saying, We have seen strange things to day.

Holiness is perfect love in action. It goes out like a fountain beyond itself and waters others. This was especially exemplified in Jesus, who went about doing good. His miracles were for the purpose of alleviating human need and distress. Thus he showed to mankind that God loved them. Those, who are partakers of his holiness, in a similar manner seek to help mankind and thus show the good will to men that is a special characteristic of our holy religion. The measure of real holiness that we possess is manifest in our desire to help others. The great busines of mankind is to glorify God and bless mankind. No wonder that, when the paralytic took up his bed and walked, the multitude glorified God. Jesus so performed his miracles that his Father got the glory. Holy people seek not their own glory but the glory of God.

The scene of this miracle was Capernaum, which was his dwelling place after he left Nazareth.

Jesus performed many miracles in Capernaum: the cure of Peter's mother-in-law; the healing of the centurion's servant; the casting of the evil spirit out of the man in the synagogue, besides the restoration of the withered hand (Mark 3:1-5) and this miracle now before us. Notwithstanding the mighty works which he did here, the people generally refused to acknowledge the truth which he spoke to them. He therefore pronounced upon this place an awful judgment (see Mark 11:23). This healing of the paralytic was one of the mighty works of which he speaks in thus pronouncing judgment on this city, that had received so much light.

On a certain day it was noised abroad throughout the city, that he was in a certain house and the multitudes came thronging the house and crowding about the door. This shows that he was very popular at this time, with the common people. And right at this time the opposition to him began. Every genuine revival will be opposed by the wicked, in the professed church as well as out of it. The most spiritual work in every age has had its greatest enemies among those who professed to be the Lord's people—the ecclesiastics. This may seem severe, but to deny it is to show ignorance of history. His popularity begat jealousy among the scribes and Pharisees. It was this that finally brought him to his death. So the Pharisees and doctors of the law were there. Holiness has always had its worst enemies in every age among the Pharisees and doctors of the law, and other ecclesiastics. They have been jealous of anything that would take from them their influence and leadership with the people.

As he was preaching, there came four men, bringing a man sick of the palsy, to have him healed. Whether it was the intense desire of the man alone, who urged them, or whether they were very anxious, being warm friends of the paralytic, we do not know. But they were desperately in earnest to have him healed. So much so that they took off the roof since they could not get at him by the door, and let him down before Jesus. Luke says they let him down through the tiling. They showed their faith by overcoming the difficulties, as much as lay in their power. Their faith was not the acceptance of any doctrine, but a deep confidence in him as one who could supply their need. People can be saved who know nothing about doctrine. It is faith in the personal Jesus that saves. This is a good test of faith—the difficulties which we overcome to bring our friends to Christ. It teaches us too that Jesus honors the faith of those who take pains to bring their friends to him. Does he see in us faith for our friends? Faith for those who have the paralysis of sin which is much worse than that of the body?

Sinners are hopeless and helpless unless we get them to Christ and let him heal them. Do we really believe that? If so, what anxiety, what pains we will take to get them to Jesus. When Jesus saw the man, he said to him, ''man, thy sins are forgiven thee.'' This same voice in the soul has made tens of thousands, ''be of good cheer,'' (Matt. 9:2) all down through the ages since. The man who does not understand why such people are of good cheer is a stranger himself to pardoning grace. It means that the guilt which dooms a soul to hell has been removed and there is now no more condemnation against him in the court of heaven. This man had his sins all forgiven. Let it be known here, *that men were forgiven before Pentecost.* How absurd the idea that the disciples were not forgiven until Pentecost, when that was the work Jesus was engaged in all the time, he was with them—three years.

Some people imagine we must have a creed and believe in it in order to be saved. But this man had only faith that Jesus could heal him. If there was no salvation possible except through believing in a creed, it would be impossible to reach many of the people of this great earth. Faith that brings salvation is faith in a personal Christ. We are not here casting any reflection on creeds. They are proper in their place. This man was pronounced forgiven and healed before he or his friends could offer a prayer with their lips. His friends were still on the roof. Jesus saw in the man's heart the real attitude of penitence for his sins and faith for forgiveness. Prayer is the real desire of the soul. This man had it and Jesus recognized it. Salvation from our sins then is an instantaneous work of God.

This was the turning point in the life of Jesus. He claimed to forgive sins and his enemies accused him of blasphemy. It was the beginning of that hate that pursued him to the cross. Some of the scribes present began at once to find fault. It shows that this was why they came. Any one who could find fault at this, was capable of finding fault at anything. Do we expect that we can escape the censure of the Scribes and Pharisees of our day? If we do, we put ourselves above Jesus. There are many professed followers of Jesus today who will attack the most sacred things. Holiness has an easier time today than it had in the time of Jesus.

With that penetration which enabled him then and enables him now to see the very inmost thoughts of the heart, which is as an open book before him, he said, ''What reason ye in your hearts?'' It was not honest criticism for they thought evil. The opposition to the truth in all ages has not been the opposition of real doubt and perplexity about understanding but it has been a malignant spirit against the truth. This is the reason so many are always misunderstanding and misrepresenting holiness. They think evil against it.

He asked them whether it was easier to say, ''Thy sins be forgiven thee,'' or to say ''rise, take up thy bed and walk.'' He did not mean the mere pronunciation of these words but that the claim to forgive is easier to make than the claim to heal the body. No one can see God's book of debit and credit, or man's heart. So that Jesus could claim that he had forgiven the man's sins and there was nothing to show to the contrary. But when he said, ''rise, take up thy bed and walk'' and the man did it, then they knew it was true, that he had healed him. And if he could heal him, then he was divine and could forgive him also. The miracle of the healing proved the miracle of forgiveness. Catholic priests claim that they have the power to pronounce men forgiven of their sins, but who knows it to be true? Where is the proof? If they could cure the people of their sickness at the same time then they would have some claim on the belief of the people that they could also forgive. So Jesus says, ''That ye may know that the Son of Man hath power on earth to forgive sins (he said unto the sick of the palcy) Arise, take up thy bed and go into thine house.'' The walking of the man proved his forgiveness. It was a double work. This man was forgiven his sins as soon as Christ spoke, but the evidence of it was not given to the others until he walked. The Pharisees themselves believed and taught that no sick man was healed, until all his sins were forgiven, so Jesus gave them an unanswerable proof from their own standpoint of his right to forgive.

When the man put forth his will power to obey Jesus then he was healed. It is true today that if we *will* be saved, God will supply the power to save us. He helps us when we have honestly done our part. And when he sees us so anxious to get rid of sin that we are *willing* to put it away, he takes away what we honestly put away.

A great lesson here is that Jesus made more account of the spiritual part of the miracle than of the physical. He was thinking more of the forgiveness of sins than of the healing of the body. The false notions of healing that are abroad in the world, make more of the physical than of the spiritual. But the physical is only secondary and of minor importance in comparison with the spiritual. Any one who claims to be able to heal the body can get a crowd, but they who seek to bring men to the great physician for salvation have difficulty in getting the ear of the people. Healing of the body is all right in its place but it is very difficult to give much attention to it without minifying soul healing which is the greater work. A man can get to heaven if he be sick all his life and die with a diseased body, but not if he die with a sin wrecked soul. Let us not minify physical healing either, but put it in its proper place.

OUR HOLY RELIGION IS A CURE FOR AVARICE. Vs. 27-32.

27   And after these things he went forth, and saw a publican, named Levi, sitting at the receipt of custom : and he said unto him, Follow me.
28   And he left all, rose up, and followed him.
29   And Levi made him a great feast in his own house : and there was a great company of publicans and of others that sat down with them :
30   But their scribes and Pharisees murmured against his disciples, saying, Why do ye eat and drink with publicans and sinners?
31   And Jesus answering said unto them, They that are whole need not a physician ; but they that are sick.
32   I came not to call the righteous, but sinners to repentance.

At this point Jesus calls one from the lowest class of society, evidently to show that he cares nothing for the class distinctions and prejudices that govern men. He calls Levi. (See Matt. 9:9.) This man's name was Levi Matthew. We see how modest Matthew was in mentioning himself. The Pharisees with their dead, formal religion made no salutary impression in the lower classes, but the holy character of Jesus did. The character of Jesus is the greatest miracle of the Bible. It impresed such characters as Matthew, Zaccheus and Mary Magdelene with a desire to be good. The world's idea of true religion is holiness. A holy man is a means of conviction to sinners. Just as far as the holy life of Jesus is lived by his followers it puts the world under conviction today. He called Matthew the publican, a great sinner, to be an apostle and a writer of the Gospel. The publicans, as a rule, were extortioners who collected the Roman tax. They were exceedingly odious to the Jews. Admitting Matthew to the circle of his disciples must have greatly irritated the Pharisees. Notice how modestly Matthew mentions it thus (Matt. 9:9). ''He saw a man named Matthew, sitting at the receipt of customs.'' Matthew was a publican, or tax gatherer, and was thus employed in the business of collecting the customs of taxes which the Jews were obliged to pay to the Roman government on all imported and exported goods, as well as almost everything else. The Jews considered that they were degraded in having to pay this tax, and consequently any one who was a tax gatherer was peculiarly obnoxious to them. The Roman government farmed out, or let his business, to certain individuals who in turn sublet it to others. These tax collectors or publicans were obliged to pay those from whom they leased their collectorship a certain sum of money. So they contrived in every way to add to the taxes by all manners of excuses, extortions, and false accusation. They stripped the Jewish farmers of about everything they had. These publicans, as might naturally be expected, became very rich by this extortion. So odious and past redemption were they considered by the Jews that The Talmud (the body of the Jewish civil law) classes them with thieves and robbers and regards their repentance as impossible. From this low class Jesus called Matthew to be a disciple, and he became also an inspired writer. Jesus taught by this, that no man is beyond redemption. In Mark and Luke, he is called Levi. Doubtless he changed his name after he met Christ, just as Saul changed his name to Paul after his conversion.

The same Jesus who did not hesitate to touch the leper which seemed to be contrary to the law, in order to cure him, did not hesitate to call the wicked publican to repentance. Matthew, or Levi, was so rejoiced in his new experience that like all new converts he wanted his asociates to find the same Christ. So he made a feast and called the other publicans to come and meet Jesus. This, with the Jews, was even worse than merely preaching to the publicans. Had Jesus only preached, they would not have found much fault, but by eating with them, he associated with them and so the Pharisees asked the disciples (they did not dare to speak to Jesus himself about it), ''Why do ye eat with publicans and sinners?'' They did not say why does he preach to them, but why does he associate with them. True holiness is never afraid to associate with sinners in order (not to approve of their course) but to save them. This is the only way we can ever reach the slum classes. If we are afraid to associate with them we will fail to reach them. Missions among the lower classes fail when the missionary lives in upper ten-dom, instead of among them. There is a right and a wrong way to associate with sinners. Paul said that he ''became all things to all men if by any means he might save some.'' Jesus never refused an invitation to mingle socially with sinners. We have seen some of the worst sinners won by holy people who were not afraid to go down to save them, and who were thus enabled to lead them to the cross.

The publicans were bad, and that made it all the more necessary that they have a Savior and so Jesus replies to the Pharisees. ''They that are whole need not a physician but they that are sick. I came not to call the righteous, but sinners to repentance.'' Matthew says, he quoted Hosea 6:6, ''I will have mercy and not sacrifice.'' If they accused him of being too lenient and compromising in going among sinners they at the same time accused the Heavenly Father who in Hosea 6:6 and in many other places, had said the same thing virtually. He wished them to understand that all religion both of the Old and New Testaments was full of mercy to all penitents of every grade of sin. He became *Saint* Matthew—a holy man made out of a corrupt man. Jesus has been performing the same miracle all along down through the ages. One of the opposers of Christianity in one of the early centuries, made this charge that Jesus came to call sinners of the worst classes about him. The reply of the Christians of that day was that it was true. He did not come to call the sinners, but he came to call them to repentance. He came to call them to be good men and forsake their sins.

HOLINESS IS LIKE THE JOY OF A WEDDING FEAST.
Vs. 33-39.

33   And they said unto him, Why do the disciples of John fast often, and make prayers, and likewise *the disciples* of the Pharisees; but thine eat and drink?

34   And he said unto them, Can ye make the children of the bridechamber fast, while the bridegroom is with them?

35   But the days will come, when the bridegroom shall be taken away from them, and then shall they fast in those days.

36   And he spake also a parable unto them; No man putteth a piece of a new garment upon an old; if otherwise, then both the new maketh a rent, and the piece that was *taken* out of the new agreeth not with the old.

37 And no man putteth new wine into old bottles; else the new
wine will burst the bottles, and be spilled, and the bottles shall perish.

38 But new wine must be put into new bottles; and both are
preserved.

39 No man also having drunk old *wine* straightway desireth new:
for he saith, The old is better.

Another class of people were mystified by the conduct of Jesus.
These were the disciples of John the Baptist. Their master was
now languishing in prison and naturally they were full of sorrow
and also perplexed that God should have allowed his enemies to
seize their master. And seeing Jesus eating and drinking while
they were in sadness and fasting was to them unexplainable. So
they asked him, ''Why do the disciples of John fast often, but
thine eat and drink?'' It was true that the Pharisees fasted a
great deal. They were only required in the law to fast once a year,
on the Day of Atonement. But they had prescribed very many fasts
of their own appointment. There were several national fasts and
some of the stricter Pharisees fasted the fifth and second days of
the week.

Jesus never prescribed any set fasts and the New Testament
church never set apart any special days for fasting. When it was
done it was always with the individual matter of his own private
observance. Jesus gives them light on their perplexity, by saying,
''Can ye make the children of the bride chamber fast while the
bridegroom is with them?'' He means that he is the bridegroom
and his church is the bride. His preachers and teachers are the
children of the bride-chamber who are bringing him and his church
together by getting men saved. The whole time between his public
ministry and his second advent is the wedding feast, during which
the children of the bridle-chamber are bringing their Lord to the
bride. The marriage supper of the Lamb in the heavenly kingdom
is the final consummation of the wedding ceremony.'' (Abbott.)
Those who are pure in heart: who have on the wedding garments of
holiness and are seeking to increase the number of the saved are
those who have the fullness of joy, of which Jesus speaks (John
15:11). This experience which his sanctified people have now, is
not a funeral occasion. It is the joy of the wedding feast. Fasting
is for those who have lost the presence of the Master in their
hearts. Let such people fast until their joy is restored, but not
those who have it.

Fasting is only for those who are really sorrowful of heart. To fast when we have no sorrow is only hypocrisy. When we have deep sorrow, abstinence of food is a natural consequence. There is no virtue in a self-inflicted sorrow. Alford says, "Fasting should be the genuine offspring of inward and spiritual sorrow, of the sense of the absence of the Bridegroom in the soul—not the forced and stated fasts of the Old covenant now passed away."

Jesus then goes on still further in his explanation to tell them that his new religion of love and heart holiness cannot be patched onto the old religious forms of the Old Dispensation any more than a man can put a path of unfinished material upon an old garment. "The new patch, undressed by the fuller, and moist, will shrink and rend the old worn garment's cloth." Jesus did not believe in a patched up, old nature, but in a religion that gives a new nature. All reformation that does not go on this basis is a failure.

He then gives another illustration drawn from the custom of keeping their wine in bottles made of the skins of animals. Just as the fermenting wine would destroy an old stiff and hardened wine skin so will the joyous, vigorous gospel upset the old stiff forms of the past. This means no set fasting, but the expression of the saved heart must be natural and unhindered. "To confine new truth to old forms only results in shattering the hold."

CHAPTER VI.

AN ORDINATION SERMON ON THE SUBJECT OF HOLINESS.

The Cause and Occasion that Led to This Sermon—Legalism Being Taught Instead of Holiness. Vs. 1-11. It Became Necessary that New Religious Teachers Should Be Chosen, Who Would Teach Holiness. Vs. 12-16. Jesus Preaches a Sermon on Holiness at Their Ordination. Vs. 17-49.

THE CAUSE AND OCCASION THAT LED TO THIS SERMON—LEGALISM BEING TAUGHT INSTEAD OF HOLINESS. Vs. 1-11.

1 And it came to pass on the second sabbath after the first, that he went through the corn fields; and his disciples plucked the ears of corn, and did eat, rubbing *them* in *their* hands.

2 And certain of the Pharisees said unto them, Why do ye that which is not lawful to do on the sabbath days?

3 And Jesus answering them said, Have ye not read so much as this, what David did, when himself was hungred, and they which were with him;

4 How he went into the house of God, and did take and eat the shewbread, and gave also to them that were with him; which it is not lawful to eat but for the priests alone?

5 And he said unto them, That the Son of man is Lord also of the sabbath.

6 And it came to pass also on another sabbath, that he entered into the synagogue and taught: and there was a man whose right hand was withered.

7 And the scribes and Pharisees watched him, whether he would heal on the sabbath day; that they might find an accusation against him.

8 But he knew their thoughts, and said to the man which had a withered hand, Rise up, and stand forth in the midst. And he arose and stood forth.

9 Then said Jesus unto them, I will ask you one thing; Is it lawful on the sabbath days to do good, or to do evil? to save life, or to destroy *it?*

10 And looking around about upon them all, he said unto the man, Stretch forth thy hand. And he did so: and his hand was restored whole as the other.

11 And they were filled with madness; and communed one with another what they might do to Jesus.

A collision between Jesus and the leading religious teachers of the day was inevitable. No such radical teaching as he uttered could gain such a hold upon the masses without producing the most intense hatred from the religious teachers of the day. For there is nothing that will stir carnal men's hatred so much as opposition to their formula of dead religion. Jesus was a preacher of holiness of heart and life. The Scribes were teachers of formal, dead religion. Holiness and this legalism are diametrically opposed to each other. There is no compromise when two such religions meet. Legalism is the attempt of man to be religious without giving up sin. Holiness is light, and sin is darkness, and the two are not only opposites but are antagonists. They can not both exist in the same place. One will drive out the other. The battle had already begun. The healing of the paralytic (Luke 5:18-26) had caused the Scribes and Pharisees to accuse him of blasphemy in assuming to forgive sins. This had been followed by the healing of the impotent man at the pool of Bethesda (John 5:1-16) at which they had accused Jesus of breaking the Sabbath. Another stage of the battle of holiness against formal, dead religion now begins in the section before us.

It was "on the second Sabbath after the first." There were seven sabbaths between the Passover and Pentecost. This was the first Sabbath after the second day of the Passover feast. It was often called *The Second-first Sabbath.* With his disciples he was passing through the fields of corn. And to satisfy their hunger, the disciples were plucking the corn and rubbing it between their hands to free it from the husk that they might eat it. This was allowable to satisfy present hunger. Jewish farmers were accustomed to indulge their neighbors in this privilege to satisfy present hunger. (See Deut. 23:25). But they did it on the Sabbath and had not the Jewish Rabbis (not God) decreed that this was breaking the Sabbath? The Rabbis had got the Sabbath law down to a very fine point, as a day—not of rest—but of misery. Their rules were very minute. None might walk on the grass on the Sabbath day, because the grass would be bruised, which would be a kind of threshing; nor catch a flea, which would be a kind of hunting; nor wear nailed shoes, which would be a kind of burden; nor, if he fed chickens, suffer any corn to lie on the ground, lest a kernel should germinate, which would be a kind of sowing. They considered this plucking of corn a kind of harvesting and consequently a violation of the fourth commandment. These hypocrites pretended that they were very zealous for religion and the keeping of the commandments of God, but their zeal was really a cover for an opportunity to condemn Jesus. Inbred sin hates holiness, and will do anything it can to wipe holy people off the earth. They wished to have Jesus and his disciples stoned for breaking the Sabbath. ''How often do men seem most religious when they are about to do the greatest wrong! Not that religion is to blame, but man's depraved heart is to blame, that makes use of the best thing wherewith to cover the worst practices.'' (Cumming.) Jesus was ready for them with scripture that they could not answer. He asks them in answer to their charge of Sabbath-breaking, ''Have ye not read so much as this?'' This was very sarcastic. It was a censure upon their professed knowledge of the Scriptures. It was as much as to say, ''If you were at all familiar with the import of the Scripture, you would have remembered what David did, when himself was ahungered and those with him.'' He hit these professed specialists of scripture, who had studied only the letter and not got at the spirit of the scripture at all. There are people today who doubtless read scripture as much as these religious teachers, but who read it to little purpose as far as getting any spiritual truth out of it. He then quotes from 1 Sam. 21:1-9 where David when pursued by Saul was very hungry and coming to the Tabernacle asked the priest for food, and the priest rather than allow the Lord's anointed to famish gave him the shew bread, that as was used in the sanctuary. It was on the Sabbath day that the priest fed David. We know this because the record is that the bread had just been put on the table fresh. This bread was always put upon the table fresh on the Sabbath day. David had arrived just as the bread was being changed—the old taken away and the new placed upon the table.

He draws a parallel between David's followers and his own disciples. The priest fed David and his followers on the Sabbath and it was not reckoned as a sin and neither should the rubbing of the stalks of grain between the hands be considered as a sin committed by his disciples. Necessity allowed David to set aside the great law of the Sabbath. The great law of necessity was greater than the law of the Sabbath, as they interpreted it. Jesus announces himself as the Son of Man who is ''Lord of the Sabbath.'' By calling himself the Son of Man, he means that he was a pattern man. THE Head of the new race of holy people—the Second Adam, the head of a new order of beings. Since he is Lord of Sabbath, the Sabbath must conform to his will. We do not see how any one can deny after this statement of Jesus, that he claimed to be divine. He asserts that he is greater than the fourth commandment. No mere man could dare make any such statement in his right mind. He gave the Sabbath command and if we seem in the eyes of some people to break the Sabbath in our service for him, we are really serving One, who is greater than the mere outward letter of the law. We are serving Him who gave the law of the Sabbath.

How many are great sticklers for the outward keeping of the Sabbath, who get no spiritual benefit from it. Legalists in every generation magnify the letter of the law so much, as to lose sight of the spiritual meaning of it. Mark says, he also added ''The Sabbath was made for man and not man for the Sabbath.'' It was intended to be a day,—not of misery and hunger,—but of delight and blessing. It is intended to be a holy day in which we shall ripen in holiness for heaven, the eternal Sabbath. Christ gave a spiritual meaning to the Sabbath such as it had never had before. Let us see to it that when we remember the Sabbath day to keep it holy, we do not fall into the error of a mere ceremonialism, but make it a day of soul rest and spiritual advancement. Let us remember that legalism is not only holiness but is one of its worst enemies, for it blocks up the path of heart advancement. Legalism—simply looking after the externals of religion—is not the holiness of the Bible. We may be ever so strict in the outside life and not have a bit of the soul rest of holiness for which the Sabbath stands as a symbol. They who are seeking to be saved by their works are Sabbath breakers, they break the real soul Sabbath or rather they seek to do away with the rest of faith—the true Sabbath of the soul. The true rest of the Sabbath is a rest from everything in the heart except the love that works for the glory of God and the good of men.

But Jesus did not cease the contest there. He might have let the matter rest. ''On another Sabbath,'' probably the next Sabbath, he went into another synagogue. Matthew calls it ''their synagogue''—the synagogue of the Pharisees. It was one in which the influence of the Pharisees predominated. Although the Jewish church was corrupt, yet it was the best and only church there was and it was dedicated to the worship of his Father. It is better to attend that form of public worship, which is nearest to scripture, even though it be corrupt rather than not honor God in a public way by public worship. Here he continued his battle with the Pharisees by healing a man, who had a withered hand. He might just as well have healed him on the next day and thus have avoided the issue. But he brought on a still fiercer battle. It is our duty at times to assume the offensive and not wait to be attacked. Often the best way to defend the truth is to attack error. The enemy was there watching him to see if he would heal in the Sabbath. They were seeking for proof that he did his miracles by the help of Satan and so they watched him to make it appear that he had broken the fourth commandment, and hence was in the employ of Satan. God had never forbidden man to take medicine or have a physician on the Sabbath, but the Rabbins had added this law to God's law, ''Let not those, that are not in health use physic on the Sabbath day.'' So Matthew says they asked him if it was lawful ·to heal on the Sabbath day. (Matthew 12:10). He asks them in return ''Is is lawful on the Sabbath day to do good or to do evil? to save life or to destroy it?'' Matthew says that he asked them if a man had a sheep that fell into a pit on the Sabbath, would he not take it out? This was a case that doubtless the doctors of the law had not thought of. They had made no law for the emergency. So they could not answer in the negative. He then clinches his unanswerable argument thus, ''How much better is a man than a sheep?'' It is said that up to this time the Rabbins had no law to cover such a case, but after this they forbade the owner of a beast, that might have fallen into a pit, from removing him on the Sabbath. We learn then that the way to use the Sabbath is for the highest good of men.

He then gave a practical illustration of the influence and office of the will in salvation. The man, whom they were expecting he would heal, had a withered hand. There is a very close and vital relation between the will and the muscular system. No one can explain how by an act of the will, we can move our muscles in any desired manner. This man had lost the link between the will and the muscles. When he willed to put forth his hand his muscles would not obey him. But when Jesus said, ''Stretch forth thy hand,'' he willed to do it, and Jesus supplied the missing link and his muscles obeyed his will. There are things in the spiritual realm as difficult, as the moving of that hand and arm. For instance, God says ''Be ye holy.'' We have no power in ourselves to be holy. But if we *will* to be holy with all the intensity of our souls, he will supply the power to make us holy. We do not have to urge him, in order to persuade him to make us holy, for he has been persuaded for two thousand years. But as sure as we will to be holy with all the power of our soul, he will make us holy. Notice Jesus made his hand whole *instantly.* So can he make the soul whole constantly. He did it with a word and not by any act. The Pharisees were even more enraged, for he did nothing. He only spoke to the man and there was no law to prevent a man speaking to another on the Sabbath day. To be holy is no more impossible than the healing of this man's hand. Who can doubt it?

Dr. Guthrie says on this miracle ''Virtue goes out of Christ. The shrunken hand instantly assumes a healthful color, and swells into its right proportions. In his joy the man shuts and opens it; moves his pliant fingers; and holds the miracle aloft to the gaze of a crowd, dumb with astonishment. Give him a harp, and with that hand he would sweep its sounding strings to the praise of Jesus. Pattern to men, who have souls to be saved, and hearts to cure, he did what he could—using all the means within his power to obtain the blessing. And did people with equal eagerness, repair to church on Sabbath, as he to the synagogue, to meet Jesus Christ, and with the same earnestness and faith, lay out their sins and soul's sorrows before him, our Sabbaths would witness greater works than this—he who healed the withered hand healing withered hearts, and, whether they required to be saved or sanctified, giving power to them that have no might.''

IT BECAME NECESSARY THAT NEW TEACHERS BE CHOSEN WHO SHOULD TEACH HOLINESS. Vs. 12-16.

12 And it came to pass in those days, that he went out into a mountain to pray, and continued all night in prayer to God.

13 And when it was day, he called *unto him* his disciples: and of them he chose twelve, whom also he named apostles;

14 Simon, (whom he also named Peter,) and Andrew his brother, James and John, Philip and Bartholomew,

15 Matthew and Thomas, James the *son* of Alphæus, and Simon called Zelotes,

16 And Judas, *the brother* of James, and Judas Iscariot, which also was the traitor.

The religious teachers of the day were teaching only the external holiness of forms and ceremonies. They had refused the light of the doctrine of heart holiness and now it became necessary to supersede them by a new set of religious teachers, so Jesus chose the twelve apostles.

Before he chose them he retired for an all night of prayer on a mountain top. Ordination of preachers should be preceded by solemn and much continued prayer. Jesus prayed on the great occasions of his life: at his baptism, his transfiguration, in Gethsemane and on the cross—a lesson for us, that we have all our actions ruled by prayer. Now the people must be shepherded by better leaders. The multitudes were too large for him to teach them, so he calls his disciples and sets them to preaching. One of the best ways of teaching young ministers how to preach is to set them at it. We do not by any means intend to say that there should not be a preparation to preach, but the practical method of having them preach while at their studies is, to our minds, most excellent. They were learning of Jesus and at the same time preaching. There may much be learned from Jesus and books today, and yet there be a need of practicing what is learned. It may be said that these men were not trained in the schools of the prophets, and therefore we have here an argument against intellectual training for the ministry. But this would be hardly a fair argument. This commission given here was only temporary. It was only for a few short months, or weeks at least. And yet in this short space he laid down some general principles for all successful ministry. If God can use an uneducated ministry, he ought to use an educated ministry to still greater advantage. He wants a sound mind, soul, and body, each cultivated the best we can, to be used in his service. Is he not as much the God of the mind as of the soul? When he had risen from the dead and ascended to heaven, he appeared to one of the most cultivated and best educated men of the times—Paul—and called him to the ministry. And even then he did not fully allow him to go to work, until he had been three years in the deserts of Arabia getting ready. Moses, the great leader of the ancient church, was one of the best educated men of his day. Verse 13 says ''He called unto him his disciples.'' They were *called*. They *came* when they wished to learn, but when sent out to preach, they were *called*. Let men be in no hurry to preach. Let them wait until He *calls* them. This is too serious a matter to rush into, as we would a business or profession. It is not a profession. It is *a calling*.

The number twelve is quite significant. The sons of Jacob, who were the heads of the tribes were twelve in number, and we read that these twelve apostles are to sit upon twelve thrones, judging the twelve tribes of Israel. (Matt. 19:28.) The wall of the city that John saw had ''twelve foundations and in them the names of the twelve apostles.'' (Rev. 21:14.) It says in verse 13 that he chose the twelve apostles from his disciples, showing that they had already followed him as disciples. Now he gives them power for his short temporary campaign. What is power? No one can tell. We see its effects but no one can define it. These same men had power after the Holy Ghost in his fullness came upon them, to be true witnesses for Jesus. But here we find that they had power before Pentecost, over unclean spirits, to cast them out and also to heal diseases. The lesson is that God gives those whom he has called in every generation, power to perform the special work he has for them to do. Here he gave them power to heal the sick and to cast out devils, that when they spoke, the multitudes would heed their words. His own miracles were his credentials, calling attention to his utterances of the truth. So now he gives them miraculous power over disease and devils as their credentials, that they might have influence over the people in laying the foundations of his kingdom. This was the power for working wonders and miracles. But the power that they got at Pentecost, which enabled them to be proper witnesses was still greater. Healing was a gift not bestowed on many even after Pentecost, as we see by reading 1 Cor. 12:28, where the gift of healing is placed fifth in importance in the list of gifts, which even all in the Pentecostal church did not possess. (See 1 Cor. 12:11.)

There are people in our day, who have made the gift of healing of more importance than entire sanctification. But we find that these disciples had the gift of healing before Pentecost. (See Matt. 12:8.)

"Whom also he named apostles." Notice the change of name from *disciples* to *apostles*. The word disciple means a learner. The word apostle means *one who is sent forth*. These disciples had been learners of Jesus and now he sends them forth especially commissioned to preach. This is the true preparation for preaching: first to learn of Jesus. We are not fit to represent him until we learn of him. As good as is intellectual equipment it can never take the place of this endowment, which comes from actual acquaintance with Jesus. He, who has had no experimental acquaintance with Jesus is not fit to preach the Gospel. Our schools of theology ought to have a special department to teach the young preachers how to get acquainted with Jesus. And he, who does not daily get better acquainted with Jesus, ought to get out of the ministry. He had tested them and proved them and now he sends them out to preach. The church will do well to follow the command of Paul "Lay hands suddenly on no man." Do not be in a hurry to ordain men, until they have been tried and proved. Luke says here that Jesus himself gave them the name of Apostles. Jesus himself is called an apostle in Heb. 3:1. He was *sent forth* by God.

There are four lists of the apostles given in the New Testament.

The three other places are Matthew 12:24, Mark 3:16-19 and Acts 1:13. There is some slight variation in these lists. Judas is left out of the list in Acts, as he was dead. Matthew mentions Lebbeus. Mark calls him Thaddeus, while Luke calls him "Judas, not Iscariot." In Acts he called Judas son of James. Though all of them did not come into like prominence, yet they all fulfilled their mission (with the exception of Judas) and sealed their testimony with their blood. The names are not given in the same order in the four lists. But Peter was placed first, not because he was superintendent or even exercised any authority over them. We find no place where he did. James, the brother of our Lord seems to have exercised more authority and to have been more of a leader than Peter in the church. (Acts 12:17, 15:13, 21:18.) Peter does not seem to have had so much to do in laying the foundations of the church as did Paul. So we can not admit the claims of Catholicism that Peter was the first Pope. There is no trace of the preeminence of Peter in any of his epistles. Peter was of that bold, impetuous nature, which would naturally bring him to the front. But we have no authority for saying that he was ever appointed to take the place of Jesus, as pope. Ecclesiastical history says that he suffered martyrdom at Rome. There is no account in the New Testament of his ever being at Rome.

Jesus called five of his apostles from the company of John the Baptist's disciples. (See John 1:36-49.) This is proof that they were regenerated at the time that he called them, for John preached regeneration and justification.

There were three pairs of brothers among them, Andrew and Peter, James and John (called Boanerges, sons of thunder), James and Judas or Thaddeus. Matthew has "Simon, the Canaanite" whom Luke calls "Simon Zelotes." Whedon says of the latter, "Less is known in regard to this apostle than of all the twelve. He is not mentioned in the New Testament out of the catalogue. The epithet Canaanite is an Aramaic word, signifying the Zealot. The name indicates that he had belonged to the fanatical sect of Judas, the Gaulonite before he became an apostle."

This first commission of the apostles was to the church.

Jesus said (Matt. 12:5) "Go not into any city of the Gentiles and into any city of the Samaritans enter ye not." Jesus never preached to the Gentiles. Matthew 12 contains a more complete account of the instructions of Jesus as they went forth.

IT BECAME NECESSARY THAT NEW RELIGIOUS TEACHERS SHOULD BE CHOSEN, WHO WOULD PREACH HOLINESS. Vs. 12-16.

17 And he came down with them, and stood in the plain, and the company of his disciples, and a great multitude of people out of all Judæa and Jerusalem, and from the sea coast of Tyre and Sidon, which came to hear him, and to be healed of their diseases;

18 And they that were vexed with unclean spirits: and they were healed.

19 And the whole multitude sought to touch him: for there went virtue out of him, and healed *them* all.

20 And he lifted up his eyes on his disciples, and said, Blessed *be ye* poor: for yours is the kingdom of God.

21 Blessed *are ye* that hunger now: for ye shall be filled. Blessed *are ye* that weep now: for ye shall laugh.

22 Blessed are ye, when men shall hate you, and when they shall separate you *from their company,* and shall reproach *you,* and cast out your name as evil, for the Son of man's sake.

23 Rejoice ye in that day, and leap for joy: for, behold, your reward *is* great in heaven: for in the like manner did their fathers unto the prophets.

24 But woe unto you that are rich! for ye have received your consolation.

25 Woe unto you that are full! for ye shall hunger. Woe unto you that laugh now! for ye shall mourn and weep.

26 Woe unto you, when all men shall speak well of you! for so did their fathers to the false prophets.

27 But I say unto you which hear, Love your enemies, do good to them which hate you,

28 Bless them that curse you, and pray for them which despitefully use you.

29 And unto him that smiteth thee on the *one* cheek offer also the other: and him that taketh away thy cloke forbid not *to take thy* coat also.

30 Give to every man that asketh of thee; and of him that taketh away thy goods ask *them* not again.

31 And as ye would that men should do to you, do ye also to them likewise.

32 For if ye love them which love you, what thank have ye? for sinners also love those that love them.

33 And if ye do good to them which do good to you, what thank have ye? for sinners also do even the same.

34 And if ye lend *to them* of whom ye hope to receive, what thank have ye? for sinners also lend to sinners, to receive as much again.

35 But love ye your enemies, and do good, and lend, hoping for nothing again ; and your reward shall be great, and ye shall be the children of the Highest : for he is kind unto the unthankful and *to* the evil.

36 Be ye therefore merciful, as your Father also is merciful.

37 Judge not, and ye shall not be judged : condemn not, and ye shall not be condemned : forgive, and ye shall be forgiven :

38 Give, and it shall be given unto you ; good measure, pressed down, and shaken together, and running over, shall men give into your bosom. For with the same measure that ye mete withal it shall be measured to you again.

39 And he spake a parable unto them, Can the blind lead the blind? shall they not both fall into the ditch?

40 The disciple is not above his master : but every one that is perfect shall be as his master.

41 And why beholdest thou the mote that is in thy brother's eye, but perceivest not the beam that is in thine own eye?

42 Either how canst thou say to thy brother, Brother, let me pull out the mote that is in thine eye, when thou thyself beholdest not the beam that is in thine own eye? Thou hypocrite, cast out first the beam out of thine own eye, and then shalt thou see clearly to pull out the mote that is in thy brother's eye.

43 For a good tree bringeth not forth corrupt fruit ; neither doth a corrupt tree bring forth good fruit.

44 For every tree is known by his own fruit. For of thorns men do not gather figs, nor of a bramble bush gather they grapes.

45 A good man out of the good treasure of his heart bringeth forth that which is good ; and an evil man out of the evil treasure of his heart bringeth forth that which is evil : for of the abundance of the heart his mouth speaketh.

46 And why call ye me, Lord, Lord, and do not the things which I say? '

47 Whosoever cometh to me, and heareth my sayings, and doeth them, I will shew you to whom he is like :

48 He is like a man which built an house, and digged deep, and laid the foundation on a rock : and when the flood arose, the stream beat vehemently upon that house, and could not shake it : for it was founded upon a rock.

49 But he that heareth, and doeth not, is like a man that without a foundation built an house upon the earth ; against which the stream did beat vehemently, and immediately it fell ; and the ruin of that house was great.

It may be well for us to more closely look at the personality of the twelve. Their names are given in sets of two, because he sent them out by twos to preach. Simon was originally a disciple of John the Baptist (John 1:40-42), Jesus changed his name to Peter or Cephas, which means a stone, thereby signifying that, nothwithstanding his naturally fickle disposition, he would became a rock, and he did after he received his Pentecost. He and his brother are named at the head of the list of the apostles, only because they were the first to follow Jesus.

Andrew was Peter's brother and he had the honor of leading Peter to Jesus (John 1:40-41); see also John 6:8 and 12:22 and Mark 13:3). Tradition says that both these brothers were crucified: Peter with his head downward and Andrew on a cross shaped like the letter X; hence this form of the cross is called St. Andrew's cross.

For an account of St. James, see Matt. 27:56 and Mark 15:40. He was killed by Herod (Acts 12:2). He and his brother John were probably cousins of Jesus (See Matt. 13:55); the term translated brethren, often indicated other relationship besides that of brothers. John was younger than James and hence is mentioned after him. He calls himself, ''The disciple whom Jesus loved.'' (John 12:23.) He and his brother, James, were naturally very quick and fiery of temper, with carnal ambitious spirit. (See Luke 9:52-55 and Mark 10:35-41.) Entire santicfication made a great revolution in their natures. Peter, James and John were the three most honored by the confidence of Jesus (Matt. 17:1; Mark 5:37; John 18:23). They were the three pillars of the Pentecostal church, according to Paul (Gal. 2:9). John wrote one Gospel, three Epistles and the Book of Revelation. He was banished to the isle of Patmos for Christ's sake. After being restored he lingered among the churches until a good old age, as a constant benediction. He was 94 when he died.

Philip was a native of the same city (Capernaum) as Peter, James, John and Andrew. He is mentioned (John 1:45) as having brought Nathaniel to Jesus, and as he and Bartholomew are always mentioned together and as Bartholomew is not a name but only a title, meaning Son of Tolmai, it is supposed that Nathaniel is the same as Bartholomew. Philip is known for but two things which would seem to indicate that he was not so spiritual as some of the others. (See John 6:7 and 14:8, 9.)

Matthew had two names, the other name was Levi. (Luke 5:27, 29; Matt. 9:9.) He was a revenue officer. His father was Alpheus. He wrote one of the Gospels. The manner of his death is unknown.

Thomas was also called Didymus in the Hebrew language. Both names mean *a twin*. Little is known of him except that he was of a very affectionate disposition and weak faith. (John 11:16; 14:5-20; 20:29; 21; 2.) He never seems to have accomplished much. People of skeptical disposition never do. We have nothing reliable concerning his death.

James was called the son of Alpheus to distinguish him from the other James. There were three in the New Testament by the name of James: the brother of John; the Lord's brother, who wrote the epistle of James, and this James, the son of Alpheus, also called James the less, to distinguish him from James, the brother of John.

Simon was called Zelotes because he belonged to the sect called Zealots, who were so called because they were exceedingly zealous and enthusiastic in the observance of the Mosaic ritual. Matthew calls him the Canaanite.

Judas, the brother of James is called the son of James in the *Revised Version.* He is called Lebbeus by Matthew, and Thaddeus by Mark. Probably he had three names. He was the author of the epistle of St. Jude.

Judas Iscariot, the son of Simon (John 6:71). He was called Iscariot, which means *of Kerioth,* a town in Judea. He was the only disciple that was a Judean. He was a good man when chosen, until Satan entered into him. Inbred sin in the special manifestation of covetousness ruined him. This is a warning to all other ministers of the Gospel, to beware of the love of money. See his downfall in John 12:1, 8, when he was angry with Mary for breaking the alabaster box and anointing Jesus.

We notice the four evangelists do not give the list of the disciples in the same order, as it was immaterial as to the order.

Jesus had talked with and ordained his disciples on the mountain side and now he came down from the mountain and healed many of the attendant people who were diseased. There went out a virtue or power from him that healed all those, who had genuine faith. Although he healed diseased people and often does today, yet we must not get our eyes upon healing as the chief thing in the atonement if we do we shall dishonor him. Pious Scott, the commentator says ''Men will regard the diseases of their bodies as greater evils than those of their souls; but the scriptures teach us to form a contrary judgment for if we could have access to Jesus, and obtain from him the most perfect cure of every disease, and the greatest degree of health that fallen man ever possessed, without deliverance from the power, guilt and pollution of sin, by the efficacay of his blood, and the virtue that ·proceeds from him, we must be miserable to all eternity.''

JESUS PREACHES A SERMON ON HOLINESS AT THEIR ORDINATION. Vs. 17-49.

Jesus now preaches a sermon to his newly appointed apostles. In this sermon he lays down the principles of his kingdom. It was a holy kingdom and its principles are holy and righteous. We pity those people who can not see holiness in the Bible unless the specific term *holiness* and *sanctification* are used. Those who see holiness only when it is so named fail to really see it at all. It is the basis of all the precepts and promises and prayers and sermons of the whole Bible. It is found everywhere throughout this sermon. By referring to the fifth, sixth and seventh chapters of Matthew we shall find virtually the same discourse. Matthew gives a more extended report of the sermon as given to the disciples alone. We are inclined to believe that having given the discourse as reported by Matthew he comes down into the plain and speaks to them now, openly, so that the multitudes can hear, and gives only a fragment of what he had given to his disciples already on the mount. Luke gives certain sections of the sermon. Verses 20-26 give a series of blessings and woes or curses. It is not unlike the responsive service of the Israelites at Mount Ebal and Gerizim (see Josh. 8:33-35), the blessings or beatitudes. There are four, as follows: ''Blessed are ye poor.'' This must be interpreted in harmony with Matt. 5:3, ''Blessed are the poor in spirit.'' He does not mean poverty in dollars and cents, or houses and lands. There is no virtue in such poverty. Some people are poor because of their sinful course of life. A misunderstanding here caused the rise of a sect in the days of the early church called the Ebionites, who taught that it was meritorious to be poor and a sin to be rich. Poverty is not a passport to heaven and wealth, is not a barrier to that holy place. Wealth makes it harder to be true to God than poverty, but a man may be far from being poor in spirit who is poor in pocket-book, and a man may be poor in spirit who is wealthy in material goods. Poverty of spirit is that humility of soul that feels that it is of no account in itself that all its riches and sufficiency must come from God. This leads to true penitence and trust in God, because of a sense of unworthiness. Unless we have come to this state, we have never genuinely repented of sin, and if we have not genuinely repented we have never been saved. He says of such ''Yours is the kingdom of God.'' Matthew says: ''the kingdom of heaven,'' Luke says ''the kingdom of God.'' In Luke this kingdom is named after the king-God; in Matthew it is named after the place or capital city—heaven. This is a spiritual kingdom; it consists in righteousness and peace and joy in the Holy Ghost, (Rom. 14:17). It is experienced in this life. Godet says ''These blessings are primarily spiritual-pardon and holiness.'' This penitence of soul is the foundation of all the other graces of Christian holiness.

''Blessed are ye that hunger.'' Luke is not attempting to give the whole sermon but the heart of it, and so he mentions the two works of salvation—justification in verse 20, whereby we get into the kingdom of heaven, through repentance and faith and sanctification in Verse 21, by which we are cleansed as the temples of God and filled with the Holy Spirit. So Matthew explains still further that this blessing is conferred on those, who hunger and thirst after righteousness. The experience of those who have met the conditions and experience of verse 20, have received the kingdom of God and are hungry for holiness. The new life in them makes them hunger and thirst after all the mind of Christ. They have more than a general, indefinite wish to be good. They have

an intense longing after God and his holiness, as intense as a
hungry child after food. No man can keep clearly justified and
lack this hunger. We may know whether we are genuine Christians by this hunger after holiness. If we have it not we need
to be regenerated. ''Our Lord pronounces this benediction here
upon those whose soul is hungering and thirsting after goodness,
after sanctification'' (Vaughan). Adam Clarke says this promise
means ''A full restoration to the image of God.'' What a
blessed encouragement for those who are really hungry for the
fullness of salvation. The same Spirit that gives us life and an
appetite for holiness supplies the want of the soul. He never
gave us that appetite to tantalize us. The third Beatitude is to
those who mourn. WE are in a world of mourning. Each one
sooner or later takes his turn. To those who have entered the
kingdom and have been filled with the Holy Spirit, there is a
consolation in the dark hours of life, such as the world knows
nothing about. In this world saved people are sorrowing and
rejoicing. Only saved people have this paradoxical experience.
There is a blessing upon all ''mourners in Zion.'' And we are
on our way to a world where there will be no tears nor heart
aches. Thank God! The fourth Beatitude is pronounced upon
those who are hated for Christ's sake (not for their own sake—
their own follies but because they are like Jesus); who are separated and cast out by men for Jesus' sake. Notice how Luke
states the real vital points of experience. Entrance into the
kingdom of God, the fullness of the Spirit and then the two
greatest trials and testings that we shall have—grief in the sorrows of life and ostracism and opposition because we are filled
with the Spirit. As sure as we are holy, we shall meet the opposition to holiness that Jesus, who was filled with the Spirit, met.
''In proportion as moral character becomes clear, definite, sharply
defined, in the same proportion will the world hate it and therefore such persons, so persecuted give evidence of their belonging
to the kingdom of heaven'' (Cumming). John Wesley says, ''He
that is a truly *righteous man*, he that *mourns*, and he that is *pure
in heart, yea, all that will live godly in Christ Jesus shall suffer
persecution*, (2 Tim. 3:12). The world will always say, 'Away
with such fellows from the earth. They are made to reprove our

thoughts. They are grievous to behold. Their lives are not like other men's; their ways are of another fashion.' '' Worldliness in the church is of the same nature as worldliness outside of the church, and hence holiness will be as bitterly opposed by the worldly part of the visible church as by those outside of the church. There can be no genuine holiness movement that is not opposed by worldly ecclesiastics. Spurious holiness is that which suits worldly people. Yes ''They shall separate you'' and then say ''it was you who withdrew yourselves and became 'clannish.' '' If you are holy they will reproach you and cast out your name. But what of that? Do not whine for you are in the apostolic succession; in the royal line. Jesus was so treated (Rom. 15:3); also the prophets (Vs. 23 and Matt. 5:12). We are commanded to bear reproaches (Heb. 13:13). ''The greatest purity of the church has been in times of persecution; its greatest corruption in the time of its wealth, its honor and its worldly prosperity'' (Abbott).

He commanded them to rejoice in that day—the day when we are reproached for holiness—not after it is over but while it is going on. He tells us to show our joy—leap for joy.'' If we have not the victory so that we can rejoice in persecution for Jesus' sake, but are constantly whining and showing our wounds and telling of our persecutions, it shows that after all we are not persecuted for righteousness' sake but for our own sake—for our folly or foolishness or inconsistencies. IF our persecution does not lead us to rejoice, that we are counted worthy to suffer for his sake, we can safely judge that we are not mistaken in thinking we are persecuted for our righteousness and holiness. There is a joy to those, who are like Jesus when persecuted. Men have rejoiced in the flames and in dungeons and showed a joy of which their persecutors were not only experimentally ignorant, but could not comprehend. All this opposition to the truth is nothing new. It may be new to us. We thought every body would bow down to our experience and worship, but it has always been thus. Every generation persecutes its righteous men, and wonders how their fathers could have persecuted the righteous of their day. History repeats itself. Each generation has been busy putting up monuments to the righteous whom their fathers killed and at the same time killing its own righteous men.

2. He now follows these four blessings with four woes which he pronounces upon states of character exactly the opposite to those which he has just extolled. The first woe is upon those who are rich. We must of course understand the word in the larger sense of riches. Otherwise if we restricted it to the smallest definition we should make Scripture contradict itself. The Bible never condemns mere possession of material wealth. Job was rich and yet God called him a perfect man. Abraham walked before God and was perfect and yet he was rich in silver and cattle. It means those who feel that they are well enough off without God and, who do not desire him. They feel self is sufficient. It is those who trust in their riches instead of God. Such people as the rich fool (Luke 12:16-21); Dives (Chapter 16:19-31); the young man (chapter 16:18-24) and the church at Laodicea (Rev. 3:17, 18). What is really the difference between a man who has money and makes it his God and a man, who wants it so bad that he makes the acquisition of wealth the chief desire of his soul. In either case it causes men to forget God. Jesus pronounces a woe on such people. The radical difference between Christ's kingdom and this world is shown in the fact that he pronounces blessings upon those who are despised by the world and woes upon those whom the world honors. The rich have received their consolation here—all they will have. This life is all the heaven that a worldling will ever have and all the hell that a righteous man will ever experience. Abraham told Dives, ''Son remember that thou in thy life time received thy good things and Lazarus evil things.'' (Chapter 16:25.) Men get what they seek. If they seek only this world, they will get it. And if they seek God with all the heart they can have Him. They who are seeking the things of this world have a woe pronounced upon them. IT is a sad commentary on the spiritual condition of those professed Christians, who are seeking to be rich when God has said that those, who make riches their god have a woe pronounced upon them.

''Woe unto you that are full.'' This refers to those who are full of the ambitions and carnal delight of this world. Weeping and gnashing of teeth through all eternity will follow a life of worldly pleasure. (Matt. 8:12; 13:42, 50.)

A woe is pronounced too upon those who laugh now—those who are of a giddy trifling spirit.

A fourth woe he pronounced upon those, who are well spoken of by every body. Such preachers are true successors of the false prophets, who antagonized no sin and made sinners feel comfortable. No preacher ever was true to his convictions without making some one feel uncomfortable. There is no greater danger to preachers than this—laying aside convictions to gain the favor of men. This woe of Jesus ought to be thundered in the ears of every preacher when he is ordained, and the echo ought to reverberate throughout his life time. Scott says "Thus the false prophet whom God abhorred, were generally applauded, even by his professed followers; while the true prophets, who declared his whole counsel, were hated, reproached and persecuted, as if they had been the vilest of mankind." It has always cost something to declare the whole counsel of God and preach full salvation unflinchingly. Since real holiness means death to every kind of sin, we must not be surprised, if we find all men of every grade of worldliness and sin arrayed against it.

These four woes are the direct opposites of holiness. No holy man is guilty of any such disposition as are here mentioned. Holiness destroys "the lust of the flesh and the lust of the eye and the pride of life," which make up the world about us.

Having blessed and pronounced woe upon certain classes of character, he now proceeds to lay down positive precepts. Some of these precepts are so high that many of his professed followers of today seem to think that he did not really mean what he said. Some seem to think that it is impossible to keep them. It takes a holy heart to keep them in their spirit. "Love your enemies." Love is a principle and affection of the inner man. He means that we are to go farther than to treat our enemies well. We are to love them. It takes an entirely sanctified heart to do this. We can not do this of ourselves only as God gives us the supernatural power to do it. This love will manifest itself by doing good to those who hate us. How sweet is revenge to the carnal heart. But grace kills the carnal nature and enables us to love those who hate us. This plant did not grow in nature's garden. It is an exotic. It was transplanted from the skies.

We are to go still further and "Bless them that curse" us. If we can not do that, how much better are we than the world about us. They can love their friends as easily as we. What evidence have we that we belong to God if we do not have the same attitude towards our enemies that God had towards us when we were his enemies? The maxim of the world is "Give them as good as they send." The maxim of Jesus is, "Pray for your enemies." The next precept must have astonished his audience. "And unto him that smiteth thee on the one cheek, offer also the other." This sounds Utopian and impossible to unspiritual people. But if this was the universal practice how soon strife of all kinds would cease in this jangling world. That professed Christian who feels that if he does not resist evil he is not showing the proper spirit acts from the feeling of pride and he may well doubt whether he is a Christian at all.

He commands to give to every one that asketh. This precept of course is to be interpreted in harmony with other scripture. It must depend upon certain conditions. God himself does not answer all requests, only those that are in harmony with the conditions of prayer that he has laid down. Certainly we are not warranted in giving where we know what we give is to be wickedly used.

He now gives the famous Golden Rule. There is nothing like it in all the religious teaching of all the world. Its universal practice would settle all the disputes that are in the world. It is this: have the same spirit and action towards men that we wish them to have towards us, and conversely do not expect any more from others than you are willing to feel towards and do to or for them.

Jesus was a great reasoner. We see a manifestation of it here, as he asks, "If you love them that love you what thank have ye? For sinners also do the same." Any one can love the loveable without any religion. But our religion has love for God and man even when the latter is unloveable as its corner stone. He clearly shows here the great principle that real Christians act entirely different from sinners. Sinners are those, who sin and the children of God do not act like sinners. They do not sin. Here Jesus shows the great difference between sinners and saints. This is the great teaching of the Bible everywhere—that when a man is saved he is no longer a sinner but ceases his sins. (1 John 3:4-11.)

Still further he lays the principle down that we are not to help men and lend to them from selfish motives—because we expect them to return the favor. But we are to help them from love for them. The Roman sages and philosophers contended that we should help men only when it was no sacrifice for us. We are to love and lend to our enemies. He does not say that we are to love our enemies in the same degree, that we love our most intimate friends. Jesus had some very intimate friends while on earth whom he loved better than others, while he loved every body.

"Be ye therefore merciful, as your Father also is merciful." In Matthew 5:48 we have the record that in this same sermon he also said, "Be ye therefore perfect, even as your Father which is in heaven is perfect." We are commanded then, to be like God in love and mercy. We are to have as pure love and mercy in our little, finite sphere as he has in his unlimited sphere. Jesus does not require us to be equal, but to be like God. Some one says that a drop of water can be as pure as the ocean but it is infinitely smaller. It is not the quantity but the quality that God cares for and requires. The last clause of verse 35 throws light on verse 36. God is kind even to the unthankful and the evil and we must be merciful even when men do not deserve it. Notice, in the graces of love, mercy and purity we are to be like God. (1 John 3:17; Matt. 5:48; Isa. 26:3; 1 John 3:3.)

Another sin to which we are all tempted is uncharitable judgment. This does not mean that we are to call bad things good and destroy moral distinctions. It is our duty to reprove. But we must do it in the spirit of love. It takes the blessing of perfect love to be able to maintain an equilibrium between charity with its sweetness and reproof that refuses to compromise the truth.

"Forgive and ye shall be forgiven." How many are deceiving themselves as regards their standing with God. They repeat the Lord's prayer and at the same time have an unforgiving spirit. Such people when they say, "Forgive us our debts as we forgive our debtors," REALLY ASK GOD TO DAMN THEM. It is bad enough to go to hell without asking God to send them there.

"Give and it shall be given unto you." How many times has this been proven. The man who gives generously to the cause of God finds that God makes it possible to give by giving him more.

We by no means understand this to mean that this is purely a matter of dollars and cents. For money is not the highest good. A holy man is a benevolent man as regards money, and God expands his soul the more he gives to God in the right spirit. It is a sad thing to be a Christian and not believe that "it is more blessed to give than receive" and to never have found it out, is to have missed some of the best experiences of the Christian life. Even a cup of cold water given in the name of a disciple shall not lose its reward. He here refers to the Jewish custom of carrying grain. In the waist of the long garments worn by the Jews, grain was often carried. A belt around the waist made it a large pocket into which the grain was poured. A careful observation of many years has enabled us to see that those who are liberal to others as a rule are treated in return the same way and vice versa. Those who are always censuring others have to take their pay in the same coin from their fellow men. We have seen this rule exemplified often in society.

By two illustrations, he now shows that preachers and teachers should be wholly sanctified. He first shows (Vs. 39) that all preachers and teachers should be regenerated. Otherwise they are "the blind leading the blind." How true this is. The unregenerated preacher is blind. He does not see spiritual things as he attempts to lead others, who are equally blind. They are both on the road to destruction. How appropriate this ordination sermon was! What a tremendous responsibility to preach doctrines that we have not experienced. There are many blind processions to hell led by blind preachers, who need to be born of God to get spiritual vision.

But that is not enough. Not only must the preacher be regenerate so that he can lead the way, but he must be in the possession of perfect love to be properly qualified. So he says still further, "The disciple is not above his master; but every one that is perfect shall be his master." We must not think that we are to be any different from the Master. We must be like him—have the same mercy that he had (Verse 36) and be perfect in love as he is (Matt. 5:48). He says this to let them understand that it is not even enough to be regenerated and be able to see as we lead our flock and keep it out of the ditch, as preachers and teachers. We must go further in our experience and be perfect in love like Jesus. It is absurd and dishonest for any intelligent reader of the Bible to deny that the Bible teaches perfection of some kind. Most opposers of the doctrine set up a man of straw and immediately proceed to knock him down, by saying no one can be perfect in this life. They mean absolutely perfect. But the scripture never enjoins such a perfection upon us. An honest man will seek to know what the Bible means by the perfection which it requires. The fact of it is thousands of religionists want every thing perfect except their religion and they seem to be afraid to have that perfect. The perfection taught in the Bible as a requirement is used in an accommodated sense. It means a perfection of love or perfect love which is the end of the commandment (See 1 Tim. 1:5). Who can object to that. People have to misrepresent the doctrine of Christian Perfection before they can bring any argument against it. So Jesus says ''The disciple is not above his master, but every one that is perfect is as his master.'' This is in addition to the command of Matthew 5:48. Adam Clarke says, ''Everyone, who is instructed in divine things, who has his heart united to God; whose disorderly tempers and passions are purified, and restored to harmony and order; and every thing perfect except their religion and they seem to be cannot be *above,* yet will *be as* his teacher, holy, harmless, undefiled, and separate from sinners.''

He now illustrates the reason, why the preacher should have perfect love that ''casts out fear'' and which is a state of purity. He compares a preacher, who seeks to have men leave off their sins and yet refuses to get rid of inbred sin to an oculist, who himself has poor eyesight and yet wants to operate on other people's eyes. He sees objects in other people's eyes, that he wanted to take out when he is looking over a beam in his own eye that is larger than the splinters, he wants to take out. The beam is depravity. The man who seeks to have sinners give up their sins and is unwilling to be cleansed from inbred sin is inconsistent, for people will say ''Physician heal thyself.'' To expect sinners to abandon sin while we hold onto our sinful nature and make excuses for not having it removed is the height of inconsistency. This interpretation may seem to the reader to be far fetched but let us look at it more closely and we will find that purity is the subject here illustrated. Notice how clearly this is taught in other passages. In Matthew 6:22 Jesus says "If thine eye be single, thy whole body shall be full of light." What the eye is to the human body, the affections are to the soul. The word from which we get the word integer, which means whole, entire, nothing lacking—not diseased. It means a pure heart, which is necessary in order to give us clear vision. Jesus said (Matt. 5:48) "Blessed are the pure in heart for they shall see God." The apostle says "holiness without which no man shall *see* the Lord." So we see that purity is necessary to clear vision. A diseased eye hinders vision. Entire sanctification which purifies the heart enables us to see clearly. Thus Jesus teaches that it is not enough to get eye sight and hence not be a blind man leading others to destruction. Regeneration enables us to do that. We must go farther and get the beam out of our eye by being wholly sanctified. So verse 39 teaches regeneration and verse 41 entire sanctification. Otherwise our views of truth will be cloudy, like a man who cannot see well because he has cataract of the eye. Actual sin is but a splinter compared with the beam of inbred sin which furnishes the splinters. Jameison Fausett and Brown say very pertinently here that the word "Splinter very well defines the meaning of the word "Mote."

He then gives an additional illustration to show that we ought to be holy if we are to be successful as Christian teachers. "For a good tree bringeth not forth corrupt fruit." How important if a man is to be a preacher or teacher that his life be pure. Our personality speaks louder than our words or acts. It is the man behind the sermon that is the strongest factor of the preaching. Even the heathen moralists insisted that if a man was to be effective in moving men as an orator he must be a good man. Character is greater than words, even as a tree is greater than its fruit.

All doctrine is known by the fruit that it produces. I am inclined to think that he is talking of the results of doctrine here. The way to tell the character and quality of doctrine is to watch its results. False doctrines produce unspiritual lives. Only true doctrine can produce holy living. "A corrupt tree cannot produce good fruit.'' We know this passage is usually interpreted as referring to the individual life and no doubt it does illustrate the truth that we shall be righteous only as our hearts are right, but this and the parallel passage in Matthew were spoken primarily as to the results of doctrine. (See Matthew 15:20 where in the parallel passage he says he is speaking of false prophets, when he uses this illustration.) The Verse 45 also indicates that this refers to doctrines, for he continues as to public teaching or talking thus ''A good man out of the good treasure of his heart bringeth forth that which is good . . . for out of the abundance of the heart the mouth speaketh.'' That is to say, if the preacher or teacher are truly born again and hence are not blind teachers of the blind, leading them into the ditch (Vs. 39) and are not trying to pull motes out of other people's eyes until they have got sin out of our own hearts (Vs. 11) or in other words, if we have the clear vision that comes from being entirely sanctified, we are the good tree whose fruits are manifest and we thus as preachers and teachers *speak* out of the good treasure of our hearts. So verse 45 sums up all the teachings of the illustrations of the blind leading the blind, the removing of inbred sin from the heart of the preacher and teacher, so that his life helps his teaching and thus he *speaks* out of the rich treasure of his heart, because he has been regenerated and has had the beam of inbred sin removed and his heart is now a clean treasury enriched by grace divine. The preacher as well as the layman is no mightier than his heart power and life—no matter however great his eloquence or gifts.

He now comes a little closer to his preachers in their private life and what he says of their private personal experience is applicable to everybody. He asks the searching question, ''Why call ye me Lord, Lord and do not the things which I say?'' To call him Lord is to acknowledge his authority. It is as much as to say I acknowledge thee to be my ruler, and I will obey you.'' Every time we call Him, Lord when we pray, we profess to be governed by his laws. A lord is one who rules those who acknowledge him as lord. Now to profess that he is our Lord by calling him so without obeying him, is like a man who swears allegiance to the government and then refuses to obey its laws. It is all lip service—to call him Lord and then disobey him. God requires his people to obey him—to keep his commandments. As sin is the breaking of the commands of God, it follows that God expects all Christians to live without committing sin. God does not expect us to obey him any further than we have light, but he expects us to have the spirit of obedience. This is the sense in which we can live without committing sin. Any profession of religion that does not enable us to do the will of God is a delusion. It is only a dead faith that does not lead to abandonment of sin.

A man who comes to God (Vs. 47) hears his sayings and does not obey them, is a backslidden Christian (for he has already *come* to God, and now disobeys). Such a Christian is like a man who builds a house on a poor foundation. When the storms of life come (as come they will) he will go down in ruin. The storms of this life and the Judgment will find him out. But the man who comes to Jesus and obeys him will build a character which the trials of life and the Judgment can not overthrow. Pious Quesnel says on this passage, ''Without a holy heart and a holy life, all is ruinous in the hour of temptation, and in the day of wrath.'' Let us have this holiness without which no man shall see the Lord'' in peace. As sure as we come to God and then resolve at any cost to obey his commandments we shall come into the experience of full salvation from all sin.

CHAPTER VII.

HOLINESS, AN ENCOURAGEMENT.

It Encouraged an Honest Heathen. Vs. 1-10. It Encouraged a Widow in Her Bereavement. Vs. 11-17. It Encouraged a Good Man in His Temptation. Vs. 18-35. It Encouraged a Penitent Sinner. Vs. 36-50.

IT ENCOURAGED AN HONEST HEATHEN IN HIS SORROW. Vs. 1-10.

1 Now when he had ended all his sayings in the audience of the people, he entered into Capernaum.

2 And a certain centurion's servant, who was dear unto him, was sick, and ready to die.

3 And when he heard of Jesus, he sent unto him the elders of the Jews, beseeching him that he would come and heal his servant.

4 And when they came to Jesus, they besought him instantly, saying, That he was worthy for whom he should do this:

5 For he loveth our nation, and he hath built us a synagogue.

6 Then Jesus went with them. And when he was now not far from the house, the centurion sent friends to him, saying unto him, Lord, trouble not thyself: for I am not worthy that thou shouldest enter under my roof:

7 Wherefore neither thought I myself worthy to come unto thee: but say in a word, and my servant shall be healed.

8 For I also am a man set under authority, having under me soldiers, and I say unto one, Go, and he goeth; and to another, Come, and he cometh; and to my servant, Do this, and he doeth *it*.

9 When Jesus heard these things, he marvelled at him, and turned him about, and said unto the people that followed him, I say unto you, I have not found so great faith, no, not in Israel.

10 And they that were sent, returning to the house, found the servant whole that had been sick.

Jesus was absolute holiness personified. Holiness means perfect love to man as well as perfect love to God, and those most like Jesus are constantly employed in helping suffering humanity.

151

It is a mark of holiness to be drawn out, in our sympathy, to help others. Holy people in their sphere and according to their ability delight to minister to humanity. This chapter is an illustration of the work and mission of holiness among mankind.

Capernaum was one of the chief cities of Galilee. It was situated probably on the north coast of the Sea of Galilee. It was a port of entry for goods coming from Syria and had a custom house. Consequently the Roman government had a company of soldiers stationed here. A nation that holds another nation in servitude, as the Romans did the Jews, usually carefully guard the custom houses, that it may possess itself of the revenues. A centurion was an officer who commanded a century or company of one hundred soldiers. This centurion like Cornelius (Acts 10) was favorably disposed towards the Jews, and had built them a synagogue or meeting house for Jewish worship. The events that are here described occurred immediately after The Sermon on the Mount, described in the last chapter. The centurion had a servant, who was very sick. He sent through a deputation of the elders of the Jews to Jesus, to come and heal his servant. Matthew (Matt. 8:5) does not mention the elders. There is no discrepancy here, as people are often said to do what they delegate others to do for them. The writers of the New Testament give the leading facts and do not attempt always to give all the details.

Not only does the fact that this heathen had built a synagogue for the Jews speak volumes for his moral character but the fact that he was so interested in the welfare of his servant, shows him to have been a man of large heart and nobility of character. Such tenderness towards a servant was unusual in that day. Adam Clarke says ''This centurion did not act as many masters do when their servants are sick—have them immediately removed to an infirmary or work house.'' This is a truth that may well be emphasized. Had we more of this spirit we should have less trouble in solving the ''Servant girl problem'' and less clashing between capital and labor.

These elders, who came to Jesus on behalf of the centurion, spoke very highly of him, saying that he loved the Jews and had built a synagogue for them. This was indeed remarkable for the Jews hated and despised the Gentiles, and called them dogs.

They especially hated the Roman soldiers, who had come to keep the peace and enforce the collection of the taxes. A heathen, who could love the Jews under these circumstances, showed nobler qualities than even the Jews themselves.

Matthew tells us (Matt. 8:7) that Jesus said ''I will come and heal him.'' When the centurion heard this, he sent another deputation declaring that he was not worthy to have Jesus come under his roof. He well knew that if Jesus should come under his roof he would be defiled in the eyes of the Jews. In our acknowledgement of unworthiness we often show our real character.

''Observe three estimates of the Centurion's worthiness: first his own, *not worthy*, because a sinner; second, *worthy*, because he had built a Jewish synagogue, the highest encomium of character that a Jewish elder could pass upon a Gentile outcast; third, Jesus's estimate, *worthy because* of his faith, and needing no commendation from Jewish elders, but himself an example and rebuke to them'' (Abbott). He says ''Say in a word and my servant shall be healed.'' What faith! He did not feel it necessary, even to have Jesus come near the sick servant in order to cure him. He did not wait to see signs and wonders before he could believe, as some people do.

Some people think they have faith when they are leagues from it. A sense of great unworthiness and great faith go together. There is much mock profession of unworthiness, which is only of the lip, that can not trust God simply because there is great pride covered with a thin veil of professed unworthiness. Real humility casts itself wholly on the promises of God. Mock humility refuses to trust. The Centurion now makes an argument thus, If a man in my position, who commands men under him, who will obey him, has such power over men, how much greater is thy power over disease, and how easy it is for thee to bid disease depart. Real faith uses great arguments in its petitions to God for favors. It bases its arguments upon the omnipotence of God. Our Heavenly Father delights to have us use such arguments. That is the way that Moses and Abraham and other saints of olden time prayed, *and God heard and answered their arguments.*

''Jesus'' when he heard these words ''marvelled at him.'' There are many things recorded of Jesus while on earth that show that he had human as well as a divine nature. He wept, had indignation and marvelled just as we do. There are only two recorded instances where Jesus marvelled: here where he found faith in a heathen soldier, where it might have been least expected; at Nazareth where he had been brought up he marvelled because he found unbelief (Mark 6:6), where faith might have been expected. Faith and unbelief mightily moved the heart of Jesus when he beheld their operations. Faith is the highest act of the soul, and unbelief is the great sin of the world, of which the Holy Ghost has come into the world to convict men. (John 16: 8-19.) A holy soul is very sensitive to its surroundings whether of faith or unbelief. Let us keep in mind that faith is more than intellectual perception. It is a moral act of the soul in throwing itself upon Jesus. Notice too that this was faith for another, not for himself. This example of the healing of this servant is an encouragement to us to pray for others and God will answer our prayers for them, as far as he can without coercing their wills. We have a right to believe that God will powerfully convict men, if we earnestly pray; for he can convict them against their wills although he will not justify or regenerate them against their wills. Jesus said ''I have not found so great faith, no, not in Israel.'' The whole Jewish church did not contain so bright an example of faith as was found in this heathen. How often does the world put to shame a worldly church!

Here was a heathen who was saved. For by reading the parallel account in Matthew 8:11-12 we see it clearly taught. ''Many shall come from the east and the west and shall sit down with Abraham and Isaac and Jacob in the kingdom of Heaven, but the children of the kingdom shall be cast out into outer darkness.'' This was said to show that the faith of the centurion would bring him final salvation in heaven although he was a Gentile. Peter said virtually the same thing about that other heathen, centurion, Cornelius, ''In every nation he that feareth God and worketh righteousness is accepted of him.'' Many of the heathen, who have lived up to their dim light will stand a better chance of heaven than favored church members, who have not walked up to their light. A man may be a church member and yet go to hell. And yet there are many who think that church membership will take them to heaven! Those who have not on the wedding garment of holiness will be "cast into the outer darkness where there shall be weeping and wailing and gnashing of teeth." (Matt. 8:12.) Weeping denotes sorrow and gnashing of teeth denotes rage. We are told that among the peculiar privileges of the church of God are "peculiar incitements to holiness from the hearing of God's word." If that be true and we do not improve our opportunities to obtain "that holiness without which no man shall see the Lord," we would stand a better chance of heaven if we had been born in a heathen land.

According to Matthew Jesus added, "As thou hast believed, so be it unto thee." The same is true today. We shall be saved up to and according to our faith. The miracles of healing performed by Jesus occurred mostly in his early ministry. Little is said about them in his later ministry except the healing of the servant's ear in the garden of Gethsemane, after Jesus' arrest. The miracles were intended to call attention to the deep spiritual truths which came later. After the miracles had established the fact of his deity then Jesus led the disciples on to deeper spiritualty.

Jesus healed this servant immediately. It was no gradual work and the healing of the soul of which these miracles was a symbol is also an instantaneous work.

IT ENCOURAGED A WIDOW IN HER BEREAVEMENT.
Vs. 11-17.

11 And it came to pass the day after, that he went into a city called Nain; and many of his disciples went with him, and much people.

12 Now when he came nigh to the gate of the city, behold, there was a dead man carried out, the only son of his mother, and she was a widow: and much people of the city was with her.

13 And when the Lord saw her, he had compassion on her, and said unto her, Weep not.

14 And he came and touched the bier: and they that bare *him* stood still. And he said, Young man, I say unto thee, Arise.

15 And he that was dead sat up, and began to speak. And he delivered him to his mother.

16 And there came a fear on all: and they glorified God, saying, That a great prophet is risen up among us; and, That God hath visited his people.

17 And this rumour of him went forth throughout all Judæa, **and** throughout all the region round about.

There is nothing that touches more deeply the heart of Jesus than the burdens of sorrowing humanity. Holiness brings its pos-' sessor into sympathy with the sorrowing world all about us. The next day after Jesus had healed the centurion's servant, he went to a little city called Nain, accompanied by quite a crowd of people. As they drew near the gate of the city they met a funeral procession on the way to the cemetery, for the Jews usually buried their dead outside the walls of their cities.

Here were two processions: a procession of life headed by Jesus, who is the life of man and who was followed by a rejoicing living multitude. They met a procession of death headed by the dead body of a dead young man, followed by a sorrowing company. The procession of life was too much for that of death and hence halted the sad company and overcome death and broke up the funeral. It is a parable of what Jesus will do in the resurrection morning. He will forever spoil the power of death over believers. Life is stronger than death. Bless God!

The only reason given for the raising of the young man is "he had compassion on her." Human sorrow then and now touches the great heart of Jesus. Our sorrow means his compassion. It draws out his sympathy. No one had asked him to raise the young man. Usually when he healed or helped people it was after he had been asked to do it. The centurion asked for the healing of his servant. The ruler requested the cure of his son Jairus besought him for the raising of his daughter, but here Jesus shows compassion which was unasked.

The chief mourner was a widow—the most helpless of all classes in Eastern countries. And this was her only son. It was about as sorrowful and despairing a condition as can be imagined. Jesus said to her, "Weep not." He was about to turn her sorrow into joy. In the resurrection morn he will do the same for the saints, who have sorrowed over the loss of their loved ones.

Then he came and touched the bier or coffin. It was considered an act of defilement to come in contact with the dead according to the law of Moses but Jesus was greater than the law. "Under the Old Testament, God raised one by Elijah, another by

Elisha living, a third by Elisha dead; by the hand of the Mediator of the New Testament he raised here the son of the widow, the daughter of Jairus, Lazarus; and, in attendance upon his own resurrection, he made a delivery of holy prisoners at Jerusalem. He raises the daughter of Jairus from her bed, the widow's son from his coffin, Lazarus from his grave, the saints at Jerusalem from their decay; that it might appear that no degree death can hinder the efficacy of his overruling command. He that keeps the keys of death, can not only make way for himself through the common hall and outer room, but through the most reserved closets of darkness.'' (Bishop Hall.)

With the touch of his hand came the accents of that voice. Notice how much is said about the voice of Jesus in resurrecting the dead, He said to Jairus' daughter, ''Maid arise.'' He said to Lazarus, ''Come forth.'' He said here, ''Young man I say unto thee, arise.'' He is coming with a voice that shall pierce the tomb. ''They that are in the graves shall hear his voice and come forth.'' We would have considered it sacred privilege to have heard that voice of him, who while on earth spake as men never spoke, but we are to hear it when, ''the Lord himself shall descend from heaven with a shout and the voice of the archangel and the trump of God.''

The dead young man sat up and began to talk with the neighbors and friends. Was there ever such a wonderful funeral and so strangely broken up?

No wonder fear fell on all the inhabitants of that country. But even then they did not grasp the truth of his Messiahship, but thought that he was simply a great prophet, who had lately arisen. He was the embodiment of holiness doing good wherever he went and showing compassion for suffering humanity. When we lay away our dead, we can be comforted with the thought that he is just as sympathetic now, as then.

IT ENCOURAGED A GOOD MAN IN HIS TEMPTATION.

Vs. 18-35.

18 And the disciples of John shewed him of all these things.
19 And John calling *unto him* two of his disciples sent *them* to Jesus, saying, Art thou he that should come? or look we for another?

20   When the men were come unto him, they said, John Baptist hath sent us unto thee, saying, Art thou he that should come? or look we for another?

21   And in that same hour he cured many of *their* infirmities and plagues, and of evil spirits; and unto many *that were* blind he gave sight.

22   Then Jesus answering said unto them, Go your way, and tell John what things ye have seen and heard; how that the blind see, the lame walk, the lepers are cleansed, the deaf hear, the dead are raised, to the poor the gospel is preached.

23   And blessed is *he,* whosoever shall not be offended in me.

24   And when the messengers of John were departed, he began to speak unto the people concerning John, What went ye out into the wilderness for to see? A reed shaken with the wind?

25   But what went ye out for to see? A man clothed in soft raiment? Behold, they which are gorgeously apparelled, and live delicately, are in kings' courts.

26   But what went ye out for to see? A prophet? Yea, I say unto you, and much more than a prophet.

27   This is *he,* of whom it is written, Behold, I send my messenger before thy face, which shall prepare thy way before thee.

28   For I say unto you, Among those that are born of women there is not a greater prophet than John the Baptist; but he that is least in the kingdom of God is greater than he.

29   And all the people that heard *him,* and the publicans, justified God, being baptized with the baptism of John.

30   But the Pharisees and lawyers rejected the counsel of God against themselves, being not baptized of him.

31   And the Lord said, Whereunto then shall I liken the men of this generation? and to what are they like?

32   They are like unto children sitting in the marketplace, and calling one to another, and saying, We have piped unto you, and ye have not danced; we have mourned to you, and ye have not wept.

33   For John the Baptist came neither eating bread nor drinking wine; and ye say, He hath a devil.

34   The Son of man is come eating and drinking; and ye say, Behold a gluttonous man, and a winebibber, a friend of publicans and sinners!

35   But wisdom is justified of all her children.

The healing of the centurion's servant and the raising of the widow's son, and other works of Jesus were told every where. The news even penetrated into the country beyond Jordan and were heard in the prisons. A grand man, John the Baptist, now languishing in prison heard the tidings. He was shut up in the castle or prison called Macherus, beyond the river, Jordan. The last we heard of John, he was baptizing the people in the river Jordan and denouncing the leaders of the church for their wickedness. Herod, the king had married the wife of another man, and John who never compromised with sin did not fail to rebuke him for his adultery. The result was Herod had him seized and cast into prison. We do not know how long John had been in prison, when he sent this delegation of his disciples. It seems that his disciples were allowed access to the prison. They had told him of the wonderful works and words of Jesus. Doubtless they had informed him of the neglect of fasting on the part of Jesus and his disciples and the reason Jesus had given for it. (Chapter 2: 18-22.) No doubt this perplexed John, as well as did the startling truths that Jesus had been speaking in the Sermon on the Mount. John could not be on the ground to hear for himself but must get all this from others. No wonder he was perplexed. Consequently he sent two of his disciples to inquire whether Jesus were really the Messiah or only an ordinary prophet. Holy men like John are always interested in the prosperity of the kingdom of God. If John could have been there in person and seen for himself doubtless he would have been convinced and would have so fully recognized Jesus that he could have said again, ''Behold the Lamb of God.'' He would have recognized Jesus as the one that he had baptized in Jordan, and on whom the Spirit had rested like a dove. But now was his hour of trial and tribulation, and he got the news second hand, and doubtless what he heard was much exaggerated, as is usual in reports. He knew that Jesus was doing the very works that had been expected of the Messiah but he could not understand the rumors that he received concerning the doctrines of Jesus, and he was doubtless bewildered at his neglect of fasting. He was anxious to know how to explain these things. Holy men all get solicitous for the cause of God and are often tempted to think it is not prospering as they think it should. Some think that John was discouraged because Jesus did not come and release him from the prison. But it seems to us that he was more perplexed at the doctrines of Jesus as they had been reported to him and feared that perhaps this was not the same person that he had baptized in Jordan, but some other prophet. He wanted to know how to reconcile the works of Jesus with the new and startling doctrines that he had preached. The cause of the kingdom of heaven lay nearer to the heart of John than his own comfort and freedom. The man who had been accustomed to the rough life of the wilderness would never have repined at the hardship of a prison.

Would that all the professed servants of God were as solicitous for the cause as was John. No doubt he thought the kingdom was not coming fast enough. Some of us sometimes get restless and want to hurry on matters in the kingdom of God. So when he asked ''Art thou he that should come? or look we for another?'' he doubtless referred to Malachi 3:1 ''The Lord whom ye seek shall suddenly come to his temple.''

So Jesus ''in that same hour cured many of their infirmities and plagues and of evil spirits; and unto many that were blind he gave sight.'' These were just the works that the coming Messiah was to perform. So Jesus said to the messengers ''Go your way and tell John what things ye have seen and heard.'' This is the proof of the genuine gospel today. It has holy fruitage. Wherever we see men being saved from their sins, we can believe that there the gospel is being preached.

Jesus added to this message ''Blessed is he whosoever is not offended in me.'' The word, *offend* means to cause to stumble. ''Blessed is the man who does not stumble because there are things in me and the administration of my kingdom that he can not comprehend and that are objectionable to his prejudices'' is the message that Jesus would still have all men hear.

''God moves in a mysterious way his wonders to perform.''

Many times we are apt to think his cause is halting. It is because we see things darkly or as in an enigma. Our vision is faulty.

We think too that John had another purpose in sending his disciples to Jesus. No doubt they were somewhat shaken in their faith by the reports they had heard and John wished them to see for themselves the works of Jesus and thus have their faith strengthened. John thus turned the hearts and attention of his disciples to Jesus. He had already said ''He must increase and I must decrease.'' That John succeeded here in confirming the faith of his disciples in Jesus is apparent in the fact that when

John was beheaded his disciples after they had buried his body went and told Jesus, as their best friend. Verse 24 also confirms this interpretation of John's action. Jesus tells the people that John was no reed shaken by the wind. His captivity had not at all shaken his faith or loyalty to God.

After Jesus had given the messengers of John some idea of who he himself was, he now turns to the people to give them some idea of who John was. He pronounces the most beautiful and glowing tribute to John that any mortal ever received. He describes the character of John and shows how that generation had treated both John and himself. Holy men have always had similar treatment from a worldly ecclesiasticism.

It was *after* the disciples of John had retired that Jesus gave this glowing tribute to that great and holy man. It is significant that he did not give this tribute until they had left. Holy people do not need public commendation and holy people do not unnecessarily puff others in public. Matthew Henry says ''He would not flatter John nor have his praises reported to him. . . . Pride is a corrupt humor, which we must not feed either in ourselves or others.'' This tribute to John shows in what esteem God holds holy people. For John the Baptist was a holy man. He was ''filled with the Holy Ghost.''

He began his commendation by asking the people what they thought they went out to hear—what kind of a man—when they went into the wilderness to hear John preach. Did they think they went out to hear a man who was as fickle and vacillating as a reed shaken by the wind? Tristam in his book ''Land of Israel'' says ''The reed of Egypt and Palestine is a tall cane, growing twelve feet high, with a magnificent panicle of blossom at the top, and so slender and yielding, that it will lie perfectly flat under a gust of wind, and immediately resume its upright position. It grows in great cane brakes in many parts of Palestine, especially on the west side of the Dead Sea, here nourished by the warm springs it lines the shore for many miles with an impenetrable fringe—the lair of wild boars and leopards—to the exclusion of all other vegetation. On the banks of the Jordan it occurs in great patches, but is not lofty.'' John was no such unstable man, as to be bold in rebuking sin and then whine when persecution came, and lose heart. He was made of better stuff. Or did they go to see "a man clothed in soft clothing?" Not at all. They went out to see a prophet clothed in a hairy garment of camel's hair. John might have clothed himself in purple and fine linen according to the latest styles of the day, if he had only let the sin of Herod go unnoticed. But he was not that kind of a man. These people went out to see in John not only the last prophet of the Old Dispensation but one who was more than a prophet. He was the Morning Star that heralded the rising of the Sun of Righteousness.

He was the forerunner of the Lord. He was a man who made people ready for the Lord. This is the object of the true gospel ministry in all ages of the world. It is the business of every true disciple to introduce people to Jesus.

To be filled with the Spirit, to be a fearless preacher of right-eousness and to be instrumental in leading men to Jesus constitutes true greatness, for, Jesus said of this man "There is not a greater prophet than John the Baptist." What a difference between di-vine and human ideas of greatness. Men call a man great if he is a little taller than his fellows, or weighs a little more, or has a brain of finer quality or larger dimensions, or has that persuasive-ness of speech called eloquence, or sits in high position. But God calls those great who like John are filled with the Holy Ghost and deliver the divine message fearlessly.

Jesus now adds to this paradox, "But he that is least in the kingdom of God is greater than he." This indicates that the kingdom of heaven has great and exalted privileges. It is so much greater than the Old Dispensation in which John lived, that its subjects are greatly exalted. A small child on a mountain can see much more and further than a great man in the valley. The holy John lived in a dispensation where his opportunities and privileges were circumscribed by dim light and imperfect revela-tion. In the Old Dispensation his opportunities for usefulness were not as great as the humblest child of God under the New Dispensation. The humblest of us have greater privileges since the Holy Ghost has been poured out so abundantly, than did the great John under the Old Dispensation. Jesus said that even his own disciples should work greater works than himself after Pente-cost. (See still further our comments on Matt. 11:7-15.)

Luke here says that the people who heard John and also the publicans justified God by being baptized by John. To justify any one is to approve of them, and vindicate their course. These people recognized the excellence of the way of salvation as preached by John. They recognized it as from God. Their baptism was a sign of this fact. Thus we have here taught that water baptism is an outward testimonial published to the world, that we believe in the salvation for which it stands, as a symbol. The common people came up to and embraced the light, as given by the preaching of John. These people were therefore ready for the greater light that was brought by Jesus. On the other hand the leaders of the church refused to accept John's baptism and doctrine and rejected the counsel of God. We see here the antithesis: justifying God on the one hand by accepting the truth, and rejecting his counsel by refusing the light. They rejected the counsel or doctrine *against themselves.* John's preaching was against their sins which he denounced threatening that God would lay his axe at the root of the tree of the Jewish church (Luke 3:7-9). It is worthy of note that the common people who had come to the light that John gave forth were the ones, who heard Jesus gladly, while the leaders of the church, who had rejected the message of John, rejected Jesus also. In every dispensation those who have rejected the light already given, rage at the new and advanced light. It is on the principle that a man in a darkened room whose inflamed eye-balls are hurt by one ray of light does not want the shutters thrown up. He has more light already than he wants. The greatest fighters of holiness as the second blessing, are those who are condemned by the light of the first blessing. Or to put it a little differently: those who are not living up to the standard of regeneration always fight entire sanctification. These are its most bitter enemies. Bitterness against holiness is a sure proof of an unrighteous life.

Luke having given this parenthetical remark in verses 29-30 as to the effects of John's preaching now takes up the talk of Jesus again which was broken off at the 28th verse. He illustrates the fact that sin and holiness are ever the same in all ages. They never change their nature. The depraved nature of man is the same that it was six thousand years ago. Sin opposed Jesus, just as it does his brethren of today. It opposed John just as it did Jesus and just as it did all the holy prophets since the world began. John came and they found fault with his austerity. He was not social enough to suit them. Jesus came exceedingly social, mingling with all classes and they did not like that any better. They complained because he mixed with all classes, especially with sinners. John was too plain in his living and Jesus was a glutton. They would not be satisfied with either. There are some simple minded people today, who suppose that we can be so holy that we will please people about us. Do they think they can accomplish what Jesus and John could not do? Jesus likened these carnal opposers to contrary children, in their games, who would not be satisfied with their comrades no matter how they played. This illustration shows how well Jesus understood human nature. When the other children played weddings these cross grained children thought the plays were too merry. When they played holding funeral services they thought the play too serious. So the other children said "We have piped unto you and you would not dance." They had played merry tunes in vain. "We have mourned to you and ye have not wept." They had laughed as at a wedding, but they said it was too gay. They had cried as if at a funeral but that was too sober they said. They were bound not to be satisfied anyway. John came after the funeral order and they did not like him. Jesus came after the order of a wedding full of joy but that suited them no better. We suppose the children, who were thus criticising would have accused the other children of making a division. Usually when there is a division in the church over holiness, the holy people are accused of making it. But the division is really caused by those, who can not have their own way and have holiness shut out.

It is the opposers of holiness who make the division for if all embraced holiness there would be no division. The accusation fits those who make it. It is easy to find fault with holiness people if we do not like holiness. "But wisdom is justified of her children." Those people who want to be right and are willing to be led of God are the children of wisdom or wise children, and their experience justifies their course. They are always eager for the truth and honestly receive it, in spite of the sophistry of those, who oppose it. Their shining experience proves the genuineness of the truth which they embrace. This is the hope of the preacher of holiness. Thank God there are people, who are the children of wisdom everywhere, who want the truth at any cost; who follow all the light they can get. God always leads them out into a large place in every generation, no matter what their surroundings may be.

IT ENCOURAGED A PENITENT SINNER. Vs. 36-50.

36 And one of the Pharisees desired him that he would eat with him. And he went into the Pharisee's house, and sat down to meat.

37 And, behold, a woman in the city, which was a sinner, when she knew that *Jesus* sat at meat in the Pharisee's house, brought an alabaster box of ointment,

38 And stood at his feet behind *him* weeping, and began to wash his feet with tears, and did wipe *them* with the hairs of her head, and kissed his feet, and anointed *them* with the ointment.

39 Now when the Pharisee which had bidden him saw *it*, he spake within himself, saying, This man, if he were a prophet, would have known who and what manner of woman *this is* that toucheth him : for she is a sinner.

40 And Jesus answering said unto him, Simon, I have somewhat to say unto thee. And he saith, Master, say on.

41 There was a certain creditor which had two debtors : the one owed five hundred pence, and the other fifty.

42 And when they had nothing to pay, he frankly forgave them both. Tell me therefore, which of them will love him most?

43 Simon answered and said, I suppose that *he,* to whom he forgave most. And he said unto him, Thou hast rightly judged.

44 And he turned to the woman, and said unto Simon, Seest thou this woman? I entered into thine house, thou gavest me no water for my feet : but she hath washed my feet with tears, and wiped *them* with the hairs of her head.

45 Thou gavest me no kiss : but this woman since the time I came in hath not ceased to kiss my feet.

46 My head with oil thou didst not anoint : but this woman hath anointed my feet with ointment.

47 Wherefore I say unto thee, Her sins, which are many, are forgiven ; for she loved much : but to whom little is forgiven, *the same* loveth little.

48 And he said unto her, Thy sins are forgiven.

49 And they that sat at meat with him began to say within themselves, Who is this that forgiveth sins also?

50 And he said to the woman, Thy faith hath saved thee ; go in peace.

This incident must not be confounded with the breaking of the alabaster box and the anointing by Mary at Bethany (John 12:3). They are two different events.

Jesus was invited out to dine with a Pharisee by the name of Simon. It was not so much an act of hospitality with Simon, as an occasion for criticising Jesus, as the sequel shows. This is in keeping with much of the hollow, insincere etiquette of society. We must not put much confidence in the pretensions of so called polite society. Many of the forms of etiquette are only hypocrisy. Although Jesus knew that the motives were insincere that prompted the invitation, yet he accepted in order that he might do good. We are to improve the opportunities that enemies of the truth throw in our way and go even when we know that we are not loved and are even hated, if there is a possibility of doing good and glorifying God even among his enemies.

It is evident that the Pharisee intended to be very condescending to Jesus in this invitation to dine. He thought like many to-day, who come to Christ formally and with mere profession, that he was doing Jesus a great honor to permit him to dine with him.. This is noticeable in the fact that he did not provide for him the ordinary courtesies of the day. He provided no water for his feet. He did not give the usual kiss of welcome, nor did he provide the usual oil for anointing the head. Jesus could clearly see the spirit of the man.

The custom of the day was not to sit at the meal on chairs or benches, but to recline on couches amid cushions. The Jews had introduced this custom which had long been in vogue among the Persians, Greeks, and Romans. "The dinner-bed (of three couches therefore) called a *triclinium* stood in the middle of the room, with a space between it and the walls, by which the guests passed to their places. The side of the square nearest the door was open, so that the servants could have access to the dinner table, which was inclosed within the area formed by the triclinium The guests when placed had their faces turned toward the table, with their feet outward or behind, toward the wall. It will be thus seen how the woman "standing at his feet behind," could easily do all that she is described as doing.

Multitudes had come to Jesus for healing of the body but this woman came for healing of the soul. It is refreshing to see such desire for salvation when so many were coming only for physical help. They sought good but she sought the highest good. There was so few like her that wanted salvation that she showed herself a remarkable character. We must despise no one, no matter how wicked or sinful they may be, for we do not know their peculiar temptations, nor know their desire to be good in spite of their sins. There are many forms of sin. Her sin was not as heinous in the sight of God as that of Simon. His sin was pride that shut up the way to God. It kept him away from the pardoning mercy of Jesus, while her sin led her to seek his mercy. The presence of Jesus made her penitent while it only hardened Simon.

She brought her sinful self to Jesus which was a present more precious in his sight than the contents of the alabaster box.

How mistaken men are in construing the motives of others. This Pharisee supposed the Master was ignorant of the character of this woman, but the fact of it was Simon was ignorant of the compassion of Jesus towards penitent sinners. He thought he had fathomed the character of Jesus when really Jesus had seen through his proud heart and estimated it at its real value. He was proudly condemning Jesus when the latter was acquitting a penitent. Men often judge the Lord and say hard things against his dealings and doings when in fact they are themselves at the very time being weighed in the divine balances.

The Pharisee ''spake within himself.'' It was not a spoken audible speech. It was only the thought of his heart, but Jesus ''answering said unto him.'' Jesus answered his unspoken thoughts. This teaches us that we are held responsible for the thoughts of our hearts as well as the words of our lips. This is a solemn thought that the purposes of our hearts as well as the words of our lips will be brought up in the Judgment.

When David committed his great sin, God sent Nathan, the prophet, to him to rebuke him with a parable. Here Jesus uses the same method, speaking by a parable, in which he likened the woman and Simon to two debtors, both of whom could not pay his creditor, God. Simon was as truly a sinner or debtor to God as the woman. She was fifty times as much in debt as he, but as neither could pay, the case of the one was as hopeless as that of the other. There are so called moral people today, who pride themselves on their goodness. But they as truly need salvation as the wickedest sinners. This is a very hard saying in the sight of moralists but it is the teaching of Jesus Christ.

Simon had little gratitude and Jesus makes him acknowledge it, when he answers the question, ''Which of them will love him the most?'' Simon was obliged to say ''I suppose that he to whom he forgave the most.''

It is only those who have had genuine conviction of sin and have heartily turned away from it and have the sweet sense of sins forgiven that really love God. The depth of our spirituality depends on the depth and thoroughness of our penitence and abandonment of sin. It is the proper attitude to sin that lies at the root of all true piety. Here is the dividing point between real orthodoxy and liberalism. Here is where all heresies begin— with the sin question. It is true as regards all degrees of sin. Those, who have little conviction of inbred sin, never make a real thorough consecration. It is only such people, who hate the sin of their own hearts, who really seek to be entirely sanctified. Others desire the Baptism with the Holy Ghost in order to acquire power, or satisfy their lust for a blessing. But those who hate the sin of their hearts, want it cleansed away. Lyman Abbott truly and pungently says ''We are not to forget the deep truth of this parable, which is forgotten, I fear, in much of the ministry of the modern church, with the result of a shallow love and an imperfect consecration.'' We fear that the reason so many professed Christians quibble against entire consecration and entire sanctification is, they have not that deep love which comes from a sense of sins consciously forgiven. The same writer adds further, ''I believe it is true, as matter of history, that those forms of theology which have treated sin lightly, have always issued in belittling Christ's divine nature and work; and that those experiences which have not led to thorough heart searchings and penitence before God, have not led to a deep love for Christ nor a thorough consecration to his service.''

We ought to note here the severity that Christ shows to those who pride themselves on their morals and outward living and have no sense of divine forgivenes. This class were the bitterest enemies that Jesus had when he was on earth, and they are the greatest hindrances to the spread of his gospel today. There is no hope for them, for Jesus came not to call such people but to call those who feel themselves sinners.

We learn again that the higher the degree of holiness, the greater the sympathy for the sinning and erring. Thank God, our Christ did not gather up his robes and repel this sinner. Had he listened to Simon and refused to sympathize with this penitent sinner, it would have cut off and blasted the hopes of a sinning world. Thank God that he did not agree with Simon. If he had, there would have been no hope for a guilty world.

"For she loved much." This does not mean that she was forgiven because she loved much. It does not mean that our depth and intensity of love has any merit in it, for he told her in verse 50 that it was her faith that saved her—not her love. Her faith begot love. The more and deeper the consciousness of our sins the more we shall love our Saviour.

Jesus tells her, as he told another woman (Chapter 8:48) that it was her faith that had saved her. Does faith save? Yes it is the medium through which God bestows salvation. It is like the trolley that reaches up and receives down the power upon our hearts. It is nothing of itself only as the connection between us and divine grace.

After the great premium that Jesus puts upon faith it is astonishing that men do not trust God more than they do. And so Jesus dismissed this loving, rejoicing, forgiven, weeping sinner with the words "Go in peace." He gives the power today to go away clothed with the garments of peace.

CHAPTER VIII.

THE RESPONSIBILITY AND ACTIVITY OF HOLINESS.

The Fidelity and Thankful Spirit of Holy People. Vs. 1-3. Holy People Are Abundantly Fruitful. Vs. 4-15. Religious Teachers Should Be Holy and Have Insight into Spiritual Mysteries. Vs. 16-18. Holy People Are Kinsfolk of Jesus Christ. Vs. 19-21. Feebleness of Faith Shows Lack of Entire Holiness. Vs. 22-25. Holiness Means the Destruction of Sin. Vs. 26-40. Holiness Ministers to the Distressed. Vs. 41-56.

THE FIDELITY AND THANKFUL SPIRIT OF HOLY PEOPLE. Vs. 1-3.

1 And it came to pass afterward, that he went throughout every city and village, preaching and shewing the glad tidings of the kingdom of God: and the twelve *were* with him.

2 And certain women, which had been healed of evil spirits and infirmities, Mary called Magdalene, out of whom went seven devils,

3 And Joanna, the wife of Chuza Herod's steward, and Susanna, and many others, which ministered unto him of their substance.

Jesus was an itinerant preacher. He set the example for itinerant preaching. He went throughout every city and village. By this is meant every city and village of Galilee where his mission was carried on at this time. He preached in both small and large places. There are many of his preachers today who chafe at having to preach in small appointments and consider it belittling. Every one can not preach in the large places and the gospel must be preached every where. As soon as Jesus became popular in one place he left and went to another. (Chap. 4:43.) He had no time for honors or emoluments. These are not the objects for which the gospel ministry was commissioned. The patience and self-denial of the ministry has everything to do with

171

the prosperity of the cause. Unless the ministry are examples of their own preaching how can they expect the flock to follow them! How many have entirely overlooked the self denial that the religion of Jesus requires, and even seem ignorant of it. He preached and showed "the glad tiding of the kingdom of God." There is a class of preachers, who preach after a fashion but they do not show the glad tidings of the kingdom. No one would imagine from their manner that there was any gladness connected with the gospel. We owe it to the people to show them that it is a gospel of gladness.

There were certain women especially, to whom this gospel had come in its power who manifested their holy joy by ministering to the physical, temporal wants of Jesus. While we cannot buy salvation with our money, yet we can show by the way we support the gospel and its messengers that we appreciate it. The world can tell by the way we use our money whether we really believe the gospel is the precious treasure that we profess it is. Real gratitude for the gospel is shown by the way we provide for those who at the divine command bring it to us.

The leading woman of those who showed their appreciation of Jesus was Mary called Magdalene. She was evidently a woman of high rank, for she is mentioned first—before Joanna, the wife of Chusa, Herod's steward. She has unfortunately and erroneously been confounded with the woman, who was a sinner and who anointed the feet of Jesus at the house of Simon. There is no ground for this at all. She had been possessed with seven devils. Whether there had been the definite number seven or whether seven is here used as a symbol for a great number, is not particularly relevant. She had been possessed by too many if by one. She was called Magdalene from Magdala, the town in which she lived. The devil was allowed for some wise purpose to possess people in those days. He has ever been attempting to oppose the work of God. When Moses worked miracles he helped the magicians of Egypt to do the same. When God sent prophets, he sent lying prophets. When Jesus came in the flesh, Satan also came in the flesh. Chusa is supposed to be the nobleman whose son Jesus healed (John 4:46, 54). His wife had been evidently healed of some malady by Jesus, and she expressed her gratitude.

Susanna was a woman whose character and history are unknown. She is however honored by having her name preserved in the Book of Books because of the expression of her gratitude to Jesus. Thus the Lord teaches us that he is not unmindful of the expression of our gratitude. And are we not commanded ''In every thing give thanks?'' God keeps a book of remembrance. (See Malachi 3:16.)

It is right that those who have been helped in spiritual things by the servant of God should minister to the preacher's temporal necessities out of their material substance. Paul shows this in 1 Cor. 9:11. It shows that we approve the Lord's plan of carrying on the gospel, as well as that we appreciate the blessings of the gospel. Jesus while on earth had to depend on the support of his people, such was his poverty. A religion supported by the civil government has no authority in scripture. Jesus endured poverty that we might become spiritually rich. (2 Cor. 8:9.) ''He only fed others miraculously; for himself he lived upon the love of his people. He gave all things to man, his brethren, and received all things from them, enjoying thereby, the pure blessing of love; which is then only perfect when it is at the same time giving and receiving'' (Olshausen). Nothing more clearly shows the estimate we have of the blessings we profess to have received from Christ, than the way we support and propagate the gospel.

HOLY PEOPLE ARE ABUNDANTLY FRUITFUL. Vs. 4-15

4 And when much people were gathered together, and were come to him out of every city, he spake by a parable :

5 A sower went out to sow his seed : and as he sowed, some fell by the way side ; and it was trodden down, and the fowls of the air devoured it.

6 And some fell upon a rock ; and as soon as it was sprung up, it withered away, because it lacked moisture.

7 And some fell among thorns ; and the thorns sprang up with it, and choked it.

8 And other fell on good ground, and sprang up, and bare fruit an hundredfold. And when he had said these things, he cried, He that hath ears to hear, let him hear.

9 And his disciples asked him, saying, What might this parable be ?

10 And he said, Unto you it is given to know the mysteries of the kingdom of God : but to others in parables ; that seeing they might not see, and hearing they might not understand.

11 Now the parable is this : The seed is the word of God.

12 Those by the way side are they that hear ; then cometh the devil, and taketh away the word out of their hearts, lest they should believe and be saved.

13 They on the rock *are they,* which, when they hear, receive the word with joy ; and these have no root, which for a while believe, and in time of temptation fall away.

14 And that which fell among thorns are they, which, when they have heard, go forth, and are choked with cares and riches and pleasures of *this* life, and bring no fruit to perfection.

15 But that on the good ground are they, which in an honest and good heart, having heard the word, keep *it,* and bring forth fruit with patience.

By consulting the thirteenth chapter of Matthew we find that Jesus gave seven parables at this time, of which the parable of the sower was the first. All these parables were illustrations of the varied aspects of the kingdom of heaven.

It is quite important to know what a parable is and why Jesus used this form of teaching. A parable is an illustration taken from nature to illustrate spiritual or moral truth. The word, parable means literally a putting side by side of two truths—a truth from nature that has a resemblance to some spiritual truth. God has two kingdoms—nature and grace. He governs them by essentially the same laws, or at least he does not contradict himself in his government of the two. Jesus often took a truth that every one acknowledged in the natural world to show some phase of spiritual truth.

The object of a parable was often to make men see unwelcome truths and acknowledge their obligations to the truths thus admitted. For instance, Nathan, the prophet, went to David (2 Sam. 12:1-15) with the parable of the rich man, who cruelly seized his neighbor's ewe lamb and slew it and made with it a feast for his guests. When Nathan had reached the climax of the story, David could not contain himself, but declared with great vehemence ''As the Lord liveth, the man that hath done this is worthy of death.'' Then Nathan said, ''Thou art the man,'' and David saw that he had pronounced judgment upon himself. If Nathan had come at him directly, it is doubtful whether he would have had an opportunity given to deliver his rebuke. A parable is a method of bringing the truth clearly and simply before people. We see in Matthew 21:28-45 and Luke 10:29-37 that by the use of parables, Jesus made the Pharisees condemn themselves. We believe the Christian teacher of today, especially when he preaches the central, unpalatable doctrine of the Bible, which is holiness, should make use of parables or parabolic teaching. The same may be said of the unpopular doctrine of eternal punishment.

He said "a sower went out to sow." Every preacher, every Sunday school teacher, every private Christian, who uses the word of God to teach men, is a sower.

"The seed is the word of God." This is a very striking comparison. David said in Psalm 19 that the word of God is like gold, because of its great value. But this comparison of Jesus is still more apt and striking. The tiniest seed that lies neglected on the hard earth has in it something that all the gold in the world does not possess. It has a germ or life principle. Plant gold and it will produce no crop. But plant the seed under favorable surroundings and it will bring forth something. Seeds that have laid dormant in the hands of Egyptian mummies for thousands of years, have been put in the ground and have produced plants. So it is with the word of God. Jesus said "the words that I speak unto you, they are spirit and they are life" (John 6:63). So the word of God planted in a nation, no matter however degraded they may be, will, if received, produce a new civilization. This has been again and again proved. The word of God planted in a human heart will produce a new experience. Peter says "Being born again, not of corruptible seed, but by the word of God, which liveth and abideth forever." No man can read the word of God honestly, and with a sincere desire to be good, without having a new experience, or without being regenerated.

Jesus now describes four classes of hearers of the word of God. There are but four classes that hear the word of God and everybody that hears it, belongs to one of these four classes.

(1) *The wayside hearers.* "Some fell by the wayside. . . . and the fowls of the air devoured it." In eastern coun-

tries where fencing material is expensive, each farm or plantation is divided from that lying next to it by pathways or roads. These intervening pathways become hard by reason of the travel over them. As the seed fell upon this hard soil, and lay exposed, the birds came and took it away. This represents a class of hearers, whose hearts are hard. Their hearts are a thoroughfare which Satan uses. As some one says ''A heart where Satan has ingress, regress, egress and progress; in a word, the devil's thoroughfare.'' It refers to those people, who hear the truth and it makes no impression upon them or if a slight impression is made, Satan takes it away soon. There are thousands, who go to church quite regularly, who will at last wake up in hell without doubt, because their hearts are hard and they refuse to yield to the truth. Satan gets their mind and attention on something else ''lest they should believe and be saved'' (Vs. 12). We believe it is one phase of the devil's business to get men's minds off the truth, by injecting wandering thoughts, the fashions, etc., in the house of God.

(2) *The stony ground hearers.* Some of the seed ''fell upon a rock.'' That is, it fell upon a thin coating of soil upon a rock or ledge. This represents hearers, who have little depth of purpose and determination of character. ''And as soon as it sprung up it withered away.'' These do not count the cost in beginning the Christian life, but rush into everything precipitately. But notice, they were in advance of the first class, who did not spring up at all, or receive the word. The first class had no new experience spring up at all. These do, although only for a season. Notice then the evidences of their being really regenerated. They receive the word. The first class did not. 2. They receive it with joy. Joy is the fruit of the Spirit. 3. They ''for a while believe.'' 4. They ''in time of temptation fall away.'' They must have had something *from* which to fall. 5. They had spiritual life for the blade of grain *sprang* up. But ''they have no root'' (Vs. 13). They have no determination of purpose. The root is that part of the plant that comes in contact with the moisture of the earth, as well as its nourishment. The will is that part of our nature that moves men to take hold of divine grace. We have seen people, who had all the evidences of salva-

tion, who wilted when the first scorching temptation came. They could not endure the persecution and opposition that they met and hence went down.

(3) *Those Christians not wholly sanctified.* ''And some fell among thorns and the thorns sprang up and choked it.'' Notice ''the thorns sprang up *with* it.'' The thorn life and the good seed were growing at the same time in the heart. They become choked, just as good seed in any field is choked with weeds, if the weeds are allowed to remain. These are ''choked with cares, and riches, and pleasures of this life and bring no fruit to perfection'' (Vs. 14). It is sometimes asked ''Where does the Bible teach that the two natures are in the soul that has been only justified?'' We reply, ''Here is one of the many passages that teach this. The thorns are cares and riches.'' These are called by St. Mark ''The lusts of other things.'' From inbred sin as from a root spring these things that defile the soul. It is this mixed state, that requires another work, to exterminate these evil propensities. This work is called Entire Sanctification. Jamieson, Fausett and Brown in their commentary say of this state, ''This case is that of ground not thoroughly cleansed of the thistles.'' Neander says ''The seed which takes root but is stifled by the thorns, which shoot up with it, figures the mind in which the elements of worldly desire develop themselves along with the higher life, and at last become strong enough to crush it, so that the received truth is utterly lost.'' Wesley, speaking of the difference between regeneration and entire sanctification, describes the mixed condition of believers, who have not been wholly sanctified thus, ''Till this universal change was wrought in his soul, all his holiness was mixed. He was humble, but not entirely; his humility was mixed with pride; he was meek but frequently his meekness was interrupted by anger, or some uneasy turbulent passion. His love for God was frequently dampened by the love of the creature.'' On the other hand Whedon has attempted to gainsay the voice of the other commentators thus ''The seed is good, the soil is good, the growth is genuine, internally everything is right, but while all this is going well within, there are difficulties without, which in time prove fatal.'' We differ from this view. Mark says it is the ''lusts of other things'' that constitute the

thorns. Lusts are not without but are *within* the soul. Cares are *within* the soul. Certainly everything is not right within when there are lusts and cares that are choking out the spiritual life. Care or worry is not an external affair.

This mixed unsanctified condition hinders perfect, spiritual fruitage. They ''bring no fruit to perfection.'' God wants perfect love and this state of heart can not produce it. Abbott says, ''They may produce fruit but it is both small in quantity and immature.'' Inbred sin in a believer as truly hinders perfect love as weeds and thorns allowed to grow in a cornfield hinder perfect corn, and for the same reason, this third class needs to advance and take the next degree.

Notice as we advance in the study of this parable, each class is a step in advance of the previous class. The backsliders of the second class went further than the first class, who did not believe at all. The mixed, third class, are in advance of the second class, who backslid. They did not backslide but they brought forth poor fruit. Now we come to the fourth class who are still further up the road of spiritual blessing.

(4) *The good ground—entirely sanctified hearers.* They are not hard like the first class, who do not believe at all, they do not backslide like the second class. They have been cleansed of all the thorn life of the third class. They are sanctified wholly and are free from the ''lusts of other things.'' They have a pure heart. All the thorn life is removed. They got weary of trying to keep the thorns down and so had them extracted and they are gone.

The Pharisees illustrated the first class. The second class was illustrated by the Galileans, who went with Jesus until he told them of the cross. (John 6:66.) The third is illuustrated by the church at Corinth, who had in them carnality. (1 Cor. 3:1-3.) They were saved, for Paul calls them ''babes in Christ.'' But brotherly love was choked in them. The fourth class is represented by the Colossians, who ''were made meet to be partakers of the inheritance with the saints in light.'' (Coll. 1:12.)

Let us beware of the common mistake of classing fruits with works. The fruit that a Christian bears is not works but *character*. Whedon says the hundredfold produced by this class is getting sinners converted. He says, ''To produce a hundred from one is a rich increase; but how rich the increase of every Christian, who converts a hundred souls.'' This is a mistake. Converting souls is *works*. If this were the fruit then Jesus himself did not bear much fruit while on earth. He had but few converts. The Bible makes a sharp distinction between works and fruits. In Galatians 5:19-23 we are told that the Flesh *works* but the Spirit *bears fruit*. ''The fruit of the Spirit is love, joy, peace,'' etc. None of this category is works but is a part of the character of the soul. There are conditions and qualities. A pure heart is the *condition* where the thorns of inbred sin are all removed and the love of the heart towards God is pure, unmixed. Our joy is full and our peace is perfect and patience has its perfect work.

Jesus says of this class ''in an honest and good heart having heard the word, keep it.'' They are determined in all things to do the will of God. This is the grand requisite for passing from the third into the fourth class. He, who with all the heart, follows after God, with a determination to do his will at all costs, sooner or later gets into the experience of the good ground, even if he does not know the name of the experience and has never heard it preached; for it is the business of the Holy Spirit to lead such souls on to holiness, whether they hear it definitely preached or not.

This fourth experience is the most favorable for growth. Some have slandered the teachers of holiness by asserting that they do not believe in growth in grace. This is contrary to the facts. This experience is the most favorable to growth, even as the removal of weeds in any crop help its growth. When God commands us to ''Grow in grace'' he means evidently that we are to put ourselves into the most favorable state for growth.

RELIGIOUS TEACHERS SHOULD BE HOLY AND HAVE INSIGHT INTO SPIRITUAL MYSTERIES. Vs. 16-18.

16 No man, when he hath lighted a candle, covereth it with a vessel, or putteth *it* under a bed; but setteth *it* on a candle-stick, that they which enter in may see the light.

17 For nothing is secret, that shall not be made manifest; neither *any thing* hid, that shall not be known and come abroad.

18 Take heed therefore how ye hear: for whosoever hath, to him shall be given; and whosoever hath not, from him shall be taken even that which he seemeth to have.

Having shown who the four classes are, he now makes a personal application to his disciples and tells them in the figure of the candle that they, as religious teachers, should be able from experience to reveal these truths. He had chosen them to reveal the mysteries of the kingdom of heaven, which he was obliged for the present to reveal dimly in parables to the common people. They ought to know what the experience of the good ground— entire sanctification is, from experience. No preacher ought to rest until he knows this experience, for every preacher is expected to preach about this good ground experience. Every preacher is called to preach holiness and he ought to be a living embodiment of what he preaches. The Lord has not lighted them up as his candlesticks to have them put under a bed or an extinguisher. It is a solemn thing for a preacher to get the light of holiness and not preach it. Samuel Clarke says in his comments on verse 17, "He means that the truth that he now tells them privately they ought to manifest themselves publicly in their life and doctrine; and though it was necessary at present to conceal some things from the multitude because of their prejudices, yet the time was coming when all these things should be published openly and plainly before all the world." In other words Jesus expects his preachers to preach all these four experiences and tell people just where they are—what class they are in. Many of the preachers are willing to preach three of these experiences but do not like to say anything about the fourth experience of a clean heart. God says, Let it shine out, but all sorts of specious excuses are made for concealing it. How many preachers have let their own light go out because they kept this precious truth of God under a bushel. It is the business of the ministry to let the light of this great fourth experience shine out.

This brings us then to the point of the parable, "Take heed how ye (preachers) hear." Jesus was interpreting his parable to the disciples. He will still interpret his truth to those preachers who ask his spiritual interpretation as did these disciples, and it is therefore their business to listen carefully. We are to get our messages from God. We are to allow no prejudice or favorite theology to color the messages that God would give us. We are to be as transparent as the glass that receives the light on one side and sends it forth on the other. How often have God's messages been distorted by human notions and prejudices.

"Whosoever hath, to him shall be given." He seems to mean that whosoever has these truths in a real, living experience, and maintains it shall reecive more. Whoever uses what light he has, shall receive more. He who refuses to walk up to the light will lose what light he has or *seemed to have* (see Chapter 11:35). Those people who reject the light will find henceforth that their Christian experience is only a *seeming*.

HOLY PEOPLE ARE KINSFOLK OF JESUS CHRIST.
Vs. 19-21

19 Then came to him *his* mother and his brethren, and could not come at him for the press.

20 And it was told him *by certain* which said, Thy mother and thy brethren stand without, desiring to see thee.

21 And he answered and said unto them, My mother and my brethren are these which hear the word of God and do it.

The mothers and brothers of Jesus now came to take him away. St. Mark says that they feared that his zeal had made him "Beside himself." (Mark 3:20.) When any one gets as earnest about religion as about any secular business, there are many people who think them insane or fanatical. Sometimes they of our own household can not understand us, in our devotion to God. Let us not be dismayed, for the family of even Jesus did not comprehend him. At the marriage feast at Cana of Galilee he had previously rebuked his mother (John 2:4) and in the temple (Luke 2:49) and now he says that every holy man is as great in his affection and esteem as his mother or brethren after the flesh. This forever condemns those who worship Mary as divine. Every holy man and woman is as divine as was Mary. All the divinity she had was that which she had as far as she did the will of God. *All who do that are on the same spiritual level with Mary.* He here shows that spiritual relationships are of more consequence than mere earthly ties and kinship. So instead of going with his mother and brethren, he declared that spiritual interests are first. Probably there have been few people, who have given themselves wholly up to the work of God, who have not been urged by earthly friends to turn away from their convictions. But Mary made her great mistake in thinking to turn her son away from the work of God. We can not consistently worship any such woman. The Bible nowhere commands us to worship any except God. It is those who do the will of God who are the mother and brethren of Jesus. John received the last commission of Jesus when on the cross, as he consigned Mary to his keeping. (John 19:26-27.) Doubtless some of us would have gladly taken the charge of Mary, if we had been there. We would have counted it a great honor to have been permitted to care for her during her last days. But according to this interpretation of Jesus, we have the mother of Jesus with us today and may care for her, for everybody who does the will of God is in as intimate relations with us if we care to improve on that relationship as if we had the privilege of ministering to Mary. *We must look upon the saints as closely related to Jesus as if they were his own mother.* We can minister to the saints of God for Jesus's sake.

"How great is the honor of faith and obedience. How blessed the consanguinity. To be born of God, and to bear the Lord Jesus Christ in our hearts; to express his image in every thought and word and action; and to be ourselves conformed to him, partakers of his holiness, and of his crown. Thus to become his brethren, and the children of God, is no empty honor, no sounding name, but gives a sure title to a share of his glory." (Stanhope.)

FEEBLENESS OF FAITH SHOWS LACK OF ENTIRE HOLINESS. Vs. 22-25.

22 Now it came to pass on a certain day, that he went into a ship with his disciples: and he said unto them, Let us go over unto the other side of the lake. And they launched forth.

23 But as they sailed he fell asleep: and there came down a storm of wind on the lake; and they were filled *with water,* and were in jeopardy.

24 And they came to him, and awoke him, saying, Master, master, we perish. Then he arose, and rebuked the wind and the raging of the water : and they ceased, and there was a calm.

25 And he said unto them, Where is your faith? And they being afraid wondered, saying one to another, What manner of man is this! for he commandeth even the winds and water, and they obey him.

Having spoken the parables concerning the kingdom of heaven, he now crosses the lake of Galilee with his disciples. He had taken this course to rid himself of the multitudes who thronged him. The Sea of Galilee on account of its peculiar location among the hills, is subject to wind-squalls of great fury. Jesus was so weary from his constant ministering to the multitudes that when one of these sudden storms burst upon the company, he slept on regardless of the storm. It shows that he had the same human nature as mankind in general. (He became weary in body.) In their fright the disciples awoke him. He arose from his cushion or pillow, on which he had been sleeping, as they cry to him in terror. By a comparison of Matthew and Mark it will be seen that their reported words are not the same. Matthew gives it "Lord, save or we perish;" Mark has it, "Master carest thou not that we perish," while Luke says "Master, Master, we perish." There is no discrepancy here; each one doubtless had something to say and they all spoke at once and reported what they individually said in the excitement of the moment. "We behold in him exactly the reverse of Jonah: the fugitive prophet asleep in the midst of danger, out of a dead conscience; the Saviour out of a pure conscience; Jonah by his presence making danger; Jesus yielding the pledge and assurance of deliverance from danger." (Trench.)

He arose and rebuked the wind and the sea, and immediately a great calm ensued. Usually the sea will roll for days or at least hours after a storm. But there it subsided immediately, showing that the winds did not merely cease from natural causes. So sudden was the cessation of wind and wave that it is called "a great calm." He rebuked the disciples before he rebuked the sea, because of their unbelief. To him the unbelief was a more terrible thing than the raging of the sea. Jesus was always estimating and measuring his disciples by their faith. He does the same today. He said to one on one occasion, ''according to your faith be it unto you.'' (Matt. 9:29.) When he found faith he always commended it and when he found unbelief he always condemned it. Jesus awakes and the only thing that he beholds is the unbelief of his disciples; his ear tells him not of the fury and wrack of the elements, but of the guilty fears of his Galilean friends. And his first reproof is for them. He lets the storm rage on unrebuked, until he has rebuked the agitation of their souls. And now they perceive that a most precious opportunity of signalizing their faith in Christ had been given, and given in vain. The elements had been let loose that their faith might gain a victory, and go on to perfection. The progress of ordinary months might have been made in an hour, had they been watchful. When will they understand that the education of faith is the most important thing going on under the sun?'' (Bowen.) They had faith but it was a very weak faith. It was a mixed faith. They need the purifying fires of Pentecost to burn out inbred sin, the cause of their doubts and fears. The disciples were astonished and asked themselves the question ''What manner of man is this, for he commandeth even the winds and the waters and they obey him.''

This scene is a picture of human life, whose sea we are upon seeking the other shore. We may have Jesus with us and yet have trials, difficulties, persecutions and temptations. It is no mark of sin to be tried and tempted severely. We may think sometimes that he is not interested in our condition, and be tempted to think bitter things against the Lord as if he had forgotten us. We may be betrayed to think that the cause of God is lost and that holiness is to be swept away from the earth. But he still says ''Where is your faith?''

We may not always get the help at the time that we expect it, according to our notions, but he wants us to learn the lesson of trust, no matter what or how severe the storm. He may seem to be absent or sleeping but he knows all about us and our circumstances and he always appears at the time, when it seems as if everything was giving way. Let us no more displease him by our doubts in the times of emergencies. The disciples got cured of the carnal mind at Pentecost and ceased then to be doubters for they were delivered from the tendency to doubt.

HOLINESS MEANS THE DESTRUCTION OF SIN.
Vs. 26-40.

26 And they arrived at the country of the Gadarenes, which is over against Galilee.

27 And when he went forth to land, there met him out of the city a certain man, which had devils long time, and ware no clothes, neither abode in *any* house, but in the tombs.

28 When he saw Jesus, he cried out, and fell down before him, and with a loud voice said, What have I to do with thee, Jesus, *thou* Son of God most high? I beseech thee, torment me not.

29 (For he had commanded the unclean spirit to come out of the man. For oftentimes it had caught him: and he was kept bound with chains and in fetters; and he brake the bands, and was driven of the devil into the wilderness.)

30 And Jesus asked him, saying, What is thy name? And he said, Legion: because many devils were entered into him.

31 And they besought him that he would not command them to go out into the deep.

32 And there was there an herd of many swine feeding on the mountain: and they besought him that he would suffer them to enter into them. And he suffered them.

33 Then went the devils out of the man, and entered into the swine: and the herd ran violently down a steep place into the lake, and were choked.

34 When they that fed *them* saw what was done, they fled, and went and told *it* in the city and in the country.

35 Then they went out to see what was done; and came to Jesus, and found the man, out of whom the devils were departed, sitting at the feet of Jesus, clothed, and in his right mind: and they were afraid.

36 They also which saw *it* told them by what means he that was possessed of the devils was healed.

37 Then the whole multitude of the country of the Gadarenes round about besought him to depart from them; for they were taken with great fear: and he went up into the ship, and returned back again.

38 Now the man out of whom the devils were departed besought him that he might be with him: but Jesus sent him away, saying,

39 Return to thine own house, and shew how great things God hath done unto thee. And he went his way, and published throughout the whole city how great things Jesus had done unto him.

40 And it came to pass, that, when Jesus was returned, the people *gladly* received him: for they were all waiting for him.

41 And, behold, there came a man named Jairus, and he was a ruler of the synagogue: and he fell down at Jesus' feet, and besought him that he would come into his house:

42   For he had one only daughter, about twelve years of age, and she lay a dying. But as he went the people thronged him.

43   And a woman having an issue of blood twelve years, which had spent all her living upon physicians, neither could be healed of any,

44   Came behind *him,* and touched the border of his garment : and immediately her issue of blood stanched.

45   And Jesus said, Who touched me? When all denied, Peter and they that were with him said, Master, the multitude throng thee and press *thee,* and sayest thou, Who touched me?

46   And Jesus said, Somebody hath touched me : for I perceive that virtue is gone out of me.

47   And when the woman saw that she was not hid, she came trembling, and falling down before him, she declared unto him before all the people for what cause she had touched him, and how she was healed immediately.

48   And he said unto her, Daughter, be of good comfort : thy faith hath made thee whole ; go in peace.

49   While he yet spake, there cometh one from the ruler of the synagogue's *house,* saying to him, Thy daughter is dead ; trouble not the Master.

50   But when Jesus heard *it,* he answered him, saying, Fear not : believe only, and she shall be made whole.

51   And when he came into the house, he suffered no man to go in, save Peter, and James, and John, and the father and the mother of the maiden.

52   And all wept, and bewailed her : but he said, Weep not ; she is not dead, but sleepeth.

53   And they laughed him to scorn, knowing that she was dead.

54   And he put them all out, and took her by the hand, and called, saying, Maid, arise.

55   And her spirit came again, and she arose straightway : and he commanded to give her meat.

56   And her parents were astonished : but he charged them that they should tell no man what was done.

This ship after the stilling of the storm quickly touched the opposite shore, which was the land of the Gadarenes. Here they encountered something even more fierce than the angry waves of the sea—a man possessed with a legion of devils. The man met them, doubtless to attack them until he saw it was Jesus. He had his dwelling in the tombs (Mark 5:3), some of which in that country, were excavated rooms in the cliffs thirty feet or more in length.

The devil has in all dispensations endeavored to counterfeit the work of God. In the time of Moses, the magicians sought to duplicate the miracles wrought by him. (Exodus 7:11-12; 2 Tim. 3:8.) When God raised up the order of the prophets, Satan sent lying prophets to the people. When God poured out his spirit in modern times the devil invented ''Spiritualism'' or ''Spiritism.'' When God revived the doctrine of Divine Healing, Satan brought forth Christian Science. So when Jesus came in human nature, Satan came also in human nature and possessed men. He has ever sought to duplicate all God has done among man. But he can never create holy character. It is beyond his power even if he so desired.

At the time of Jesus' Advent, the devil was having his way almost entirely. Spirituality was at a low ebb. It has never been lower since. Satan had nearly wrecked the world. He had invaded all the religions of mankind, both of the Jews and Gentiles, and as a finishing touch he had begun to possess men's natures; controlling their souls and afflicting their bodies.

Jesus came in the flesh and so did the devil. He had done his worst towards God and man when Jesus came to destroy his works. There could be no more terrible influence and power over men than the power he at this time exerted. He had come to the height of his influence. It has never been so great since that time It was necessary for Jesus to meet and conquer the devil in this highest, strongest manifestation of his power, in order to reveal himself as having all power. The great lesson for us is that as Jesus expelled devils from the souls of men while on earth, *so he can expel all sin from the souls of men today for* humanity has never gone lower. The remedy that cures the worst forms of disease is more than equal to the lighter varieties. Sin in the heart is the work of the devil. He who expels the devils can destroy sin, the work of the devil. If Jesus can expel devils he can as easily destroy the ''Old Man.'' He can as quickly destroy sin as he can cast out devils. Here is one of the many proofs of the *immediateness* of the work of entire sanctification. Who will honestly oppose the work of entire cleansing of sin from the soul, as an instantaneous work, when he remembers that Jesus by a word cast these devils out at once Who will say that he can not *as easily* cast out sin as he did the devils?

We have had occasion several times to note that the miracles of Jesus are illustrations of the salvation of the soul from sin. All the miracles of Jesus are not given. There would not be space enough to give them. Only those that especially illustrate different phases of salvation from sin are mentioned.

This was *not* a case of insanity. Jesus and the four evangelists carefully distinguished between demonical possession and lunacy. To be sure the indwelling of evil spirits might cause insanity, but it was only an effort.

Sin is moral insanity. The sinner is not in his right mind— the mind that God originally gave man. He is possessed of the carnal mind, whose captive he is, like the man in Rom. 7:24. This man *illustrated* the working of the carnal mind. There were two wills in him. With one will he ran to Jesus to worship him. With the other he drew back from Jesus, and said ''What have I to do with thee!'' It was exactly the same kind of contest that takes place in those who have the carnal mind.

We note some illustrations here of the nature of sin. 1. It brings men into strange places and associations. This man lived in the tombs among the dead—a strange place for a living man! Into what strange places and associations sin brings men. See the slums of our cities; the prodigal among swine; the trusted friend Judas among the enemies of Christ; the companionship with devils throughout eternity of those who once bore the image of God. To live among the dead on earth is bad enough. To live with them throughout eternity is unspeakably horrible.

2. Human power is helpless in bringing relief. Men had attempted with fetters to bind this man, but all in vain. Men have been trying by all sorts of bonds to suppress sin but all in vain. Reform, pledges, resolutions and will-power have all been snapped asunder by sin. *Sin can not be suppressed or repressed.* God never intended to repress it. Jesus never repressed it while on earth. He was a physician who worked radical cures. He does the same to-day. ''The carnal mind is not subject to the law of God; neither indeed can be.''

3. This possession was destructive. The man was cutting himself with stones. When the devils entered the swine, they were the means of destroying them. The devils by destroying

the swine cut off their own refuge and were compelled to retire to their native hell. Sin is self-destructive. He that sins against God ruins his own soul. All the calamities of the human race are self-inflicted—caused by sin.

When the afflicted man saw Jesus afar off he ran and worshipped him—not with the adoration we feel when we worship, but with a recognition of the superior power of Jesus. As he ran he cried ''What have I to do with thee, Jesus, thou Son of the most high God.'' These evil spirits, who spoke through this man, were more orthodox in their belief in the Messiahship of Jesus than many of the professed church of that day, who see nothing divine in Jesus. Here we have illustrated the sentiment of St. James which shows that a good creed does not make its confessors good. ''Thou believest that there is one God; thou doest well: the devils also believe and tremble.'' (Jas. 2:19.) But they remain devils. Saving faith is not of the head but of the heart. ''Art thou come to torment us before the time?'' (Matt. 8:29.) The devils know the time of torment for all the wicked is to come.

''I adjure thee by God, that thou torment me not.'' The very presence of the holy Jesus was a torment to the devils. We sometimes say a wicked man would be in torment if permitted to be in heaven. It is equally true that one holy man in hell would increase the torments of the damned. Thus we see why holy people—those most like Jesus—have so much persecution in this world. *They are a torment and constant rebuke to those who do not propose to give up sin.* Now we know why Jesus, John, Paul and the holy of all ages have been so opposed. We know why the modern holiness movement is a torment to some people.

These devils whose delight it was to torment this afflicted man, are now tormented themselves. No doubt this is the reason they love to torment men. ''Misery loves company.''

The only recorded words of Jesus here are '' Come out of the man thou unclean spirit.'' (Mark 5:8.) It seems there are different kinds of evil spirits, whose wickedness predominates in special directions. Some are unclean; others fierce and others lying spirits, etc. It seems there are *specialists* in wickedness in hell.

It was the voice of Jesus that brought forth the devils from the man. The same voice had just stilled the stormy sea. It drew Lazarus from his grave. It pronounced the leper, clean. It will raise the dead in the last day. It speaks forgiveness to the penitent sinner and the cleansing of the heart from all sin to-day, *as instantaneously.*

Just as the Angel of the Covenant asked wrestling Jacob "What is thy name?" so Jesus asks the same question here. Before the man can reply, the spokesman of the devils answers, "My name is Legion." The Roman soldiery had been among the Jews so many years that they well understood the Roman military terms. A Roman legion was a division of the Roman army containing about six thousand men. He meant to say there were a great number of devils. Doubtless he lied about the exact number, although there were many.

Notice the prayer of the devils, *for every devil prayed here.* They prayed that "he would not command them to go out into the deep." This gives us a glimpse into the awful torments of hell. These devils, through the one who had acted as spokesman, dreaded to go back to their native hell. Consequently their prayer was to be allowed to enter a herd of swine that was feeding near by. Jesus gave them permission to enter the swine but did not command them to go. Hence the criticism of infidels, that Jesus destroyed the property of these people is not valid. The swine thus possessed ran violently down the steep incline to the sea and were choked in the sea. The ceremonial law forbade the use of swine's flesh. These swine were doubtless the property of certain Jews who hired some one else to herd their swine. The Jews were forbidden to eat swine's flesh. It was an unlawful business, and its ruin was a just punishment to the owners. Because there were two thousand swine, it does not necessarily follow that there were two thousand devils—one for each of the swine. Doubtless many of these swine were frightened at the commotion of the others and thus they were stampeded.

The swineherds fled in fear and told the news to everyone that they met. One would suppose that they would want Jesus to remain with them, after such a wonderful display of his power and such deliverance of the man possessed with the devils. But not so. "They began to pray him to depart out of their coasts." (They did not want such a person within their coast or borders.) They were sorry for the loss of their swine. They preferred swine rather than Jesus. There are many such to-day, who prefer their unclean idols, impurity and sin. They love swine, pleasure, possessions, and sin rather than to have Jesus dwell in them. We must make the choice—swine or Jesus, Christ or Barabbas, holiness or hell.

They saw a wonderful sight as they were pleading with Jesus to leave them—the man in whom were so many devils; who had been raging and naked now sitting quietly "clothed and in his right mind." He had been in his wrong mind and now he was in her right mind. Sin is a moral insanity. God never intended man should be in such a condition. A sinner acts as unreasonably in continuing in sin, as if he were a lunatic, for sin is the worst form of insanity.

Notice the difference in the praying. The devils prayed to be permitted to enter the swine. The people prayed Jesus to depart out of their country. The man prayed to be permitted to remain with Jesus. All three prayers were answered. The first and second were answered as prayed. The third received a better answer than was asked. It was better for the man to go home and tell of his deliverance than to accompany Jesus. He had conferred upon him the honorable commission of being a witness for Jesus. Prayer is the desire of the heart. The first and second prayers were answered as desired, but there had better never have been such desire. It is thus to-day. If we desire to have Jesus leave us, he will go. If we keep excusing ourselves from having him and the holiness he brings, he will excuse us from having it. But it will be a sad day for us if he answers such desire.

The man received more than he asked. He wanted to be with Jesus. He had the high honor put upon him of being a witness for Jesus in his own country and among his own people. Would that we all realized the great honor conferred upon us of being his witnesses. We need be in no hurry to go to heaven to live with Jesus if he will let us have the privilege of staying on earth to witness for him. There will be time enough to be with him in heaven later.

So the man went forth publishing the story of his cure everywhere. This is what we are all called to do—witness to the power of Jesus, who has cast sin out of us. A holy man's tongue is consecrated to testimony. The man was commanded, not only to "live it" but to tell that the Lord had cast the devils out of him. We are commissioned to tell that the Lord has cast the *works* of the devil—sin—out of us. How unscriptural and wicked are those people who seek to repress testimony. God commands it. To withhold it is a sin. So the man went out and published the story through all Decapolis. (Mark 5:20.) The word Decapolis is Greek and means *the ten* cities. These ten cities were in the northeast of Palestine. Doubtless they had some special privilege granted them by the Roman government and the region therefore went by that name.

While Jesus was yet speaking a ruler of the synagogue, probably at Capernaum where he was speaking, came to him and prostrating himself before him said, "My little daughter lieth at the point of death: I pray thee, come and lay thy hands on her that she may be healed." (Mark 5:23.)

As Jesus was going accompanied by his disciples and a great crowd, he stopped to heal an unfortunate woman who had been grievously afflicted for twelve years with what was considered an incurable disease. He stopped to do good everywhere he went. "On his way to perform one act of love he turned aside to give attention to another. The practical lesson is this: there are many who are so absorbed in one set of duties as to have no time for others; some whose life business is the suppression of the slave trade—the amelioration of the state of prisons—the reformation of abuses. Right, except so far as they are monopolized by these, and feel themselves discharged from other obligations. The minister's work is spiritual; the physician's temporal. But if the former neglect physical needs or the latter shrink from spiritual opportunities on the plea that the care of bodies, not of souls is his work, so far they refuse to imitate their Master." (Robertson.)

Jesus was ever ready while on earth to do for humanity wherever he knew their needs. And the man who is holiest is like his Master, doing good where he finds opportunity. There is nothing like full salvation to make an "all around man." Holiness is as much misunderstood now as it was in the time of Christ. Those who know nothing about its workings, or are too careless to inquire, or too prejudiced to give it credit, have asserted that it means one-sided development—a specialism that neglects the most important and practical duties. But the holy man or church is just the reverse. Such a man, or church will be found abundant in good deeds to the poor and unfortunate, zealous for foreign and home missions, straight on the Temperance and Prohibition question, always on hand at the revival meeting, and ever anxious to lead sinners to Christ. Any denial of this is either made in ignorance or prejudice, or both. Facts can be brought to substantiate this. Every holy man, like Jesus, has a heart of sympathy for the sad, sorrowing world all about him. It is a consolation to us to know that Jesus is just as sympathizing to-day as He was when on earth.

This woman was like the soul that tries to find earthly cure for sin. She had tried all kinds of doctors and had suffered many things of them. A good deal of the doctoring of that day, and perhaps some of to-day, makes the patient worse. The soul that has tried Drs. Morality, Reformation, Good Works, Evolution and the like, has fared as did this woman. As she saw Jesus going by she said "If I may touch but his clothes I shall be whole." So, as the multitude were thronging him, she touched the hem of his garment. The hem of the garment had a religious significance. The Jews were required by law to have the borders of the garments made with a fringe on which was a ribbon of blue to keep them in constant remembrance of God's law. (See Numbers 15:37-40.) She seemed to think he was surcharged with divine power like a person full of electricity, and that this fringe of the garment had an especial sanctity. Jesus dressed like the rest of the Jews, evidently. He did not rebuke this woman's superstitious faith but honored it. This teaches a great lesson, viz: that we ought to be very charitable towards the ignorant and superstitious, if they have any faith in Christ at all, even though it be mixed with error. Better the superstitious faith of the ignorant than the cold unbelief that attempts to explain away the supernatural entirely. It shows how lenient Jesus is towards those with blind faith in Him. He healed her immediately. He saw her heart all the time and saw the movement of faith, unseen by the eyes of the crowd. The healing power did not go out of him unconsciously. Holiness is the state of perfect soul health, the result of being cured of the malady of sin. This woman's cure illustrates the cure of the soul, of the disease of sin. Her confession illustrates our duty to confess to holiness of heart, which has been secured by the destruction of the sin principle.

Consequently Jesus did not propose to let her off with an unconfessed cure and Jesus said "Who touched me." The disciples tell him that everybody is thronging him and it is useless to ask who touched him. This was not true. There were many who thronged him but only one who definitely put forth the finger and touched him. Is this not often true to-day? In the great assemblies where many take part in the singing, and even in the outward forms of prayer, there are often only a few who really touch him and get healing power in their souls. There are frequently great assemblies, with crowds going through the motions and only a few really saved!

"And when the woman saw that she was not hid she came trembling and falling down before him, she declared to him before all the people for what cause she had touched him, and how she was healed immediately." She knew instantly that she was healed. Jesus still does cures so marked that the subject knows that he is cured immediately. He did not ask her to come and confess as if he did not know who touched him. Some people object to a confession and coming to an altar in public. They make all sorts of excuses against it. But Jesus made an altar of confession right here and he did in many other instances. God says, "Ye are my witnesses." "With the heart man believeth unto righteousness and with the mouth confession is made unto salvation." He says that if we confess him before men He will confess us before His father and the holy angels. And if we deny Him before men He will deny us before His father and the holy angels. Those people who make excuses against confessing what Christ has done for them are unscriptural and disobedient.

"And he said unto her, Daughter, be of good comfort." The saved person who testifies to the power of God to save, from a real desire to glorify him, will find a wonderful comfort imparted by the Spirit of God. This is the reward given by Him who says, "Them that honor me will I honor." But this is not all. He gives her more light and makes her more intelligent. He says, "Thy faith hath made the whole. Go in peace." He shows her that it was not the hem of the garment that cured her, but it was her faith. As sure as we have a sincere faith and a clear testimony we will find we are in his school and he will add to our faith, light, knowledge and experience. "Go in peace." It may be translated "Go *into* peace." It is our privilege to live in the atmosphere of peace. He assures her that the cure was permanent. This is an illustration of the fact that "Christ will have himself openly confessed and not secretly sought: that our Christian life is not as it is sometimes called, merely a thing between ourselves and God: but a 'good confession to be witnessed' before all people." (Alford.)

He also gives her comfort saying "Go in peace." He not only cures but he gives comfort and peace to those *who confess the cure.* He puts a special blessing on those who thus testify. What a pity that any of us by withholding testimony should rob our souls of the peculiar blessing he gives to those who confess him!

Jesus now continued on his way to the house of Jairus the ruler. Had Jairus had no trouble he would hardly have sent to Jesus. It is strange but true, that men will often refuse to come to Jesus until some great trouble comes upon them. This is one of the blessings that come out of sorrow. It leads us to God. It leads us to see how weak we are and helpless in the great emergencies of life. We prosper best some one says, when we have just enough trouble to keep us on our knees a good deal of the time.

When they arrived at the house they found the people and the minstrels making a great noise, according to the custom of the day. This was something like the custom of "wakes" in some parts of Ireland today. He told them that she was not dead but asleep. He meant to show them that death is not to be regarded as of any more account than sleep, which in some respects it resembles. Why should we be so afraid of death when the Master regarded it as nothing of any more consequence than sleep. This was his way of bidding us not fear, for the girl was really dead, for when he took her by the hand "her spirit came again."

"They laughed him to scorn." He put out of the room all but the father and mother, and Peter, James and John. These three disciples were with him on the important occasions of his life. Some of the commentators think the others were put out because he did not wish the faith of the people to rest on his miracle. But it seems to us he put out the hired mourners, who had laughed and scorned him, as he wanted only those near who had faith and were in sympathy. Then he took her by the hand and "called saying, Maid, arise, and her spirit came again, and she arose straightway." He then commanded them to give her something to eat, to show them that it was a reality that they saw, and not an apparition. They must use the natural means to keep her well, after she had been supernaturally raised to life. Young converts who have been raised from the death of sin need to be fed also. The glorious lesson here for us is that Christ is Lord of death! has the power over it, and will raise us all from the dead. "Christ raised three dead men to life—one newly departed, another on the bier, a third smelling in the grave—to show that no degree of death is so desperate that it is past help." (Bishop Hall.)

"Walking was an evidence of her restoration. One who had been at the point of death (Vs. 42) and was simply aroused from syncope, could not have walked, except by miraculous impartation of strength. The command to give her something to eat evidenced the reality of the resurrection: it was a tangible proof to her parents that it was no apparition that they saw." (Abbott.)

Since these miracles are parables of salvation and this illustrates the truth that Jesus can resurrect souls from the death of sin, it is an encouragement for us to bring our unsaved friends to Jesus, to be resurrected into newness of spiritual life.

He commanded them to give her something to eat. Young converts need spiritual food as truly as this resurrected girl needed food. Some think the only thing to do is to set them to work. This is only a part of it. Work without food brings death. Peter says "As newborn babes desire the sincere milk of the word that you may grow thereby."

We also learn from this miracle that it is right to ask for temporal blessings. While this parable illustrated spiritual healing it by no means is confined to that illustration. It is our privilege to ask for temporal as well as spiritual blessings upon our friends.

It will be noticed that although Jesus raised the girl miraculously, he did not propose to keep her alive in that manner, but expected her friends to feed her. There is a place for miracles and there is a place for our duty, which can never be superceded. It would have been of no use for Jesus to raise the girl if her parents were to let her starve. Of what use for God to give converts to some churches, when they are sure to starve.

CHAPTER IX.

THE VERSATILE POWER OF HOLINESS.

It Radiates Forth to Bless the World. Vs. 1-6. It Disturbs Guilty Consciences. Vs. 7-9. It Blesses Mankind. Vs. 10-17. It Means Death to the Carnal Nature. Vs. 18-27. It Has Glorious Revelations Even in the Initial Degree. Vs. 28-36. The Church Is Weak without It. Vs. 37-45. It Kills Unholy Ambition. Vs. 46-48. It Destroys Sectarianism. Vs. 49-50. It Roots Out a Revengeful Spirit. Vs. 51-56. It Demands Entire Consecration. Vs. 57-62.

Holiness is well rounded Christian manhood. It affects the whole man and strengthens for every duty and relation of life. Far from being the one sided development, as some unacquainted with it suppose, it is aggressive and active in all directions. There is nothing that so strengthens the church and individual in the whole orbit of duty and privilege. Far from being a ''one idea'' it is the source and success of all good endeavor in all directions. As the ocean rolls itself up to and conforms to all the indentations of the coast so holiness fits all the relations of life. It is a power everywhere and there is naught but weakness and failure where it is lacking. We have in this chapter illustrations of its diversified blessings.

IT RADIATES FORTH TO BLESS THE WORLD. Vs. 1-6.

1 Then he called his twelve disciples together, and gave them power and authority over all devils, and to cure diseases.

2 And he sent them to preach the kingdom of God, and to heal the sick.

3 And he said unto them, Take nothing for *your* journey, neither staves, nor scrip, neither bread, neither money; neither have two coats apiece.

200 COMMENTARY ON THE GOSPEL

4 And whatsoever house ye enter into, there abide, and thence depart.

5 And whosoever will not receive you, when ye go out of that city, shake off the very dust from your feet for a testimony against them.

6 And they departed, and went through the towns, preaching the gospel, and healing everywhere.

Jesus had already chosen his disciples (Chapter 6:13-16). He had given them his platform of principles in The Sermon on the Mount. He had been performing miracles to confirm the teachings of The Sermon on the Mount. He had aroused the enmity of the Pharisees and Scribes, who were the dominant church party, by his denunciation of their practices, in The Sermon on the Mount.

The more these churchmen hated him, the more his popularity increased with the common people, who rallied about him and gladly heard him. Because it was impossible for him to preach to all these vast multitudes, for whom his holy soul went out in compassion, and because he needed to have his preachers in training, in order to take up the work after his crucifixion, he therefore commissioned the twelve to commence preaching. True holiness gives a longing for the souls of men. It begets an earnest desire to save men.

One of the best methods of teaching young ministers to preach is to set them at it. We do not by any means say there should be no special preparation, but they should be encouraged to begin even while engaged in their studies. It might be said that these men went to preaching without any special preparation and therefore special preparation is not sanctioned by Scripture. But this is hardly a fair argument. This commission here mentioned was only temporary. It was only for a few weeks. Nevertheless for that short period of evangelistic labor he laid down some eternal principles, which should guide the ministry in all subsequent time. When he arose from the dead, he appeared to one of the most cultured scholars of the times—Paul—*and called him to be his leading preacher.* And even then he did not allow him to enter fully into the work until he had been three years in the deserts of Arabia, getting ready. Moses, although skilled in all the wisdom of Egypt, yet passed forty years in the desert before he entered upon his great work as a prophet of God.

The call and ordination of the apostles had been given at the time of the Sermon on the Mount. (Matt. 5:1.) At that time it is said "When he was set his disciples came to him." Now, when he commissions them for this evangelistic tour it says "he called his disciples." They came when they wished to learn, but when he sent them out to preach, he *called* them. Let men be in no hurry to preach. Let them wait until he *calls* them. This is too serious business to rush into, as we would any secular calling. It is not a profession. It is a *calling*.

The number twelve is significant. The sons of Jacob were twelve, and we read that the twelve apostles are to sit on twelve thrones judging the twelve tribes of Israel (Matthew 19:28). The wall of the New Jerusalem that John saw had "twelve foundations and in them the names of the twelve apostles." (Rev. 21:14.) It says in verse 1, "His twelve disciples" showing that they already belonged to him. He had already chosen and ordained them. He gave them power for this short campaign. What is power? No one can give a good definition. We see its effects but are not able to define it. These same men had power after the Holy Ghost came upon them, but it was not the same kind of power that they had previously. Then, it was to be qualified to be his witnesses. Now it was to work miracles. The power conferred at Pentecost was a higher power than this. Witnessing power is therefore of more importance than miracle working power. Let those remember this, who are seeking the special gifts of the Spirit. If we have the real experience of salvation and have been qualified by the baptism with the Holy Ghost to testify, we have arrived at the highest degree of power. The sanctifying power, that they received at Pentecost, was greater than this miracle working power. The lesson is that God gives those that he calls in every generation, to any special work, all the power needed for that work, if they are true to him. The reason he gave them power at this time to heal the sick and cast out devils was because he wished to convince the people of the truth which they preached.

His own miracles had already awakened great interest in the truth which he spoke and now he wished to give them favor with the people for they are now out in the business of laying the foundations of his kingdom. Healing was a gift not bestowed on all even after Pentecost, as we see by reading 1 Cor. 12:2, where the gift of healing in the church after Pentecost is placed fifth in importance in the list of the gifts, which even all did not possess in the Pentecostal church, but it was given as the Spirit saw fit.

There have been people in our day who have put healing above sanctification. But we find here that the disciples had this gift before they came to Pentecost. It belongs to the degree of grace below entire sanctification. The Gospel is so well established to-day that we do not need this miraculous gift to call the attention of men to the truth. These twelve men, commissioned to cast out devils, certainly could not have been unsaved men, for Satan can not cast out Satan. Jesus would not give sinners power to cast out devils. How absurd the assertion of some that these men were not saved before Pentecost.

They were to provide no money for their journey. This was to be a short evangelistic trip and it was not necessary for them to make great preparations for it. They were not to take any scrip. This was a bag usually made of sheep skin, in which the traveler took his food. He intended that they should trust the Lord and the people for supplies.

Some times the ministry wish they had a fund so they need not be dependent upon those who begrudge what they give, for the support of the Gospel. But if the preacher had abundance of means so as to be independent it would be a damage to the people and would make them penurious. God wants men to open their hearts by benevolence, so that they may develop. God has usually called poor men to preach his gospel. He has made it his order that they that preach the Gospel should live by the Gospel. They were not to take any superfluous clothing. These commands were for an evangelistic trip of a few weeks and yet these fundamental principles contained much. ''It is no more just to assume that the minister must always be itinerant and without a stated support, than to conclude that they must never preach to the Gentiles, and must confine their preaching to a mere heralding of the kingdom of heaven. (Vs. 2.) In subsequent directions to the ministry, Christ gave his disciples commands directly opposite to certain precepts here, and his own practice did not ordinarily conform to the principles here given, forbidding to take money and provision. The band had a treasurer and usually carried both money and provision (John 12:6; Matt. 14:17; 15:34; 16:6, 7); and Christ himself expressly declared later that those directions were not applicable to their subsequent ministry. (Luke 22:35., 36.)'' (Abbott.) But the underlying principles of unostentatious attire and simple food are still applicable.

They were to be very particular where they were entertained. They were to stop with those who had proved themselves worthy, by gladly receiving the Gospel. Wherever they found the people of the house worthy, they were to stop there and not waste their time in social visiting. This is a good suggestion to the evangelists of today. When they came to a house, they were to salute it. (See Matt. 10:12.) That is they were to pronounce a blessing upon the household. This was a custom of those days. The ambassador of Jesus Christ is to be courteous.

If they were not received they were to shake the dust off their feet, as they departed. It signified that the iniquity of that house or place had defiled the very earth, and they wished to separate themselves from it. The Scribes and Pharisees, when they came from a journey in a heathen country were accustomed to shake the dust off their feet as if the soil of the heathen country was a defilement. It was a custom, whose significance was generally understood. Matthew says that he declared that it would be more tolerable for Sodom and Gomorrha in the Day of Judgment, than for such a city. It was because they had greater light than Sodom and Gomorrha. These two cities were beastly in their sins, for which they were destroyed. It is a serious matter to reject light. An indecent, vile sinner will have a better lot in the world to come than a church member who rejects great light. Suppose a church member, who has once tasted the powers of the world to come, turns his back upon holiness and rejects it after he has had great light, the vilest sinners will not have to meet so fearful a doom as he.

IT DISTURBS GUILTY CONSCIENCES. Vs. 7-9.

7 Now Herod the tetrarch heard of all that was done by him: and he was perplexed, because that it was said of some, that John was risen from the dead;

8 And of some, that Elias had appeared; and of others, that one of the old prophets was risen again.

9 And Herod said, John have I beheaded: but who is this, of whom I hear such things? And he desired to see him.

Herod, the tetrarch, heard of these things done by Jesus. *Tetrarch* meant originally, one who rules over a fourth part of a kingdom. It came to mean any petty ruler. He was named Herod Antipas. He was a son of Herod the Great and ruled over Galilee and Perea. He was perplexed. He had killed John the Baptist and now his guilty conscience made him fear that John had risen from the dead. He had destroyed the preacher but the message of the preacher still stuck. Truth can never be destroyed. Men may kill the messenger but it is too late to stop the effect of the message when once it has been delivered. The triumphing of the wicked is short. The present accusations of a guilty conscience are premonitions of the coming Judgment Day. Herod was a Sadducee and according to his creed did not believe in a resurrection. But conscience made him forget his creed. Conscience cares little for men's creeds. It speaks in spite of them.

Matthew tells us that Herod really thought that John had arisen from the dead. We read in chapter 23:8 that this same Herod wanted to see Jesus later hoping that he would work a miracle. But Jesus never worked miracles to satisfy curiosity. It must be remembered that John was a holy man. This was acknowledged by Herod himself. (Mark 6:20.) Holy men are faithful in their rebuke of sin. They are a constant reminder to men of sin. The holiest men like John and Jesus are a constant rebuke to sin. It is often said by opposers of holy men that they make trouble in church and state. There is no doubt of it. Here we see the reason. A holiness that allows men to feel comfortable in sin is not the kind that Jesus and John exemplified. ''Woe unto you when all men shall speak well of you,'' said Jesus. Yes Herod wanted to see him. He did see him later but it only increased his guilt.

IT BLESSES MANKIND. Vs. 10-17.

10 And the apostles, when they were returned, told him all that they had done. And he took them, and went aside privately into a desert place belonging to the city called Bethsaida.

11 And the people, when they knew *it*, followed him : and he received them, and spake unto them of the kingdom of God, and healed them that had need of healing.

12 And when the day began to wear away, then came the twelve, and said unto him, Send the multitude away, that they may go into the towns and country round about, and lodge, and get victuals : for we are here in a desert place.

13 But he said unto them, Give ye them to eat. And they said, We have no more but five loaves and two fishes ; except we should go and buy meat for all this people.

14 For they were about five thousand men. And he said to his disciples, Make them sit down by fifties in a company.

15 And they did so, and made them all sit down.

16 Then he took the five loaves and the two fishes, and looking up to heaven, he blessed them, and brake, and gave to the disciples to set before the multitude.

17 And they did eat, and were all filled : and there was taken up of fragments that remained to them twelve baskets.

The history leading up to the event of the feeding of the five thousand is this : Jesus had sent his disciples out to preach the gospel in the villages (Vs. 6) while he preached in the cities. This preaching on the part of himself and disciples had extended the fame of Jesus so that Herod Antipas had heard of it, and thought that John the Baptist had arisen from the dead, and was doing mighty works. When Jesus knew of Herod's state of mind he withdrew from Herod's territory and went across the sea of Galilee into the dominions of the king's brother. The people gathered near the shore of the sea, near Bethesda, bringing their sick, that he might heal them. It was, so John tells us, at the time of the Passover (John 6:3-5). Jesus, full of compassion, had retired to a mountain. He had come down from the mountain and spent the day in healing the sick. It was now eventime and some of the disciples recognized the need of feeding the people. John tells us that Jesus had previously asked Philip, "Shall we buy bread for so many to eat?" He wanted Philip to see his own heart and the measure of his faith. So he said this to test him. The spiritual lesson of the parable was unfolded in his sermon next day (John 6:26-55), on the theme Christ, the Bread of Life, and eternal life conditioned upon feeding upon Christ. This miracle was not given merely to do good by feeding the multitude and satisfying their hunger but to illustrate by a striking object lesson, that he could as easily satisfy their souls as their bodies. Like all his miracles, it illustrated spiritual truth.

(1) Notice Jesus expected his disciples to feed the multitudes. He said "give ye them to eat." He expects the church today to have that on hand, which will feed the multitude. He expects us to be well fed that we may be able to help rescue the perishing all about us. (2) If we have but little and it is genuine food, he will multiply that little for the use of others. They began with five loaves and two fishes. (3) There was enough It ran over. There were twelve baskets of fragments—one for each disciple. It looks as if each one of the disciples had a basket and helped pick up the fragments. Jesus set an example of frugality. He would not allow any of the bread to be wasted. The miracle was not the suspension of appetite on the part of the people but an actual multiplication of bread. As truly is there an abundance of salvation now for those who will accept it.

Jesus looked up to heaven and blessed the bread. He gave thanks. It was the custom of the Jews always to give thanks before eating. It is heathenish not to give thanks for our food.

"Like the widow's crust when a part was taken, its place was instantly supplied by divine power. The loaf remained still as large as when the piece was broken off, and each piece in hand became imperceptibly as large as the loaf. Was this an original act of creation? Not necessarily. He, who guided through the water the fishes to Peter's net, could guide the invisible atomic elements in however gaseous a form, through the air, to form the loaf, the material bread. This but hastened the process that ever is taking place in the growth of the corn or wheat. There is but the additional modification produced by heat in the oven; but even this is only a different arrangement of the particles." (Whedon.) The grand lesson of the parable is that there is virtue sufficient in the atonement of Jesus, made once for all, for the salvation of the whole world. And his people can go to all the world and distribute the bread of life to all, for there is plenty for the whole human race. The holy man will like Jesus do all he can to bless the world.

IT MEANS DEATH TO THE CARNAL NATURE. Vs. 18-27.

18 And it came to pass, as he was alone praying, his disciples were with him : and he asked them, saying, Whom say the people that I am?

19 They answering said, John the Baptist ; but some *say*, Elias ; and others *say*, that one of the old prophets is risen again.

20 He said unto them, But whom say ye that I am? Peter answering said, The Christ of God.

21 And he straitly charged them, and commanded *them* to tell no man that thing ;

22 Saying, The Son of man must suffer many things, and be rejected of the elders and chief priests and scribes, and be slain, and be raised the third day.

23 And he said to *them* all, If any *man* will come after me, let him deny himself, and take up his cross daily, and follow me.

24 For whosoever will save his life shall lose it : but whosoever will lose his life for my sake, the same shall save it.

25 For what is a man advantaged, if he gain the whole world, and lose himself, or be cast away?

26 For whosoever shall be ashamed of me and of my words, of him shall the Son of man be ashamed, when he shall come in his own glory, and *in his* Father's, and of the holy angels.

27 But I tell you of a truth, there be some standing here, which shall not taste of death, till they see the kingdom of God.

Matthew gives the fullest account of the events herein described. We shall combine the account of Luke and Matthew that we may get the full story. Jesus was alone praying, when his disciples came to him. They were on the borders of Caesarea, Philippi. There were two cities by the name of Caesarea. One was on the sea coast on the southern borders of Samaria. This city where Jesus was at this time was named Caesarea Philippi in honor of the family of Augustus Cæsar. It was situated at the very northernmost boundary of Palestine. This was the farthest north that Jesus ever went in his journeyings. He had now arrived at the climax of his ministry. He had performed his miracles and imbued his disciples with his doctrines and now he begins to prepare them for the work of spreading his kingdom after his decease. Here apart from the world, he goes a step farther and requires of them a positive declaration of what they estimated him to be. He now begins to lay the foundations of his church. He was *alone praying* when they came to him. He was alone praying a good deal of the time of his earthly ministry. He gave us the example of secret prayer. He was praying when he was baptized and the Spirit like a dove rested upon him. He spent the night in prayer just before he called his twelve disciples. He prayed in Gethsemane and on the cross. He lived a life of prayer. So should and will all his true disciples.

He now asks his disciples what the people were saying about him or, in other words, what they thought of him and his dictrine. They replied that some thought he was John the Baptist, resurrected; others thought he was Elijah returned to earth; while others thought he was Jeremiah or one of the prophets of old. We sometimes hear people say that it is difficult now to believe but if they had lived in the days of Jesus and seen his miracles they would have believed on him. But there were multitudes who lived in the time of Christ and saw his miracles who did not believe on him.

There are the same differences of opinion in society today concerning Jesus. Some think he was only a good man. Others think he was the world's greatest teacher. Others know from experience that he was the Son of God. Having learned what the people think of him, he now turns to his disciples and asks them, "But whom say ye that I am?" He asks that they may give their candid opinion, after having lived with him and seen his miracles and heard his teachings for so long a time. This is the vital question with every disciple of Jesus; not what do others think of Jesus, but what do we think. What can we affirm concerning Jesus from our personal knowledge of him and his acts and words? What does our experience teach?

Our opinion of Jesus makes all the difference in the world as to our destiny. It does not make so much difference what we think about Napoleon Bonaparte, or George Washington, or Julius Cæsar, but it will make a great deal of difference with us to all eternity as to what we think of Jesus. Right opinion is necessary to right action. If we see in him only a human character we shall fail of eternal salvation. If we fail to see in him a Saviour we shall fail to obtain salvation.

Our real opinion of Jesus is our life and testimony combined. Our opinion is incomplete without either. These disciples were acquainted with Jesus. And we can know him too. Paul said he was willing to suffer the loss of all things that he might know Jesus. It is possible to know a good deal about Jesus without being acquainted with him.

We are to tell what we have found out about Jesus to the world about us. The world expects a man's friends to give him a good recommendation. We are called to go out and tell from personal experience what we know about Jesus. This is our whole busines in life as disciples. Peter replied from personal experience that he had found that Jesus was the Christ, the Son of the living God. Happy is the man today who does not have to depend on argument to know that Jesus is divine, but can speak from a genuine experience, and can tell the world, that he knows Jesus is, divine, because of the divine work that he has wrought in his own soul. Testimony is the greatest preaching that there is. Christianity is the only religion that has any witnesses because it is the only religion that gives men an inner soul experience. Satan does not care how many great sermons are preached or arguments framed for Christianity, if there is no testimony. He would like to have it all appear as merely a beautiful impracticable theory. When Peter had given his testimony Jesus said to him, ''Blessed art thou Simon Bar-Jona (Son of Jona); for flesh and blood hath not revealed it unto thee but my Father which is in heaven.'' (Matt. 16:17.) Since Bar-Jona means Son of Jona, some of the commentators have seen an allegorical meaning in the name Jona as it means a *dove*. It would then mean Simon son of the dove, that is, son of the Holy Spirit, who is likened to a dove. It would indicate that Peter was a saved man. But we have some very positive proofs that Peter was a saved man at this time. Let those who contend that Peter and the other disciples were unregenerate before Pentecost notice the proofs that he was regenerate at this time. (1) Jesus calls him *blessed*. Who ''blessed'' him if not his Heavenly Father of whom Jesus here speaks? He certainly could not have been a blessed sinner, for that would be a contradiction of terms.

(2) Peter was so spiritual that the Father had revealed the truth to him concerning the deity of Jesus Christ. This was a truth that most people of that day had not yet apprehended. Spiritual truth is not revealed to unspiritual people. ''The nat-

ural man receiveth not the things of God, for they are foolishness to him; neither can he know them for they are spiritually discerned.'' (1 Cor. 2:14.) The great truth of the deity of Jesus that the whole Jewish Church had failed to see was revealed to Peter, because he was a *blessed*, spiritual man. Paul says ''No man can say that Jesus is the Lord but by the Holy Ghost.'' (1 Cor. 12:3.) And John says ''Whosoever shall confess that Jesus is the Son of God, God dwelleth in him, and he in God.'' (1 John 4:15.) So we must admit from the teachings of Scripture that Peter was a regenerate man, to whom God could in advance of the whole Jewish people, reveal the Messiahship of Jesus when his enemies were calling Jesus a blasphemer. But some have taken the position that people were not regenerate before Pentecost. They forget that Jesus told Nicodemus before Pentecost that he must be born again. He did not tell Nicodemus that he must wait three years until Pentecost to be born again. It was an experience that it was the duty of Nicodemus to possess at that time.

This proves conclusively that there is such an experience as having a revelation of spiritual things. So we have here the truth revealed to us that God reveals truth to men. (For a fuller discussion of the lessons of this event we refer our readers to our Commentary on Matthew, chapter 16.)

Jesus now charged them to tell this revelation of his deity to no man. The time had not yet come for it to be proclaimed, for they had not received the Holy Spirit in his fullness, which would fully qualify them as witnesses. No Christian is fully qualified, as a witness, until he receives the Holy Ghost. Jesus said this when he said, ''Ye shall receive power after that the Holy Ghost has come upon you and ye shall be witnesses unto me.'' (Acts 1:8.) Just as taking the oath qualifies a man and gives him the authority of the government to be a witness, so God gives his witnesses full authority when he baptizes them with the Holy Ghost, and then men have to do something with their testimony when they hear it. The Spirit accompanies it and men have to come to some decision. There was no embargo put on their testimony after Pentecost, when they had received the Holy Ghost.

He now tells them that he was to be rejected by the leaders of the church and killed and resurrected on the third day after his death. For some time he had been in seclusion, because of his enemies. Now that his disciples had recognized him as the Messiah, a new epoch begins. They had received the light and confessed that Jesus was the Messiah; now he gives them more light and tells them that he was to be the *suffering Messiah,* who was to be killed by the leaders of the church. As sure as we welcome light and acknowledge it and confess it as did these disciples, we shall have more light given us. If we like the light we have, we shall be glad to receive more. We are all in the pathway of increasing light if we are honest. We, if we are, have been born again and can say from a living experience, like the disciples that Jesus is the Christ, will be led on to the crucified life. We will have fellowship with his suffering. There is as truly a crucified life for us as there was for Jesus. It is the crucifixion of the carnal nature. God does not intend that we shall stop with the elementary experience of knowing Christ. In the language of Paul we are to be ''Crucified with Christ.'' The same things are said of the experience of the believer that were said of the earthly life of Jesus: both are born of the Holy Spirit, crucified and resurrected. Paul says, ''If ye be risen with Christ, seek the things that are above.''

This announcement was a staggering truth to Peter. He had an entirely different idea of what the Messiahship of Jesus meant. He was thinking of earthly, worldly grandeur. He thought Jesus would drive out the hated Romans, and sit on the throne of his father David and have the twelve apostles as his cabinet and chief officers. And now to be told that Jesus was to be rejected and even killed by the chief men of the church was too much for Peter's ambitions. There are many who profess the religion of Jesus in these days who have the same carnal notions of religion. When told of the crucifixion of their carnal nature and that it is an unpopular notion with the leaders of ecclesiasticism, they will not accept it. The religion of the cross will never be popular in this world.

Peter began to rebuke the Lord, so Matthew tells us (Matt. 16:22). The trouble with Peter was he had yet the carnal mind, just as Paul told the church at Corinth who were saved but they were ''*yet carnal.*''

Jesus now goes on to tell these disciples (or according to Matthew) more particularly Peter that if they were to follow him they must take two steps, (1) deny self. The word deny here is used in the sense of *renounce.* ''If any man is coming after me, let him renounce himself.'' This is the first step in the blessed life. These disciples had already renounced the world. This is what every true converted soul does. It will be noticed that ''Come after'' in the first clause and ''Follow'' in the last clause mean the same thing. Between these two clauses are the two works of grace or the two degrees of salvation, which are known as regeneration and entire sanctification. (1) Regeneration. The life of regeneration results in renunciation of the self life. The really converted man renounces the old self life and all that is dear to it. He takes the advice of Paul and makes ''no provision for the flesh.'' He cuts off the supplies or food of the carnal nature. He comes out from the world and is separate from it. He gets victory over its allurements. ''Whosoever is born of God overcometh the world.'' This is not putting the standard of conversion too high, for it is a high experience. It is thought by some that they who profess entire sanctification make a high profession. So do those who profess regeneration. The Christian life of any degree is a great experience. Those churches that require a baptismal covenant, in so doing require a very high profession of those baptized. Here is the baptismal covenant: ''I renounce the devil and all his works, the vain pomp and glory of this world together with the covetuous desires of the same so that I will neither follow nor be led by them.'' It will be noticed that this covenant required by the church, acknowledges that the ''Carnal desires of the flesh are all in converted man.'' He promises no longer to be led by these carnal desires. The difference between the converted and unconverted man is that the former is not led by these desires while they lead the latter. Paul says to a converted church (we use conversion here in the sense of regeneration), ''In time past ye walked according to the course of this world, according to the prince of the power of the air, the spirit that now worketh in the children of disobedience, among whom we all had our conversation in times past in the lust of the flesh, fulfilling the lust of the flesh and of the mind: and were by nature the children of wrath even as others.'' When we are born again we no longer are led by the flesh but renounce it—make war upon it. *But this is the first degree of salvation only.* (2) ''And take up his cross daily.'' This is the second step. It is singular what strange notions people have of the nature of cross-bearing. We have seen those who thought it means to testify to the glorious experience of sins forgiven. We have heard others say that it means to perform our duty as God bids us. Is it a cross to tell to sinners what a dear Saviour we have found? Is it a cross to do what the dear Lord that loves us bids us do? Away with such trifling. The cross was the instrument of ignominious death. The man who carried it was on the way to be nailed to it until he was dead, and to die in derision and disgrace in the eyes of the world. It was the punishment meted out to the worst criminals. It meant more than saying a few words in a classmeeting surrounded by sympathizing friends, or doing a few errands for the Lord, who bought us from captivity to Satan and sin. It means the death of the old nature within us. It means the crucifixion of the ''Old man,'' and the reproach that comes to those, who are thus crucified. It means the reproach that comes from living the life and professing the unpopular doctrine of entire sanctification. The offense of the cross will never cease while the world stands, or while the carnal mind is enmity against God. The offense of the cross seems to have ceased with all religions of today except the profession of the experience of entire sanctification. Notice, Jesus did not say we must bear the cross that is laid upon us, but we must *ourselves take it up.* We must embrace it from choice. We must take it up because we love Jesus so much that we propose to follow him. Paul took it up because he loved it. He said ''God forbid that I should glory save in the cross of our Lord Jesus Christ by whom the world is crucified unto me and I unto the world.'' When we have renounced the old self life, have consequently been converted, and have resolved to go with Jesus all the way to Calvary, and consequently have been entirely sanctified, we are willing to have our names cast out as fanatics, disturbers, enthusiasts for Jesus' sake and glory in it, as Paul did. Do we love Jesus enough to go with him all the way?

This is where and why so many shrink and make all sorts of

excuses against sanctification. They do not want the old carnal nature to die. Verse 25 gives the reason why sanctification is and always will be unpopular. "Whosoever will save his life shall lose it." There are thousands, who claim to love Jesus but are afraid to be out and out Christians lest their reputation shall suffer. They are trying to save their lives. They fear their social lives will suffer. They want an easy religion that will allow the old life of the flesh to live. All the arguments against holiness are simply excuses for letting the old carnal life continue. In the early days of Christianity men were willing to give their physical lives and become martyrs for Jesus, but it takes more decision today to be willing to die out in the carnal nature and face the loathing that men feel for a dead man. When we get to the real dying out place we shall find that we have just begun to live.

He now asks an unanswerable question, "For what is a man advantaged if he gain the whole world and lose himself?" This text is almost always applied to sinners but it refers here to disciples. It refers to the question of holiness too. It means that the professed Christian who refuses to go on and have the carnal nature crucified is in danger of losing his soul. The great reason usually why professed Christians are unwilling to be sanctified is they want to save the old carnal life. If we make our own life and its security the chief object we shall fail. This is true even in spiritual seeking. The man, who is seeking only happiness and joy for himself will fail. Here is a subtle snare even to well meaning people. There are such whose highest ambition in spiritual things is to be happy and have religious joy. The end of spiritual life is not joy but the will of God. There is a real selfishness in all the time asking the Lord to make us happy. It is a subtle self seeking. It requires self forgetfulness to reach the highest stages of spiritual life. Seeking happiness is one of the characteristics of a carnal Christian.

"For whosoever shall be ashamed of me and my words." What was the temptation here to be ashamed? It was because of the cross that he was now prophesying. What were the words of which there was danger that they would be ashamed? These words about crucifixion (Vs. 23). How many so called followers of Jesus are ashamed of his real cross today and the words that describe crucifixion—such as sanctification, holiness and perfection, which describe various phases of the crucified life. These are very distasteful to carnal Christians and false professors even to-day. Death to sin is a shameful subject to many. Here is the crucial point with many camp followers of Jesus. They do not want to be separated from the multitude and walk in the middle of the narrow way. That is the reason they shrink from the call to holiness. Dr. Hanna says on this passage, ''What hinders many from a full embrace of Christ and all the blessings of his salvation, is a desire to go with the multitude; a shrinking through shame, from anything that would separate them from the world.'' Let us of this day remember that we are not to deny Christ for a temporary worldly gain. The early disciples had many temptations to do it. And we have just as many though of a different kind. But all our sufferings for his sake are only temporary for he is coming again in all his glory. And then he will confess us or be ashamed of us according as we have treated him in the matter. His denial or confession of us will be just as *real* as ours is of him. Because of the imminence of the Great Day, we are to have that holiness without which no man shall see the Lord. We are to take up the humiliating cross. That means a profession of holiness, in order that Jesus on that Great Day may not be ashamed of us.

''There be some standing here who shall not taste of death until they see the kingdom of God.'' Matthew, Mark and Luke, all three, report this saying, but with a difference of statement. Matthew has it ''till they see the Son of Man coming in his kingdom.'' Mark says ''Till they have seen the kingdom of God come with power.'' Each seems to have supplied the words that the other left out. Jesus evidently refers to the outpouring of the Holy Ghost at Pentecost, when the kingdom of God was established with power upon the earth. In Matthew 10:23 we have a similar passage, ''Ye shall not have gone over the cities of Israel until the Son of man come.'' This must have referred to his coming at Pentecost. This is not to be confounded with his second coming in visible form. (See our note on Matthew 10:23.)

IT HAS GLORIOUS REVELATIONS, EVEN IN THE INITIAL DEGREE. Vs. 28-36.

28   And it came to pass about an eight days after these sayings, he took Peter and John and James, and went up into a mountain to pray.

29   And as he prayed, the fashion of his countenance was altered, and his raiment *was* white *and* glistering.

30   And, behold, there talked with him two men, which were Moses and Elias:

31   Who appeared in glory, and spake of his decease which he should accomplish at Jerusalem.

32   But Peter and they that were with him were heavy with sleep: and when they were awake, they saw his glory, and the two men that stood with him.

33   And it came to pass, as they departed from him, Peter said unto Jesus, Master, it is good for us to be here: and let us make three tabernacles; one for thee, and one for Moses, and one for Elias: not knowing what he said.

34   While he thus spake, there came a cloud, and overshadowed them: and they feared as they entered into the cloud.

35   And there came a voice out of the cloud, saying, This is my beloved Son: hear him.

36   And when the voice was past, Jesus was found alone. And they kept *it* close, and told no man in those days any of those things which they had seen.

There are those who mistake great raptures and emotional blessing and revelations, for The Blessing of Full Salvation. They must remember that the three disciples, Peter, James and John had the great revelation on the mountain top, before Pentecost.

A careful study of divine revelation will show that it has always been gradual. God has not flashed all his truth upon mankind at once; for man could not bear it. This may be seen in the revelation of truth in the Old Testament and also in the revelation of the Messiah in both Old and New Testaments. Perhaps the best illustration of this gradualism is seen in Matthew.

Jesus, having now established in the hearts of his disciples the great truth that he was divine, as evinced by the confession of Peter, and having revealed the advanced truth that he was to suffer and die for the sins of the world, lest his disciples become discouraged at the prophecy of his approaching ignominious death, reveals to them on the mountain top as much of the heavenly glory, which he had before the foundation of the world as they could bear, in order to strengthen their faith. This is just like the Lord, he always comes at the time when we need encouragement. It revived their staggering faith and prepared them for Gethsemane and Calvary. The nearly three years of training under Jesus must have been a constant series of surprises to them. The revelation of Christ to the soul of the believer is much the same. It is a gradual unfolding of truth from the time of awakening and conviction. Jesus said on another occasion, "I have many things to say unto you but ye can not bear them now."

This great manifestation which they received on the mountain was not entire sanctification. He had already been telling them about the gift of the Holy Ghost. But this manifestation was not that gift. They did not receive it until Pentecost. We have seen those who thought that some wonderful mountain top experience that they had received was the Baptism with the Holy Ghost. Not so: we may have many blessings before we have the gift of the Holy Ghost—the crowning blessing. We may have many gifts of the Holy Spirit before we receive *the* Gift of the Holy Spirit himself, as our abiding comforter and cleanser. The disciples had a wonderful experience on the mountain but it was not cleansing from all sin. Let us not rely on great manifestations but let us seek the great blessing that destroys inbred sin— that kills the Old Man. "A great blessing" is one thing, but *the blessing* that cleanses the heart from all sin is something else, and is greater.

Jesus took Peter, James and John up on a mountain to pray. What fellowship there is between souls, who go away often to pray. It binds them wonderfully together. Why did he take these three disciples and not the other nine? We do not know, but it seems that they were of stronger spiritual character than the rest. There are various degrees of character among even true followers of the Lord. No doubt they were more closely intimate with Jesus than the others. Jesus was human and had his special friends as well as we. Paul calls Peter, James and John, the three pillars of the church. (Gal. 2:9.) These three were with Jesus at the raising of Jairus' daughter and in Gethsemane. They evidently had a larger share in the founding of the church than the rest. It was necessary that they should be well rooted and grounded in the faith.

It has been thought that this mountain was Mt. Hermon. Why did he go upon a mountain? We suppose because there was more privacy up above the world. There were many notable scriptural events that occurred on mountains. Sinai, with the Law; Horeb with the burning bush; Carmel, and the revelation of fire to Elijah, and the Mount of the Beatitudes are instances of the remarkable manifestations of God on mountain tops.

He was praying when he was transfigured. We have had occasion to note before that he prayed on the great occasions of his life. When he was baptized by John and the Spirit came upon him, he was praying. An angel came and ministered to him when he was praying in Gethsemane. ''The fashion of his countenance was altered.'' Matthew says ''his face did shine as the light.'' Some of the glory which he will manifest when he comes the second time shone out of his person. It was this that overpowered the soldiers who kept his tomb, and they fell as dead men. His body was the same yet it glowed with an effulgence, such as we believe, he will show forth in his person when he comes again. These disciples saw some of the heavenly glory. Peter never forgot it. Years after he wrote concerning this scene, and refers to it as a convincing proof of the deity of Jesus. (See 2 Peter 1:16-18.) Peter in verse 20 had just testified that he believed Jesus was the Messiah and now he got a revelation that was a confirmation or witness to the fact. He had believed on sufficient evidence, but now he had the full proof revealed to his sight in the transfigured Christ, and to his hearing in the voice from the cloud. Yet there are people, who in order to maintain a theory would have us believe that these three men to whom Christ revealed his glory were unsaved, unregenerate sinners. What will not people believe rather than accept the truth. Jesus said that he revealed himself unto his disciples *as he did not to the world.* The believer of today, who will act on the evidence that God has given will receive a revelation and assurance that will be unmistakable. He may not see the transfiguration as these disciples did, but he will receive assurance that will be satisfactory. Let us then confess our faith in Christ as a means to further revelations. The Pharisees said the work was only a cunning fraud—the work of the devil, that Jesus had palmed off on the people. But Peter says in his second epistle "We have not followed cunningly devised fables, when we made known unto you the power and coming of our Lord Jesus Christ but were eye witnesses of his majesty. For he received from God, the Father, honor and glory, when there came such a voice from the excellent glory. This is my beloved Son in whom I am well pleased." Let us not suppose that there are no revelations in the experience of regeneration. There are. We must not belittle them even if we have been raised to the higher degree of entire sanctification. But they are not permanent like the revelations of the indwelling Comforter. There are gradual revelations all the way along as we are fitted for them. Jesus could not have given these disciples this revelation a few weeks before this. They were not prepared for it. But this was not the only revelation that they received. "And behold there talked with him, two men, which were Moses and Elias." We also learn what they were talking about—"his decease which he should accomplish at Jerusalem." The great theme of holy prophets and martyrs of old was the atonement through the blood of Jesus—his sacrificial death. There are those who assert that the great object of the coming of Jesus to earth was to set us an example for godly living. But this is a mistake. The great object of his mission was to atone for our sins by his death. Moses and Elias on the Mount do not say a word about his perfect example, concerning which our Unitarian friends prate so much. They speak of his death—the great event of human history.

How did the disciples know who Moses and Elias were? We suppose they could gather it from the conversation, or they might have been told by Jesus; or they might have had divine revelation on the subject as Peter did of the Messiahship of Jesus in verses 18-20. It was necessary that these disciples, who were to be the pillars of the church should hear this testimony from Moses, the leader of the Old Dispensation and Elijah, leader of the dispensation of the prophets concerning the death of Jesus, that they might see how the dispensations all centered upon and agreed concerning the death of Jesus as the sacrifice for the sins of mankind.

Here the Law and the Prophets and the disciples are all testifying to the Messiahship of Jesus of Nazareth, just as Peter had just done a few days previously. It was a grand assemblage. The like of it has never been seen on earth since. It shows that Moses and Elias were still alive and are today and that death is not unconscious sleep in the grave. "They spoke not of his miracles, nor of his teaching, nor of the honor which he put upon the scriptures, nor of the unreasonable opposition to him and his patient endurance of it. They spoke not of the glory that they themselves were enshrouded in, and the glory which he was soon to reach. Their one subject of talk is his *decease,* which he was going to accomplish at Jerusalem. One fancies that he might hear them say 'Worthy is the Lamb, which is to be slain.'" (Brown.)

"Peter said unto Jesus." He seems to have been the spokesman of the apostles; probably the readiest to talk. Some have the gift of speech in greater measure than others. They can talk even when they do not know how it sounds or really what they are saying. Peter was naturally talkative.

"Let us make three tabernacles." This was unselfish. He wanted to make three tabernacles for Jesus, Moses and Elijah. He wanted to keep them on earth and be in their company all the time. He said this "Not knowing what he said." Mark says the disciples were "sore afraid." While Peter was yet speaking a bright cloud overshadowed them. This was probably the Shekinah, the cloud that manifested itself in the tabernacle and temple of Solomon. And there was a voice that came out of the cloud, saying "This is my beloved Son hear him." So they had the evidences of sight and hearing as to the deity of Jesus. The voice said "hear him." If ever there was an excuse for worshiping the saints it was at this time. But there is no hint of it even. We shall have to deny the claims of Roman Catholicism that the saints are to be worshipped. We are to listen to no one but Jesus. It is often our duty to keep silent. Happy the man who knows when to keep still.

Matthew tells us that the disciples fell on their faces, overcome with fear. What must there have been in that voice! While they were delighted and astonished at the sight of the glory, the voice appalled them. There is something in the voice of God that takes hold of the very depths of the heart, the very soul. At Mt. Sinai the people besought Moses to pray that God speak no more to them. That voice, says the author of Hebrews, once ''shook the earth.'' (Heb. 12:26.) Matthew says they fell on their faces and were sore afraid.

They lifted up their eyes, but Moses and Elijah had vanished. Jesus remained, and they saw no man save Jesus only. Thank God, if every one else in the universe shall disappear we may see Jesus. He is the central figure in history and the center of the affections of his people. And if we lose sight of every one else we shall not be desolate as long as we can see Him. Let us determine to see no man save Jesus only.

At the command of Jesus they kept these things, that they had seen and heard, to themselves. The revelation was not for the world, but to confirm his own desciples in their faith.

THE CHURCH IS WEAK WITHOUT IT. Vs. 37-46.

37 And it came to pass, that on the next day, when they were come down from the hill, much people met him.

38 And, behold, a man of the company cried out, saying, Master, I beseech thee, look upon my son: for he is mine only child.

39 And, lo, a spirit taketh him, and he suddenly crieth out; and it teareth him that he foameth again, and bruising him hardly departeth from him.

40 And I besought thy disciples to cast him out, and they could not.

41 And Jesus answering said, O faithless and perverse generation. how long shall I be with you, and suffer you? Bring thy son hither.

42 And as he was yet a coming, the devil threw him down, and tare *him*. And Jesus rebuked the unclean spirit, and healed the child, and delivered him again to his father.

43 And they were all amazed at the mighty power of God. But while they wondered every one at all things which Jesus did, he said unto his disciples,

44 Let these sayings sink down into your ears: for the Son of man shall be delivered into the hands of men.

45 But they understood not his saying, and it was hid from them, that they perceived it not: and they feared to ask him of that saying.

When they arrived at the foot of the mountain they found a remarkable sight. They found the disciples, who had remained at the foot of the mount apparently defeated by the devil and his hosts. It reminds us of the coming down of Moses from Mt.

Sinai, where he had glorious communion with God to find the people dancing around the golden calf, the idol god of Egypt. Jesus, Peter, James and John found the disciples baffled in their attempts to cast the devil out of an afflicted boy.

There are some people who have wickedly applied this transaction as an illustration to wound the holiness people. They have said that these people spend their time on the mountain top of enjoyment when the world needs them, as in this case. Such people really reflect on Jesus for he was on the mountain top and the boy did not get healed until he came down. It shows to what inconsistencies some people will go in fighting holiness. Besides this it does not apply at all for the disciples had not yet had their Pentecost. They were yet in the initial experience—regeneration. Either they were in this experience or Jesus showed his glory and was on the most intimate terms with sinners.

Mountain top experiences are real and blessed. God wants us to have them in a certain sense in this life, but he does not intend that we shall be in such a state all the time as far as raptures are concerned. The body would not endure the strain; nor is religion chiefly emotion. This is only one of the accompaniments which God allows us as far as we need it. Alas, that there are so many who think that feeling and emotion are all that there is in religion! The Holy Spirit is the author of a great variety of experiences. Our great business is not to enjoy ourselves but to do the will of God.

While the Scribes according to Mark were taunting the disciples with their failure to cast the evil spirit out of the boy, Jesus comes to their rescue and asks the scribes "what question ye with them?" Before they had time to answer a man comes out of the crowd and kneeling before Jesus, tells him the victim is his son, who had been driven insane by the possession of the evil spirit, whom he had brought to his disciples, who were powerless to cast out the devil. The afflicted father cries to Jesus in the bitterness of his spirit, for him to have mercy and help him. The father takes the case of his son on his own heart as if it were himself that was thus possessed of the devil.

Jesus breaks forth with words of heart weariness thus, "O faithless and perverse generation, how long shall I be with you and suffer you?'' This outburst of Jesus shows what a humiliation it was for Jesus, the pure and holy One, to be associated with unbelief in any form. What a transition it was from the glories of the Mount of Transfiguration to come down to these weak believers, who had no power over evil because of their unbelief. We can hardly comprehend how heinous and odious unbelief was to him. He was constantly exclaiming against it and constantly especially commending those who had faith. He is we believe similarly affected today with those who have unbelief. He adds: "Bring him to me.'' This is a good suggestion for us, when we have tried in vain with human sympathy to comfort the distressed, or have sought to get men saved in vain. Let us be sure to bring the case to Jesus and put it in his hands, the best we can. He can do what we can not. Jesus then rebuked the devil and he came out of the child from that hour.

Matthew tells us that the disciples came to Jesus and asked him why they could not cast out the devil and he replied "Because of your unbelief.'' It must be remembered that Jesus had sent them out with power to cast out devils, when he commissioned them to preach. (See Matthew 10:1.) Great powers then are nothing without faith. They may be, dormant because of lack of faith. Their faith was like that of sinking Peter in the lake. It was mixed with unbelief, with sinful tendencies that made it weak. Before Pentecost their success was intermittent, because of the carnal nature within them. After Pentecost we hear no more of failure in their faith or in their work.

IT KILLS UNHOLY AMBITION. Vs. 46-48.

46 Then there arose a reasoning among them, which of them should be greatest.

47 And Jesus, perceiving the thought of their heart, took a child, and set him by him,

48 And said unto them, Whosoever shall receive this child in my name receiveth me: and whosoever shall receive me receiveth him that sent me: for he that is least among you all, the same shall be great.

So it seems that these men who had been commissioned to preach the gospel were at variance among themselves in their efforts to assume leadership. Lust for leadership is one of the traits of the carnal mind. No matter how loudly people may profess to have been entirely sanctified, if they have the itch for leadership, they have an indubitable evidence that they are far from the lowly spirit which marks one who is cleansed from all sin. Jesus had so emphatically emphasized his claims of Messiahship upon their minds that they now believed it and began to scramble for power in the new kingdom, which they believed was now to be set up. This lust for power in the church in our day is known as Clerical Politics. Would that it had died out of the church at the time of the apostles. This trait of unsanctified human nature if there were no other reason would be sufficient to prove the need of entire sanctification. These men, it will be seen, were not cleansed from all sin when they left all to follow Jesus.

Luke says, "there arose a reasoning among them which of them should be greatest." They argued the matter. Each trying to convince the other of his fitness to be leader of the band. One of the most ridiculous things on earth is to see a man who is unfit for leadership, aspiring and trying to get into office in the church. How many there are who are not as open in their office seeking as these disciples were; to see the tricks and wire pulling resorted to even in ecclesiastical circles is worse than disgusting. It is wicked and a positive damage to the kingdom of God. Poor old carnal nature has not improved with the flight of time. It still shows the same evil manifestations.

Matthew Henry characterizes their scramble for office thus, "Peter was always the chief speaker and had the keys given to him; he expects to be lord chamberlain or lord chancellor of the household, and so to be the greatest. Judas had the bag and so expects to be the head treasurer, which, though now it comes last, he hopes will then discriminate him first. Simon and Jude are nearly related to Christ and they hope to take the place of all the great officer of state, as princes of the blood. John is the beloved disciple, the favorite of the Prince, therefore he hopes to be the greatest. Andrew was first called, and why should he not be the first preferred." Men have always an excuse when they really want anything.

Jesus perceived their thoughts and gave them a very practical lesson and rebuke at the same time. He took a little child, as a model for their imitation. None of the great teachers or philosophers of the world ever did such a thing as making a child a model for older people. Usually older people have been set up as models for the young. Jesus was startling in his methods. No wonder carnal minded people never enjoy his teachings. A child is a most excellent model for us in our relations to our heavenly Father. For we bear the same relation to him spiritually that our children do naturally to us. A child is teachable and confiding. In these respects we must be like little children. Jesus used object lessons to enforce truth—an excellent example for teachers and preachers.

"Whosoever shall receive this child in my name, receiveth me." Children are in the kingdom of heaven through the merits of Jesus' death, until they sin and fall out when they come to the years of accountability. This was a *very little* child; so the Greek word here signifies. If we receive our children as already members of Jesus' kingdom and as from him, we are receiving him. How many fail to look on children as members of his kingdom. How many parents are out of the kingdom that their little children are in. We are to receive them by considering them as in the kingdom of God and seeking to so bring them up that they need never drop out of that kingdom. We should so train them and regard them. When a child is born into the home we should rejoice that we have another member of the kingdom of heaven in our midst. Those who thus regard their children and seek to thus bring them up have received Jesus. So he teaches the greatness of childhood with its artlessness and simplicity. It is above human greatness and this we should aspire to, instead of seeking to have some place above our brethren in our lust for leadership. The greatness of humility is that for which we should aspire; and those who are seeking to eclipse others show that they have missed true greatness as Jesus estimates it. The carnal mind in them needs killing. Thank God the baptism with the Holy Ghost can kill out this desire and make us truly great. The humblest is the greatest in the kingdom of God.

Some of us sometimes wish we were back to childhood that we might again live a life free from care and worry. Perhaps if we had no more carnal ambition and evil desires than we had in childhood we might be as free now. Much of our fret is because we con not occupy places that we are not in, or can not have things that we covet, or wield power that we desire. He who finds his satisfaction in God has escaped much worry, disappointment and sorrow. Here these disciples were disputing as to who should be greatest in the kingdom, when they were all in danger of missing the kingdom entirely because they sought to be great. The essence of our holy religion is not, as some have thought, in climbing to sublime heights, but it is in going down into the depths of the lowly valley of humility. A humble man is not necessarily one who has no good opinion of himself, or a proper estimate of his powers, but who is willing to take a lowly position where God wants him and rest there until God bids him come up higher. He is one, who is seeking nothing in this life but what God can give him.

IT DESTROYS SECTARIANISM. Vs. 49-50.

49 And John answered and said, Master, we saw one casting out devils in thy name; and we forbad him, because he followeth not with us.

50 And Jesus said unto him, Forbid *him* not: for he that is not against us is for us.

Jesus had said in verse 48 that, whosoever received this little child in his name received him. This did not please John. He did not like the idea that any one no matter however humble could be accepted if it was in the name of Christ, and so he thought he would bring up an instance of some one who had used the name of Christ unwarrantedly. So he tells the Master of a man whom he had seen casting out devils in *the name* of Jesus, who did not belong to the company of disciples. The case was so aggravated as he saw it that he and the other disciples had forbidden the man to cast out any more devils. It was as much as to say "Master, you are giving the authority of your name to unworthy people. Surely people will take advantage and too much license if you put such a premium on your name." But Jesus rebuked John saying, "Forbid him not; for he that is not against us is for us." This man, who was casting out devils was probably some disciple of Jesus, who was not of the twelve but to whom Jesus had given the power to cast out devils and God had honored his faith and his work was successful. Sectarianism in religion is one of the marks of the carnal mind. It can see no good in any one unless he has the same tag or belongs to the same company. It thinks more of building up a sect than in building up the kingdom of Christ. It does not ask, Was the devil really cast out under the ministry of some other worker, but did he belong to our crowd? How much there is of this damnable stuff. One of the fruits of real santification is a recognition of spirituality in others, who are not of our religious persuasion on non-essentials to salvation.

There are thousands, who call themselves Christians, who consider the great holiness movement, a gigantic fanaticism, notwithstanding thousands of sinners are genuinely converted under its ministry every year. One of the strange contradictions is that there are preachers, who are glad to receive the converts, who call the movement that produced them, a species of fanaticism. Abbott says ''The principle here inculcated forbids *discouraging any work, by whomsoever undertaken, minister or layman, man or woman,* which is really accomplishing spiritual results.''

What shall we say about those who see God blessing the labors of women preachers, who still refuse to endorse or encourage them?

IT CONDEMNS A REVENGEFUL SPIRIT. Vs. 51-56.

51 And it came to pass, when the time was come that he should be received up, he stedfastly set his face to go to Jerusalem.

52 And sent messengers before his face: and they went, and entered into a village of the Samaritans, to make ready for him.

53 And they did not receive him, because his face was as though he would go to Jerusalem.

54 And when his disciples James and John saw *this,* they said, Lord, wilt thou that we command fire to come down from heaven, and consume them, even as Elias did?

55 But he turned, and rebuked them, and said, Ye know not what manner of spirit ye are of.

56 For the Son of man is not come to destroy men's lives, but to save *them.* And they went to another village.

To us this is one of the most sublime statements that has been made of the acts of Jesus. Knowing that he was soon to be offered up as a sacrifice for the sins of the world; foreseeing the awful sufferings of soul and body that he was to pass through, he nevertheless steadfastly *set* his face towards Jerusalem, and commenced his last journey to that wicked city. It was one of the most sublime acts of heroism recorded in history. Unshrinking and undaunted he went forth to die. His disciples were amazed no doubt to hear him say, he was going to the very place where they had tried to kill him, and even prophesying that they would do so. He *set his face* with determination to fulfill his Father's will. His death was voluntary, He might have avoided it, He has left on record an example to us of the way we should face duty when the divine will requires it.

He had to pass through Samaria to get to Jerusalem, He might have avoided it and gone around (as the Jews usually did), because of their hatred to the Samaritans. The Samaritans hated the Jews also. There was a religious quarrel between them, as to the place where God should be worshipped. There is no quarrel so bitter, as a religious quarrel. Jesus had no such feeling towards the Samaritans although he did not endorse their error that God could only be worshipped in Samaria.

The Samaritans would not receive him in one of the villages through which they passed. This was contrary to the laws of hospitality of the times. To rightly understand the incident we must remember that the disciples had just had the revelation that Jesus was the Messiah and a sense of his dignity and authority must have possessed them. Not to receive him was a repudiation of his claims as Messiah. It was really a rejection of him. Seeing the laws of the times thus broken, James and John were filled with a righteous indignation, because the dignity of the Lord should be thus outraged. So they wanted to call down fire from heaven and burn up these impudent people. Here is the danger: that righteous anger may be carried too far and become sin. Here we see the difference between indignation and righteous indignation. It is unrighteous not to be indignant against sin. Salvation is not an opiate that so benumbs us that we will not recognize sin, or know when a wrong has been done. It is not a sweetish sentiment. But it is a sweetness that prevents us from desiring to wreak vengeance upon people. Inbred sin in the heart betrays good people sometimes to wish to wipe out people who do not behave towards us as we desire or who injure us. This is what ailed these preachers. They had not been delivered from the carnal mind. Here we have the manifestation of inbred sin in men who were so spiritual that Jesus had called and sent them out to preach and reveal himself in his heavenly glory on the mount of Transfiguration a few days before, He revealed himself to them as he did not to the world. And yet they still needed the destruction of their carnal nature, as here revealed. Inbred sin wants to wipe out sin by wiping out the sinner, but a holy man while he hates sin still loves the sinner. James and John never behaved that way after Pentecost. Trench says, "With all of carnal and sinful mingled with this proposal of theirs, yet what insight into the indignity and the greatness of the outrage, does it reveal?" Matthew Henry says, "There may be much of corruption, lurking, nay, stirring, too, in the hearts of good people and they themselves not be sensible of it." Thus we see they needed the second work of grace-full salvation. This fiery John after Pentecost became the apostle, who was the best embodiment of love that the religion of Jesus ever produced. It was holiness that did it.

"Ye know not what . . . spirit ye are of." It is the outbreathing of the carnal mind when we want to have other people removed from the world who are obnoxious to us or do not think as we do. It was this that led to the institution of the Spanish Inquisition that burned men at the stake for their doctrinal beliefs. It is this same devilish spirit that dwells in those fanatics who profess holiness and condemn every one who does not subscribe to their theories and practice. When a man thinks he is sanctified wholly who has such a spirit, he is grievously in error. He knows not what manner of spirit he is of.

Those who seek to premote holiness with a vindictive harsh or intolerant spirit have made a great mistake. No one wants that kind. They may have a correct theory but the samples they carry are not wanted in the market of public demand.

So Jesus went to another town. He waived his rights. He might have demanded his rights in accordance with the laws of hospitality of that day. He set us an example. Personally we are afraid of and avoid those people who are always standing up for their rights. If Jesus had stood up always for his rights we should have had no atonement and no salvation. If men were more willing to concede some things to each other instead of standing up for their rights there would be no strife between capital and labor, wars and fighting and tumults would cease. If men were wholly sanctified, they would be ''in honor preferring one another.''

IT DEMANDS ENTIRE CONSECRATION. Vs. 57-62.

57   And it came to pass, that, as they went in the way, a certain *man* said unto him, Lord, I will follow thee whithersoever thou goest.

58   And Jesus said unto him, Foxes have holes, and birds of the air *have* nests; but the Son of man hath not where to lay *his* head.

59   And he said unto another, Follow me. But he said, Lord, suffer me first to go and bury my father.

60   Jesus said unto him, Let the dead bury their dead: but go thou and preach the kingdom of God.

61   And another also said, Lord, I will follow thee; but let me first go bid them farewell, which are at home at my house.

62   And Jesus said unto him, No man, having put his hand to the plough, and looking back, is fit for the kingdom of God.

We now come to a very well known character—the man of irresolution and indecision, who wants to follow Christ but is handicapped by his vacillating disposition. A certain man met them in the way and announced his purpose to become a disciple of Christ. He announced very vehemently, ''I will follow thee withersoever thou goest.'' Matthew says he was a Scribe. He was a man of high position in the church and it would be considered by many, as an act of great condescension to follow Jesus, who was now so unpopular with the leaders of the church. No doubt the disciples must have felt greatly honored to have this great man express his desire to become a member of this despised company. If Jesus had been like many ecclesiastics he would have been eager to get such a follower. But he never catered to men because of their rank. Would that this professed church had done likewise. But this man would have been a detriment to the cause. He was only halfhearted. Jesus told him that he was poor. He had even less land than the foxes and not so much of a dwelling as the birds. Jesus thus told him of his poverty.

Jesus was a very discouraging preacher, to all half hearted people. He is today and so is his real gospel. The reason he was so discouraging was, he did not wish to be followed by a cheap crowd. He challenged the heroic in the man and found it evidently lacking. This is the way preachers should do today. There is such a thing as making it too easy for people and consequently they never come to a point of decision. This appointing inquiry meetings and failing to bring men to an open confession is all wrong. It proceeds from an emasculated gospel that fails to put men under urgent conviction. The gospel ought to be so sharp and clear cut that men will be so convicted that they will be willing to do anything—cut off a right hand or pluck out a right eye to save themselves from hell. Much of the so called "revivals" are not deep enough to last the converts all the way to their residences because no line of demarcation is drawn. This preaching of real gospel truth is far different from the so called signing a card "revivals" of today.

To what a life of humility did the King of Heaven submit that we might have eternal riches? He calls himself here "The Son of Man." He gave himself the title because he is the real man—the ideal man; just as God wants man—holy. He left a throne that we might sit on a throne.

Then another came desiring to be his follower in the future. He wanted to put the matter off as many do today. It is the same old excuse of procrastination, that we hear in every revival meeting. It is the excuse that has sent so many people to hell. This man said when urged to follow him (so we see that Jesus urged and exhorted men. Do we ever do much exhorting?) "Lord suffer me first to go and bury my father." He did not mean that his father was dead and he wanted to attend the funeral for the Jews always held the funeral on the same day that the person died and he could have attended the funeral and then followed Jesus. He meant that he wanted to take care of his father during his declining years and after his father was buried he would feel at liberty to be a preacher of the gospel. How many have treated the call to preaching the same way? For this was a call to preach. God never calls a man to preach without making it possible for him to preach. He will not require any duty that conflicts with other duties. It has been supposed that this disciple was Philip.

Jesus replied, ''Let the dead bury the dead.'' Here he uses the word ''*dead*'' in two senses. It is what is called a play upon words. He meant, let the spiritually dead bury the physically dead. They can do that as well as you, but I want you to preach the gospel. There are a lot of people who might be helping the preachers called to preach the gospel. There are plenty of unconverted people who can take care of the aged as well as those called to preach, but they can not preach.

Still another man came and said, ''Lord I will follow thee; but let me first go home and bid them farewell, which are at home at my house.'' To understand this we must remember the fierce opposition that had arisen against Jesus and his doctrine. To go back home and declare that he was intending to preach the gospel of the lowly Nazarene meant that all manner of opposition, ridicule or persuasion would be used to dissuade him. The man, tremendously in earnest to follow Jesus, would know better than to go home and face all this. ''The case of Elisha (8 Kings 19:19-21) though apparently similar to this, will be found quite different from the 'looking back' of this case, the best illustration of which is that of those Hindu converts of our day who, when once persuaded to leave their spiritual fathers in order to 'bid them farewell which are at home at their house' very rarely return to them.'' (Brown.)

Jesus utters a proverb, ''No man having put his hand to the plough and looking back is fit for the kingdom of heaven.'' Notice he is talking of *fitness* for the kingdom of heaven. The man who looks back to this world has in him the love of this world. He does not say the man who *turns* back, but the man who *looks* back. So a man may be on the way to heaven with his eyes toward the world—going to heaven backwards. Like Lot's wife looking back at Sodom. No wonder such people say they make crooked paths. We are certain that if a farmer undertook to plow the land and kept his eyes behind him, he would make crooked furrows. Inbred sin in the heart is what makes people unfit for the kingdom of heaven and is the cause of their crooked paths. God can not not only take away the ''go back'' but also the ''look back'' from our hearts.

These three men—the scribe, the man who wanted to go and take care of his father and the man who wanted to go back and say good bye illustrate three phases of inbred sin the first by his self confidence, the second by his vacillation and the third by his worldly mindedness were unfit for the kingdom. Their consecration was incomplete. Jesus demanded a complete consecration. People may quibble all they please about the perfection demanded by Jesus. But no candid man can deny that he demanded a complete, perfect consecration.

CHAPTER X.

HOLINESS AND ACTIVITY.

It Sends Forth Its Influences to Bless the World. Vs. 1-20. It Rejoices at the Revelation Made to the Lowly. Vs. 21-24. It Is Perfect Love to Man as Well as to God. Vs. 25-37. Holiness Can Not Be Substituted by Mere Activity. Vs. 38-42.

IT SENDS FORTH ITS INFLUENCES TO BLESS THE WORLD. Vs. 1-20.

1 After these things the Lord appointed other seventy also, and sent them two and two before his face into every city and place, whither he himself would come.

2 Therefore said he unto them, The harvest truly *is* great, but the labourers *are* few : pray ye therefore the Lord of the harvest, that he would send forth labourers into his harvest.

3 Go your ways : behold, I send you forth as lambs among wolves.

4 Carry neither purse, nor scrip, nor shoes : and salute no man by the way.

5 And into whatsoever house ye enter, first say, Peace *be* to this house.

6 And if the son of peace be there, your peace shall rest upon it : if not, it shall turn to you again.

7 And in the same house remain, eating and drinking such things as they give : for the labourer is worthy of his hire. Go not from house to house.

8 And into whatsoever city ye enter, and they receive you, eat such things as are set before you :

9 And heal the sick that are therein, and say unto them, The kingdom of God is come nigh unto you.

10 But into whatsoever city ye enter, and they receive you not, go your ways out into the streets of the same, and say,

11 Even the very dust of your city, which cleaveth on us, we do wipe off against you : notwithstanding be ye sure of this, that the kingdom of God is come nigh unto you.

12 But I say unto you, that it shall be more tolerable in that day for Sodom, than for that city.

13 Woe unto thee, Chorazin! woe unto thee, Bethsaida! for if the mighty works had been done in Tyre and Sidon, which have been done in you, they had a great while ago repented, sitting in sackcloth and ashes.

14 But it shall be more tolerable for Tyre and Sidon at the judgment, than for you.

15 And thou, Capernaum, which art exalted to heaven, shalt be thrust down to hell.

16 He that heareth you heareth me; and he that despiseth you despiseth me; and he that despiseth me despiseth him that sent me.

17 And the seventy returned again with joy, saying, Lord, even the devils are subject unto us through thy name.

18 And he said unto them, I beheld Satan as lightning fall from heaven.

19 Behold, I give unto you power to tread on serpents and scorpions, and over all the power of the enemy: and nothing shall by any means hurt you.

20 Notwithstanding in this rejoice not, that the spirits are subject unto you; but rather rejoice, because your names are written in heaven.

There are two kinds of activity—creature and spiritual. One is human and the other divine. One springs from the activities of a sanctified nature. The other is an imitation. One seeks to bless mankind, because of the love for the race. The other compasses sea and land to make proselytes for the upbuilding of its own sect and communion. Jesus was the personification of holiness absolute, and he was the center of a spiritual activity that was ever seeking to bless the world and so are those who are most like him. We find him here sending forth seventy more preachers. He was not satisfied simply to put the twelve in training for their apostleship when he sent them forth to preach (see Chapter 9) but he sent forth seventy others also. The twelve already appointed corresponded to the twelve tribes of Israel, and the seventy corresponded to the number of elders of Israel (Numbers 11:24-25). He sent these seventy out two by two for mutual sympathy and support. He sent these as forerunners into places where he purposed to come. Every gospel preacher today prepares the way for the coming of Jesus, both to the hearts of man and in the clouds of heaven. Our commission is to persuade men that he wants to come and will come to them if permitted. Men ought to feel encouraged whenever they see a gospel minister, for it is a sign that God has not left them, but wants to come to them, and will do so if they will permit. If we are not apostles we must not feel that we are not called to preach the word in some manner or other. The seventy were not apostles but they were to prepare the way for the coming of Jesus and he wants us to do that by urging men to receive Jesus.

A reference to chapter 9, verse 1, will show that the twelve disciples has greater power and authority than the seventy had given them when they went out to preach. He gave the former authority over devils and disease. He gave no such authority or power to the seventy. The latter were laymen, who went forth as heralds of his coming. They were not ordained like the twelve. Here we have the authority and sanction of lay preaching, by Jesus himself. He told them that the harvest truly was great but the laborers few. This was his reason and is still the reason for lay preaching. The emergency is great. One great hindrance to the salvation of men is the scarcity of laborers to tell the story. We live in a day when the denominations are inquiring why so few are willing to give themselves unreservedly to the ministry. Many reasons have been given, but the real reason is because so few are willing to heed the call of Jesus. It shows a lack of spiritual life in the professed church. When the church has been most spiritual it has had a comparatively easy time in finding candidates for the ministry.

Jesus here commands them to pray the Lord of the harvest to send more laborers into the harvest. We believe it would be a good plan for those denominations, who just now are seriously considering the matter of the decreasing number of preachers to make special prayer for an increase of preachers. A day of fasting and prayer for this purpose occasionally would not be amiss. Every one ought to have an interest in the welfare of the cause of God.

Jesus said he sent them forth as ''lambs among wolves.'' This would seem to indicate their character. It means that they were saved men and the world about them were unsaved and like wolves ready to devour them. Let those who endeavor to teach that these men were not saved before Pentecost ponder this statement and note that he did not send them out as wolves among wolves—unsaved men among unsaved men. They were to carry neither purse nor scrip (a sheep skin bag for provisions). They were to trust to the people among whom they labored for their support. They were to salute no man by the way. The oriental method of salutation was very lengthy and made up of many expressions of friendship that were mere pretence. They had no time for such trifling. They were not to accommodate themselves to the hollow hearted, insincere forms of etiquette. Into whatever house they entered they were to pronounce a blessing upon it in the name of their master. The house would prove itself worthy by receiving them for their master's sake. Wherever a servant of Jesus is welcomed for the value of the message he brings and for the sake of the gospel he preaches, the blessing of God will abide upon that home. If the dweller of the house was a son of peace—had peace with God—then their prayer for increased peace would be granted. If he was not, then the blessing would return to them and belong to them.

He had commanded them to abide only with those, who were in sympathy with their mission. They were therefore to contentedly share in the same kind of food and living of the people with whom they were entertained. The ministry today, who hope to reach men, must live among them and make them feel that they are of them. Jesus came to earth and set us this example by becoming one of us and living as we do.

They were not to go from house to house as if seeking better fare: or for social visiting. They were to deliver their message telling the people that the kingdom of heaven had come right to them. And if it were embraced it would come *into* them.

But if the people refused to hear their message they were to tell them that they would wipe even the dust of the streets off their feet against them. When Jews came into their own country after sojourning in heathen lands, they always wiped the dust from their feet to show that they were clean from the ceremonial pollution which they considered they had contracted in the land of the heathen. The ministry are to show by their life and example that they are entirely clear of the spirit of the world about them. This is quite different from the modern idea of joining worldly organizations in order to gain an influence over them, as some preachers claim to do. If men will not hear our message without attempts to become of their spirit, then we ought to separate ourselves from them. Pious Scott says, ''If our message be obstinately rejected, we ought to, in the most decided manner, bear testimony against them and separate ourselves from them.''

He now pronounces a woe on Chorazin and Bethesda, two cities of Galilee, where he had taught and worked miracles, doubtless. He contrasts them with Tyre and Sidon, two heathen cities of the northern country. If Tyre and Sidon had had the light that these cities had, they would have repented. This teaches us several things. (1) No matter how wicked cities or individuals may have been if they repent God will forgive them. (2) It were better never to have been converted if we do not walk up to the light constantly. The greater the light the greater the condemnation if we do not walk up to it. It is a remarkable fact that while the location of Tyre and Sidon can be pointed out today, the site of Chorazin and Bethesda can not be decided. The heathen cities, Tyre and Sidon will have less condemnation in the judgment than these cities. Notice that he shows there will be degrees of punishment in the next world according to the light that the sinner has here. The sin of rejecting God is worse than the sins of fornication, sodomy and adultery, of which Sodom and Gomorrha were guilty.

He also declares that Capernaum had been exalted to heaven. It was at Capernaum that he had healed a great multitude, including Peter's wife's mother; here he had cast out an unclean devil (Chapter 4:38-42); here he had healed the paralytic (Mark 2:1), also the centurion's servant. Truly this city had been exalted to heaven in point of privilege, in comparison with some other cities. ''The name and perhaps the remains of Sodom are still to be found on the shore of the Dead Sea, while that of Capernaum on the Lake of Gennessaret, has been utterly lost.'' (Stanley.)

God was with the seventy as he always is with every true embassador of his truth. The seventy returned with joy saying that even the devils were subject to them. But there is always a danger even in success in preaching the gospel, lest we get puffed up. There are very few ministers but have come under the spell of this temptation. Pride easily creeps into the very best work in the world unless we are on our guard and of all kinds of pride, spiritual pride is the most subtle and dangerous. Satan fell from heaven because of pride. And so Jesus cautions them, saying, ''I beheld Satan as lightning fall from heaven.'' Satan was once a good angel but fell through this subtle sin.

He then declared that he gave them power over all the forces of the devil, which he likens to serpents and scorpions. ''The language here is symbolical: serpents and scorpions signify the poison and sting of sin, with all its dangerous, deadly effects. These results of the fall, are conquered in redemption, being utterly put underfoot, through him who makes us more than conquerors.'' (Rom. 18:37.) (Abbott.) Here he clearly shows the mighty power of the gospel over sin. Too few of professed Christians believe it. He makes the strong statement, ''Nothing shall by any means hurt you.'' This promise was for their encouragement in carrying on the work of God. ''A man is immortal until his work is done.'' ''All things work together for good to them that love God.'' This ought to make us brave in preaching and testifying.

Nevertheless we must not rejoice in these things and give way to spiritual pride. We ought to feel glad that God is willing to use us, but we should not be exultant over it. It ought to make us very humble. We ought to rejoice that our names are written in heaven. Ancient cities kept a book in which were enrolled the names of the citizens. Hence the allusion. God says he keeps a book. It is the Lamb's Book of Life. This shows that these servants of God were saved before Pentecost, although those who wish to dodge the necessity of the second work of grace attempt to deny it. We also notice that great deeds for the Master are not of so much consequence as the fact that we are counted worthy, because of our faith, to have our names written in the book of life in heaven. We may show off in the church and do great thing in the name of religion, but are our names written in heaven? We learn from this again that we may know that our names are written in heaven. It is more than in an inference or an induction from some passage of scripture. We may have divine assurance of the fact.

Again we learn that we ought to rejoice both at the thought of present salvation and future reward.

Personal salvation is of more importance than to have a great name as a soul saver. Lastly we learn that the disciples had the power to work miracles before Pentecost, hence the Pentecostal blessing was not as some suppose, the power to work miracles. They had that before Pentecost. The blessing of Pentecost was heart-purity. (Acts 15:9.)

IT REJOICES OVER THE REVELATION MADE TO THE LOWLY. Vs. 21-24.

21 In that hour Jesus rejoiced in spirit, and said, I thank thee, O Father, Lord of heaven and earth, that thou hast hid these things from the wise and prudent, and hast revealed them unto babes: even so, Father; for so it seemed good in thy sight.

22 All things are delivered to me of my Father: and no man knoweth who the Son is, but the Father; and who the Father is, but the Son, and *he* to whom the Son will reveal *him.*

23 And he turned him unto *his* disciples, and said privately, Blessed *are* the eyes which see the things that ye see:

24 For I tell you, that many prophets and kings have desired to see those things which ye see, and have not seen *them;* and to hear those things which ye hear, and have not heard *them.*

On another occasion when he was rebuking an apostate church, he rejoiced that God had revealed his truth to humble souls. It is worthy of special notice as being the thing that rejoiced Jesus. He was more interested in the humble, child like souls of earth than in worldly ecclesiastics and as he is the same yesterday, to-day and forever we must believe that he still rejoices in the humble, who are so spiritual that God can reveal truth to them. He wept and rejoiced while on earth. He had a human nature like ours. Why does God hide spiritual truth from the worldly wise? Because the worldly wise are not particularly interested in spiritual truth. God never casts his pearls before swine. To all sincere seekers he gives light. This is often forgotten when churches wax rich and worldly. The tendency then is to place book knowledge, human culture and intellectual power above spiritual things, and men are estimated not for their piety and knowledge of spiritual things but for their worldly condition. In fact as churches grow worldly they are apt to discount or deny spiritual revelation. But it is better to be a humble, fully saved child of God than an unsaved doctor of divinity. And the revelations that God gives such humble children are worth more than all the acquirements of the human intellect. We are by no means decrying human knowledge and power but simply trying to show that it is not the chief thing. Spiritual truth is the *real* truth and will shine when the world is on fire. Much of the boasted human philosophy is simply the starting of questions which no one can answer.

He now goes on to say that all things are delivered into his hand. This is the same statement virtually that he makes in Matt. 28:18, "All power is given unto me in heaven and in earth." We ought then to go about our publication of his gospel without fear. He further states that no one can understand the nature of God or is able to fully interpret Him. Only Jesus can understand God. We cannot know God in the sense of understanding Him, and yet if Jesus has revealed himself to us we may know him. We know many things in the natural world that we can not comprehend. Verse 22 seems to explain verse 21 and show that the lowly can know God by personal acquaintance. "God has revealed in his word enough to enlighten, sanctify, save and comfort, but he has not given a line to gratify mere curiosity, or to answer those endless questions which do not minister to our edification." (Cumming.)

Then he turned to his disciples and said, "Blessed are the eyes that see the things that ye see." This must be read in connection with verse 21 where he is rejoicing at the fact that the lowly and humble, see what the grand and lofty do not see. They are of the lowly classes and therefore their eyes and ears are blessed because of what they see and hear. Even kings and prophets of old did not have such a privilege as the humblest in the kingdom of grace. It is not possible for us to realize how highly favored we are in this Holy Ghost dispensation. Those of the Old Dispensation looked forward to this dispensation. Hence this dispensation is a fulfillment of the Old Dispensation.

IT IS PERFECT LOVE TO MAN AS WELL AS GOD.
Vs. 25-37.

25   And, behold, a certain lawyer stood up, and tempted him, saying, Master, what shall I do to inherit eternal life?

26   He said unto him, What is written in the law? how readest thou?

27   And he answering said, Thou shalt love the Lord thy God with all thy heart, and with all thy soul, and with all thy strength, and with all thy mind; and thy neighbour as thyself.

28   And he said unto him, Thou hast answered right: this do, and thou shalt live.

29   But he, willing to justify himself, said unto Jesus, And who is my neighbour?

30   And Jesus answering said, A certain *man* went down from Jerusalem to Jericho, and fell among thieves, which stripped him of his raiment, and wounded *him,* and departed, leaving *him* half dead.

31   And by chance there came down a certain priest that way: and when he saw him, he passed by on the other side.

32   And likewise a Levite, when he was at the place, came and looked on *him,* and passed by on the other side.

33   But a certain Samaritan, as he journeyed, came where he was: and when he saw him, he had compassion on *him,*

34   And went to *him,* and bound up his wounds, pouring in oil and wine, and set him on his own beast, and brought him to an inn, and took care of him.

35   And on the morrow when he departed, he took out two pence, and gave *them* to the host, and said unto him, Take care of him; and whatsoever thou spendest more, when I come again, I will repay thee.

36   Which now of these three, thinkest thou, was a neighbour unto him that fell among the thieves?

37   And he said, He that shewed mercy on him. Then said Jesus unto him, Go, and do thou likewise.

Now we have another character, a lawyer, that is one, who was versed in the laws of Moses and the Jewish Rabbins. He was not unlike the theologians of today in some particulars. Like many theologians of today he seemed to think that his knowledge was sufficient for salvation. We do not say such people think so or so assert it but they have that appearance. He was an illustration of the spiritual blindness of unspiritual people, mentioned in verse 21 while the Samaritan was an illustration of that understanding given to common people.

He attempts to test Jesus with a theological question.   He

asks the same question asked by the young ruler in Chapter 18:18, "What shall I do to inherit eternal life?" This is indeed a great question, and worthy the attention of all mankind. His question indicates his spiritual blindness. He asked, "What shall I do to inherit eternal life?" To inherit, one must be an heir; and to be an heir one must belong to the family. Like all the Jews he claimed to belong to the family of God, because he belonged to the family of Abraham. To be an heir then is not a question of doing but of being. The moralist today makes the same mistake. He thinks he can gain heaven by doing something —by his good works.

Jesus replies and tells him what the qualification is—"Thou shalt love the Lord thy God with all thy heart, and with all thy soul, and with all thy strength, and with all thy mind; and thy neighbor as thyself." Here Jesus states that perfect love or holiness is the necessary qualification for heaven. This lawyer did not deny it; nor was he ignorant of it, as are many so called Christians of today. To love God thus is to have a heart in which all the affections are towards God, with nothing contrary to the love of God; in other words—a clean heart. Wesley says, "That is, thou shalt unite all the faculties of thy soul, to render him the most intelligent and sincere, the most affectionate and resolute service." We may safely rest in this general sense of these important words; if we are not able to fix the peculiar meaning of every single word. If we desire to do this, perhaps the heart, which is a general expression, may be explained by the three following: *with all thy soul*, with the warmest affection; *with all thy strength*, the most vigorous efforts of thy will, and *with all thy mind*, or understanding, in the most wise and・reasonable manner thou canst, thy understanding guiding thy affections. Matthew Henry says, "It must be an entire love; he must have our whole souls, and must be served with all that is in us." Inbred sin can not serve him and hence must be cast out, before we can love God with the whole heart. This candid man acknowledged that we must render to God a holy service.

"This do and live." Here Christ plainly tells this church member that holiness is essential to everlasting life. "Willing to justify himself." All the arguments that people raise against obtaining holiness as a present experience are really offered as their excuse for not seeking it. This man thought by a quibble he could dodge his duty. So he asked, as he thought, an unanswerable question, ''who is my neighbor?'' As much as to say, God has given the command but who knows what he means? It is impossible to do it.

It is like people today who say, no man ever did live a holy life. We reply that, even if no man ever did, nevertheless God requires it.

So he asked, ''Who is my neighbor?'' As a Jew, he loved only Jews, and probably of the Jews he had no special love except for a few congenial acquaintances. He thought that his neighbors were only the people who lived in his *neighborhood.* There are people today who claim to believe the Bible who deny the possibility of loving their neighbors as themselves. But it all depends upon the way we love ourselves. We must love ourselves properly. And we can not do this until God makes our hearts right. If we love Him with perfect love, it will be with a heart free from sin. With such a heart we can love our own selves properly, and then we can love our neighbors in the same way—with pure hearts fervently. Paul sums up the whole matter in Rom. 13:9: ''Love worketh no ill to his neighbor.'' We can not love ourselves properly until we are living for our own highest good. We can so live, as far as consistent with duty, so as to be serviceable to the highest good of our neighbor. Our actions towards men are to be the fruit of perfect love. This may be seen in the teaching of the Sermon on the Mount; first have pure love then our relations to men will be right. Thus we fulfill the spirit of the law which is, ''Be ye therefore perfect, even as your Father which is in heaven is perfect.'' (Matt. 5:48.) Thus Christian perfection is simply perfect love. Godet, the great French commentator says, ''How is such love to be obtained?'' This would have been the question put by the scribe had he been in that state of soul which Paul describes in Rom. 7, and which is the normal preparation for faith. He would have confessed his impotence and repeated the question in a yet deeper sense than at the beginning of the interview. What shall I do? What shall I do in order to love thus?

But instead of this, feeling himself condemned by the holiness of the law which he has formerly expressed he takes advantage of his ignorance, in other words, of the obscurity of the letter of the law, to excuse himself for not having observed it. ''What does the word neighbor mean? How far does its application reach?'' So long as one does not know exactly what this expression signifies, it is quite impossible he means to ''fulfill this commandment.''

So Jesus gives this illustration which like all the illustrations of Jesus is so clear as to leave the man no excuse. Often the best argument can be put into an illustration. Here is a hint to the teacher and preacher, use illustrations as Jesus did. The world is indebted to the quibbling of this lawyer for one of the greatest narratives and illuminations of practical truth. God can make all things work for good. What a wonderful story is this of the good Samaritan.

Jesus uses popular language when he says *by chance.* That is the way it would be regarded by men. But God is watching over all the affairs of life. This Samaritan improved his opportunity as he went along. That is what we should do and we can find our neighbors and find an opportunity to help them every day. Jericho was a city of priests. There were twelve thousand who lived there. It ought to have been a very holy place. The road to Jericho was much infested with robbers. It is today because of the numerous caves along its side which make good hiding places. The priest might have plead that he feared for his own life. It was a serious matter not to help one in distress for the law demanded it. (See Deut. 22:1-4.)

''A Levite.'' As we would say today, a church janitor or sexton. He did more than the priest who passed by on the other side. The Levite went and *looked* at him.

''A certain Samaritan.'' The Jews hated the Samaritans and would have no dealings with them. It was a stiff dose to give this Jewish lawyer when Jesus held up the Samaritan as a model. The priest, Levite and Samaritan are good illustrations of the truths of verse 21. The former were of the class who can not see spiritual truth although religion was their special calling (there are such preachers), while the despised Samaritan saw the spiritual meaning of God's law. Wesley says, "Is it not an emblem of many living characters, perhaps of some who bear the sacred office? O house of Levi and of Aaron, is not the day coming when their virtues of heathen and Samaritans will rise up in the judgment against you?"

This Samaritan had compassion on the poor sufferer. So we see that all he did for him subsequently was because of this compassion which he felt stirring in his heart. Thus we see what it is to love our neighbor as ourselves. It is to have compassion on our neighbors whether we see them afflicted physically or spiritually. And all who need help according to this parable are our neighbors.

Since everybody who needs help is our neighbor, therefore our neighborhood covers the entire world. Opposition and indifference to foreign missions is contrary to perfect love, for perfect love to man is the result of perfect love to God. We can not have the latter without the former. Holy people are therefore imbued with the missionary spirit and zeal to make the whole world partakers of the same blessed salvation.

Some of the commentators have used this story of Jesus in an allegorical sense. It is more than an allegory. It was a real scene. So said Jesus. We do not mean to say that it may not be used symbolically. It can, because it contains great truths. The allegory is this: Human nature on its way from the holy city to the city of the world is attacked by Satan and left half dead. The priesthood and the law pass by and give no help. In this desperate condition the Great Physician heals him. "Only that true Samaritan, beholding, was moved with compassion, as he is all compassion, and poured oil into the wounds, purifying their hearts by faith." (Trench.)

Jesus makes the lawyer give answer to his own question. Notice the lawyer dislikes to pronounce the name "Samaritan" and evades it by saying, "he that showed mercy." This is a fine use of illustrations where the caviller is made to answer his own question and pronounce judgment on himself and his own attitude of heart.

HOLINESS CAN NOT BE SUBSTITUTED BY MERE ACTIVITY. Vs. 38-42.

38 Now it came to pass, as they went, that he entered into a certain village: and a certain woman named Martha received him into her house.

39 And she had a sister called Mary, which also sat at Jesus' feet, and heard his word.

40 But Martha was cumbered about much serving, and came to him, and said, Lord, dost thou not care that my sister hath left me to serve alone? bid her therefore that she help me.

41 And Jesus answered and said unto her, Martha, Martha, thou art careful and troubled about many things:

42 But one thing is needful: and Mary hath chosen that good part, which shall not be taken away from her.

Martha was a Christian troubled with inbred sin. Rev. John Cumming says, ''There can be no doubt, therefore from the testimony of John (John 11:27) that she was a Christian.'' Her conduct proved it. At the time that Jesus was hunted by his enemies she received him into her house; it was a reproach at that time to be known to receive him. We may see here some of the traits of inbred sin in a Christian. (1) It takes the attention away from our Lord as in the case of Martha. She was cumbered. Literally it means *drawn away*. She was drawn away from communion with Jesus in her anxiety to provide for his wants. There are many such souls in the church today. People who want to be good, who substitute churchly activity for communion with God. They work hard to build up the church without having the soul rest they should have and communion with Jesus. They starve their souls while helping to bless other people. It is no credit to the Lord to have his people starved in soul; nor is it necessary. Many substitute church work for holiness. It is a mistake and a detriment both to their own souls and to the cause of God. We can do more good to be intensely spiritual. She gave too much attention to meat and drink instead of the kingdom of God which is ''righteousness, peace and joy in the Holy Ghost.'' Too much time is often spent in preparing food for preachers instead of seeking spiritual food. (2) Display of bad temper. This is seen in her question, ''Dost thou not care that my sister hath left me?'' There is such a thing as showing sinful temper towards the Lord. Some people do it when they complain of other people and try to find excuse for their own short comings. "Lord you allow other people to do so and so, or Lord you allow other people to have things and do not permit me." Cumming says, "This was evidently the language of temper." (3) She was mixed in her experience. She was afraid the feast would not be a success. Some people take great pride in being entertainers. And it would sometimes be difficult to tell which they are most interested in, religion or housework. "A mind divided between concern respecting the inward and outward life is always perturbed, never knowing the perfect peace of the mind that is stayed on God." (Abbott.) It was a case pure and simple of worry which is one of the marks of perfect inbred sin. (4) Fault finding. This is a mark of the carnal mind. Farrar says, "An imperfect soul, seeing what is great and good and true, but very often failing in its attempt to attain, is very apt to be very hard on its judgment of the failings of others. But a divine and sovereign soul—a soul that has attained the more nearly to the stature of a perfect man—takes a calmer and gentler, because a large-hearted view of those weaknesses which it can not but daily see. And so the answer of Jesus, if it were a reproof, was an infinitely gentle and tender one, one which would purify, but would not pain the faithful heart of the busy, loving matron, to whom it was addressed." There is no place wherein entire sanctification is needed more than in the kitchen for there are jars, heat and stews, often started there that do not come from the kitchen range. The fact of it was Martha was consecrated to work and Mary was consecrated to Jesus. There are many today who see in consecration only being set apart for work, when it means more than to do the will of God; it also means to suffer His will.

"Mary hath chosen that good part." We like the word *that*, here used. It refers to a definite experience. There is such a thing as having definite experiences. Character is more than conquest. God cares more for what we are than for what we do. He has put us here to make character for eternity. Barnes says, "The most lovely female is she who has the most of Jesus. The least amiable, she who neglects her soul; who is proud, thoughtless, envious and unlike the meek and lowly Redeemer. At his feet is peace, purity and joy.'' ''To hear, believe and obey the Gospel, and to have him for our 'wisdom, righteousness, sanctification and redemption' comprises all that is necessary for this world and the next; and without this, all the rest will leave us forever miserable.'' The only thing then that is needful is salvation in all its degrees.

CHAPTER XI.

HOLINESS ATTRACTIVE AND REPULSIVE.

The Influence of Holiness Upon Those Who Desire to Be Good. Vs. 1. Prayer for Holiness. Vs. 2-4. Why and How We Should Pray for Holiness. Vs. 5-10. The True Doctrine of Holiness. Vs. 11-13. The Result of Opposing Holiness. Vs. 14-26. An Interruption of the Discourse. Vs. 27-28. The Result of Refusing Light on Holiness. Vs. 29-36. Spurious Holiness Condemned. Vs. 37-54.

THE INFLUENCE OF HOLINESS UPON THOSE WHO DESIRE TO BE GOOD. Vs. 1.

1 And it came to pass, that, as he was praying in a certain place, when he ceased, one of his disciples said unto him, Lord teach us to pray, as John also taught his disciples.

This chapter is an illustration of the effect holiness has upon different classes of people. We are accustomed to think that holiness is attractive. There are those who think that holiness is repulsive. It is repulsive to certain people. While holiness never changes, yet its effects are often different because those who come in contact with it, are different. If all mankind were alike, holiness would have the same effect every time and everywhere. The old illustration is very fitting here. The same sun that melts the wax hardens the clay. The same sun that helps ripen the fruit helps rot it after it is ripe, if exposed to it. So here we see Jesus, who was holiness incarnate, so attractive, that when his disciples saw him praying they were moved to learn how to pray. They wanted to do as he did and be as he was. On the other hand, the same absolutely holy Being was accused by his enemies of working in league with Satan. We must remember that no matter how sincere our motives or righteous our deeds we shall be misrepresented, especially if we have in any degree the holiness of Jesus. People say sometimes, they would as soon have the devil around as holiness and holy work. We do not doubt it. Simply because they do not like holiness. But it is no sign because holiness is an offense to certain people, that it is not of God. Usually it is a sign when certain people do not iike it, that it is of God.

This shows the power of holy character upon those, who desire to be good. We all have a threefold influence. (1) *The influence of our words.* Words spoken are but sounding breath modulated and modified by the vocal organs. But there is a mightier influence that attends these feeble expulsions of the breath, than the most destructive tornadoes that ever devastated the face of the earth. The fate of nations and the history of the world has been affected by spoken words. When God ordained that his Gospel should be carried on by words, he set in motion great powers for good. He might have written his truth on the sky, but he saw fit to have it committed to preaching. All of us have a mighty influence in our words. (2) *Our acts.* They are mighty. They will help or hinder the best words that have ever been spoken. We can emphasize or neutralize our words according to the quality of our actions. Men are creatures of imitation. What one man sees another do, he wants to do also. This is the rule. Children learn first by imitation. It was said by Jesus of the Pharisees, ''they say and do not.'' (3) The influence of ourselves. This is our real influence. We may speak most correctly, and live as perfect as possible, and yet if the influence of ourselves is against our words and acts, they will be neutralized. This influence is the subtle silent force that pervades all our doing and talking. It is the hidden man of the heart projecting himself upon people. It is the spirit that we manifest when we bear our trials. It is the manner in which we do the little things of life, when we are not on our guard. It is ''The man behind the gun,'' as they said in the Spanish war. It is the man behind the sermon that is the great factor in preaching. It is impossible to be among men without their estimating what the man is back of all our talking and doing. Men will know of what spirit we are. We can not deceive them as to that. Sooner or later like perfume it will betray itself.

How important then that we be holy first of all, and then ourselves will confirm and strengthen the influence of our words and actions.

And so as Jesus was praying, there was such a heavenly atmosphere that pervaded his act that the disciples desired to learn to pray also. Happy is the man who is so good and holy in his religious exercise, that he incites a hunger in other people to be like him, because of his holiness. So Jesus taught his disciples to pray. He never taught them to preach, because if a man is called to preach by God, and is faithful in prayer he can preach with success. The trouble with many preachers is that they do little praying. The greatest business God ever called a preacher to engage in, is not preaching but praying.

PRAYER FOR HOLINESS. Vs. 2-4.

2 And he said unto them, When ye pray, say, Our Father which art in heaven. Hallowed be thy name. Thy kingdom come. Thy will be done, as in heaven, so in earth.

3 Give us day by day our daily bread.

4 And forgive us our sins; for we also forgive every one that is indebted to us. And lead us not into temptation; but deliver us from evil.

We have here the best known prayer in the world. Usually called the Lord's Prayer, although he gave it to his disciples to use for their own devotions. Some one has said therefore it ought to be called the Disciples' Prayer. He does not mean that we are always to use these set words when we pray. It is a model of the various subjects that we may pray for and the relative importance of them. It is rather an explanation of the way we should pray. All things that a Christian can desire in prayer are here included. This is not exactly the same form as the prayer used or given in Matt. 6. This is to show us that we are not to be necessarily confined to the same set form of words. It is the ideas and principles that should dominate us when we pray. It is possible to pray without a prayer book or set forms of prayer. And yet they can be made useful.

''Our Father.'' The first word, OUR shows the unity of God's children. The second shows the universal fatherhood of God.

Notice, this prayer was not given to the world but to the disciples. The Universalist has much to say about the divine fatherhood of all men. But the scriptures say that the fatherhood of God applies only to those who are *born*, not of natural, but by supernatural birth (John 1:12). Adam was created a son of God, but died on the day that he ate the forbidden fruit. He died spiritually, that is, he lost the divine image.

Chrysostom says of this prayer, "He who says, 'Our Father' sums up in this word, forgiveness of sins, justification, sanctification, redemption, adoption, inheritance, brotherly fellowship with the only begotten Son, and the gifts of the Holy Ghost in their fullness." The Fatherhood of God towards his saints and their fellowship with each other are all contained in these words.

"Which art in heaven," God is everywhere, and yet there is a place of his abode, the place of his especial majesty, His capital city. "This then instructs us to come before God with deep humility and adoring reverence of his majesty and condescension; with abstraction of mind from external objects and carnal imaginations; with spiritual desires and large expectations, and aspiring to the purity and felicity of his heavenly worshippers." (Scott.)

"Hallowed be thy name." Or may thy name be hallowed or made holy. This is the literal translation. This is a prayer for holiness—that holiness may spread everywhere. The rest of this prayer is but the expansion of this petition.

We now notice the two steps necessary to fulfill this prayer in our own experience. The next two sentences contain the two degrees of grace whereby we obtain full salvation or complete holiness. Notice them.

(1) "Thy kingdom come." A kingdom is that portion of territory and the people included in it who obey the laws and are subjects of that king and kingdom. To have the kingdom come to us and be set up in our hearts, we must surrender and become loyal subjects. So the sinner surrenders—quits his rebellion and becomes a loyal subject. This is the experience of regeneration and justification which is called Conversion. This is the first step in having his name hallowed in us. The kingdom having begun in us, then our prayer will be that it may be set up in the hearts of all mankind. Surely we can not pray consistently to have it

set up in the hearts of others until it has been set up in our own hearts as Jesus said, ''The kingdom of heaven is within you.''

''Thy will be done in earth as it is in heaven.'' This indicates the state of experience which is the second work of grace or entire holiness. The holiness of the first degree whereby the kingdom comes into us is completed when this prayer (Thy will be done in earth as it is in heaven) is fulfilled. What is the will of God? Paul says, ''This is the will of God, your sanctification.'' Albert Barnes says, ''The will of God is that men should obey his law and be holy.'' Cumming says, ''Thy will be done on earth which is our sanctification.'' Adam Clarke says, ''This petition certainly points out a deliverance from all sin: for nothing that is unholy can consist with the divine will, and if this be fulfilled in man, surely sin shall be banished from his soul. This is further evident from these words, AS IN HEAVEN—i. e., as the angels do it: that is with all zeal, diligence, delight and perseverance. Does not the petition plainly imply that we may live without sinning against God?

Surely the holy angels never mingled iniquity with their loving obedience; and as our Lord teaches us to pray that we do his will here as they do it in heaven, can it be thought that he would put a petition in our mouths, the fulfillment of which is impossible? This certainly destroys the assertion *''There is no such state of purification to be attained here, in which the soul is redeemed from sinful passions and desires;* for it is *on earth* that we are commanded that his will, which is our sanctification, may be done.''* (Clarke.)

This ends the first part of the prayer which is for the spread of holiness in our own hearts and the hearts of all mankind. The second part of the prayer is for our personal needs. Notice: we are to pray for holiness first, and then for our personal needs. We are to do all we can to answer all these petitions.

''Give us day by day our daily bread.'' While it is true that we can most properly pray for spiritual food, yet the bread particularly meant here is literal bread that nourishes the body. Thus we are taught that we may pray for other things besides spiritual needs—our food, business, raiment, shelter, etc. The Lord shows here that he is interested in everything pertaining to our needs of every kind. The marginal reading translates ''day by day'' by the phrase ''*for the day.*'' We like this rendering. We are to pray only for the needs of a day at a time and not for a whole life time. We need to daily acknowledge our dependence upon God. Notice, it is our bread. That bread which we have fairly earned and made our own—not bread of idleness. We can not expect God to bless laziness. But we can ask Him to bless our daily toil and not allow anything or any one to defraud us of what we have earned. After we have plowed and sowed we need to ask God to give us the right conditions of weather in order to succeed. These are the conditions under which we have a right to pray for ''the meat that perisheth.'' Matthew Henry says, ''If our chief desire and care be that God's name be sanctified, his kingdom come and his will be done, we may then come boldly to the throne of grace for our daily bread, which will then be sanctified to us when we are sanctified to God, and God is sanctified by us.'' How few people apparently pray for their daily bread in this spirit.

''Forgive us our sins.'' In Matthew it is *debts* instead of *sins*. In the Church of England prayer book it is ''forgive us our trespasses.'' And many of the liturgies have followed the form of the prayer book. The word *debts* means more than *tresspasses*. The latter means only positive breaches of the law. The former means sins of commission and omission—all that is due. Even when we do not violate intentionally the will of God, we must ever regret one inability to come up to the absolute standard of right and wrong because of our feeble intellect and judgment. And whenever we see that we have even unintentionally done a wrong, or made a mistake we feel like making an acknowledgement just as we ask pardon of a dear friend whom we have unintentionally wounded. To whom we say, ''Forgive me, I did not intend to injure you.'' These people who say ''the holiness people think they have got beyond saying the Lord's prayer'' are either grievously mistaken or willfully misrepresent. But after all the chief point of the petition is, *our asking God to treat us as we treat other people.* What a prayer this is—asking God to forgive us as we forgive other people. This is an awful prayer for some people to make. In uttering it, they really ask God to damn them. It is bad enough to be among the damned, but it is awful to ask God to do it. The prayer here then is, ''Forgive us our sins because we forgive.'' If we do not forgive them it is useless to ask forgiveness. Godet says, ''He therefore passes naturally from sins to be forgiven to sins to be avoided. For he thoroughly apprehends that sanctification is the superstructure to be raised on the foundation of pardon.''

''Lead us not into temptation.'' The Greek word here translated *temptation,* means literally, *trial, testing, affliction* and is so translated in various passages of the New Testament. The common interpretation is solicitation to evil. But that meaning is too narrow and is not the idea here. God never leads us into temptation to do evil. St. James says ''God can not be tempted with evil, *neither tempteth he any man.''* So when we read that God tempted Abraham (Gen. 22:7) we are to understand it, that God *tested* Abraham. There are trials and afflictions ahead of us all. Some God permits, others he inflicts, for wise purposes, usually for the development of character. We are to pray this prayer like all our praying in submission to the divine will, ''Lead us not into testing'' if it can be possible to take us to heaven some other way. God help us to so live that testing will not be necessary, for do we not have enough of trial naturally which God does not send?

''Deliver us from evil.'' The Revised Version omits this clause. It is however found in Matt. 6:13. This is a prayer for holiness. Some have translated it, ''deliver us from the evil one.'' But it means more than that. Of what good is it to deliver us from the Evil One, if we must still be in bondage to sin which is the work of the Evil One. Dr. Whedon says, ''The evil here named does not mean simply the Evil One; but all evil, including all sin, and hell, as well as the devil.'' A child of God wants deliverance from all sin and will gladly offer this prayer. But what folly to offer this prayer if we can not have it answered! Godet thus paraphrases it, ''Keep me in the sphere where thy holy will reigns.''

WHY AND HOW WE SHOULD PRAY FOR HOLINESS.
Vs. 5-10.

5 And he said unto them, Which of you shall have a friend, and shall go unto him at midnight, and say unto him, Friend, lend me three loaves;

6 For a friend of mine in his journey is come to me, and I have nothing to set before him?

7 And he from within shall answer and say, Trouble me not: the door is now shut, and my children are with me in bed; I cannot rise and give thee.

8 I say unto you, Though he will not rise and give him, because he is his friend, yet because of his importunity he will rise and give him as many as he needeth.

9 And I say unto you, Ask, and it shall be given you; seek, and ye shall find; knock, and it shall be opened unto you.

10 For every one that asketh receiveth; and he that seeketh findeth; and to him that knocketh it shall be opened.

As we have shown that the central petition of this preceding prayer is for holiness, so now we have a parable showing how to pray, or the spirit with which we should pray for it. He uses an illustration from the every day life of that country. This is a good hint for preachers. Use illustrations from every day life. A man comes to the house of a friend at the unseasonable hour of midnight and asks for three loaves of bread, because he has had company come unexpectedly, who must be fed. We must remember that in Eastern countries people travel a great deal in the night to avoid the heat. This man was out of bread. Here is a lesson for us. We may be out of spiritual food that we ought to give the hungry world about us. We have known such instances. We knew a professed Christian asked by a dying sinner to pray, and she could not do it, because she was not in the habit of praying much. She was out of bread. If we today are out of bread, thank God, we have a friend who has plenty and will give us all the bread we need. So he went to the home of his friend and knocked until he awoke him. The man within the home replied, "Trouble me not. The door is now barred (this is the literal rendering) and my children are with me in bed." That is, his children as well as himself were in bed. To arise and unbar the door was quite an inconvenience when one was sleepy. He felt that it was too much bother, just for three loaves of bread. Here we have the thought of the apparent delay of the answer of our prayers. Augustine says, ''When sometimes God giveth tardily he commends his gifts, he does not deny them; and again, God for a time withholds his gifts, that thou mayest learn to desire great things greatly.'' Human friends are sometimes selfish when it must cost them something to help us. Nevertheless as the friend on the outside of the door is so urgent in his request, he feels that he must arise and give him not merely three loaves but *all that he needs.* The point of the parable is the argument of Jesus that if importunity will overcome human selfishness, much more will it prevail with God who loves us. God loves to have us importunate in asking for that bread and sustenance of spiritual life—holiness of heart, that experience which is wrought by the reception of the gift of the Holy Spirit. The lesson of the parable is in verse 9 ''*Ask* and it shall be given you; seek and ye shall find; *knock* and it shall be opened unto you.'' *Ask, seek,* and *knock* do not express the same idea. This is a climax. To our *asking* we must add *seeking.* If we are asking to be delivered from evil. or to be cleansed from sin (Vs. 4) we must *seek* to know if we are fulfilling the conditions and we must *seek* to find out the proper way of obtaining. But we must do more than *ask* or *seek.* We must *knock.* We must be importunate. This means the intensest urgency. We do not like this dry-eyed lazy way that some have of seeking (?) holiness. They ''take it by faith''—faith of the head rather than of the heart. Let us be dead in earnest when we seek spiritual things—and especially the great blesing—the gift of the Holy Ghost.

THE TRUE DOCTRINE OF HOLINESS. Vs. 11-13.

11 If a son shall ask bread of any of you that is a father, will he give him a stone? or if *he ask* a fish, will he for a fish give him a serpent?

12 Or if he shall ask an egg, will he offer him a scorpion?

13 If ye then, being evil, know how to give good gifts unto your children: how much more shall *your* heavenly Father give the Holy Spirit to them that ask him?

Jesus now uses another illustration to show how anxious God is to give us the Holy Spirit—more anxious than a parent is to give his children food. (Who believes this? Let him then act as if he believed it.) Notice the similarity of the two illustrations. *They are both concerning the obtaining of bread.* Why does he make food so prominent in these two illustrations? Because the real hunger of all God's children is for the gift of the Holy Spirit. This is to the Christian's spiritual nature what bread is to the body.

There are some things that we are not certain are in the good pleasure of God to give us, and when we pray we need to qualify them by saying, "If it be the will of God." But we do not need to say this as regards the gift of the Holy Spirit. He tells us to pray for deliverance from evil (Vs. 4) and he says God is more willing to give the Holy Spirit, who cleanses our hearts from evil, than we are to give food to our children. These disciples did not receive the answer to their prayers until Pentecost, because they did not fulfill the conditions. J. P. Thompson says, "By the virtue of that is lodged in the prayer of faith, whosoever will may approximate himself to God in character. This is the will of God, your sanctification." Jesus tells us here that the gift of the Holy Spirit is to be *asked* for. It is to be made a subject of prayer.

"Will he give him a stone?" This parable teaches us that if we sincerely ask for the Holy Spirit in his cleansing, filling power and God blesses us in so doing, we are not to call it something else or by some indefinite term. We are to be definite. Call it by the same name that we used when we asked for it, *if it was a scriptural* name, just as a son would call bread, *bread* and not a stone, so when we ask definite blessings of the Lord, whether justification or santification, and are blessed in so asking, let us not dodge the terms when we testify to it. He will not give us a stone too hard to eat; nor a serpent to sting us. Some people have queer ideas of the fullness of the blessing of the Holy Spirit. They say, "I fear if I should be filled with the Spirit, I would become fanatical, or do something clownish." Do not be afraid, this blessing is never dangerous nor harmful. It is neither a stone, a serpent or a scorpion. The devil is crying "mad dog," and frightening people over this the sweetest, richest gift within the grasp of the Christian.

Jesus clinches this illustration with an incontrovertible argument in the words of verse 11, "If ye being evil know how to give good gifts unto your children; how much more shall your heavenly Father give the Holy Spirit to them that ask him." *We quote this verse in full as we consider it one of the most important passages in the New Testament.* He says first, "If ye being evil." We think he meant to tell these disciples, who had embraced the gospel preached by John the Baptist (which was regeneration and justification, and in acceptance of which they had been baptized), that their nature was still evil. They had inbred sin and needed to be wholly sanctified. We give some of our reasons for considering this one of the most important passages in the New Testament.

1. This passage connects the Old and New Testaments . We have the great promise of the Old Testament (Is. 44:3; Joel 2: 28) which he called *The Promise of the Father* (Acts 1:4), now promised as an experience.

2. We find the doctrine of the Trinity contained in this verse. Here is Jesus, the second person promising that the Father, the first person should give the Holy Spirit, the third person.

3. This passage shows Jesus as a preacher of holiness. John had been preaching the same doctrine to them. (Matt. 3:11.) It is a fine thing when the succeeding preacher gives the people the doctrine of holiness, just as his predecessor did. People ask why do you preach holiness so much? One reason is because Jesus and John the Baptist set us the example.

4. This passage shows Jesus preaching holiness to young converts. These disciples had already been converted under the ministry of John the Baptist. Some people say the preaching of holiness discourages young converts. Jesus and John did not think so.

5. This passage shows Jesus preaching and urging holiness upon young preachers. It is just what young preachers need.

6. This passage reveals the real doctrine of holiness and exposes many erroneous views. We notice some of them. (a.) It reveals the error of holiness being only power for service. Some one has very pertinently remarked that the third person is called the *Holy* Spirit, not because his nature is more holy than that of the two other persons of the Trinity, but because His special office is to make his people holy. He is the Holy Spirit or Spirit of Holi-

ness. Scott says on this passage, ''The gift of the Holy Spirit is twofold: his immediate inspiration made men prophets, his regenerating and sanctifying influence renders men *saints* or holy persons. No sober man can suppose that every one who prays for the Holy Spirit will be made a prophet, or enabled to work miracles. His renewing, enlightening, sanctifying and comforting power is, no doubt, exclusively intended.'' It is more than power for service—is it cleansing from sin.

(b.) It uncovers the error that we obtain the gift of the Holy Spirit at the time of regeneration. When regenerated we have the work wrought by the Holy Spirit. We find later (John 14:17) that the disciples had come to have and know the Holy Spirit in a sense, but had not yet received him as an abiding indwelling Comforter.

Here Jesus uses an illustration just as earthly parents give food to their children, much more will God give the Holy Spirit to his children. These disciples were already the children of God. Jesus says, ''How much more shall your Heavenly *Father* give the Holy Spirit.'' He taught these *disciples* to pray the prayer ''Our Father.'' He never taught sinners to pray this prayer. Sinners are dead in trespasses and sins. To say sinners are eligible to the gift of the Holy Spirit is to spoil this illustration. It is as much as to say, if earthly parents give good things to other folks' children how much more will your Heavenly Father give the Holy Spirit to the children of the devil, for sinners are of their father, Satan.

(c.) Another error abroad is, that we grow into this cleansing power of the Spirit. This too would spoil the illustration of Jesus. He does not say earthly parents make the giving food to their children a matter of growth. A child can not grow into a gift. A gift is something imparted to him. The growth theory is not only contrary to experience but it is ridiculous. No parent says to a hungry child, ''I will let you grow into your food.'' He gives it to him.

(d.) Again some have said ''we cannot receive this gift until we die.'' But this too would spoil the illustration of Jesus. He does not say that a parent would put off a hungry child and refuse to give him bread until he died. *He gives him the food while he is alive.* And God gives his children the Holy Spirit when they are alive—in this world.

(e.) It is a definite experience. The child asks for something definite—bread, an egg, a fiish—not something general and indefinite. How much indefinite seeking there is in religion. Many people like to be indefinite. They want ''a deeper work of grace,'' ''more religion,'' etc. But Jesus says it is not religion in general but the gift of the Holy Spirit. People go to the altar thus indefinitely and never know what they get if they get blessed or what to call it. God wants us to call things by their right names. Call bread, *bread;* call holiness, *holiness,* and not ''a deeper work of grace'' or ''more religion.''

(f.) We learn too that holiness is to be made a specialty. A hungry child is a specialist on the question of bread and butter, and the longer he is put off, the more of a specialist he is too. So is a child of God a specialist on the subject of holiness. The man who keeps clearly regenerate has an insatiable appetite for holiness. When we seek it as a hungry child does food, we will get it.

(g.) The gift of the Holy Spirit is not the same as the gifts of the Holy Spirit. Some want the latter who do not desire the former. The gifts of the Spirit are the fullness of joy, love, etc. Many wish these who do not want Him, the source of the gifts. They want power more than they desire the indwelling Comforter. Dr. Keen tells of a man who went to California and got rich. He kept sending beautiful presents to his family. They finally wrote and said, ''Father we enjoy your gifts but we want you.'' How many want the gifts of the Spirit, instead of the gift of *Himself.*

(h.) A gift is not a gift until we take it. No one can make us a present against our own will. It is so with the Spirit. We must receive Him.

(i.) The Holy Spirit in his cleansing power is a gift. Hence he can not be bought nor earned by money, toils, prayers, sufferings or tears. He must be received by faith. The late Bishop Edwards once said in prayer, ''Lord, why do I not receive this blessing? Thou hast said 'Ask and receive.' O, I see it. I have been asking but have done no receiving. Lord I receive.'' And he received the blessing at once.

(j.) Notice the wonderful argument that Jesus uses. "How much more shall your Heavenly Father give the Holy Spirit to them that ask Him." How much more. Moody showed the force of the "much more" used five times in Rom. 5. But this "How much more" of Jesus far transcends them all. He deigns to reason with us to convince us by argument because we are so loath naturally to believe in holiness.

(k.) Notice again another truth that is difficult of belief, that God *loves* to give the Holy Spirit to his children. He loves to do it even more than we love to feed our children. Who believes it? Then we do not need to tease God for the gift, but empty our hands of everything and take it.

THE RESULT OF OPPOSING HOLINESS. Vs. 14-26.

14 And he was casting out a devil, and it was dumb. And it came to pass, when the devil was gone out, the dumb spake; and the people wondered.

15 But some of them said, He casteth out devils through Beelzebub the chief of the devils.

16 And others, tempting *him*, sought of him a sign from heaven.

17 But he, knowing their thoughts, said unto them, Every kingdom divided against itself is brought to desolation; and a house *divided* against a house falleth.

18 If Satan also be divided against himself, how shall his kingdom stand? because ye say that I cast out devils through Beelzebub.

19 And if I by Beelzebub cast out devils, by whom do your sons cast *them* out? therefore shall they be your judges.

20 But if I with the finger of God cast out devils, no doubt the kingdom of God is come upon you.

21 When a strong man armed keepeth his palace, his goods are in peace :

22 But when a stronger than he shall come upon him, and overcome him, he taketh from him all his armour wherein he trusted, and divideth his spoils.

23 He that is not with me is against me : and he that gathereth not with me scattereth.

24 When the unclean spirit is gone out of a man, he walketh through dry places, seeking rest; and finding none, he saith, I will return unto my house whence I came out.

25 And when he cometh, he findeth *it* swept and garnished.

26 Then goeth he, and taketh *to him* seven other spirits more wicked than himself; and they enter in, and dwell there : and the last *state* of that man is worse than the first.

A study of Matthew 12:22-32 will show that Jesus charged the Pharisees with committing the unpardonable sin of ascribing the work of the Holy Spirit to the devil. If it was true then it is true now. There are people, who in this day have done this very thing in relation to holiness. They have said ''they had rather have the devil around them that those who profess holiness.'' It is bad enough to oppose holiness, but to ascribe it to the power of the devil is infinitely worse. It is perilous. These Pharisees said it of Jesus, who was absolutely holy. We have no doubt but there have been people who committed the unpardonable sin in opposing the Holiness Movement, which is the work of the Holy Spirit. So when Jesus cast out a devil, the holiness fighters of the day declared that the devil helped him. Just as if devils could cast out devils. Still others after all the light he had given them (the casting out of the devil of itself was sign enough of his divinity) asked for a sign of his divinity. He uses an illustration thus. If the house of Satan is divided against itself it can not stand. *Notice his enemies could not* deny that he had wrought a miracle but they try to destroy the force of it by attributing it to Satanic agency.

He now asks an unanswerable question. Notice his logical method of driving his enemies into a corner by his searching questions. ''And if I by Beelzebub cast out devils, by whom do your sons cast him out?'' There were exorcists among the Jews, who were the disciples (or children of the Pharisees), who claimed to cast out devils. Jesus does not here admit that they really did cast out devils but he shows that on their own principles if their disciples did cast out devils by their own power, they ought not to deny that Jesus could also do it. We do *not* believe these disciples really did cast out devils because in Matt. 9:33 the people said when Jesus cast out devils, ''It was never so seen in Israel.'' But his power over the devils was a proof to them that the Kingdom of God had come. He now gives another parable. He represents Satan as ''a strong man'' who has taken possession of a palace (the human soul) and Christ (a stronger than he) has driven him out. Only divine power can drive the devil out of the soul. He now makes a sharp thrust at the multitude who had been standing by as belonging really to the party of the devil and the Pharisees, because having seen his miracles they refused to side with Him. It is true today. There is no neutral ground. "He that is not with me is against me" is still the declaration of Jesus. It applies in the twentieth century as well as the first. Every man who does not gather the influence of his life for Christ is scattering and wasting his talents and opportunities. There is no neutral, passive ground in this great battle between Christ and his enemies.

He then applies this parable still further to the spiritual condition of the Jewish people. Dean Alford says, "The direct application of this parable is to the Jewish people, and the parallel runs thus: The old demon of idolatry brought down on the Jews the Babylonish captivity; and was cast out by that captivity. They did not, after their return, fall into it again, but rather endured persecution, as under Antiochus Epiphanes. The emptying, sweeping and garnishing may be traced in the growth of Pharisaic hypocrisy and the Rabinnical schools between the Return, and the coming of our Lord. The re-possession by the one and the accession of seven other spirits more malicious than the first, hardly needs explanation. The desperate infatuation of the Jews after our Lord's ascension, their bitter hostility to the church, their miserable end, are known to all."

It shows the cunning of Satan. When a person begins to reform by merely human will power and human strength, Satan will let him alone for a time and even leave him that he may glory in his fancied victory. But such reform is not of God and the Holy Spirit does not come in the heart to dwell. After a while Satan returns and finds the soul empty and re-enters it and takes up his abode, and relapse into evil, when complete, makes the case worse than ever. It paralyzes the will, and God lets that paralysis take place.

AN INTERRUPTION OF THE DISCOURSE. Vs. 27-28.

27 And it came to pass, as he spake these things, a certain woman of the company lifted up her voice, and said unto him, Blessed *is* the womb that bare thee, and the paps which thou hast sucked.

28 But he said, Yea rather, blessed *are* they that hear the word of God, and keep it.

A woman moved by the manifestation of his power and his reply to his enemies here interrupts him by calling his mother blessed in having such a son. It was the exclamation of an honest woman, convinced by the words and work of Jesus. All women as a rule rejoice in having honored sons. This was especially the case with Jewish mothers. . . . And when this woman thus expressed herself concerning Jesus, this Jewish young man of a little more than thirty, she implied in the exclamation that she wished she had such a son. Truly Mary the mother of Jesus was blessed above all women by being the mother of Jesus. She herself said, ''From henceforth all generations shall call me blessed.'' Chap. 1:48. She was blessed or ''happy,'' for that is what the word means. But that is no reason why she should be considered divine or should be worshipped.

''Blessed are they that hear the word of God and do it.'' He destroys all foundations for the worship of Mary. Any woman who hears the word of God and does it, is just as holy as Mary. This word must have been a comfort to the honest woman who made this speech. She could be just as holy and blessed as Mary, and so can we if we obey God, for he gives the Holy Spirit to them that obey him (Acts 5:32), and the gift of the Holy Spirit insures holiness of heart and life. So the Roman Catholic doctrine that Mary was from her birth without sin falls to the ground.

THE RESULT OF REFUSING LIGHT ON HOLINESS.
Vs. 29-36.

29 And when the people were gathered thick together, he began to say, This is an evil generation: they seek a sign; and there shall no sign be given it, but the sign of Jonas the prophet.

30 For as Jonas was a sign unto the Ninevites, so shall also the Son of man be to this generation.

31 The queen of the south shall rise up in the judgment with the men of this generation, and condemn them: for she came from the utmost parts of the earth to hear the wisdom of Solomon; and, behold, a greater than Solomon *is* here.

32 The men of Nineve shall rise up in the judgment with this generation, and shall condemn it: for they repented at the preaching of Jonas; and, behold, a greater man than Jonas *is* here.

33 No man, when he hath lighted a candle, putteth *it* in a secret place, neither under a bushel, but on a candlestick, that they which come in may see the light.

34 The light of the body is the eye: therefore when thine eye is single, thy whole body also is full of light; but when *thine eye* is evil, thy body also *is* full of darkness.

35 Take heed therefore that the light which is in thee be not darkness.

36 If thy whole body therefore *be* full of light, having no part dark, the whole shall be full of light, as when the bright shining of a candle doth give thee light.

Jesus now goes on with his discourse taking up the demand for a sign which his enemies had made (see Vs. 16). He tells them that the only sign that should be given them was the sign of the prophet Jonah. Just as Jonah was a sign to the Ninevites, so should he be to that generation. Jonah in being resurrected from the whale was a sign of the Resurrection of Jesus. Jonah and Jesus were both hid away from the light for three days. The idea is this. The resurrection of Jesus from the grave would prove his deity and the truth of Christianity. These cavillers had but to wait and see if he rose or not. This would be sign enough for them. They had more light than the Ninevites, who repented at the preaching of Jonah.

Likewise the Queen of Sheba who came a long distance to visit Solomon (See 1 Kings 10:1-13) and acknowledged his wisdom would rise up and condemn those people who had a greater than Solomon close to them. Jesus professed here to be greater than Solomon, the wisest man of the whole world. Jesus was all he professed to be, or he was an imposter for he made great claims. Thus we see Jesus believed the much ridiculed narrative of Jonah. Some even in evangelical churches today, say the story of Jonah was an allegory. If so then the resurrection of Jesus was an allegory for Jesus said, "As Jonah was three days and nights in the whale's belly, so shall the Son of Man be—in the heart of the earth." Rejecting the Old Testament miracles is only a step towards rejecting the New Testament miracles.

He gives a parable of a man lighting a candle. The purpose of lighting a candle is for people, who have eyesight to perceive objects. God has given light sufficient for those who desire to know the truth. The affections are to the soul what the eye is to the body. Purity and seeing go together. "If thine eye be single." The Greek word here translated "single" means simplicity, or singleness that is free from any compound or mixtures. It means that the affections and intentions are pure— not mixed with any sinfulness. It means an entirely sanctified heart. If we have that experience we will be in the light and the light will flood our whole being.

The warning he then throws out to these holiness fighters is "Take heed therefore that the light that is in thee be not darkness." A diseased eye can keep us in darkness and a bad heart can do the same to our moral nature. Men whose souls have been darkened by sinful affections become darkened in their minds. No wonder prejudiced minds can not see holiness in the Bible, for prejudiced minds could not see Jesus himself. How many by fighting holiness have gone into darkness. The Pharisees could not see the sign already given or they would not have asked for another sign. They had made themselves blind, by resisting truth. Godet says, "Jesus means that from the inward part of a perfectly sanctified man there rays forth a splendor which glorifies the external man, as when he is shone upon without. It is a glory as the result of holiness."

SPURIOUS HOLINESS CONDEMNED. Vs. 37-54.

37 And as he spake, a certain Pharisee besought him to dine with him: and he went in, and sat down to meat.

38 And when the Pharisee saw it, he marvelled that he had not first washed before dinner.

39 And the Lord said unto him, Now do ye Pharisees make clean the outside of the cup and the platter; but your inward part is full of ravening and wickedness.

40 Ye fools, did not he that made that which is without make that which is within also?

41 But rather give alms of such things as ye have; and, behold, all things are clean unto you.

42 But woe unto you, Pharisees! for ye tithe mint and rue and all manner of herbs, and pass over judgment and the love of God: these ought ye to have done, and not to leave the other undone.

43 Woe unto you, Pharisees! for ye love the uppermost seats in the synagogues, and greetings in the markets.

44 Woe unto you, scribes and Pharisees, hypocrites! for ye are as graves which appear not, and the men that walk over them are not aware of them.

45   Then answered one of the lawyers, and said unto him, Master, thus saying thou reproachest us also.

46   And he said, Woe unto you also, *ye* lawyers ! for ye lade men with burdens grievous to be borne, and ye yourselves touch not the burdens with one of your fingers.

47   Woe unto you ! for ye build the sepulchres of the prophets, and your fathers killed them.

48   Truly ye bear witness that ye allow the deeds of your fathers : for they indeed killed them, and ye build their sepulchres.

49   Therefore also said the wisdom of God, I will send them prophets and apostles, and *some* of them they shall slay and persecute :

50   That the blood of all the prophets, which was shed from the foundation of the world, may be required of this generation ;

51   From the blood of Abel unto the blood of Zacharias, which perished between the altar and the temple : verily I say unto you, It shall be required of this generation.

52   Woe unto you, lawyers ! for ye have taken away the key of knowledge : ye entered not in yourselves, and them that were entering in ye hindered

53   And as he said these things unto them, the scribes and the Pharisees began to urge *him* vehemently, and to provoke him to speak of many things :

54   Laying wait for him, and seeking to catch something out of his mouth, that they might accuse him.

We now come to an incident which Jesus used to show the difference between mere outward holiness and inward holiness. Jesus was invited to dine at the house of a Pharisee and as he looked upon the scrupulously clean dishes upon the table he saw an opportunity to illustrate spiritual truth. He told them they lived outwardly clean, like their cups and platters. But they neglected the inner life. They were like legalists of today, much concerned about outward holiness and neglectful of inward holiness. They put their religion on the outside and made it consist in *doing*. Like people today who act as if they had no inward nature. The fact of it is while true holiness is seen on the outside, the biggest part of it is on the inside where the human eye can not see it. Pharisees in all ages have been unable to appreciate or comprehend inward holiness. So they are always looking after only the outside—going to church, saying prayers, fasting, tithing, "all manner of herbs," washing and baptizing and attending to everything except the most important thing—the heart. "But rather give alms of such things as ye have." The Revised

Version gives the true meaning thus, ''But rather give alms of those things which are within.'' Abbott says, ''Christ says not *give alms,*—the outward gift, but give *compassion*—the inward feeling; he says not *of such things as ye have,* but those things which are *within;* thus he does not make mere alms giving an atonement and reparation for sin, but he declares that works of mercy out of a sincere heart are a condition of true spiritual cleansing.'' We would have liked Abbott here better if he had said ''A proof of true spiritual cleansing.'' ''All things are unto you.'' When the heart is clean all the outside life will be clean. ''To the pure all things are pure.'' A profession of holiness, no matter how exemplarily we may live is nothing more than the washing of the Pharisees, if we are devoid of inward sanctifying grace. Crosby says, ''The pure heart will need no outer rule (Gal. 5:23).''

He then gives three characteristics of this spurious holiness: (1) an exceedingly scrupulous observance of the minutest things (Vs. 42) and neglect of the love of God in the heart. (2) Self-seeking (Vs. 43). The really holy man is humble and seeks nothing for his own glory. (3) Hypocrisy (Vs. 44). Seemingly so fair, they are really like graves. Men walk over them and they seem so fair and pure. But really they are full of uncleanness. Any one who is not on the inside what they appear to be is a hypocrite.

Jesus preached in such a way that people knew what he meant. The lawyers or Scribes—those who interpreted the Mosaic law and the traditions of the elders—took offense and one of them acknowledged that the sermon had hit them also, saying ''thou reproachest us also.'' He is a gospel preacher who like Christ can make men feel that the truth applies to them. We do not believe a man is a gospel preacher who does not make people see their condition, or who does not probe their consciences. The reason men cry out against the truth is because it reproaches them.

He then more specifically accuses them of lading men with heavy burdens, and not doing a thing to help them bear them. These heavy burdens were requiring the people to keep the traditions of the elders. There is a great deal of burdensome religion in the world. All religions that do not bring soul rest are burdensome. How much there is of it in the world today! Jesus said his yoke is easy and his burden light. How little false religionists seem to care about the people.

He then utters the great truth—ever true in all generations—that each generation builds monuments to the prophets that their fathers killed and at the same time kills its own prophets. In building the monuments to those persecuted in the past, it condemns its fathers and itself too.

Who today are being persecuted with the same vindictive spirit of past ages? Those who seek to be holy. Dead ecclesiasticism was the bitterest foe of the Apostles, the Reformers, the Puritans, the Quakers, the early Methodists and the Holiness People of today.

By "the wisdom of God" in verse 49 he means himself. (See Matt. 23:34.)

He represents the blood of the martyrs, by a figure of speech, as flowing down upon the Jewish nation in a mighty flood, for by treating their own saints as they did, they had ratified all the guilt of the martyrdom of the past, and were essentially guilty of it, by really showing the same spirit to their prophets that their fathers had shown to theirs. Zacharias was slain in the temple (2 Chron. 24:20-22). It was one of the foulest murders in the estimation of the Jews that ever took place and they were accustomed to say that the blood was never cleansed away until the temple was burned. He said that all these things should come upon this generation. He meant that all these crimes were treasured up by divine justice and the punishment would come upon this generation. God punishes nations in this world; individuals in both worlds.

He then accuses the lawyers of taking away the key of knowledge. This is a metaphor referring to the custom of initiating or inaugurating the doctors of the law into their office of interpreters of the law. They were solemnly admitted by being presented with a key and a table book. So we understand that by key is meant the interpretation and understanding of the Scriptures. By taking away the key of knowledge is meant not only that "they arrogated to themselves the true understanding of the

Scriptures but that they had conveyed away the key of knowledge, neither using it themselves, nor suffering others to use it.''

And now his enemies are malignant and determined upon his reprovers of sin must expect to have many enemies.'' Now Jesus destruction. They attack him with all sorts of questions, hoping to confuse him and make him say something that they can twist and use against him. Matthew Henry says ''Faithful who had shown great tenderness to the penitent and compassion on the weary-hearted multitudes shows a new phase of character firmness, courage and outspoken boldness—against the inconsistency and wickedness of the Pharisees.

CHAPTER XII.

HOLINESS MILITANT.

Holiness Antagonizes False Doctrine. Vs. 1-12. Holiness Antagonizes Covetousness. Vs. 13-21. It Condemns Worry. Vs. 22-34. It Is a State of Readiness to Meet the Lord. Vs. 35-48. Holiness Is the Occasion of Division. Vs. 49-53. It Is Stern in Its Rebuke of Sin. Vs. 54-59.

HOLINESS ANTAGONIZES FALSE DOCTRINE. Vs. 1-12.

1 In the mean time, when there were gathered together an innumerable multitude of people, insomuch that they trode one upon another, he began to say unto his disciples first of all, Beware ye of the leaven of the Pharisees, which is hypocrisy.

2 For there is nothing covered, that shall not be revealed; neither hid, that shall not be known.

3 Therefore whatsoever ye have spoken in darkness shall be heard in the light; and that which ye have spoken in the ear in closets shall be proclaimed upon the housetops.

4 · And I say unto you my friends, Be not afraid of them that kill the body, and after that have no more that they can do.

5 But I will forewarn you whom ye shall fear: Fear him, which after he hath killed hath power to cast into hell; yea, I say unto you, Fear him.

6 Are not five sparrows sold for two farthings, and not one of them is forgotten before God?

7 But even the very hairs of your head are all numbered. Fear not therefore: ye are of more value than many sparrows.

8 Also I say unto you, Whosoever shall confess me before men, him shall the Son of man also confess before the angels of God:

9 But he that denieth me before men shall be denied before the angels of God.

10 And whosoever shall speak a word against the Son of man, it shall be forgiven him: but unto him that blasphemeth against the Holy Ghost it shall not be forgiven.

11 And when they bring you unto the synagogues, and *unto*

magistrates, and powers, take ye no thought how or what thing ye shall answer, or what ye shall say :

12 For the Holy Ghost shall teach you in the same hour what ye ought to say.

It is considered pugnacious to attack false doctrine. It is called sour holiness by some if we expose error. So there has arisen a wishy washy sentiment supposed to be a mark of holiness. But holiness is as far removed from and as antagonistic to sin as light is to darkness. One of the principal marks of true holiness is intense antagonism to sin. Holiness is the foe of all crookedness whether in life, practice or doctrine. Hence Jesus and the disciples always attacked the doctrinal errors in their neighborhood. He here warns his disciples against the hypocrisy or leaven of the Pharisees. He had shown in the previous chapter that their hypocrisy consisted in pretended holiness on the outside, when the inside was corrupt. He said this right before a great multitude who had been drawn together by the casting out of the evil spirit. (See Chapter 11:14.) Dean Alford thus shows the connection of verses 1-12. ''The connection may be thus concluded: Beware of hypocrisy (verse 1) for all shall be made evident in the end (verse 2), and ye are witnesses and sharers in this unfolding of the truth (verse 3). In this work ye need not fear men; for your Father has you in his keeping (verses 4-7). And the confession of my name is a glorious thing (verse 8), but the rejection of it (verse 9) and especially the ascription of my works to the evil one (verse 10) is a fearful thing. And in this confession ye shall be helped in the hour of need (verses 11-12).

The Holy Ghost is ''the conservator of orthodoxy'' for the Holy Spirit in the heart kills out the Old Man; and one of the workings of the Old Man is heresies. (Gal. 5:20.) Holy people are not found in the ranks of the agnostics or the semi-infidel higher critics. The old fashioned Bible and its old fashioned doctrines are good enough for them. The religion of the outside only, is false doctrine, and that is all many are preaching today as did the Pharisees.

He told his disciples not to fear men. The man fearing spirit is a trait of the carnal mind. Jesus with all his gentleness and love was the most searching preacher of hell fire that the world has ever known. His denunciation of sin and portrayal of its punishment did not compromise his gentleness and love in the least. There is a hell according to Jesus for those, who fear man so much as not to fear God. The fear of man will drive out the fear of God, and the fear of God will drive out the fear of man. The fear of hell tends to drive us to fear God. In other words there is a hell for those, who fear man more than God.

If we truly fear God he will take care of us. We need not fear what men can do against us. For God watches over the insignificant birds—the sparrows and will he not take care of us? If we are delivered from the carnal mind, we shall be delivered from worry and anxiety. Our God who is the ruler and maker of the Universe is mighty enough to look after sparrows, number the hairs of the billions of heads in the earth and take care of us all. He loves us. Pious Quesnel says, ''The providence of God is the comfort of the righteous. His wisdom can not be surprised, his power can not be forced, his love can not forget. He alone knows our value, because he alone knows how much he loves us, and because he is himself the price of our love.''

Why then should we fear to confess him? He promises to confess us before his Father and the Holy angels. And if we deny him before men he will deny us before his Father and the Holy angels. *The confession and denial will be just as real there as here.*

He seems to refer back to the charge made against him in Chapter 11:15 that he performed his miracles by the help of Satan (see our exposition of Luke 11:14-26). To blaspheme means to slander. They had slandered the Holy Spirit, and so do those today who attribute his work to Satanic power.

Such fearless people should have help in the hour of need. If they feared God and confessed him before men, when brought before magistrates they were not to fear, for God would help them and tell them what to say in their own defense. They did not need to prepare their defense beforehand. It is singular that some have interpreted this to mean that preachers do not need to prepare beforehand to preach the Gospel. It has no reference to that at all.

HOLINESS ANTAGONIZES COVETOUSNESS. Vs. 13-21.

13 And one of the company said unto him, Master, speak to my brother, that he divide the inheritance with me.

14 And he said unto him, Man, who made me a judge or a divider over you?

15 And he said unto them, Take heed, and beware of covetousness: for a man's life consisteth not in the abundance of the things which he possesseth.

16 And he spake a parable unto them, saying, The ground of a certain rich man brought forth plentifully:

17 And he thought within himself, saying, What shall I do, because I have no room where to bestow my fruits?

18 And he said, This will I do: I will pull down my barns, and build greater; and there will I bestow all my fruits and my goods.

19 And I will say to my soul, Soul, thou hast much goods laid up for many years; take thine ease, eat, drink, *and* be merry.

20 But God said unto him, *Thou* fool, this night thy soul shall be required of thee: then whose shall those things be, which thou hast provided?

21 So *is* he that layeth up treasure for himself, and is not rich toward God.

There is no sin so often rebuked in the Bible as covetousness. And there is perhaps less preaching about it, than upon any other sin. It is the most insidious of all sin. It creeps upon good people stealthily like a savage upon his foe. It inoculates the soul like a secret deadly poison. God says a covetous person is an idolater (Eph. 5:5) and also that he abhors him. (Psalms 10:3.) Covetousness works its way into even the highest places in the church. It ruined Judas. It was the destruction of Ananias and Sapphira. It thrusts its hideous presence into the most solemn surroundings. Happy is he who has been delivered from this leprosy. At this most solemn time when Jesus was in the heat of his controversy against the Pharisees and had been discoursing on the awful sin of blasphemy against the Holy Ghost, a bystander recognizing the justice of his attack upon the hypocrisy of the Pharisees, thought it would be a fine thing to turn matters to his own profit. So he selfishly asked Jesus at this solemn moment to speak to his brother and request him to "divide the inheritance with him." It seems the other brother had all the patrimonial estate which he had refused to divide. All this man wanted to do with Jesus was to use him for his own financial interests. There are many today who use religion as a stepping stone to their selfish gain. ''It was covetousness that caused the unjust brother to withhold; it was covetousness which made the defrauded brother indignantly complain to a stranger.'' (Robertson.) What a sad thing it is when people use the sun to put out their eyes. And what a sad thing when people use religion that was intended to kill covetousness, just to increase their covetousness. Jesus rebuked him just as he did the Pharisees asking him indignantly ''who made me a judge.'' As good an office as it might be, Jesus had a higher mission than to be a judge. A hint to the ministry—to stick to their calling.

So Jesus to his solemn warning adds the parable of the rich fool. Let us notice why Jesus calls this rich farmer a fool. Covetousness contradicts Providence. Such a man acts as if money and crops were of more consequence than Almighty God. He acts as if he were to live forever. He really cheats himself, by robbing himself of a home in heaven. He thinks that happiness comes from what a man has instead of what he is. He does not understand that man's life is not in his goods; that it amounts to nothing except it be in God. This fool forgot too that all he possessed came by the permission of God, so he said *my* barns, *my* goods, *my* fruits. He did not realize that by giving him weather, soil and health God had really allowed him to be only his steward. He was a fool too because he forgot that he must die and leave all these goods. He robbed himself of God. This is the experience of a worldling. Let us remember that the man that the world calls prudent and wise is a fool in the sight of God. It is not intimated that he had unjustly acquired these goods. So a man may be honest in the sight of men and dishonest in robbing God. A holy heart is free from covetousness. And the holy Jesus attacked this sin. Scott says, ''Yet after all that the Lord hath said on the subject how few are those among professed Christians, who do not desire to be rich, and to make their children rich. And many are apt to point out to them similar characters with this in the parable for their imitation, and as proper persons for imitation, and as proper persons with whom to form connections.'' (Scott.) The question that God asks him shows he was a fool. Hear it ye who are hoarding up money! "Thou fool—then, whose shall these things be which thou hast provided?" It is folly to lay up money for some one else to squander after we are gone. Many a fool denies himself to hoard up money thereby shrivelling up his own soul and furnishing means for the riotous living of those who come after him, while the cause of God goes limping and halting for lack of means to carry it on.

Is it wicked to be rich? No. Abraham and Job were rich and true to God. It is not wrong to have money but it is wrong to love it. Rich men can help the cause of God as poor men can not, if they will. But for Joseph of Arimathea the precious body of Jesus would have been buried in the potter's field. (See our exposition of Matthew 6:24-34.)

IT CONDEMNS WORRY. Vs. 22-34.

22   And he said unto his disciples, Therefore I say unto you, Take no thought for your life, what ye shall eat; neither for the body, what ye shall put on.

23   The life is more than meat, and the body is *more* than raiment.

24   Consider the ravens: for they neither sow nor reap; which neither have storehouse nor barn; and God feedeth them: how much more are ye better than the fowls?

25   And which of you with taking thought can add to his stature one cubit?

26   If ye then be not able to do that thing which is least, why take ye thought for the rest?

27   Consider the lilies how they grow: they toil not, they spin not; and yet I say unto you, that Solomon in all his glory was not arrayed like one of these.

28   If then God so clothe the grass, which is to day in the field, and to morrow is cast into the oven; how much more *will he clothe* you, O ye of little faith?

29   And seek not ye what ye shall eat, or what ye shall drink, neither be ye of doubtful mind.

30   For all these things do the nations of the world seek after and your Father knoweth that ye have need of these things.

31   But rather seek ye the kingdom of God; and all these things shall be added unto you.

32   Fear not, little flock; for it is your Father's good pleasure to give you the kingdom.

33   Sell that ye have, and give alms; provide yourselves bags which wax not old, a treasure in the heavens that faileth not, where no thief approacheth, neither moth corrupteth.

34   For where your treasure is, there will your heart be also.

Having spoken this parable to condemn the covetousness of this self-seeking man, Jesus turns to his disciples with an exhortation against worry about daily needs.   He had just told them that God looked after the insignificant sparrows and numbered the hairs of the head of his children, and now he says "therefore" there is no need of worry over daily needs.   He who worries doubts Providence.   Worry is one of the traits of the carnal mind.   An entirely sanctified heart is one out of which unbelief has been cleansed.   And as he trusts God implicitly such a man is free from anxious forebodings of the future.   So Jesus says "Take no thought for your life."   The old English word thought often meant anxiety.   We do not now so use it.   The Revised Version gives the true meaning thus: *"Be not anxious about your life."*   This is the meaning of the word *thought* in verses 25-26 also.   This command of Jesus is equivalent therefore to a command to obtain the blessing of a pure heart.   He does not mean that we are not to have a wise forethought for the things necessary for our existence.   The farmer with his crop, and the merchant with his investments, have to look ahead.   But we are not to worry.

"Consider the ravens."   If God takes care of the birds who can not plow or sow or raise their own food, will he not take care of his children?   He does not mean that we are not to sow or reap or work, but we are not to worry, when true to God about our daily food and raiment any more than the birds do.   Another reason why we are not to worry is it does no good.

"Which of you by being anxious can add to his stature, one cubit."   Worry will not enable a person to grow one thousandth of an inch.   And if it will not increase the height of the body, it certainly will not feed and clothe it.   Some one says there are two things about which we ought not to worry—those things we can not help and those things we can help.   Worry does no good and it often does harm.

The Greek word rendered here *stature* is rendered *age* in John 9:21.   Consequently some commentators have thought that he meant here "Which of you by being anxious can add to the length of your life."   It means all the same thing.   Worry will add neither to the length of the body nor the life. No one will live any longer by worry and usually not so long.

"Consider the lilies." Jesus often went to nature for his illustrations—a hint to the teacher and preacher. Nature and grace are two kingdoms ruled by the same God. His workings in nature are fine illustrations of his workings in grace.

"Solomon in all his glory was not arrayed like one of these." Solomon reigned in more glory than any other of the Jewish kings. His reign was looked upon by the Jews as the most splendid of all history. They believe today that its magnificence has never been equalled on earth.

Yet Jesus says all this glory is surpassed by the perishing lilies of the field. Take the most splendid human fabric whether of gold, silver or cloth and put it under the microscope and it will appear coarse and imperfect. But put any of the smallest and most delicate flowers that God has made under the glass and it will be found to be perfect. Abbott thinks in this illustration he is rebuking those who fret because they can not dress and make as much display as their neighbors. "Our worry and anxiety are for the most part, not for food and clothing that are necessary, for our life and usefulness, but for the means to equal and surpass our neighbors in display; and yet with all our strivng the wild flowers of the field surpass us." If we were as splendidly arrayed as Solomon at his best, the flowers are more so, *and God takes care of them.* The grass that God takes so much care of is cast into the oven for fuel, or withers away. God who takes cares to make the flowers so beautiful will take care of his children.

"O ye of little faith!" There is nothing in the record of the life of Jesus that so excited his censure as lack or littleness of faith. He upbraids his disciples more for this than for anything else.

He tells them that these things are the chief pursuits of "the nations of the world." But the disciples were to pursue something higher and grander. If we make the same things our chief objects in life that the world seeks, how are we better than they when we act as they do? Let the world worship mammon if they will, but let us worship only God. Our business is to "seek first the kingdom of God'' and those other things—food, raiment, etc., shall be added to us. Who believes it? Let him so act. It is a comforting thought to the trusting soul that ''your Father knoweth that we have need of these things.'' If we are wholly the Lord's we will not set our hearts on the things that this wicked world delights in. We have better things to seek after and hope for. ''If we have a relish for spiritual pleasures, and know the value of 'the beauty of holiness' we shall not crave the luxuries of life.'' (Scott.) How assuring are his words that follow! ''Fear not little flock.'' How precious are the ''Fear nots'' of the Bible. God's people have always been a little flock in the midst of devouring wolves. They have always been few in comparison with the raging world about them. But we need not fear for he has promised to give us a kingdom—*the kingdom* of righteousness, peace and joy in the Holy Ghost. ''God has already given you that kingdom, which consists in righteousness, peace and joy in the Holy Ghost, and has undertaken to protect and save you to the uttermost, therefore fear not, the smallness of your number can not hurt you, for omnipotence itself has undertaken your cause.'' (A. Clarke.)

But notwithstanding God has freely given us this kingdom yet it must be bought. It takes all we have to purchase it. If we have but little it costs little; if we have much it costs much. But it is worth more than it costs. No matter how great the price, we get it for nothing because it is so great. So we can invest all we have in this kingdom and the investment is safe. ''Every one lays up treasure on earth if he take not great care; and his earthly treasure is whatever he loves that is contrary to the will of God, and in which he seeks his own satisfaction. One person has gold, silver, furniture; his estate, position, power; his business, diversions, pleasure. Another his learning, books, reputation, ease; his friends, their affection, esteem, approval, and companionship.'' ''For where your treasure is there is your heart also.'' What our heart worships is our god—our idol. You heart is set on the kingdom or on the things of this world.

IT IS A STATE OF READINESS TO MEET THE LORD.
Vs. 35-48.

35   Let your loins be girded about, and *your* lights burning;

36   And ye yourselves like unto men that wait for their lord, when he will return from the wedding; that when he cometh and knocketh, they may open unto him immediately.

37   Blessed *are* those servants, whom the lord when he cometh shall find watching: verily I say unto you, that he shall gird himself, and make them to sit down to meat, and will come forth and serve them.

38   And if he shall come in the second watch, or come in the third watch, and find *them* so, blessed are those servants.

39   And this know, that if the goodman of the house had known what hour the thief would come, he would have watched, and not have suffered his house to be broken through.

40   Be ye therefore ready also: for the Son of man cometh at an hour when ye think not.

41   Then Peter said unto him, Lord, speakest thou this parable unto us, or even to all?

42   And the Lord said, Who then is that faithful and wise steward, whom *his* lord shall make ruler over his household, to give *them their* portion of meat in due season?

43   Blessed *is* that servant, whom his lord when he cometh shall find so doing.

44   Of a truth I say unto you, that he will make him ruler over all that he hath.

45   But and if that servant say in his heart, My lord delayeth his coming; and shall begin to beat the menservants and maidens, and to eat and drink, and to be drunken;

46   The lord of that servant will come in a day when he looketh not for *him,* and at an hour when he is not aware, and will cut him in sunder, and will appoint him his portion with the unbelievers.

47   And that servant, which knew his lord's will, and prepared not *himself,* neither did according to his will, shall be beaten with many *stripes.*

48   But he that knew not, and did commit things worthy of stripes, shall be beaten with few *stripes.* For unto whomsoever much is given, of him shall be much required: and to whom men have committed much, of him they will ask the more.

He now uses a very expressive figure. "Let your loins be girded about." When the Jews were about to go on a journey, the loose flowing robes which they wore were gathered up in a belt which they wore about the waist, so as not to hinder their walking. The man thus *girded* was ready to go and could walk quickly. In other words we are to be in a state of readiness all the time to meet the Lord. Anything that hinders us from meeting the Lord at any time must be taken out of the way. The only thing that hinders our readiness to meet him is sin. Therefore to be ready to meet him, we must be entirely sanctified, for without holiness "No man shall see the Lord." We must be with our "lights burning." It takes constant grace to keep our lamps burning. A past dead experience is no help. We must not let the light go out. We are to be "like men that wait for their Lord." The New Testament nowhere tells us to prepare to die, but to be ready to meet the Lord. This keeping ready to meet the Lord was the inspiration to holy living in the early Christian church. It was then that Christianity achieved its greatest triumph. It is the inspiration for holy living. If we have a genuine hope of seeing Jesus we will either have or be seeking holiness. There are many who hold dear the *doctrine* of the Second Advent who care little for holiness. They are the most inconsistent people in the world. They would flee as soon as sinners if He should come. Notice the Bible never tells us to get ready but to *be* ready. If the summons should come at midnight during the next twenty-four hours and you would have to get ready to meet the King, it would be because you were not ready. Holiness is the only state that keeps us always ready.

Watching for the coming of Jesus does not mean setting a time and threshing our fellow servants who do not agree with us as to the time of His coming. Watching is to be living a holy life each day as if it were our last day.

"If he should come in the second watch." The ancients divided the night from 6 P. M. to 6 A. M. into four watches. He uses the illustration of a householder, who has his property taken unawares by a burglar. If he had known what hour the burglar was coming he would have been ready and saved his property. We are to *be* ready to meet the unexpected coming of Jesus. "The church has not the task of fixing beforehand that unknown and unknowable time; she has nothing else to do, in virtue of her very ignorance, from which she ought to wish to escape than to remain invariably on the watch. This attitude is her security, her life. The principle of her virgin purity." One thing is sure, Jesus will come when the majority are not expecting him.

Peter interrupted the Lord at this point asking if this parable applied to the disciples or to all people. Jesus replies to his question by asking him the question, ''Who then is that faithful and wise householder,'' etc. This is an indirect answer to Peter's question. He meant this: The parable applies most certainly first of all to you disciples as ''stewards of my household,'' but also to all preachers of the gospel, and all other servants of lesser degree. Preachers are stewards of the mysteries of the gospel. Paul so recognized his calling. It is the preacher's duty first of all to preach to the church (Eph. 4:11-16). Such a preacher is preaching in order to have a prepared, ready, holy church for the coming of the Lord. If he is not preaching entire sanctification in technical terms, he is in substance preaching it. Such a preacher wants his people to be fully saved and ready. That preacher is ''blessed'' (vs. 44) because his Lord finds him so doing—feeding the household, having a ready church, not telling them to expect to get ready, or get rid of sin gradually, but be *ready now*. But if that servant preaches ''my Lord delayeth his coming,'' he will not come for thousands of years; if he begins to spend his time in contentions with his fellow servants and to live for selfish ends and purposes, he will be cut off by the sudden coming of the Lord and have his portions with unbelievers. Whether Jesus comes while we live or when we die, he comes virtually in the end for us. Readiness for the one means readiness for the other. The great thing is to be faithful. ''The condition of fidelity being constant watching for the master's return, this servant, to set himself more at ease in his unfaithfulness, puts the thought of that moment far off. So the minister of Jesus does, who in the place of watching for the Parousia (Greek word for the second advent) substitutes the idea of indefinite progress.'' (Godet.) Those who teach the removal of sin by growth are not living each day so as to be ready to meet Jesus. The second coming of Jesus and the second work of grace in the heart by which the carnal nature is destroyed are usually denied by the same class of preachers, who make both indefinite. It is a most solemn thing to be commissioned to preach the gospel if we are not endeavoring to have the church as a waiting bride for the coming Heavenly Bridegroom. The traditions of men have been foisted upon the church instead of the plain teaching of Scripture. Matthew Henry says, ''Our looking upon Christ's second coming as a thing at a distance is the cause of all the irregularities which render the thought of it terrible to us. *He* saith in his heart, my Lord delayeth his coming.''

It all depends on the amount of light we have as to our punishment for unfaithfulness. Light graduates guilt. It is a fearful thing to have known the doctrine of holiness and not have the experience. We had better have been born heathen. Notice he says that *servant* which knew his Lord's will and did it not should be ''cut asunder'' or cut off and have his portion with unbelievers. This does not refer to a sinner, but to a believer. So the error ''once in grace always in grace'' is here condemned.

HOLINESS IS THE OCCASION OF DIVISION. Vs. 49-52.

49 I am come to send fire on the earth; and what will I, if it be already kindled?

50 But I have a baptism to be baptized with; and how am I straitened till it be accomplished!

51 Suppose ye that I am come to give peace on earth? I tell you, Nay; but rather division:

52 For from henceforth there shall be five in one house divided three against two, and two against three.

Those who criticise the preaching and advocacy of holiness because it is the occasion of division must criticise Jesus, for he came to cause divisions. He came to start the *fire* of holiness in the earth. The fire that consumes sin and scorches and angers those who cling to sin. Fire is a great separator. It separates dross from the pure metal. Olshausen, the great commentator, says of this fire, ''The highest spiritual element of life which Jesus came to introduce into this world, with reference to its mighty effects in quickening all that is akin to it and *destroying all that is opposed.* To cause this element to take up its abode in earth, and wholly to pervade human hearts with its warmth was the lofty destiny of the Redeemer.''

''I have a baptism to be baptized with.'' He refers to the baptism of suffering which was before him. The mysterious sufferings of Gethsemane and Calvary are in this verse. ''How am I straitened.'' The marginal reading is ''How am I pained.''

He thus sums up his whole talk of the chapter on hypocrisy, covetousness and watching thus, ''My conflict hastens apace; mine over, yours begins; and then let the servants tread in their Master's steps, uttering this testimony fearlessly, neither loving nor dreading the world, anticipating awful wrenches of the dearest ties in life, but looking forward as I do, to the completion of their testimony, when, reaching the haven after the tempest they shall enter into the joys of their Lord.'' Let us therefore as we seek to live a holy life not wonder at the opposition and division it causes, sometimes in our own households too. Jesus met it and his gospel must divide sin from holiness.

IT IS STERN IN ITS REBUKE OF SIN. Vs. 54-59.

53   The father shall be divided against the son, and the son against the father ; the mother against the daughter, and the daughter against the mother ; the mother in law against her daughter in law, and the daughter in law against her mother in law.

54   And he said also to the people, When ye see a cloud rise out of the west, straightway ye say, There cometh a shower ; and so it is.

55   And when *ye see* the south wind blow, ye say, There will be heat ; and it cometh to pass.

56   *Ye* hypocrites, ye can discern the face of the sky and of the earth ; but how is it that ye do not discern this time?

57   Yea, and why even of yourselves judge ye not what is right?

58   When thou goest with thine adversary to the magistrate, *as thou art* in the way, give diligence that thou mayest be delivered from him ; lest he hale thee to the judge, and the judge deliver thee to the officer, and the officer cast thee into prison.

59   I tell thee, thou shalt not depart thence, till thou hast paid the very last mite.

He now turns away from his disciples and asks the people why they can read the face of the sky and predict the weather, but can not *discern this time.* As much as to say that the signs of the times were as easy to read as the signs of the sky. Notice this is at the close of the address when they were asking him for a sign. (Chapter 11:16.) The signs of the time were so apparent that if they had not been blinded by sin they could not have helped seeing that prophecy was being fulfilled in and by him. The scepter had departed from Judah. (Gen. 49:11.) Even secular writers tell us there was a general expectation of the immediate coming of the Messiah. The prophets had foretold him. The seventy weeks of Daniel had been accomplished (Dan. 9:25) and John the Baptist, the greatest of the prophets had already announced him. These were the blinded reprobates that asked for a sign, when the religious sky was full of signs. He calls them hypocrites, to ask for a sign under these circumstances. How often has a dead ecclesiasticism failed to discern the signs of the times!

"Yea and why even of yourselves judge ye not what is right?" If they had not seen the signs of the times, they ought to have formed a correct opinion of Jesus. He now seeks by an illustration to warn them. The hated Romans ruled them and made them pay taxes. God was going to permit the Romans to bring this wicked nation to the bar of judgment. The *adversary* here mentioned is God. Had the Jews remained true to God they would never have been delivered up to the Romans. God deals with nations as such in this world. He deals finally with individuals in the world to come, but to some extent in this world also. He sends dispensations of providence to men often in this world to warn them and if they come to terms they will be saved from the final doom of the Judgment day.

"Till thou hast paid the very last mite." This must be eternal, for we can never pay the last mite due to justice. If our suffering could atone for all the past, yet unrenewed in spirit during the period of suffering, we would still have the sins of that period to atone for, and so on forever. We are redeemed by the precious blood of Christ, not by our suffering. If we depend upon ourselves to make the payment we shall always be bankrupt.

CHAPTER XIII.

HOLINESS SENSIBLE.

This Great Holiness Preacher Discoursed on Repentance. Vs. 1-5. He Clearly Pointed Out the Doom of Unfruitful Church Members. Vs. 6-9. And Rebuked Dead Ecclesiasticism. Vs. 10-17. The Mighty Power of Our Holy Religion. Vs. 18-22. Holiness Is a Rebuke to Idle Questioners. Vs. 23-30. Holy Men Can Not Be Frightened Away from Their Work and Duty. Vs. 31-35.

We have denominated the leading thought of this chapter, *Holiness Sensible* because it always adjusts vexed questions in a sensible manner. Fanaticism is not holiness, although it is sometimes so considered. The holy Jesus met the inquiry if those who perished at the hand of Pilate were destroyed as a punishment of their sins. He also showed that calamities are not necessarily judgments (Vs. 10-18) in a sensible, reasonable manner and in two parables in the chapter shows the beauty and reasonableness of the kingdom of heaven, and answers wisely the foolish questions of Vs. 23 and shows his tenderness of heart at the approaching doom of Jerusalem, which he sorrows over even while he condemns it. Truly the reasonableness of holiness is well illustrated in this chapter.

THIS GREAT HOLINESS PREACHER DISCOURSED ON REPENTANCE. Vs. 1-5.

1 There were present at that season some that told him of the Galilæans, whose blood Pilate had mingled with their sacrifices.

2 And Jesus answering said unto them, Suppose ye that these Galilæans were sinners above all the Galilæans, because they suffered such things?

3 I tell you, Nay: but, except ye repent, ye shall all likewise perish.

4 Or those eighteen, upon whom the tower in Siloam fell, and slew them, think ye that they were sinners above all men that dwelt in Jerusalem?

5 I tell you, Nay: but, except ye repent, ye shall all likewise perish.

The Jews at this time were exceedingly restless under the Roman yoke and frequent insurrections broke out. In order to promptly quell these outbreaks a Roman garrison was stationed in the tower of Anthony, built close by the temple. Some Galileans had created a tumult and the Roman soldiers had rushed down upon them and slain many right in the temple itself, so that the blood of these rioters had actually mingled with the blood of the sacrifices being offered in the temple.

This awful tragedy set the people to talking. Death and calamity are some of the means God uses to set men to thinking on eternal truths. There have ever been in the world those who have attributed all calamities to the divine action of God in punishing on account of sin. The friends of Job accused him of great sin because he suffered greatly. While it is true that all suffering is caused by the sin of Adam and the righteous as well as the wicked have to suffer in this world, yet it is not true that every calamity is sent as a punishment for some special sin. There might have been some special sin committed by those, who perished. But there were others who did not perish, just as wicked or more so. It is a mistake to apply a general truth to all individual cases. Just as some people because sickness is the result of sin have maintained that every one who is sick is undergoing punishment for some sin that they have committed. Suffering is not always penal. It is sometimes for our good as Christians. "Whom the Lord loveth, he chasteneth." Some one says it is our weakness not to see that blessing comes from God as well as suffering. Anything terrible or destructive is attributed to God. But prosperity and happiness are attributed too much to ourselves.

Jesus tells these false philosophers that except they repented they too would perish. He showed the right use we should make of the calamities of others. We should consider them as loud calls to be true to God. This massacre of the Galileans was only a faint type of the awful calamity which was to come upon the impenitent Jewish nation at the destruction of Jerusalem. And the destruction of Jerusalem was but a faint picture of the awful doom of hell for impenitent men.

"Except ye repent." To repent is to turn away from all known sin. Unless we do this we are not the children of God. Repentance today is one of the neglected doctrines of the Bible although it is the foundation doctrine of the gospel. It ought to be preached often. Jesus and John the Baptist and Paul preached it much.

HE CLEARLY POINTED OUT THE DOOM OF UNFRUITFUL CHURCH MEMBERS. Vs. 6-9.

6 He spake also this parable; A certain *man* had a fig tree planted in his vineyard; and he came and sought fruit thereon, and found none.

7 Then said he unto the dresser of his vineyard, Behold, these three years I come seeking fruit on this fig tree, and find none: cut it down; why cumbereth it the ground?

8 And he answering said unto him, Lord, let it alone this year also, till I shall dig about it and dung *it:*

9 And if it bear fruit, *well:* and if not, *then* after that thou shalt cut it down.

He now follows up his exhortation to repentance by a parable of warning. The fig tree represented the Jewish church. He tells them that God is delaying the great disaster—the destruction of Jerusalem—of which the massacre by Pilate and the fallen tower of Siloam prefigured, in order that they may repent. Here was an instance of a *church* that needed to repent. After all God had done for this church he had a right to have the fruits of righteousness from them. There could be no excuse for this church being like the barren fig tree. For *three years* now Jesus had been laboring among them. This parable is a plea for a holy life, and applies to us all. Are we bearing fruit in proportion to our opportunities? The condition of abundant fruitfulness is cleansing—heart purity. "Why cumbereth it the ground?" The word cumber in the original means, *to make useless* or *unproductive.* The tree sucked from the soil nourishment that would have produced fruit in a good tree. A church member that is not right is a positive hindrance to the work of God.

"Till I shall dig about it." This illustrates the care of a professed Christian whom God spares for the purpose of giving him the privilege of recovering from backsliding. He gives him further light to lead him on to full salvation. Trench says, "Allusion is here more immediately made to that larger, richer supply of grace—that freer outpouring of the Spirit which was consequent on the death, and resurrection, and ascension of our Lord."

"After that thou shalt cut it down." While this refers primarily to the Jewish people, it also refers to every unfaithful church member, for God deals the same with all men. His mercy is extended as long as there is any hope that the unfruitful servant will turn from his wayward course. Unfruitful church members will do well to ponder this parable.

AND REBUKED DEAD ECCLESIASTICISM. Vs. 10-17.

10   And he was teaching in one of the synagogues on the sabbath.
11   And, behold, there was a woman which had a spirit of infirmity eighteen years, and was bowed together, and could in no wise lift up *herself.*
12   And when Jesus saw her, he called *her to him,* and said unto her, Woman, thou art loosed from thine infirmity.
13   And he laid *his* hands on her : and immediately she was made straight, and glorified God.
14   And the ruler of the synagogue answered with indignation, because that Jesus had healed on the sabbath day, and said unto the people, There are six days in which men ought to work : in them therefore come and be healed, and not on the sabbath day.
15   The Lord then answered him, and said, *Thou* hypocrite, doth not each one of you on the sabbath loose his ox or *his* ass from the stall and lead *him* away to watering?
16   And ought not this woman, being a daughter of Abraham, whom Satan hath bound, lo, these eighteen years, be loosed from this bond on the sabbath day?
17   And when he had said these things, all his adversaries were ashamed : and all the people rejoiced for all the glorious things that were done by him.

Although Jesus knew that the great mass of religionists (at least the leading ecclesiastics) were hypocrites yet he attended their church services and let his light shine endeavoring to do all the good he could. The temple and the Jewish religion were all the visible representation of Jehovah on earth. We ought to frequent the sanctuary even when religion is at a low ebb because it is the representation of Jehovah's name. If the visible organization is not what it should be, one ought to try to help it at least by our presence.

There was one temple located at Jerusalem, but there was a synagogue or meeting house in every town. One Sabbath there was a woman with "a spirit of infirmity" in the synagogue where Jesus was teaching. From verse 16 we judge that it was a case of demonical possession, for "Satan had bound her" for many years. According to this Satan had some control over bodies as well as souls in those days. John Wesley says, "To many doubtless it appeared a natural distemper. Would not a modern physician have termed it a natural disease?" It had been a long, painful and humiliating affliction.

As all affliction is the result of the original introduction of sin into the world, therefore disease of the body is often used to illustrate disease (or sin) in the soul. There are many daughters of Abraham (Vs. 16) members of the church who have a spirit of infirmity worse than a crooked body. A sin warped soul is very much worse. "Unsanctified hearts are under *the spirit of infirmity;* they are distorted, the faculties of the soul are quite out of place and order; they are bowed down towards things below. They can in no wise lift up themselves to God and heaven; the bent of their soul in its natural state is quite the contrary way. Such crooked souls do not seek Christ, but he calls them to him, lays the hand of his grace and power upon them, speaks a healing word to them by which he looses their infirmity, makes the soul straight, reduces it to order and raises it above earthly regards and directs its affections and aims heavenward." (Henry.) This woman went to the church notwithstanding the pain of body and sensitiveness which her deformed figure would occasion. What a lesson to people who let little things keep them from the house of God. Be punctual. Had she remained away from church that day she would not have met Jesus. Thomas remained away from meeting and failed to meet Jesus who appeared to the other disciples. (John 20:24). The people who willingly ab-

sent themselves from the house of God rarely ever meet the Lord.
God has made it a proof of our love for him that we forsake not
the assembly of his house.

"Jesus saw her." He sees us all with whatever burdens and
weaknesses we may have. He called her to him, just as now, he is
calling a sin-burdened world to him, and told her that she was
loosed from her infirmity. The word *loosed* is used in verses
twelve and sixteen. This same word in the Greek is translated
destroy in 1 John 3:8 thus, "For this purpose the Son of God
was manifested that he might *destroy* the works of the devil."
Jesus destroys sin or *looses* us from it, so that we are as free
from it as this woman was from her crookedness. Her infirmity
was not suppressed but entirely removed.

It would naturally be supposed that all religious people would
rejoice to see this woman delivered from this awful condition. It
might be supposed too that all religious people would rejoice to
see a soul freed from sin. But such is not the case. Then and
now such acts, whether of this woman's deliverance or of the
deliverance of the soul from sin, find their most determined enemies among religionists—false religionists. The ruler of the synagogue was very angry and sand to the people, "There are six days
in which men ought to work, then therefore come and be
healed, and not on the Sabbath." He did not have the courage to
say this to Jesus or the woman but said it *to the people,* who had
no particular interest in the miracle. Was there ever a complete
work done in a soul that was not antagonized by dead, formal
ecclesiastics? It was so in the days of the Wesleys. The mob
was often stirred up and sometimes led by the clergy. "It is a
fact in the history of Christianity that almost all—and this is a
question you ought not to forget, and I speak very advisedly—the
heresies that have been introduced into the church have come
from the presbyters, or the bishops, of the ministers of Christianity, or ecclesiastics, and that when the whole priesthood has
become degraded, the mass of the people have continued more
or less orthodox and Christian. I fear more the domination of
the priest, than I fear the domination of the people." (Cummings.) The first great doctrinal apostasy in the great Methodist
church—the denial of the second work of grace, entire sanctifica-

tion has received its greatest support from some of the ministry. So also has the denial of the resurrection of the body had its support from leading ecclesiastics.

The ruler of the synagogue (the same as the minister of a church today) was apparently angry, not because Jesus had healed the woman, but because he did it on the Sabbath. At least that was his excuse. But usually when men oppose the work of God the objection they make is not the real objection they have in their hearts. The carnal mind is opposed always to displays of spiritual or divine power. That is the real cause of the opposition and excuses are usually made, which are only pretenses. How inconsistent carnality is! He admitted that the woman had been healed. If so divine power did it; and the very fact that divine power was with Jesus sanctioned whatever he did. So he could not have really broken the Sabbath. He only broke the ruler's notion of Sabbath keeping. We have known ecclesiastics to fight soul healing by charges that some ecclesiastical law or usage had been broken when the real reason was they did not like holiness and sought some other excuse, because they did not dare to say they were opposed to holiness.

As long as the ruler could not heal the woman himself he ought to have been glad that some one else could. We have seen all this illustrated in the fight against holiness work. Adam Clarke says truly ''It is not an unfrequent case to find a person filled with rage and madness while beholding the effects of Christ's power upon others. Perhaps like this ruler, he pretends zeal and concern for the honor of religion. These preachings, prayer meetings, convictions, conversions, etc., are not carried on in *his* way, and therefore they can not be of God.''

''There are six days.'' Works of mercy and necessity are always in order on the Sabbath. This was surely a work of mercy.

''Thou hypocrite.'' Jesus called him a hypocrite because he was pretending to have a great zeal for religion which was not his real motive. Jesus did not defend himself for breaking the law of the Sabbath. He goes on to deny that he had broken it. The only idea of the Pharisees in Sabbath keeping was keeping the day but not the *spirit* of the Sabbath at all. So Jesus reasons to show the absurdity of their position thus: If an animal was thirsty their law would allow them to lead it to drink, but if a human being was rescued from the power of Satan their law condemned it. They would treat an animal better than a human being. It will be seen that the reasonable, common sense method of solving questions when solved from the stand point of holiness is a rebuke to the consummate absurdities of Phariseeism. Notice still further that the ruler said in verse 14 "ought" and Jesus replies with "ought not" in verse 16. Jesus turns the word back on him.

This answer of Jesus shamed his adversaries and won the confidence of the people. The common people have often been more orthodox than the ecclesiastics in times of religious declension.

THE MIGHTY POWER OF OUR HOLY RELIGION.
Vs. 18-22.

18 Then said he, Unto what is the kingdom of God like? and whereunto shall I resemble it?

19 It is like a grain of mustard seed, which a man took, and cast into his garden; and it grew, and waxed a great tree; and the fowls of the air lodged in the branches of it.

20 And again he said, Whereunto shall I liken the kingdom of God?

21 It is like leaven, which a woman took and hid in three measures of meal, till the whole was leavened.

22 And he went through the cities and villages, teaching, and journeying toward Jerusalem.

The prosperity of the world depends upon its morals; and its morals depend upon its religion, and the power of its religion depends upon the amount of its holiness. The reason Christianity has prospered is because it is a holy religion. Its brightest days have been when holiness has been most popular with its devotees.

He gives two parables illustrating the power of the kingdom of God. (See our commentary on Matt. 13:31-33.) The parable of the mustard seed illustrates the aggressive power of our holy religion manifested in its spread in the earth. Is it not astonishing that Jesus should have so prophesied of the final success of this cause when it was so feeble at the time.

The second parable shows the way in which our holy religion elevates society as yeast or leaven raises bread. Some have misinterpreted this parable because they have not needed the symbolism. Leaven is often used in a bad sense in the Bible. But here its raising power is shown. It does not mean that all the world is to be converted. *The leaven or yeast does not turn the whole mass of dough into leaven.* It *lifts* it. Our holy religion lifts society and civilizes it although it does not convert the whole of it.

Jesus now went on an evangelistic trip through the towns and villages of Perea (probably). He was a travelling evangelist. Those who are opposed to evangelists are opposed to the work that Jesus did, for he was an evangelist.

HOLINESS IS A REBUKE TO IDLE QUESTIONERS.
Vs. 23-30.

23 Then said one unto him, Lord, are there few that be saved? And he said unto them,

24 Strive to enter in at the strait gate: for many, I say unto you, will seek to enter in, and shall not be able.

25 When once the master of the house is risen up, and hath shut to the door, and ye begin to stand without, and to knock at the door, saying, Lord, Lord, open unto us: and he shall answer and say unto you, I know you not whence ye are:

26 Then shall ye begin to say, We have eaten and drunk in thy presence, and thou hast taught in our streets.

27 But he shall say, I tell you, I know you not whence ye are; depart from me, all *ye* workers of iniquity.

28 There shall be weeping and gnashing of teeth, when ye shall see Abraham, and Isaac, and Jacob, and all the prophets, in the kingdom of God, and you *yourselves* thrust out.

29 And they shall come from the east, and *from* the west, and from the north, and *from* the south, and shall sit down in the kingdom of God.

30 And, behold, there are last which shall be first, and there are first which shall be last.

A holy man has no time to waste either in idleness or in foolish speculation. Many of the so called theological discussions and fine discriminations are a waste of precious time. Jesus rebuked such idle speculation. A man at this juncture asked him, "Lord are there few that be saved?" Perhaps this questioner was judging of the merits of the cause by the number of its adherents. Many today so judge. But we are to keep our eyes off other folks and attend to our own salvation. It is not our business to pry into the Lord's affairs or tell who or how many are saved. If we knew the number of the saved it would do us no good. Jesus never attempted to satisfy idle curiosity, but to keep man's attention on the central theme of salvation. "I am sure you must have seen in reading the Bible how much there is in it to sanctify, how much to comfort, how much to strengthen, but how little to gratify an anxious and itching curiosity. Now if I wanted to make a book extremely popular what would I do? I would try to gratify the curiosity of mankind: and if I wanted to write a book extremely unpopular, I would try to sanctify the hearts and correct the sins and vices of mankind. It is a striking trait in our fallen nature that we are more curious to know an interesting speculation than we are anxious to feel the force of a sanctifying and saving truth." (Cummings.) For this reason a sensational preacher will always be more popular than a preacher of entire sanctification.

It is our business to "strive" to enter in at the narrow gate. The Greek puts this more forcibly, by using the word "agonize." We are to be tremendously in earnest to enter the narrow gate of eternal life. Striving of itself will not bring us in except the Spirit himself strive with us. (Col. 1:29). Our part is to be dead in earnest in the matter of our salvation.

Many will seek to enter but will not be able, for several reasons. 1. They only *seek*. They do not *strive* with all earnestness. 2. They try to get in some other way except the gate. The gate is so narrow that we can not take a single sin with us. "No one can enter it but naked men who are stripped of all worldly lusts." (Erasmus.) Many who do not want to give up their sins are trying to get in some other way. 3. Because they do not strive to enter at the right time. (Vs. 25.) There is a time when striving is too late.

He represents the Master of the house at a feast as sitting now, because it is the day of probation but the time will come when God will rise up—probation will be ended. When those whom he desires as guests are prepared he will shut the door.

He represents those shut out of the heavenly feast as saying in astonishment, "We have eaten and drunk in thy presence."

But the answer will be, "I never knew you. Depart from me." This applies to those who have had a mere profession of religion, but never got better acquainted with the Lord. There are many religionists who do not seem to know that religion is anything more than forms. It never occurred to them that it means to get acquainted with the Lord. That will be the time when holiness will be popular. It is unpopular now. "No nearness of external communion with Christ will avail in that great day in place of that 'holiness without which no man shall see the Lord.' Observe the style which Christ intimates that he will then assume, that of absolute disposer of men's eternal destinies, and contrast at this time." (Brown.) Matthew Henry says of these rejected souls that while on earth "they had a good mind to happiness and a good opinion of holiness, and take some good steps towards both." Jesus calls these rejected church members, "workers of iniquity." According to this those who have only a profession of religion are workers of iniquity.

He then pronounced sentence upon them thus: "There shall be weeping and gnashing of teeth." Weeping denotes sorrow and gnashing of teeth denotes rage. Sorrow and rage are the conditions in hell.

"Ye shall see Abraham." The identity of these patriarchs will be preserved in the other world. We shall know them and we shall know our friends in heaven. These bodies shall be raised and glorified. Abraham, Isaac and Jacob were the three founders of the Jewish church. We see here that it is possible to be loyal to our church and be cast into hell.

"You yourselves cast out." He says in the parallel passage in Matt. 8:12 "the children of the kingdom shall be cast out." This condemns the unscriptural teaching "once in grace always in grace." So a church member once in grace may be cast out into outer darkness because he stops *striving;* leans on an empty past experience; thinks his denominational standing will admit him to heaven.

To the question, "Are there few that be saved?" (Vs. 23) he gives this answer (Vs. 29), "They shall come from the four quarters of the earth to sit down in the kingdom of God." (See Matt. 8:11-12.)

He further tells them that high places in the church will have no influence in making our place in heaven. "There are last that shall be first" and vice versa.

HOLY MEN CAN NOT BE FRIGHTENED AWAY FROM THEIR WORK AND DUTY. Vs. 31-35.

31 The same day there came certain of the Pharisees, saying unto him, Get thee out, and depart hence: for Herod will kill thee.

32 And he said unto them, Go ye, and tell that fox, Behold, I cast out devils, and I do cures to day and to morrow, and the third *day* I shall be perfected.

33 Nevertheless I must walk to day, and to morrow, and the *day* following: for it cannot be that a prophet perish out of Jerusalem.

34 O Jerusalem, Jerusalem, which killest the prophets, and stonest them that are sent unto thee; how often would I have gathered thy children together, as a hen *doth gather* her brood under *her* wings, and ye would not!

35 Behold, your house is left unto you desolate: and verily I say unto you, Ye shall not see me, until *the time* come when ye shall say, Blessed *is* he that cometh in the name of the Lord.

The Pharisees unable to overcome Jesus in argument, tried to frighten him by telling him that Herod was seeking to kill him. This was evidently a lie, for if Herod really wished to kill him, he would have easily have found him and taken him. It is quite evident that Herod had not sent them to drive him away by threatenings for Herod and the Pharisees were enemies. If Herod had really desired to kill him, the Pharisees would have been only too glad to have it so, for they hated him. Holy people trust too implicitly in God to be frightened away from the post of duty.

"Jesus replied, "Go ye and tell that fox." This is the only word of contempt that is ever recorded as having passed the lips of Jesus. It described the character of Herod with exactness. He was a cunning, paltry hypocrite; false to every body, that had anything to do with him. Men often exhibit the traits of animal creation. The same eye that discerned the hypocrisy of the Pharisees, discerned also the craftiness and deceit of Herod, and called him by the right name. He sees through us all. No man can deceive him. He knows the character of each one. John said on Patmos his eyes were like flames of fire. (Rev. 1:14.)

"Behold I cast out devils." From this same phraseology employed in verses 32 and 33 we conclude that he had determined to remain in Perea (where he was not teaching) for two days longer, and then on the third day he could return to Judea to finish his passion, which ended or was perfected, when on the cross he cried, "It is finished." Trench thus paraphrases it, "My danger is not in Galilee, nor yet from Herod. I shall not perish here but in Jerusalem, your seat, your headquarters, where you reign supreme. When the day of my death or my consummation arrives, you and not Herod, will be the authors of the murderous deed." It would not be a treacherous world but a backslidden church that would slay him. His death would not be in semi-heathen Peres but in Jerusalem, where all the prophets were martyred.

"O Jerusalem, Jerusalem." This most pathetic apostrophe ever put into human language was addressed to an apostate church. "It is the very heart of God pouring itself through human flesh and speech. It is this incarnation of the innermost life and love of deity, pleading with men, bleeding for them, and ascending only to open his arms to them and win them back by the power of this story of matchless love, that has conquered the world, that will yet 'draw all men unto him' and beautify and ennoble humanity itself."

CHAPTER XIV.

HOLINESS RADICAL AND UNCOMPROMISING.

The Holy Jesus Unmasks an Inconsistent Religion. Vs. 1-6. Our Holy Religion Rebukes Selfseeking. Vs. 7-11. Holiness Levels Class Distinction. Vs. 12-14. Holiness Ferrets Out and Discerns the Weakness of Carnal Excuses. Vs. 15-24. Holiness Is to Love God Above All Things Else. Vs. 25-33. The Insipidness of Backsliders. Vs. 34-35.

Holiness means hatred of sin and all the imitations that sin endeavors to palm off for true religion. In this chapter its uncompromising nature may be seen in the attack of Jesus upon a false religion (Vs. 1-6); upon self-seeking, (Vs. 7-11); upon false benevolence (Vs. 12-14); upon weak excuses (Vs. 15-24); upon half heartedness (Vs. 25-33) and upon empty and dead profession (Vs. 34-35).

THE HOLY JESUS UNMASKS AN INCONSISTENT RELIGION. Vs. 1-6.

1 And it came to pass, as he went into the house of one of the chief Pharisees to eat bread on the sabbath day, that they watched him.

2 And, behold, there was a certain man before him which had the dropsy.

3 And Jesus answering spake unto the lawyers and Pharisees, saying, is it lawful to heal on the sabbath day?

4 And they held their peace. And he took *him,* and healed him, and let him go;

5 And answered them, saying, Which of you shall have an ass or an ox fallen into a pit, and will not straightway pull him out on the sabbath day?

6 And they could not answer him again to these things.

The Revised Version says it was the house of a ruler (not a Pharisee) into whose house Jesus came. His enemies from this time constantly watched him. Jesus was invited here to eat bread. The rulers or chief ministers of the synagogue watched him. They pretended to extend hospitality but really were trying to ensnare him. Very much of the so called politeness of society is hypocrisy. True politeness comes from divine love in the heart. "Love doth not behave itself unseemly." It crops out in the little acts of life. Love may not be according to all the rules of etiquette as laid down in the books on decorum, but it is not the hypocrisy of saying one thing and meaning another. Holiness means perfect love to man. It is more than form.

There was a certain man there afflicted with the dropsy. Doubtless he came hoping to be healed. He got healing, the others got nothing. Just so now, some get something of Christ. Others get nothing, because they seek nothing.

The all seeing eye of Jesus beheld their thoughts and inward questionings and answered them just as if they had been spoken, and he answered their questioning by asking them a question. "Is it lawful to heal on the Sabbath days?" He did not wait to be attacked. He brought on the battle. We are to attack error. He here teaches us that no false idea of politeness on social occasions should muzzle us when the truth is at stake. We ought not to accept any hospitality that will close our mouths.

They were silent. No one attempted to answer the question. If they said it was wrong to heal on the Sabbath it would be like cruelty to the sick man. If they said yes, why did they make the Sabbath so uncomfortable for men both sick and well? Why did their traditions forbid works of mercy? They made the Sabbath ridiculous by their traditions. A Jew could not quit his camp or village or city on the Sabbath. He might not begin a journey; if going along a road, he must rest from sundown until the same event next day. He might not carry a pencil, a kerchief of a shekel in his belt; if he required a handkerchief for use, he had to tie it around his leg. If he offended against this rule he was held to deserve the doom awarded the vilest sinners. "Their rules were very minute. None might walk upon the grass on the Sabbath because it would be bruised, which would be a kind of threshing; nor catch a flea which would be a kind of hunting; nor wear nailed shoes which would be a kind of burden; nor, if he fed chickens, suffer any corn to lie on the ground lest a kernel should germinate, which would be a kind of sowing.'' (Abbott.)

So he healed the man and let him go. We can but admire his fearlessness. If we have the Christ life in us can we have the man-fearing spirit? Matthew Henry well says ''The cure of a dropsy, as much as of any disease, one would think would be gradual. Yet Christ cured even that disease, perfectly; cured it in a moment.''

He showed them that it took more labor to pull an animal out of a pit than to heal this man. They would allow the greater amount of work and condemn the lesser work. The man had dropsy of the body. They had dropsy of the soul—inflation with pride.

They could say nothing. Their mean little plot to snare him had failed.

OUR HOLY RELIGION REBUKES SELFSEEKING. Vs. 7-11.

7 And he put forth a parable to those which were bidden, when he marked how they chose out the chief rooms, saying unto them,

8 When thou art bidden of any *man* to a wedding, sit not down in the highest room; lest a more honourable man than thou be bidden of him;

9 And he that bade thee and him come and say to thee, Give this man place; and thou begin with shame to take the lowest room.

10 But when thou art bidden, go and sit down in the lowest room; that when he that bade thee cometh, he may say unto thee, Friend go up higher: then shalt thou have worship in the presence of them that sit at meat with thee.

11 For whosoever exalteth himself shall be abased; and he that humbleth himself shall be exalted.

He found his illustrations in the action of the people going on about him. So can we. If we wish to see the workings of the carnal mind, all we need to do is to look around us on every hand. Here he saw it in the selfseeking going on at this feast, where he was now being entertained. They were seeking the best rooms (seats, Revised Version). That is characteristic of the carnal mind. It takes holiness of heart to be "in honor preferring one another." Holiness and self seeking are as far apart as the poles of the earth. Let not those people who aspire to be leaders, suppose for a moment that they are entirely sanctified. There have crept into even the great holiness movement as Satan crept into Eden, little popes and bosses, who think acceptance of doctrine is a mark of holiness. We may be as orthodox on the doctrine as the devil himself and as unholy as he. True holiness means the deepest humility.

The chief seats (mistranslated rooms) were in the middle of the couches on which they reclined in taking their meals. Each guest undertook in such feasts to indicate his rank by taking the place of which he judged himself worthy. Hosts often had to re-arrange seats to harmonize conflicting ideas of the guests as to their places. The Pharisees always took the highest places. "When we know our real character in the sight of God, and we are made well acquainted with our own hearts, we shall proportionately be disinclined to aspire to the chief places in the church, and shall be contented and thankful for the most obscure and be made willing to have others honored and ourselves neglected and slighted in comparison." (Scott.) This illustrates the 13th chapter of First Corinthians. Let no one say there is no need of entire sanctification when they look about and see the scramble for position and place in the church today. Let us remember we shall never have a high seat in heaven if we are eager for high seats on the earth. "He that exalteth himself shall be abased."

So he thus begins his parable: "When thou art bidden to a wedding." This is an extract from Jesus Christ's book of etiquette. If all the world practiced the spirit of these precepts, there would be truly "Peace on earth and good will towards men."

"Give this man place." How much mortification and bitterness of heart and sore disappointment there is in this world because men seek to fill places for which they are not qualified, and then they have to be ousted. The sainted Payson once said that he never got to any place of satisfactory experience until he ceased his ambition to be a great man. When he sought only to be humble and lowly he became an eminent saint. How many foolish little people never become entirely sanctified until they gave up their ambitions to be president of the United States. Today there are people sour at everybody because they were turned out of positions for which they were not qualified.

"Friend go up higher." This is the true order in the kingdom of God: be humble and you will be promoted if you deserve it. If not, a high place will only make a greater fall. He that is faithful in a small position, will be faithful in a higher. It is only those who are faithful in a justified experience, who are fit to go up higher into the next degree—entire sanctification. A lot of people are seeking holiness, who are not justified.

HOLINESS LEVELS CLASS DISTINCTION. Vs. 12-14.

12 Then said he also to him that bade him, When thou makest a dinner or a supper, call not thy friends, nor thy brethren, neither thy kinsmen, nor *thy* rich neighbours; lest they also bid thee again, and a recompence be made thee.
13 But when thou makest a feast, call the poor, the maimed, the lame, the blind:
14 And thou shalt be blessed; for they cannot recompense thee: for thou shalt be recompensed at the resurrection of the just.

He hits one of the leading principles of society—to invite those who invite us, to call upon those who call upon us; to invite only those to eat with us who can pay it back. He does not mean by this that we can not invite our friends to eat with us for he did that very thing himself. But if we are doing these things in order to obtain a recompense and are neglecting God's poor, then we are acting on the principles of selfishness. Entertain your friends, but feed the hungry, and relieve the distressed. It is a matter of motives. It is blessed to help those who can not help themselves.

"And thou shalt be blessed." This is another of the Beatitudes of Christ. The Psalmist says virtually the same thing thus "Blessed is he that considereth the poor." (Psalms 41:1.) Our recompense will come at the resurrection of the just. True benevolence will have its reward in the Great Day, if done for Jesus' sake. (Matt. 25:31-40.) Jesus and the Jews generally believed in the doctrine of the Resurrection—and that there was a special reward for the good at that time. Notice we shall not be saved for our good works, but we shall be rewarded according to our good works.

HOLINESS FERRETS OUT AND DISCERNS THE WEAKNESS OF CARNAL EXCUSES. Vs. 15-24.

15 And when one of them that sat at meat with him heard these things, he said unto him, Blessed *is* he that shall eat bread in the kingdom of God.

16 Then said he unto him, A certain man made a great supper, and bade many :

17 And sent his servant at supper time to say to them that were bidden, Come ; for all things are now ready.

18 And they all with one *consent* began to make excuse. The first said unto him, I have bought a piece of ground, and I must needs go and see it : I pray thee have me excused.

19 And another said, I have bought five yoke of oxen, and I go to prove them : I pray thee have me excused.

20 And another said, I have married a wife, and therefore I cannot come.

21 So that servant came, and shewed his lord these things. Then the master of the house being angry said to his servant, Go out quickly into the streets and lanes of the city, and bring in hither the poor, and the maimed, and the halt, and the blind.

22 And the servant said, Lord, it is done as thou hast commanded, and yet there is room.

23 And the lord said unto the servant, Go out into the highways and hedges, and compel *them* to come in, that my house may be filled.

24 For I say unto you, That none of those men which were bidden shall taste of my supper.

At this discourse of Jesus concluded one of the company spoke up and said ''Blessed is he that shall eat bread in the kingdom of God.'' According to the notion of the Jews the setting up of the Messiah's earthly kingdom was to be ushered in by a great festival of which all the members of the kingdom should partake. So his remarks signified ''Blessed are we Jews who will be partakers of the Master's kingdom.'' He seemed to thing that when Jesus came revealing the fact that religion was spiritual, it did not concern himself as he was a church member in good and regular standing. That is the same idea that many church members today have. They think when the gospel of full salvation is preached that it does not concern them, for their salvation is secured through church membership. So Jesus spoke this parable to show that the Jewish guests, who were bidden to the real, spiritual Kingdom of God had refused the call and now the Gospel was to be given the Gentiles instead. This is a lesson to us of today. Trench says of this man who asked the question, ''He had not considered at all whether in their refusal to enter into the higher spiritual life of the Gospel, to which Christ was now inviting him, there was not involved his own ultimate rejection from the heavenly festival. For his warning, and for the warning of all likeminded with him, the parable is spoken.''

We notice that the Gospel is here likened to a feast. What a feast is to physical man, the blessings of the Gospel are to the soul.

''Eternal wisdom hath prepared
A soul-reviving feast
And bids your longing appetites
The rich provisions taste.''

A feast usually implies not only choice food, but plenty of it. This is true of salvation. There is plenty of it to satisfy every craving of the soul.

So the man sent out his servants to invite the people to the feast. This refers to the custom among the Jews to give out a general invitation and then a second one when the supper was ready. The first invitation had been given by the prophets and the second by John the Baptist and Jesus. The feast was now ready. Since that time supper has always been ready. In addition to the invitations of John and Jesus we have those of the Spirit and the Bride. The invitation, ''Come,'' is ringing throughout the whole world.

The invited guests began right away to ''make excuse with one consent.'' The word, *consent* is not in the original. It is the easiest thing in the world to make excuses if a person does not want to do a thing. Notice the character of the excuses. The excuses were not that they wanted to do anything wrong. No sinful occupation kept them away. Many people let employments and pursuits not sinful in themselves keep them from the salvation of their souls. The reason these guests did not come to the supper was there were other things that they liked better than the supper. To refuse to come to supper in such cases was considered an insult to the host. "The carnal mind gives everything the preference to Christ and his salvation, instead of using all in subserviency to it." (Scott.) It is an insult to God to refuse to come to the Gospel feast. There is no reasonable excuse for refusing the Gospel. An excuse is only a guarded, sugar coated lie. It covers up the real reason. These who made excuses were all united. Some people praise unity and talk about a united church, as if unity were always a blessing and division a calamity. It depends on what kind of unity it is. Sometimes unity is a calamity, and division a mark of divinity. If a church are all united in fighting holiness or excusing themselves for not seeking it, such union is a serious affair. John Cumming says "The mere fact of being united in a transaction does not prove it good, or the parties combined to be personally holy."

Of course these parties all told lies. The man who had bought the land was not obliged to go and see the land he had already bought: nor was the second obliged to try oxen already purchased. They both had plenty of time now that the property was theirs. The third could have brought his wife to the feast. None of the parties had anything to say against the quality of the feast. These excuses must be read in the light of verse 26.

The Master of the house was angry at these insults. God is angry with those who persistently refuse the offer of salvation, because it has been provided at so great cost and because it is of so much worth. There is such a thing as the wrath of God.

The angry Master of the house now turns away from these unappreciative insulting people and tells his servants to invite the unfortunates of the city. This represents the fact that God gave the Jews the first call and as they turned away he has called the Gentiles—the unchurched masses. Several times in history, God has had to turn away from the nominal church and send his servants after the unchurched, neglected masses. The church refused to come up higher because dead, and God has had to form a new church out of the unchurched. Under Luther, God made a new church, repudiating the dead ecclesiasticism of Rome; under the

Wesleys a new church in place of the worldly church of that day. Will history repeat itself in the passing by of the modern worldly church?

He told them to ''go out into the highways and hedges'' after guests. The neglected corners, the back circuits in the great harvest field often contain the richest sheaves. God needs some one to reap the corners of the field where the great harvesting machines can not go. Let us not as preachers and teachers neglect the highways and hedges, where the gospel neglected throngs are.

''Compel them to come in.'' Compelling them by the sweet compulsion of love—entreating, urging them with a heart so loving that they will feel compelled to come.

He means to have a full heaven. Though thousands refuse the invitation yet thank God there will be a great company in heaven that no man can number. There will be enough saved out of every generation to make a full heaven.

He clearly shows too that he is ''*the man*'' in the parable who gave the invitation, for he says ''I say unto you'' and ''my supper.'' (Vs. 24.) None of these scorners should receive the salvation they had refused—neither salvation in this world, nor final salvation in the world to come.

Paul says ''He that is spiritual judgeth (or discerneth) all things, yet he himself is judged (or discerned) of no man.'' (1 Cor. 2:15.) A spiritual man like Jesus can clearly detect the sham excuses of carnal men.

HOLINESS IS TO LOVE GOD ABOVE ALL THINGS ELSE.
Vs. 25-33.

25 And there went great multitudes with him: and he turned, and said unto them,

26 If any *man* come to me, and hate not his father, and mother, and wife, and children, and brethren, and sisters, yea, and his own life also, he cannot be my disciple.

27 And whosoever doth not bear his cross, and come after me, cannot be my disciple.

28 For which of you, intending to build a tower, sitteth not down first, and counteth the cost, whether he have *sufficient* to finish *it?*

29 Lest haply, after he hath laid the foundation, and is not able to finish *it,* all that behold *it* begin to mock him,

30   Saying, This man began to build, and was not able to finish.
31   Or what king, going to make war against another king, sitteth
not down first, and consulteth whether he be able with ten thousand to meet him that cometh against him with twenty thousand?
32   Or else, while the other is yet a great way off, he sendeth an
ambassage, and desireth conditions of peace.
33   So likewise, whosoever he be of you that forsaketh not all that
he hath, he cannot be my disciple.

He now still further answers the excuses of verses 18-20 and
shows that if a man is intending to follow him he must break
every hindering tie and cast off every weight. The teachings of
Jesus were revolutionary. He uttered startling truths often in
the form of a paradox as here. Notice his assertion of authority.
Had he been only a Jewish peasant, he would have been one of
the most fanatical and insane men that ever lived to insist that if
any man followed him, he must sunder every tie no matter however dear. If he had not been divine, then his claims were the
most preposterous and ridiculous. He made demands on all men
that no one else has ever dared or dreamed of making. He demands that all men shall follow him even if they have to lose
everything near and dear to them. But his pure life and spotless
character prove him to have been a truth teller. Therefore his
claims of divinity are genuine.

He says if a man comes after him and ''hates not his father
and mother and wife and children'' and his own life he cannot be
his disciple. This is pretty stringent doctrine. It requires much
to enter the *first* degree of grace. Some people think entire consecration whereby we are wholly sanctified is a severe condition. It
is to be feared that they do not know about the conditions of regeneration. The man who has been really converted has paid a
great price in forsaking all for Christ and he has gone too far now
not to put himself wholly on the altar. Much of the struggling of
people seeking the second work of grace is because they have failed
to comprehend the rugged conditions of the first work of grace.

The word ''hate'' here means to love less. It is best understood by reading the parallel passage in Matthew 10:37. ''Loveth father and mother more than me.'' If any social or temporal
interest stands in the way of our loyalty to Jesus it must be aban-
doned.

"Whosoever doth not bear his cross and come after me." But we must not only forsake all for Christ, but also bear the cross. Here are indicated the two works of grace—justification and entire sanctification. (See our commentary on Matt. 16.) When we are converted in the language of the baptismal covenant "we renounce the devil and all his works, the vain pomp and glory of the world, with all the covetous desires of the flesh, so that we will neither follow nor be led by them." This is a great and high experience. But it is only the beginning. The next step is to take up the cross. Were it another subject, it would be amusing to hear the notions expressed as to the nature of bearing the cross.

Some people have mistaken the crucifix for the cross. So we see it worn as a charm placed on church buildings and spires, represented by picture and painting as really a lovely thing.

Others think cross bearing means the performance of duty. This is absurd—to call it a cross to do the will of God, who gave himself for us. Think of a man being loyal to his wife and calling it "bearing the cross." Think of a man doing the will of God and considering it cross-bearing.

Others still think it means to speak in a religious asembly. Try to imagine a sinner taken out of the miry pit; the shackles of sin stricken off; the peace of God in his heart; the evidence that his name is written in the Lamb's Book of life. He goes to a religious assembly and tells the joys of his new experience and calls it "Bearing my cross!"

The fact is the cross was the ignominious instrument of death. The man who bore the cross was going to the place where he was to be nailed to it until he was dead. It meant death. It means death to the old carnal nature. To bear it means to take the daily reproach that comes to those who are crucified with Christ. Jesus not only bore his cross when going to Calvary but he bore it in the shame and reproaches heaped upon him as he hung upon it. Cross bearing means all this. If we do not propose to go clear through and have the carnal nature destroyed, we *can not* be his disciples.

He now gives two illustrations to show that we must renounce everything for his sake. He cites the case of a man who attempts to build a tower and does not have the means to finish it. So we if we attempt in our own strength to build up a holy character, will fail. We might as well understand it and renounce our own striving and let God make us holy. The sooner we find that we are teetotal failures and renounce everything and let him make us holy the better for us. How many a Christian has been justified by faith, but expects to complete his sanctification by works, growth, gradualism and human effort. *This is the great error of Protestantism, today.* How many backsliders there are who started well but failed because they did not go on to entire sanctification by faith. And the world mocks them because they began to build and were not able to finish.

He gives another illustration of the king who goes out to battle and fails because he tries to meet an army of 20,000 with only 10,000 and sues for peace. The Christian who attempts to carry on the war without being wholly sanctified is hindered by indwelling sin and the resistance is two to one against him. It is uphill business getting to heaven with inbred sin. It is as hard and sure of defeat as a king who goes with a small army to attack one double the size. No wonder the country is full of backsliders. Better not be a Christian at all, unless we are going clear through and propose to bear the crucifixion of the cross. (See verse 27.) Let us go *clear through.*

THE INSIPIDNESS OF BACKSLIDERS. Vs. 34-35.

34 Salt *is* good: but if the salt have lost his savour, wherewith shall it be seasoned?

35 It is neither fit for the land, nor yet for the dunghill; *but* men cast it out. He that hath ears to hear, let him hear.

In Matt. 5-13 his followers are called the salt or purifying element of the earth. What salt is to preserve from putrefaction holy men and women are in the world. The moral condition of the world depends upon the kind of religion it has. A religion without holiness is worthless. How many kinds of worthless religions there are. God wants a pure church to purify the world, for only a pure church can do it. The idea the unconverted world have of the nature of the religion of Jesus is holiness. They often say if they were to get religion they would have a kind of religion that would make them right, or none. An unholy religion is of the devil and is worthless. Notice then the connection from verse 26 to the end, thus. We must forsake all and be crucified to sin. If we are just intending to build a Christian character and then backslide instead of getting holiness then we are like worthless salt, despised of the world about us.

CHAPTER XV.

HOLINESS A REBUKE TO UNCHARITABLENESS.

The true experience of holiness is the opposite of uncharitableness. The lesson here is that those church members who are opposed to the urgent and immediate efforts for the salvation of sinners are not in sympathy with Jesus Christ. Real holiness of heart is a standing rebuke to any religion not employed in the salvation of men. There are many useful lessons and doctrines in this chapter, but the chief point of the whole chapter is Jesus' rebuke of the Pharisees. The three parables were given for this purpose. This is then the point of the parable. *Unholy church members are not in sympathy with work that seeks the salvation of sinners.* The Pharisees had outside holiness. But external holiness is not interested in the salvation of sinners as a rule. We notice then the three parables which Jesus here utters to rebuke the Pharisees.

The preaching of Jesus had attracted the lowest classes—publicans and sinners. This called forth the criticism of the Pharisees. They said ''This man receiveth sinners'' and even worse than that ''eateth with them.'' To eat with anyone was regarded as putting one's self on an equality with them. It is even so today. There is one section of this country that can hardly forgive an ex-president because he ate with a negro. These Pharisees could not understand how Jesus could be good and be on speaking terms with these low classes. They knew nothing about associating with sinners to do them good. This fact is a comment on the force of verse 7. ''Joy shall be in heaven over the one sinner that repenteth more than over ninety and nine just persons that need no repentance.'' If we do not therefore keep in mind the criticism of the Pharisees we shall lose much of the force of verse 7.

Trench says ''Of the three parables the first two, those of the lost sheep and the lost piece of money, set forth to us mainly the *seeking* love of God; while the third, that of the Prodigal Son, describes to us rather the rise and growth, responsive to that love of repentance in the heart of man. It is in fact only the same truth presented successively under different aspects. God's seeking love being set forth first, and this not without reason, since we are thus taught that all first motions towards good are from him, that grace must go before as well as follow us. But yet it is the same truth in all; for it is the influence of this drawing and seeking love from without, and of the faith awakened by the same power from within—the influence of these two streams, the grace and the faith—out of which repentance springs.

Some commentators see in the three parables the office work of the Trinity shown. They say the first parable shows the redemptive work of the Son; the second the convicting work of the Holy Spirit represented in the diligent searching of the house; the third presents the great truths of adoption and justification which are the work of the Father.

The parables of the lost sheep and lost coin seem to represent the rescue of backsliders. It was a sheep that was lost—not a goat; that of the prodigal more especially illustrates the experience of a backslider. The first and second represent God seeking the lost; the third represent the lost seeking God. All three parables are illustrated in the conversion of every soul. For no one desires to seek God until God has first sought him, as in the first parable, and convicted him by his Spirit (as represented in the seeking and sweeping and lighting of the lamp, of the second parable).

THE LOST SHEEP. Vs. 1-7.

1 Then drew near unto him all the publicans and sinners for to hear him.

2 And the Pharisees and scribes murmured, saying, This man receiveth sinners, and eateth with them.

3 And he spake this parable unto them, saying,

4 What man of you, having an hundred sheep, if he lose one of them, doth not leave the ninety and nine in the wilderness, and go after that which is lost, until he find it?

5   And when he hath found *it,* he layeth *it* on his shoulders, rejoicing.

6   And when he cometh home, he calleth together *his* friends and neighbours, saying unto them, Rejoice with me; for I have found my sheep which was lost.

7   I say unto you, that likewise joy shall be in heaven over one sinner that repenteth, more than over ninety and nine just persons, which need no repentance.

"What man of you." He uses the same style of argument as in Chapter 14:5 and Chapter 13:15. If men will take so much care and pains to look after sheep, how much care ought the church to take for lost souls. He likens backsliders to that simple, silly animal, the sheep, who is so easy to go astray. There is no animal on earth more helpless in the matter of finding its way home when lost. The prophet says "All we, like sheep have gone astray." (Isa. 53:6.)

We notice in the illustration of the Shepherd seeking the *one* sheep the truth is brought out that God is interested in us as individuals. God convicts men singly and converts them singly. We ought to realize the importance of individual effort in the salvation of souls. "Hand picked fruit keeps the best." Christ passed by millions of worlds to come to this little planet.

The Shepherd went "after that which was lost." He went where the lost one was. If our great cities where the majority of the lost are today, are to be evangelized there must be more going to them, to live with them as Christ came to live with us. Here is one element in the solution of the problems of saving the cities; and that is the great problem of the times. We must not merely send others, but go ourselves, as far as divine providence will permit. The way to show our hatred of sin is to do as Jesus did— not keep aloof from sinners but go to them and persuade them to flee the wrath to come.

The shepherd kept after the lost sheep *until he found it.* He was persistent. How many make a few faint endeavors and then quit the field. Jesus persisted in his efforts until the Jews absolutely refused his invitations.

Then the shepherd lays the lost (found) sheep upon his shoulders and carries it home. The sheep is worn out from its wanderings and has not the strength to get back home. So the backslider is especially weak and helpless. If he yield up in true penitence he will be carried back into the fold by Jesus. Undershepherds—pastors, teachers, parents—who see wayward souls turning to God know something of the emotions of the Shepherd who has found his lost sheep, as he comes with rejoicing, over the sheep recovered.

No wonder such a Shepherd would say to his friends ''Rejoice with me.'' No wonder Jesus, who loved us so as to die for us should want all heaven to rejoice when a soul is saved. ''He shall see of the travail of his soul and be satisfied.'' One of the blessings of good news is the privilege of telling it and rejoicing over it. It always does us good to rejoice over good news.

''I say unto you.'' In this utterance he displays the authority and dignity of his character. As much as to say ''I am one who knows all about heaven and what they do there.''

We notice then that the inhabitants of heaven know some things that take place upon the earth. Either they perceive it or it is told them. Why may not the former be the case?

One of the causes of joy in heaven is the salvation of men. It is possible then for mortals to increase the joy of heaven. *We can then be felt in our influence even in heaven.* How great is the influence of man. It affects three worlds—earth, hell and heaven.

See then in this verse the rebuke of the Pharisees. The conversion of one sinner stirs heaven, but the *attempt* to convert them makes Pharisees murmur. This shows Phariseeism in an awful light.

From so slight a foundation as this text Romanists deduce the doctrine of praying to angels and saints.

Notice he says ''Just persons which need no repentence.'' We learn from this that there are just or justified persons. No man is just by nature but he becomes just by being justified. God justifies because sin was repented of and faith exercised in Jesus. Being just he does not need to keep repenting or turning from sin each day. He has quit the sin business. So here we see Jesus recognizes that there is a class of persons, who do not need to repent, *because they do not commit sin.* This is the normal experience of every child of God.

THE LOST COIN. Vs. 8-10.

8 Either what woman having ten pieces of silver, if she lose one piece, doth not light a candle, and sweep the house, and seek diligently till she find *it?*

9 And when she hath found *it,* she calleth *her* friends and *her* neighbours together, saying, Rejoice with me; for I have found the piece which I had lost.

10 Likewise, I say unto you, there is joy in the presence of the angels of God over one sinner that repenteth.

The parable of the lost sheep is especially interesting to men. This of the lost coin is especially interesting to women; while the parable of the lost son particularly appeals to the affection of parents for their children.

The original calls the ''ten pieces of silver'' ''ten drachma.'' The drachma was a piece of money worth about eight pence—a day's wages in that country. ''Commentators have recognized the increasing value of the *sheep,* the *coin* and the *son* by the diminishing number from which they are lost. The *sheep* is but the hundredth part of the flock; the *coin* is but the tenth part; the *son* is one of the two.'' (Whedon.)

The women of that day wore these coins in their head dress. They were property that descended from mother to daughter and were considered very sacred. This woman owning only ten must have been a very poor woman and it was a great loss. No wonder she lighted a candle because the houses had no windows, and sought diligently with the broom to find the lost coin.

Commentators have noticed that the coin had the stamp of the government upon it. The human soul is like it in this particular. It has the image and superscription upon it—not of Cæsar but of the King of the Universe, for God created man in his own image. Man like the coin, while he is lost, is lost for all useful purposes.

The penetration of truth into the heart, the illumination of the Holy Spirit and the providences of life are like the lighting of the candle and the sweeping of the house. These produce conviction.

We think these two parables are an argument too for foreign missions. The great mass of the world are in the darkness of heathendom. If the shepherd could leave ninety nine saved sheep to go after one, how much more would he go if only *one* was in·

the fold and ninety nine were lost. There are more unsaved than saved in the world.

It takes a holy church to light the candle of conviction. Such a church will by its prayers and testimonials keep the unsaved under conviction. Dr. Whedon says here, ''The woman here is the Lamb's wife, the church. But if we adopt the interesting view that while the *Shepherd* is the *Son* of God, the woman, the *Holy Spirit,* and the *father,* in the third parable, God, the Father Almighty, then we may view this woman as the Church, in which the Holy Spirit dwells, and through which He works. Then as the Son was incarnated in the Christ, and the Father embodied in the creation, so the Holy Spirit is here impersonated in the living church of God.''

THE PARABLE OF THE LOST SON. Vs. 11-32.

11   And he said, A certain man had two sons:

12   And the younger of them said to *his* father, Father, give me the portion of goods that falleth *to me.* And he divided unto them *his* living.

13   And not many days after the younger son gathered all together, and took his journey into a far country, and there wasted his substance with riotous living.

14   And when he had spent all, there arose a mighty famine in that land; and he began to be in want.

15   And he went and joined himself to a citizen of that country; and he sent him into his fields to feed swine.

16   And he would fain have filled his belly with the husks that the swine did eat: and no man gave unto him.

17   And when he came to himself, he said, How many hired servants of my father's have bread enough and to spare, and I perish with hunger!

18   I will arise and go to my father, and will say unto him, Father, I have sinned against heaven, and before thee,

19   And am no more worthy to be called thy son: make me as one of thy hired servants.

20   And he arose, and came to his father. But when he was yet a great way off, his father saw him, and had compassion, and ran, and fell on his neck, and kissed him.

21   And the son said unto him, Father, I have sinned against heaven, and in thy sight, and am no more worthy to be called thy son.

22   But the father said to his servants, Bring forth the best robe, and put *it* on him; and put a ring on his hand, and shoes on *his* feet:

23 And bring hither the fatted calf, and kill *it;* and let us eat, and be merry:

24 For this my son was dead, and is alive again; he was lost, and is found. And they began to be merry.

25 Now his elder son was in the field: and as he came and drew nigh to the house, he heard musick and dancing.

26 And he called one of the servants, and asked what these things meant.

27 And he said unto him, Thy brother is come; and thy father hath killed the fatted calf, because he hath received him safe and sound.

28 And he was angry, and would not go in: therefore came his father out, and intreated him.

29 And he answering said to *his* father, Lo, these many years do I serve thee, neither transgresed I at any time thy commandment: and yet thou never gavest me a kid, that I might make merry with my friends:

30 But as soon as this thy son was come, which hath devoured thy living with harlots, thou hast killed for him the fatted calf.

31 And he said unto him, Son, thou art ever with me, and all that I have is thine.

32 It was meet that we should make merry, and be glad: for this thy brother was dead, and is alive again; and was lost, and is found.

This, greatest of parables, is usually called The Parable of the Prodigal Son. This is no doubt an expressive title, but it is not scriptural—at least the term is not found in the Scripture. It illustrates the repentance of a backslider and the treatment he often receives from unholy church members. The older son represents the Pharisee and the younger the Publicans. There are many great truths, and lessons in this parable.

I. *It shows some phases of sin.* 1. Independence of God. He said "Father give me the portion of goods." He feels that he can set up business for himself, independent of God. This is the attitude of sinners, and backsliders. They feel competent to take care of themselves, independent of God. 2. Departure from God. "He took his journey into a far country." 3. A state of soul poverty. He "wasted his substance."

II. *The results of sin.* These are seen in verse 14. 1. Prodigality. Wasting and squandering his God given powers. 2. Famine. "A mighty famine" always exists where the soul is away from God. There is nothing to satisfy. 3. "Want." Soul starvation. 4. Service of Satan. "Joined himself to a citizen of that country.'' 5. The misery of sin—to feed swine. The devil makes sinners feed his swine. The Jews were taught to look upon swine as unclean animals. The lowest depths of wretchedness possible, in the conception of a Jew, was herding swine. But herding swine was a step up from his condition when feasting with harlots. It was an attempt at reformation. It shows that even human reform does not get us back to God.

III. *The accompaniments of true repentence.* We say *accompaniments* because these accompaniments are often taken for repentance itself. 1. Conviction. ''He came to himself.'' He began to see his condition. 2. A sense of his unfitness for dwelling with God. ''Servants of my father have enough.'' 3. A perception of the destructiveness of sin. ''I perish with hunger.'' 4. A determination to return to God. ''I will arise.'' 5. Sorrow for sin. ''Father I have sinned.'' 6. Confession of guilt and unworthiness. ''I am no more worthy.'' 7. Humility. ''Make me as . . . hired servant.''

IV. *True repentance.* This is especially described in verses 20-21. (a) Abandonment of sin. ''He arose and came to his father.'' (b) Confession to God. ''Father, I have sinned.''

We also see: 1. The compassion of God displayed at the faintest turning to him. ''When he was yet a great way off his father . . . had compassion.'' 2. The welcome which God gives returning wanderers. 3. Pardon. 4. Righteousness and holiness imparted. ''The best robe.'' Notice in verse 21 that while he confesses himself to be unworthy to be a son, he does not ask to become a servant. God does not wish to make sinners servants, but sons. ''Being clothed with holiness, *married* as it were to Jesus Christ (2 Cor. 11:2)'' (Clarke). John Wesley says, ''He arrays him with the robe of a Saviour's righteousness, with inward and outward holiness, adorns him with all the sanctifying graces and honors him with tokens of adopting love.'' Notice the robe of holiness is given *after* pardon.

Let us now look more closely at this parable. Having provided the best robe, the ring and shoes, the father now calls for the fatted calf with which to make a feast. This illustrates the fact that salvation is a joyful feast, a satisfying portion as far as the saved man is concerned. More than that the father too is glad. This is akin to verses 7 and 10—joy in the presence of the angels—and is a rebuke aimed at the Pharisees.

So they began to be merry. Of all people in the world, the truly saved ought to and will be joyful. Our religious joy on earth is the echo of joy in heaven.

Now comes in more forcibly the point at which the three parables are aimed—the Pharisees represented by the condemnation of the elder brother. ''He heard the music and dancing.'' Dean Alford tries to make an argument for dancing from this passage. Everything that Jesus mentions in parables he does not necessarily sanction. For instance in verse 12 it was illegal to ask for his portion, according to Jewish law, and the father was over indulgent to grant it. But this would not sanction lax family government. We must never try to make an illustration mean what the speaker did not intend.

The elder brother demanded ''what these things meant.'' This is akin to the objections and fault finding that carnal professors of religion offer against the demonstrations of those who are rejoicing over their own salvation and that of others. So he does not go into the feast but stands outside and finds fault. He can not see why so much fuss should be made over the restoration of his brother.

He boasts of his morality. He says ''neither transgressed I at any time.'' The proud Pharisees thought it was a feast in honor of his brother when in fact it was a feast expressive of the joy of the father, in the restoration of his son. Jealousy is one of the strong characteristics of the carnal mind.

He complains ''thou never gavest me a kid.'' He who rests his salvation in an outward service only, a merely moral performance, will receive nothing, kid, lamb, peace, joy or happiness. Godet says ''Do not these sayings which Jesus puts into the mouth of the righteous legalist, contain the keenest criticism of a state of soul wherein men discharge duty, all the while, abhoring it, and wherein, while avoiding sin, they thirst after it?'' He adds a fling at his brother as having been ''with harlots.'' Pharisees never forgive a man's past life even when the Lord does. Thank God, He never brings up the past, when he forgives. He says he ''will remember our sins against us no more.'' It is better to fall into the hands of God rather than man.

And so the elder brother, with his self righteousness and churlishness becomes himself the *lost* son. He has lost the filial brotherly spirit.

The father reasons now with the elder son and tells him that he would lose nothing if he was a true son. Forgiving the younger would not injure the rights of the elder son. If we are true to God, the favor which he bestows upon others will not rob us. If we are uncharitable to others we shall lose the favor of God.

Wesley says God will not raise sinners to a state of glory equal to that of those who have always served him, if the latter have, upon the whole, made a greater progress in inward as well as outward holiness.

CHAPTER XVI.

HOLINESS AN ENEMY OF COVETOUSNESS.

A Parable Against Covetousness. Vs. 1-18. A Revelation Against Covetousness. Vs. 19-31.

The two forms of inbred sin most common in the church are pride and covetousnes. Jesus rebuked the first in the three parables of the previous chapter. He now utters two rebukes against the second—covetousness.

A PARABLE AGAINST COVETOUSNESS. Vs. 1-18.

1 And he said also unto his disciples, There was a certain rich man, which had a steward; and the same was accused unto him that he had wasted his goods.

2 And he called him, and said unto him, How is it that I hear this of thee? give an account of thy stewardship; for thou mayest be no longer steward.

3 Then the steward said within himself, What shall I do? for my lord taketh away from me the stewardship: I cannot dig; to beg I am ashamed.

4 I am resolved what to do, that, when I am put out of the stewardship, they may receive me into their houses.

5 So he called every one of his lord's debtors *unto him,* and said unto the first, How much owest thou unto my lord?

6 And he said, An hundred measures of oil. And he said unto him, Take thy bill, and sit down quickly and write fifty.

7 Then said he to another, And how much owest thou? And he said, An hundred measures of wheat. And he said unto him, Take thy bill and write fourscore.

8 And the lord commended the unjust steward, because he had done wisely: for the children of this world are in their generation wiser than the children of light.

9 And I say unto you, Make to yourselves friends of the mammon of unrighteousness; that, when ye fail, they may receive you into everlasting habitations.

10 He that is faithful in that which is least is faithful also in much: and he that is unjust in the least is unjust also in much.

11 If therefore ye have not been faithful in the unrighteous mammon, who will commit to your trust the true *riches?*

12 And if ye have not been faithful in that which is another man's, who shall give you that which is your own?

13 No servant can serve two masters: for either he will hate the one, and love the other; or else he will hold to the one, and despise the other. Ye cannot serve God and mammon.

14 And the Pharisees also, who were covetous, heard all these things: and they derided him.

15 And he said unto them, Ye are they which justify yourselves before men; but God knoweth your hearts: for that which is highly esteemed among men is abomination in the sight of God.

16 The law and the prophets *were* until John: since that time the kingdom of God is preached, and every man presseth into it.

17 And it is easier for heaven and earth to pass, than one tittle of the law to fail.

18 Whosoever putteth away his wife and marrieth another, committeth adultery: and whosoever marrieth her that is put away from *her* husband committeth adultery.

The true interpretation of this parable is the stewardship with which God has entrusted us over our money, property, time, talents, friends, position, etc. We must give an account of the way we use these.

This steward had wasted his lord's goods. It is just as truly stealing for a steward to waste as to commit highway robbery or rob his lord's purse. Is not the man who is misimproving his talents and opportunities robbing God? God gave us all we have for a purpose—to glorify him.

This is a lesson in entire consecration. Covetousness is one of the great hindrances to entire consecration. See examples of Achan, the young man (Luke 18:18-28), Ananias and Sapphira. This man *wasted.* There are two extremes, one is to live beyond one's means, and therefore use other people's property; the other is to live below our means for the sake of hoarding. The miser and the spendthrift are the two extremes. They both rob God.

The lord of this steward had heard that he was living beyond his income and therefore called him to render an account. When a man is living beyond his means, it is usually a fact that someone is being or will be robbed.

As sure as we live, we shall all be called to render an account to God of *our* stewardship. The unprofitable steward is condemned already. The judgment day only fixes his punishment. The righteous steward will continue his trust and have higher employment in the world to come. While death will close the accounts of the unfaithful.

The steward began to ask himself the serious question, ''What shall I do?'' He was in a dilemma. He was not accustomed to labor. He could not do that to any profit. His pride kept him from begging. So he hit on an expedient. He expected to be put out of his stewardship and he resolved on a trick that would benefit him for the time being in two ways. 1. He would persuade the tenants to falsify in their accounts. Where a tenant should have paid a hundred measures of oil, he allowed him to call it fifty, or a hundred measures of wheat, he called it fifty. Thus the lord would not see that he had been cheating him, and there would not be as much required of the tenant in the future. Thus the tenants became partners in his rascality. 2. The tenants were in consideration of the discount, to take care of him, if he lost his position. So he concealed much of his fraud and at the same time provided for his future necessities. This is what the world calls shrewdness—wisdom. This is what many a niggardly rich man tries to do with the Lord. He makes benefactions in his will to the cause of God or charitable objects in hopes of bribing the Lord.

''And the lord commended the unjust steward.'' Many have been puzzled with this passage as to how the Lord could commend an unjust man. They have got the wrong lord in their minds. Verse 8 is the words of our Lord Jesus Christ. He is telling how the lord of the steward was pleased at the latter's ''shrewdness.'' It is not our Lord Jesus Christ who is commending an unjust steward, who ''had done wisely'' from his standpoint, as he saw things. Jesus means if we would do as wisely from our standpoint as he, we would make our money our friend in the future life, as this man attempted to make his stewardship help him in his time of future emergency. Money is an awful enemy or a means of grace, according to the way we use it.

He (Jesus) says, ''The children of this world are wiser in their generation than the children of light.'' In other words the children of the darkness of this world are wiser in their darkness than the children of light are in their light. The Revised Version translates it, ''The children of this world are wiser *for* their generation.''

Justin says ''The children of this world have for the most part a steady regard for the end which they pursue; they are wise in choosing proper means, and finding out the nearest way to compass their end; they are vigilant and active, constant and resolute in their pursuits. On the other hand the children of light sometimes quite overlook and forget the great concern, have intervals of remissness and indifference and are easily deterred and unsettled, and drawn aside by every impediment and discouragement.'' The point therefore held up for imitation is the *foresight* of the unjust steward. God's professed people with the true riches do not often use the same foresight as the children of this world do with mammon. This is an argument for holiness or whole heartedness in religion. Are we using our money with foresight as to how it will affect our condition in the everlasting habitation of heaven? Are we making our money our friend so that its use will enrich and expand our souls here and make our seat higher in heaven? Or are we so abusing it by misuse as to shrivel our souls and fatten our covetousness?

Mammon meant literally *that in which we put our trust.* It is usually applied to money because that is the god of this world, in which they trust. Jesus does not mean to say that we shall have no money if we belong to him. But we must not make it our God. It is only entrusted to us for a little time as God's stewards. The professed Christian who finds inbred sin in his nature in the form of covetousness is in awful danger, as much as if he had a licentious disposition. Any use of money except for the glory of God makes money our enemy, to curse us. Who believes it? Covetousness is one of the most often described sins in the Bible. Yet how few sermons we hear against it. Rich men are the most envied but really the most to be pitied of all men. They have a hard time getting to heaven. Jesus said so. If we have little, thank God. If we have much thank God that he has confidence enough in us to let us have the stewardship of it, and let us have it, as an evidence of the fact that he believes he has grace enough to get us through, in spite of it, if we will cling close to him.

''Faithful in that which is least.'' Nothing is great or small in our affairs as seen by God. He judges our attitude of will towards all things great and small. If we are unfaithful in the use of money, how can we expect that God will entrust the greater riches of heaven? We believe God has higher employments in heaven, but only for those who have been faithful in the lesser responsibilities of this life. Money will not buy our way into heaven. But its use here will determine the measure of our reward in heaven.

The depravity which causes us to be unfaithful in the use of money will shut us out of heaven entirely.

"Another man's" (Verse 12). Represents our trust given by God.

Jesus now goes on to give a still further lesson drawn from the parable thus, "No servant can serve two masters." The two masters referred to here are God and Mammon. He did not say we ought not but we *can not*. The heart can obey God and Mammon at the same time. We can not be worldly and spiritual at the same time. We are all serving one or the other. We can not live without serving some one. Bishop Huntington says, "It has been said that the difference between one man and another is in their choice of their Masters. Some master every human being has, and none are in so complete a bondage as those who fancy themselves to be absolutely independent. There are people who scorn the idea of working at all, who yet work harder, put up with more humiliations and part with more real liberty, for vanity, for fashion, for a certain standing in society or a certain amount of prosperity, or a sensual pleasure, than the serf that is bought and sold and whipped. So it appears that men are always serving their own masters. Every heart chooses."

The result of this discourse was the covetous Pharisees derided him. The shot struck home. Jesus did not preach concerning the sins of the children of Israel in the Wilderness. But he struck home at the sinners of his own day. He preached in such a manner that they knew what and whom he meant as he uncovered their sin of covetousness.

As they derided him, he spoke still more pointedly and plainly, telling them that they justified themselves before men, but God knew the condition of their hearts and did not estimate men according to human standards.

People who are not wholly given to God are much like these Pharisees. They are all the time trying to preserve their reputation among men, rather than with God. They were trying to make up their lack of holiness of heart by outward display.

Jesus tells them ''that which is highly esteemed of men is an abomination to God.'' In other words God is not satisfied with external righteousness, which men think is sufficient. He wants holiness of heart and that is what carnal men hate. These holiness fighters when he probed their hearts acted as holiness fighters do today. Scott says ''Such characters are commonly the bitterest enemies to the power of godliness; and whilst those who know the worth and danger of their souls are pressing through dangers and temptations into the kingdom of God, they are carping at the doctrines or exhortations of faithful ministers, and explaining away the Scriptures which run counter to their sins, making void the law of God, by their own notions or traditions, and attempting to prejudice better disposed persons against the truth.

At the time these Pharisees were boasting of their righteousness, they were violating the spirit of the law. Godet says, ''The law itself which they violate at the very moment they make their boast shall remain as the eternal expression of divine holiness and is the dreadful standard by which they shall be judged.'' Jesus declares of that law that it would be easier for heaven and earth to pass away than one least bit of the law, which has for its essence, holiness.

(He adds a word concerning divorce, right here between these two rebukes. He is evidently referring to the Pharisees who had been putting away their wives and re-marrying. He calls it adultery).

A REVELATION AGAINST COVETOUSNESS. Vs. 19-29.

19 There was a certain rich man, which was clothed in purple and fine linen, and fared sumptuously every day:

20 And there was a certain beggar named Lazarus, which was laid at his gate, full of sores,

21 And desiring to be fed with the crumbs which fell from the rich man's table: moreover the dogs came and licked his sores.

22 And it came to pass that the beggar died, and was carried by

the angels into Abraham's bosom: the rich man also died, and was buried;

23   And in hell he lifted up his eyes, being in torments, and seeth Abraham afar off, and Lazarus in his bosom.

24   And he cried and said, Father Abraham, have mercy on me, and send Lazarus, that he may dip the tip of his finger in water, and cool my tongue; for I am tormented in this flame.

25   But Abraham said, Son, remember that thou in thy lifetime receivedst thy good things, and likewise Lazarus evil things: but now he is comforted, and thou art tormented.

26   And beside all this, between us and you there is a great gulf fixed: so that they which would pass from hence to you cannot; neither can they pass to us, that *would come* from thence.

27   Then he said, I pray thee therefore, father, that thou wouldst send him to my father's house:

28   For I have five brethren; that he may testify unto them, lest they also come into this place of torment.

29   Abraham saith unto him, They have Moses and the prophets; let them hear them.

30   And he said, Nay, father Abraham: but if one went unto them from the dead, they will repent.

31   And he said unto him, If they hear not Moses and the prophets, neither will they be persuaded, though one rose from the dead.

In this revelation of the rich man and Lazarus, he shows the awful results of a life of covetousness. This revelation concerning the future life was given as a warning to his hearers who had been deriding him when he exposed their covetousness, (Vs. 14) to show them the awful doom of the covetous. The former part of the chapter is the introduction to this revelation, especially verses 14, 18. Godet says, ''This is given to show the Pharisees the end of their paraded show of righteousness and the advent of true holiness.'' This seems to be the meaning of verse 16.

Man has in many respects shown his greatness in his mighty achievements, in science, in literature, in art, in his use and adaptation of the forces of nature to useful ends. But there is one sinmple thing that he can not with all his achievements bring to pass. It is the power to read the future.

But there was one on earth once to whom the unseen world and the future life were as an open book. It was Jesus Christ. He here lifts the curtain and gives us a view of the unseen world.

We refuse to call this a parable or nothing but a parable. All the narratives Jesus used were parabolic, as all true stories are that are told to illustrate truth. But we have no reason to call this a parable. No one can prove that it was a parable. It is as truly a history as is the life of Jesus a history. Where is the proof that it was a parable? If it is a parable then we may with equal authority say that the narrative ''now when Jesus was born in Bethlehem of Judea'' is a parable and the whole history of Jesus also. The fact of it is we have allowed Universalists and Annihilationists to call it a parable until we use the term ourselves and almost believe it to be so. To those who say that this was only parabolic or symbolic we say nevertheless, symbols point to realities. If symbolic, the truths symbolized are of no less force. *But rather the thing symbolized is always greater than the symbol.* The great feature of narrative is the sharp contrasts all the way through. Notice them.

1. *The contrasts in the social conditions of the two men.* Their clothing was radically different. The rich man was clothed in purple and fine linen. Garments dyed in purple were extremely costly in those days and fine linen no less so. Only the very wealthy could afford thus to dress. The poor man wore rags, which were not sufficient to cover his sores. What a contrast. The rich man had servants to wait upon him. The poor man had only dogs. The rich man fared sumptously—had more than he could eat. The poor man was so hungry that he was glad to eat the scanty morsels of food that fell on the floor. The rich man and the poor man were not unlike the two extremes of society today— the multi-millionaire and the tramp. The rich man has been called Dives. His real name is not given. It was not worth re- membering. Dives is the Latin word for *rich man.* The beggar's name was Lazarus, which means *the help of God.*

The rich man's sin was not in being rich. It is no sin to be rich and no virtue to be poor. Abraham, Job and Joseph of Ari- mathea were rich. Wherein then lay the sin of the rich man? It was here: his covetousness made him forget his poor brother. The law required that wherever a Jew saw another in want he must relieve him if he had the power. ''If there be among you a poor man of thy brethren within any of thy gates in thy land which the Lord thy God giveth thee, thou shalt not harden thy heart, nor shut thine hand from thy poor brother. But thou shalt

open thine hand wide unto him and shalt surely lend him sufficient for his need, in that which he wanteth.'' (Deut. 15:7-8.)

We suppose few latter day church members realize their duty
to the poor. God says much about it in his Book, and declares
that the reward of the last day will be apportioned according to
our faithfulness in regard to God's poor. (See Matt. 25:34-46.)

Notice a similarity—they both died. As far as this world
was concerned death treated them both alike. Their bodies saw
corruption. Death makes no class distinctions.

Notice another contrast in their burial. The beggar dies.
Probably he did not have a decent burial. Nothing is even mentioned of his burial. It says with a divine sarcasm in view of
what follows, ''The rich man died and was buried.'' It was probably a great funeral with pomp and parade. It was the last honor
he ever received and he was not there to receive it; so it was
lavished on his decaying body. Yes, he was ''buried.''

Another contrast is seen in the attendants. The friends of the
rich man could go with him only to the grave, but angels went
with Lazarus to Abraham's bosom. The world did not miss Lazarus, but God loved him. The world doubtless thought the rich
man would obtain great honors and place in heaven for was he
not a rich churchman?

But the scene is reversed in the other world. This world is all
the heaven that sinners will have and all the hell that the righteous will know and in the world to come the rich man found his hell
and the poor man his heaven. What a change for Lazarus. One
moment cared for by dogs, another moment cherished by angels.
We learn in this passage that angels come for the good. Do
devils come for the wicked? What a contrast for the rich man;
waited on by servants at one moment, the next moment in the
company of devils. Lazarus is no longer lying at the gate of the
purse proud rich man, but in *Abraham's bosom*. The rich man
is in Hades—the place of departed spirits. The Jews who gave
much of their time to the study of the Scriptures understood,
1. That while the body was in the grave, the soul was in the
other world. 2. That there were two conditions of destiny in the
world to come—Paradise called Abraham's bosom, and Gehenna,
the place of punishment. Jesus did not contradict these ideas,

but added to them showing here that the covetous will go to hell. "As far as bliss is from misery, so far is holiness from depravity." (Crosby.)

The Jews spoke of all true believers as going to Abraham. He was the father and founder of the church to which they all belonged. This was the Paradise of which Jesus spoke to the dying thief on the cross. (Luke 23:43.) It is the intermediate state where souls await the full joys or penalties awarded at the Judgment. It is incipient heaven for the righteous or incipient hell for the wicked.

The rich man there sees (he still sees) Lazarus afar off and he cried "Father Abraham." The Roman Catholics believe in praying to departed saints. Wesley says here, "It can not be denied that there is one precedent in Scripture of praying to departed saints, but who is it that prays, and with what success? Will any who consider this be fond of copying after him?" The rich prayed to Abraham in vain.

He wanted the aid of Lazarus. He was more anxious for the company of Lazarus than formerly. Notice the scene in the other world is just as graphic and real as the scenes of this world. Why believe Christ's statement of the scene on this earth and not believe his statement of the scene in the spirit world? Crosby says of the rich man, "He does not seek holiness, but only relief from suffering."

We now see the key to the parable and connect it with verse 9. It is this: the rich man had failed to make his money his friend, as a faithful steward. This scene in hell is the result.

See the contrast again. Crumbs of bread for the poor man on earth; not even the wished for drops of water for the rich man in hell.

He is now in the tormenting flame. The hell fires of covetous lust kindled on earth, consume him. This torture to the soul is worse than fire in its awful pains in the body. The hell fire of sin in us will torment us forever if it is not driven out by Holy Ghost fire.

Abraham replied to the piteous call for drops of water. "Son remember." One of the tormenting things about hell is to have to remember occurrences of this life. An eternity-quickened memory will be a scorpion lash to the lost.

"Son remember that thou . . . hadst thy good things." They were his good things because he made them so by choice. He put a supreme value upon them, and let spiritual things alone. He thought they were all there is in life worth living. He chose them rather than divine things. He had them while they lasted, but they were only for a season. He could not take them into eternity with him. He made the mistake of choosing things that were to perish. They were his *good* things because he thought they were the highest good.

Lazarus had evil things. They were all the evil things he ever had. They were not so evil after all, because they did not interfere with his religion. They did not hinder his possession of eternal riches. The rich man had the real evil things. His good things, food, raiment, money and so forth, were not evil in themselves. But everything is evil (no matter however good in itself) that hinders our race for glory. Sometimes good things become evil because they hinder the soul. We shall find when we get to heaven a different standard of judging things. The very worst things we had to deal with on earth will be found to be our choicest valuables, and we shall pity those we thought richest favored because their "good things" were only snares to their souls. This passage shows that the real object of the narrative is to warn against covetousness.

Another contrast is that the rich man comforted on earth is tormented in the other world and the poor man tormented on earth is comforted in Paradise.

"But besides all this . . . there is a great gulf fixed." It is not a narrow ditch or seam but a great gulf. These two men were far apart in the other world. In one sense—that of character they were far apart in this world. There is a great gulf between the character of a proud, covetous worldly debauchee and a plain, simple, humble child of God. The state of character is fixed in the world to come. There is no further probation. The gulf begins in this life. It grows wider and wider and becomes fixed in the world to come (Rev. 22:11). Each one of us is now on the side of the gulf that we love best—holiness or sin. The rest of the verse goes on to say that souls could not cross the gulf if they would. If we do not like holiness in this world, we shall not like it in the world to come. The rich man did not lament his sins, but only the consequences of them. These words of Christ are worth pondering for he knew what he was talking about. How anxious then should we be to be holy in this life.

The rich man now that his doom is sealed has a desire to keep his brothers from coming to him. He feared that their presence in hell would add to his misery. People sometimes say if their friends are in hell, they do not wish to be saved themselves. How ungrateful! If our friends are lost shall we join them to increase their misery? This would be just the reason why we should not join them. The rich man in hell was a gentleman in comparison with some who make no effort to get their family saved.

He wanted Lazarus to go as a witness—not as a preacher. The greatest method of disseminating the truth is by testimony. He thought a living witness risen from the dead here of great effect in persuading his brothers.

Jesus replied that they had Moses and the prophets. This was the Bible of that day as the New Testament had not yet been written. The first five books of the Old Testament were written by Moses. Wordsworth observes that this is ''a remarkable testimony from Christ himself that the canon of the Old Testament is what it was believed by the Jews, to be, the Word of God speaking by Moses and the prophets; and that it had been preserved by the Jewish church to our Lord's age (whence it has come down to ours) in purity and integrity: that it is genuine, authentic and divine, and that they who will not receive it as such are in so hardened a state that they would not be persuaded though one should rise from the dead. It is here intimated also, that men come into the ''torment'' of Hades, as Dives did *because* they will not hear the Old Testament Scriptures. What then will be the condition of those who refuse to hear Christ and the apostles speaking in the New?''

One would naturally suppose that to see a man rise from the dead would convince the most skeptical and cause them to repent. But Jesus said that was not true. A man may be intellectually convinced of the truth of Christianity and yet refuse to yield, for it takes belief of the heart to bring salvation. If God had to work the miracle of raising some one from the dead every time he wanted to convict a man, very soon these occurrences would be common and lose their force and cease to be miraculous. In fact Jesus did rise from the dead. But the Jews generally refused to believe him. If men would not believe when Jesus himself rose from the dead they would not believe if any other man came from the regions of the dead. They would probably say he did not really die and hence the resurrection and revelations were only a hoax.

God gives every man light sufficient for salvation, if he will walk up to that light. If he refuses to walk up to that light, it is of no use to waste further light upon him. The five brethren had Moses and the prophets, if they walked up to the standard there laid down they would be saved. So Jesus here teaches that there is light enough in the Holy Scriptures to lead men to salvation. Bengel says, ''We are saved by faithful believing and not by ghosts.'' The rich man thought his brethren who would not believe the Bible would believe a ghost. Abraham says they would not be even *persuaded.*

Ingersoll used to say, ''show us a miracle and we will believe.'' God has done it and he did not believe. The Book of God to which the rich man himself refers is miracle enough to cause men to believe. (See Isa. 55:10-13.) In verse 13 of that chapter the prophet, Isaiah says of the word of God, ''It shall be to the Lord for a name, for an everlasting *sign* (miracle) which shall not be cut off.'' The power and achievements of God's Word, amidst opposition in all ages that would have destroyed any other book is miracle sufficient to convince all candid people. With the immutable word, which shall not return to its author void, we do not need to hold any communications with departed spirits. Modern Spiritism (often miscalled Spiritualism) is unscriptural and therefore of the devil.

CHAPTER XVII.

THE IMPORTANCE OF HOLINESS BY FAITH.

Holiness Is Obtained by Faith. Vs. 1-6. Holiness Is Not Obtained by Works. Vs. 7-10. A Miracle Showing How to Exercise Faith for Holiness. Vs. 11-19. Holiness Has Its Seat in the Heart. Vs. 20-21. The Importance of Holiness to Keep Us Always Ready. Vs. 22-37.

We have given the title ''The importance of holiness by faith'' because the two parables and parabolic miracle treat of holiness obtained by faith and the remaining part of the chapter shows the necessity of holiness as a kingdom within us to keep us ready for the coming of the Son of Man. We have thus divided the chapter.

HOLINESS IS OBTAINED BY FAITH. Vs. 1-6.

1 Then said he unto the disciples, It is impossible but that offences will come: but woe *unto him,* through whom they come!

2 It were better for him that a millstone were hanged about his neck, and he cast into the sea, than that he should offend one of these little ones.

3 Take heed to yourselves: If thy brother trespass against thee, rebuke him; and if he repent, forgive him.

4 And if he trespass against thee seven times in a day, and seven times in a day turn again to thee, saying, I repent; thou shalt forgive him.

5 And the apostles said unto the Lord, Increase our faith.

6 And the Lord said, If ye had faith as a grain of mustard seed, ye might say unto this sycamine tree, Be thou plucked up by the root, and be thou planted in the sea; and it should obey you.

In order to understand this chapter, we must refer back to the opening of chapter 15. The Pharisees and Scribes had found fault with Jesus for preaching to publicans and sinners. Jesus therefore spoke the three parables of chapter 15 and one parable of chapter 16, and gave the narrative of the rich man and Lazarus to rebuke the sins of the Pharisees and Scribes. Now he turns in chapter 17 to his disciples. Doubtless some of them were converted publicans, who would feel disheartened at the treatment of the Pharisees. He tells them that they must expect ill treatment in this world.

So he says, ''It is impossible but offences will come.'' We all must expect harsh treatment, especially from a worldly church, if we seek to live spiritual religion. The word offence means a stumbling block or occasion to stumble or backslide. In other words there is plenty of occasion to get sour and lose our religion over the treatment of others. If we think we are on a picnic in this world and every one will treat us as they should, we shall be mistaken. We shall meet the same treatment that Jesus met. There will always be found sinful, worldly people in and out of the church who will be a hindrance to those who are seeking to be godly. How many have been turned from the way of life by harsh treatment and persecution. In our day how many have got discouraged in the way of holiness by severe persecution, sometimes right in the church too. An awful woe is pronounced here on those who hinder others. The devil himself could not act meaner against those who profess holiness than some who profess to be followers of Jesus Christ. Hebrews 12:13-15 is very significant. How much we all need holiness of heart to enable us to exert a proper, salutary influence.

''It were better for him that a millstone were hanged about his neck.'' This shows the awful fate of fighters of holiness. If a man were taken into the middle of the ocean and thrown overboard with a millstone about his neck, he would go to eternal glory, if he were a child of God. But to be an opposer of one person seeking to live a humble prayerful life means an awful doom. It is an awful sin to so oppose any one as to cause them to let go on their hold upon God.

''Take heed to yourselves.'' Having said so much as to the fate of opposers, he now turns to his disciples and tells them that the opposition of others is no excuse for their backsliding. If people put stumbling blocks in our way we are to blame if we fall over them. We can not throw responsibility upon them. We ought to pity them when we consider the awful fate that awaits them, but we have no excuse for backsliding over their persecutions. It is astonishing how some people will ill treat the Lord because some one ill treats them. Would not a man be foolish to go home and abuse his wife because some one had abused him? And yet some people will give up serving God and backslide because they have been ill treated by man. The worst injury any one can do us is to cause us to lose our religion. We ought to realize when men ill treat us, that it is simply an artifice of Satan, who is back of the whole business trying to upset us. ''Take heed to yourself.'' God gives us salvation and then gives us our brother man to practice the principles of salvation upon.

''If the brother trespass against thee.'' Sometimes the most trying things we have to meet come from our brothers in the household of God, who will infringe upon our rights. To have the grace to put up with disagreeable and unkind people is a high state of experience. Even where every body is wholly sanctified it takes a good deal of grace to put up with each other's whims, notions and practices. But when we reflect on the numbers in our churches who are carnal, it become on especially difficult matter to keep churches harmonious. The third chapter of First Corinthians is a good illustration of the quarrels that arise in churches whose members are not wholly sanctified. Doddridge says of this passage, ''This contains a strong and important intimation of how much sin and scandal are occasioned by a severe, quarrelsome temper in the disciples of Christ, as it not only stirs up the corruptions of those with whom they contend but lead others to think meanly of a profession which has little efficacy to soften and sweeten the temper of those who maintain it.'' The greatest hindrance to the spread of the gospel is the display of unsanctified temper among professed followers of the Lord Jesus Christ.

Jesus says, if he trespass ''rebuke him.'' Most any one is willing to obey this command. We are all glad that it is given and how ready we are to rebuke. But he says in the next sentence, ''But if he repent forgive him.'' Ah! we are not so ready to obey this as the former command. ''Love and holiness meet together in this precept; holiness begins with rebuking, then, when the rebuke has once been taken, love pardons.'' (Godet.) There is a weak, maudlin idea quite current that holiness is a spineless, jelly fish arrangement that smiles on sin and allows it to go un-rebuked. The Scriptural idea is that proper rebuke (in the proper spirit) will lead to penitence. It takes a holy heart to rebuke in the proper spirit. In any other spirit rebuke will fail. We must have the forgiving spirit, if we expect God to forgive us. ''He who will not forgive others breaks down the bridge over which he must travel himself.''

We are to forgive even if he sins against us ''seven times in a day.'' While we must cherish the forgiving spirit, yet we can not pronounce forgiveness until it is asked. And then we can forgive only personal wrongs. No priest, potentate or human being of any kind can forgive sins against God.

When the disciples heard the command to forgive seven times in a day they were astounded. It almost took their breath and they cried, ''Lord, increase our faith.'' They thought they would have to receive a great increase of faith in order to do that.

This is the only instance on record where the disciples ever asked any spiritual blessing of Jesus. They made a great mistake in asking for an increase of faith. In one sense it is an insult to ask God for an increase in faith; an increase of faith in whom? in God? It certainly is an insult to ask an increase of faith in man. Suppose we have known a man intimately for a number of years and we tell him we wish we had more faith in him. He would take it as an insult. But if we are acquainted with a worthy man, the more we know him the stronger will grow our faith in him. Instead then of asking God for more faith in him, we ought to ask for a better acquaintance with him. We can become better acquainted with him and if we do, we shall certainly have a firmer faith in him.

So Jesus tells them that if they have faith as a grain of mustard seed, they would be able to command ''this sycamine tree to be plucked up by the roots.'' These are figurative expressions. Of course we are not to ask for things outside the realm of faith. It can not be taken literally. It is not the pulling up of literal forest trees. In another place he speaks of faith that will move mountains (Matt. 17:20), not literal mountains. This was a figure of speech to denote the removal of difficulties. Let us notice then what is meant by the sycamine tree and the faith like a grain of mustard seed.

1. *The sycamine tree.* This was the Egyptian mulberry tree —a tree whose roots were so numerous and so spread out and intertwined as to be impossible of extraction by any natural means. What then was the difficulty here as great as to extract a sycamine tree from the earth? If we study the context we shall see. They had been commanded to forgive a trespassing brother seven times in a day. This seemed impossible from a human standpoint. And so they asked for increase of faith. Why did it seem impossible? Because of the natural disposition in man that makes it hard to forgive. Our old evil nature likes to get even and have revenge. But if we have faith like a grain of mustard seed we can have that evil nature removed. Some people ask where does it teach the doctrine of eradication in the Bible? Here is one of the many places where it is taught. We might ask where does the Bible teach anything else?

2. *Mustard seed faith.* We have a parable in Matthew 13:31-32 spoken by Jesus in which he said the kingdom of heaven was in its growth like the thrifty development of the lively flourishing seed of mustard. In other words the mustard seed was an illustration of a healthy genuine divine faith, the fruit of the Spirit (Gal. 5:22) allowed to develop in the heart of a child of God, who goes straight on being loyal to God after his conversion. The man who does not backslide but grows up into Christ, his living head in all things has a vigorous faith. And when he sees it his privilege to have sin removed from his heart does not stagger at the promise but easily trusts God to do it.

The reason so many people have so weak faith when it comes to trusting God for a clean heart is because they have had so many backslidings and such an up and down experience that their faith is sickly. It has not grown like a mustard seed. No wonder such people find it hard to believe and try to explain their failure by saying, ''I am different from other people. It comes natural for them to be religious.'' If we had more real experiences of justification, there would be less unbelief as regards entire sanctification.

HOLINESS IS NOT OBTAINED BY WORKS. Vs. 7-10.

7 But which of you, having a servant plowing or feeding cattle, will say unto him by and by, when he is come from the field, Go and sit down to meat?

8 And will not rather say unto him, Make ready wherewith I may sup, and gird thyself, and serve me, till I have eaten and drunken; and afterward thou shalt eat and drink?

9 Doth he thank that servant because he did the things that were commanded him? I trow not.

10 So likewise ye, when ye shall have done all those things which are commanded you, say, We are unprofitable servants: we have done that which was our duty to do.

Having shown that we can be entirely sanctified by faith he now speaks a parable to teach that we can not be saved by works. Why does this parable follow immediately the other? Most people are trying to get saved by works rather than by faith. Salvation by faith is not popular with the carnal mind. You will not hear its praises sounded in the daily paper, or in the markets, or places of worldly associations, or with formalists or religionists generally. We know to be sure that the Reformation, that improved the whole world on all lines, was brought about by the doctrine of justification by faith, but nevertheless the way of faith for individual salvation, "the faith that works by love and purifies the heart and overcomes the world" is not popular. Men love to be saved by their own works. It gives the credit to themselves. The carnal mind does not enjoy being dependent on either God or man for salvation. So the moralist brings forward his good works as an excuse for not being justified by repentance towards God and faith in our Lord Jesus Christ. And having been justified by faith the carnal Christian seeks to be entirely sanctified by some other means, although the Word of God as clearly declares we are sanctified by faith (Acts 26:18) as that we are justified by faith. Hence theories of getting rid of the carnal mind by evolution, growth, works, etc., are very popular in the church today. On a Roman Catholic tombstone in Ireland is recorded the good deeds of the departed "*which made heaven her debtor.*" The man who seeks any kind of salvation from sin in any way except by faith is trying to make the Lord his debtor and expects to be paid off with salvation.

The parable is of a servant ploughing in the field all day, who after his day's work gets supper for his employer, who does not thank him for getting supper because he pays him for it. We are under no obligation to thank those whom we pay. If we can earn our salvation we are under no obligation to the Lord for it. We can never put the Lord in debt to us. After we have done all that we can do we are unprofitable servants—we have done that which it was our duty to do, and had no time to square up our past sins or atone for their guilt. ''The law is that you should love God with all your heart, and your neighbor as yourself; and when you have done all, you have no claim upon God for a reward; you have only done your duty.'' (Cumming.)

A MIRACLE SHOWING HOW TO EXERCISE FAITH FOR HOLINESS. Vs. 11-19.

11 And it came to pass, as he went to Jerusalem, that he passed through the midst of Samaria and Galilee.

12 And as he entered into a certain village, there met him ten men that were lepers, which stood afar off:

13 And they lifted up *their* voices, and said, Jesus, Master, have mercy on us.

14 And when he saw *them,* he said unto them, Go shew yourselves unto the priests. And it came to pass, that, as they went, they were cleansed.

15 And one of them, when he saw that he was healed, turned back, and with a loud voice glorified God.

16 And fell down on *his* face at his feet, giving him thanks: and he was a Samaritan.

17 And Jesus answering said, Were not there ten cleansed? but where *are* the nine?

18 There are not found that returned to give glory to God, save this stranger.

19 And he said unto him, Arise, go thy way: thy faith hath made thee whole.

As we have previously remarked the recorded miracles of Jesus are parables of what he can do for the soul. The majority of his miracles for healing are not given. Only those are recorded that especially illustrate soul healing. We know his miracles illustrate the salvation of the soul because in several of them he so illustrates. (See Mark 2:10 and John 9:39-41 and many other instances.)

Here were ten lepers that met him. We know leprosy was
the type of sin because this was the only disease that rendered
a man ceremonially unclean; and when healed by divine power,
it was the only disease that required a religious ceremony when
cured. Says Hanna in his life of Christ, ''This strange, loath-
some, creeping, fatal disease appears to have been selected as the
one form of bodily affliction to stand, in the legal impurity attached to it, and in the penalties visited on that impurity—as a
type of the inward pervading, corrupting, destroying malady of
sin. Among the Jews the leper was excommunicated.''

To heal leprosy was considered by the Jews as one of the
works the Messiah, when he came, would perform. These lepers
''stood afar off'' and cried to Jesus to have mercy upon them.
The law forbade them to come near other people. Leprosy banished them from healthy people, just as sin will banish its subjects from a holy God and a holy heaven.

''As they were companions in suffering they were also companions in prayers. Prayer should be strong and earnest, when
the disease is great and inveterate. Sin is the worst of all lepro-
sies; it not only separates those to whom it cleaves from the
righteous, but separates them from God; and nothing but the
pitying heart and the powerful hand of Jesus Christ can set any
soul free from it.'' (Clarke.)

When Jesus heard their piteous cry for mercy and saw their
condition he did not consider it necessary to call them to him,
but spoke to them saying, ''Go show yourselves unto the priests.''
It was commanded in the law that when a man was cured of leprosy he should go to the priests and let him examine him and
when the fact of his cure was established thus he was to offer
sacrifices (Lev. 13:2; 14:2). Notice, they believed he was healing them before they had the knowledge of it. Some might have
told them that they were on a fool's errand when they started
for the temple and the priest. Many today want the Lord to heal
them of sin first and then they are willing to trust him *afterwards*. These men took Jesus at his word and started off for the
temple just as if the work were already done. Thus believing and
obeying the work was done. Here is a practical definition of
saving faith. It is to *trust the Lord for salvation and then go*

off and act as if we believed he was saving us. "As they went they were cleansed." Jesus said, "Whatsoever things ye desire when ye pray believe ye receive and ye shall have them."

Notice these ten started out to the priest to confess what the Lord had done for them, before they were conscious of the healing. People often say they believe but have not the evidence. No man believes without some kind of evidence or assurance. Our faith is our evidence. "Faith is the evidence of things not seen." (Hebrews 11:1.) They acted just like well people— went to the priest. If we believe that Jesus saves from inbred sin we shall act if we believed it. "To such the command of Christ is, Go, assume that I will and can cleanse you, begin the life of one that has been cleansed." (Abbott.) Matthew Henry says, "Though the means will not heal thee of themselves, God will heal thee in the diligent use of the means."

But alas! only one of the ten lepers thought of glorifying God. How rare a virtue is gratitude! How few thankful hearts there are in this world! And it costs nothing, no man is poorer for giving thanks, but is richer in spirit.

This man glorified God with *a loud voice.* We do not believe in noise for the sake of noise. But there are some blessings that it would be wrong to keep quiet about. Let people keep quiet who can, but there are some secrets too big, there are some blessings too great to allow us to keep quiet. When Elizabeth was filled with the Holy Ghost, she spoke out with a *loud voice.* (Luke 1:42.) Some thing is the matter with those people who complain when souls are blessed because they make so much noise. The trouble with them is they are not in sympathy with the blessing that God has given these rejoicing souls. The nine were so contented with the cure that they forgot everything else. This one man forgot the cure for the time being in the sense of gratitude he felt. This man had never heard the modern, unscriptural, nonsensical sentiment. "Live it but do not say anything about it." It was true then although Paul had not written it, that "with the mouth confession is made unto salvation."

And this man fell down on his face in adoration of Jesus. He appreciated what had been done for him.

The most remarkable thing about it all was, the man was a

Samaritan. He belonged to the nation whom the Jews hated. (See chapter 9:52.)

Then Jesus turned and asked ''Where are the nine?'' Jesus demands the testimony of saved men, in order that others may know of his power. If all who had been cleansed from sin in the United States during the past years had been true to their testimony, spiritual religion would have swept the country like a mighty tidal wave. ''All this springs from the want of a broken heart, a deep sense of their need of free salvation, and a real application to Christ to cleanse from the leprosy of sin. For when a man is convinced of his sin and pollution, and that he must be forever excluded from the company of God and his saints, unless he is cleansed by the divine Saviour he will earnestly seek mercy.'' (Scott.)

This man ''returned to give glory to God.'' Some people accuse those who testify to salvation of boasting. It is not boasting ''to give the glory to Jesus except it be boasting in him. Some say we are boasting when we tell what God has done for us. This proves they know nothing themselves of the mighty power of God.

And it was a stranger who gave this praise to Jesus—an alien—one outside of the church. In chapter 7:9 we have a similar case. Jesus dismisses this alien with a richer blessing than the others had received. God always rewards those who testify and glorify him. Let us remember it. Gratitude for one blessing always brings another and greater. There is always a peculiar blessing given to those who testify to salvation. Reader do not rob your soul of this blessing by withholding testimony. God says ''Them that honor me will I honor.''

Then Jesus gives him further light and assurance, saying, ''Thy faith hath saved thee.'' (This is the correct translation.) He not only was cured of leprosy but saved. He got more than the other lepers—even salvation. It was a faith cure, instantaneously applied. He did not have to outgrow either sin or leprosy. There is no such thing as outgrowing sin taught in the Bible. Lyman Abbott's remarks on this case of salvation are so good that we want all our readers to ponder them. He says, ''Christ now gives him assurance of something more; a cleansing of inward sin, which the outward leprosy was but a type. All had faith enough to go show themselves to the priest while as yet there was no cure, but only the one had the faith that is perfected in love. They all had faith and hope, but only one had the greatest of the graces, that love which is the consummation of salvation.''

HOLINESS HAS ITS SEAT IN THE HEART. Vs. 20-21.

20 And when he was demanded of the Pharisees, when the kingdom of God should come, he answered them and said, The kingdom of God cometh not with observation:

21 Neither shall they say, Lo here! or, lo there! for, behold, the kingdom of God is within you.

It was a question of great concern at that time as to when the Messiah should come and set up his kingdom. The Jews had entirely mistaken the nature of that kingdom. They failed to see in the prophecies that it was a spiritual kingdom because they were unspiritual. They were looking for the splendor and pomp of a secular, political kingdom. Jesus had to tell them that the kingdom of heaven was not to come with ''outward observation'' that is outward display, for it was an inward condition. The trouble with the churchmen of that day was they believed only in outward holiness. There are many such religionists today. It is Churchism, which looks at crowds of people, elaborate, ritualism; or others esteem simplicity in dress and severity in worship to the neglect of heart holiness. Many today are looking like the Jews for the immediate coming of Christ who have no love for or experience of heart holiness, ''without which no man shall see the Lord.''

They looked at the question from the wrong standpoint. They did not comprehend that ''the kingdom of heaven is righteousness, peace and joy in the Holy Ghost'' (Rom. 14:17) and that it was in the heart. A kingdom is that ruled by a king; and wherever the heart is in subjection to God, there is the kingdom of God. Complete subjection brings complete sanctification.

THE IMPORTANCE OF HOLINESS TO KEEP US ALWAYS READY. Vs. 22-37.

22 And he said unto the disciples, The days will come, when ye shall desire to see one of the days of the Son of man, and ye shall not see it.

23   And they shall say to you, See here; or, see there: go not after *them,* nor follow *them.*

24   For as the lightning, that lighteneth out of the one *part* under heaven, shineth unto the other *part* under heaven; so shall also the Son of man be in his day.

25   But first must he suffer many things, and be rejected of this generation.

26   And as it was in the days of Noe, so shall it be also in the days of the Son of man.

27   They did eat, they drank, they married wives, they were given in marriage, until the day that Noe entered into the ark, and the flood came, and destroyed them all.

28   Likewise also as it was in the days of Lot; they did eat, they drank, they bought, they sold, they planted, they builded;

29   But the same day that Lot went out of Sodom it rained fire and brimstone from heaven, and destroyed *them* all.

30   Even thus shall it be in the day when the Son of man is re-vealed.

31   In that day, he which shall be upon the housetop, and his stuff in the house, let him not come down to take it away: and he that is in the field, let him likewise not return back.

32   Remember Lot's wife.

33   Whosoever shall seek to save his life shall lose it; and whoso-ever shall lose his life shall preserve it.

34   I tell you, in that night there shall be two *men* in one bed; the one shall be taken, and the other shall be left.

35   Two women shall be grinding together; the one shall be taken, and the other left.

36   Two *men* shall be in the field; the one shall be taken, and the other left.

37   And they answered and said unto him, Where, Lord? And he said unto them, Wheresoever the body *is,* thither will the eagles be gathered together.

Having uttered verses 20-21 to the inquiring Pharisees, he now turn to his disciples and speaks still further on the question of the coming of the kingdom of God.

He tells them that the pure church of Jesus Christ, sur-rounded by worldliness, skepticism and blatant infidelity, amidst a host of backsliders, and the waning love of many, will long for one of the days of Jesus on earth, and will look for his visible coming. They would wish to see him, on earth, again, as he had been, if it were only for one day. And all this because he had al-ready come to them spiritually and set up his kingdom in their hearts.

Hence we see there are two comings of Jesus, one spiritual, one visible. He prophesies a decay of faith at the time of his second coming. (Ch. 18:8.) The great thing is not to be setting the time, when men cry, ''See here'' he comes, or ''See there'' he comes, but to be holy and therefore ready. Verse 23 says Alford ''is a warning to all so called expositors of prophesy, who cry, See here! or See there! every time war breaks out or revolutions occur.''

His coming will be as swift and startling, as the lightning flashes from one part of the heaven to the other. The lightning is seen in an instant in all quarters of the heaven at once. So will Jesus be seen by all nations simultaneously.

By that generation slighting him his kingdom would become invisible to the eye until his second visible coming in the clouds of heaven.

''As it was in the days of Noe.'' It is very significant that Jesus refers back to the days of Noah. The days of Noah ended the first dispensation when the world was so wicked God had to destroy the wicked. Now the Jews were closing the second great dispensation with awful wickedness, and the destruction of Jerusalem was the result. And Jesus prophesies that the Gospel dispensation shall close with a similar tragedy. Dr. William Smith in his New Testament History says, ''Each of God's three dispensations toward the disobedient is closed by a catastrophe; and all three are included in our Lord's discourse; the reckless security of those who perished in the flood being a pattern of the folly of the Jews and of the finally impenitent.''

There need be no wonder at the mention of the flood, the destruction of Jerusalem and the Second Coming of Jesus. They are similar terminations of the three great dispensations; sent for similar purposes, because similar causes required them. The Jews acted like the antediluvian world and sinners at the time of the second coming of Christ will act in the same manner.

Jesus here endorses the account of the Flood, which some people have attempted to explain away. Notice, still further the similarity preceding the Flood and the Second Advent. 1. The religion of the day was secularized. Only eight saved people on earth after 2,000 years of the world's history. Only a few righteous Jews at the time of the destruction of Jerusalem. 2. The experience of that company. "Noah was a just man and perfect in all his generations." (Gen. 6:9.) Only the sanctified church of the Pentecost were ready when Jerusalem was destroyed. 3. The people who were warned of the Flood did not believe it. It was so when Jesus warned Jerusalem of its coming destruction. 4. Worldliness predominated both at the time of the Flood and of the destruction of Jerusalem. 5. The majority were unprepared for the event. 6. Both events were sudden. And as regards the Second Advent, the occurrences of the Flood and the Destruction were similar and symbolical.

"Also in the days of the Son of man." Dr. Whedon says this means, "The days preceding the second advent." Dr. Brown says, "Though the antediluvian world and the cities of the plain were awfully wicked, it was not their wickedness but their worldliness, their unbelief and indifference to the future, their unpreparedness that is held up as a warning." In these days there is a growing sentiment that if we only belong to the church we can get to heaven if we are not completely saved; that by an indefinite gradualism, or in old age or on a sick bed we can complete the consecration which we are not willing to do now. Salvation means *being ready* for death or the coming of Jesus, all the time. If we are not ready for the coming of Jesus as was Noah, for the flood, we shall have no escape. If we are ready to meet Jesus we are ready for death. If we are ready for death, we are ready for the coming of Jesus. Holiness is the only preparation. It is folly to be looking for the second advent if we are not saved from all sin. If we do not have the kingdom fully set up in our hearts, we will not be recognized by the king.

The destruction of Jerusalem and of the world will be as complete and awful as was that of Sodom, from which Lot fled.

Commentators generally have agreed that Luke has introduced in verse 31 an account of the siege of Jerusalem. The verse should be joined in thought not with the previous verses but with Matthew 24:16 which is an account of the siege of Jerusalem. Certainly no saved person would want to flee from the coming Christ.

"Remember Lot's wife." Centuries after the tragic fate of

this lost woman, a command is given to remember her. She is a standing monument, a beacon of warning, to all who love the world. When Jerusalem was being surrounded by the Roman armies, the Christians, having been forewarned by Jesus had just time to and did escape to Pella, a little city near by. Not one Christian was killed in the destruction of Jerusalem. The trouble with Lot's wife was a carnal nature that loved Sodom. Her heart was in Sodom while fleeing from it. Many a man has a profession of fleeing from the world's allurements when his heart is fixed upon them. Many are trying to go to heaven backwards, and it is hard work. No wonder they complain of making crooked paths. Let us remember Lot's wife by getting the same evil nature that ruined her, cast out of us!

He then lays down a lesson drawn from the fact of the coming destruction of Jerusalem, which is applicable to us in view of the approaching Judgment Day. "Whosoever shall seek to save his life shall lose it." This is one of the paradoxes of Jesus whereby he was accustomed to put stern truth in a startling form of expression. He says here that entire devotement and obedience to God, which is considered by the world to be ruinous, is really the gateway to eternal salvation. Eternal ages of heaven will more than compensate for all we give up in this life.

According to Jesus, his coming will be in the night. He says "one shall be taken and the other left." The righteous will be taken. This shows that the righteous and wicked will be associated together until the end. Brown says, "Awful truth! Realized before the destruction of Jerusalem, when the Christians found themselves forced by their Lord's directions (ch. 21:21) at once and forever away from their old associates; but most of all when the second coming of Christ shall burst on a heedless world."

The disciples then asked Jesus *when* these things should take place. He replied by quoting a common parable of the day, "where the body is, thither will the eagles be gathered together." By the eagles is meant the Roman armies, whose standard under which they marched was an eagle. In other words wherever there is corruption, the punishment of God will come, as it did in the days of Noah and Lot. Thus it came upon the corrupt Jewish nation. Thus it will come upon a wicked world.

CHAPTER XVIII.

HOLINESS GIVES LIGHT.

How to Retain the Experience of Holiness—by Constant Praying. Vs. 1-8. Church Membership Does Not Save. Vs. 9-14. The First Degree of Holiness. Vs. 15-17. The Second Degree of Holiness. 18-30. Crucifixion, the Central Truth of Christianity. Vs. 31-34. Blinded Eyes Opened. Vs. 35-42.

We have given this title to this chapter because Jesus, who was holiness incarnate gave light in this chapter on these important subjects: the attitude of the church waiting for the return of her Lord—constant prayer; union with the visible church does not bring salvation; light on the plan of salvation—first step; acceptance of the Gospel with the humility of children; increasing light shows the need of entire consecration; light on his great mission and a miracle illustrating light to the spiritually blind.

We have here then more definitely

HOW TO RETAIN THE EXPERIENCE OF HOLINESS—BY CONSTANT PRAYER. Vs. 1-8.

1 And he spake a parable unto them *to this end*, that men ought always to pray, and not to faint;

2 Saying, There was in a city a judge, which feared not God, neither regarded man:

3 And there was a widow in that city; and she came unto him, saying, Avenge me of mine adversary.

4 And he would not for a while: but afterward he said within himself, Though I fear not God, nor regard man;

5 Yet because this widow troubleth me, I will avenge her, lest by her continual coming she weary me.

6 And the Lord said, Hear what the unjust judge saith.

7 And shall not God avenge his own elect, which cry day and night unto him, though he bear long with them?

8 I tell you that he will avenge them speedily. Nevertheless when the Son of man cometh, shall he find faith on the earth?

Having told his disciples in the previous chapter their duty to be always ready—looking for the coming of the Lord, Jesus now tells them what they must be always doing to keep thus ready—praying and maintaining their courage. As certain as holiness is the preparation for the coming of the Lord, so sure is it that prayer is necessary to the maintenance of a holy life. We are commanded by the apostle as well to "pray without ceasing." Jesus gives a parable here for this purpose. Matthew Henry has well observed, that this parable differs from most of the parables of Jesus in that he gives the lesson before he utters the parable. Most of the parables have the lesson at the close of the parable.

He does not teach here that men ought to pray, but that men ought *always* to pray. It is hardly necessary to command men to pray, any more than to eat. It is natural to pray. Nowhere in the Bible is the abstract duty of prayer taught. Men will pray sooner or later, more or less. Even if they deny the value of prayer in prosperity,—adversity or calamity brings them to their knees. So the Bible seeks to systematize praying. It tells how, when, where and for whom to pray (1 Tim. 2:8). He tells us here when we ought to pray, *always*, "and not to faint." Having fulfilled the conditions of true prayer, we ought to be persistent in it. In the last chapter, he had been telling the disciples to be prepared for his coming. This parable is given to teach that when things seem to go hard while waiting for his coming; when the love of many waxes cold; when the god of this world seems to triumph; we are not to be discouraged, but by constant communion with God, we are to be kept holy and courageous in spite of the corruption all about us. We can pray always even if we can not be on our knees; our hearts can be constantly uplifted to God.

"Pray and not faint." We shall surely get faint hearted as we see error abounding on every hand if we do not pray a good deal. The faint hearted Christians are those who pray little. The atmosphere of the world will dim the fine gold of our experience if we do not pray much. So it is more than a duty, it is a *necessity* that we pray much.

Pious Quesnel says, ''to pray always and to speak but little, is one of the paradoxes of the Gospel; this duty requires little of the tongue, much of the heart. A man may justly be said to always pray when he has God always in his mind, and always desires him; whether he do it standing or kneeling, in rest or labor, in grief or joy.''

He mentions the unjust judge, first. The parable teaches by contrast that if so unjust a man could relent and grant a petition, because of its persistency, much more will the just and merciful God hear the persistent prayer of his children, though sometimes he appears like the unjust judge, not to hear their prayers.

Widows in eastern countries are peculiarly helpless and defenceless. This is the fact wherever the gospel of Jesus has not had sway. She kept coming and crying, ''Avenge me of mine adversary.'' Some one was injuring her in some extreme way. The church is like a widow. Her Lord is gone into the heavens. She is oppressed by the sin and wickedness of the world and these words wonderfully express her attitude to the corruption of sin all about her. While we pray daily to be delivered from evil, we long for the time to come when sin and iniquity shall be overthrown. We long to see justice meted out and the wrongs in society righted.

The judge was so annoyed by the persistency of the widow that he ''said within himself though I fear not God.'' A man who can thus unblushingly admit his wickedness is a hardened sinner indeed.

''Though he bear long with them.'' The Revised Version has it ''And he is long suffering with them.'' God often *seems* to be acting like the unjust judge in not hearing the prayers of his people.

''God will avenge his own elect speedily.'' He will come and rescue his people from the fires of persecution just at the right time. He will not leave them unavenged longer than is necessary. He may be slack ''As men count slackness,'' but not really so. His coming will adjust matters. (Rev. 6:9-10.) We can afford to have the Lord delay justice for it still gives men time to repent. (2 Peter 3:9 and 15.) Sometimes when men become intolerable, it becomes necessary to pray them out of the way. We have known such instances.

He then asks one of the saddest questions of which we have any record in the history of his sayings. ''When the Son of Man cometh shall he find faith on the earth?'' He saw that in his un-sanctified church is the tendency to backslide, because of inbred sin. If Jesus felt that way is it any wonder that those who live nearest him should sigh and cry for the worldliness and abomination all about them? A blessing is upon such. (Ezek. 9:4.) How much we need to watch and pray in these days of religious indifference lest our faith fail! Dr. Whedon says, ''Notwithstanding therefore the certainty that Christ will in due time *avenge his elect,* the prayer of the church may hardly last and faith upon earth may scarcely be found.'' When Christ comes the faith of the church then on the earth will be weak. It will not do to get our eyes upon the average professor of religion that is near us.

CHURCH MEMBERSHIP DOES NOT SAVE.   Vs. 9-14.

9   And he spake this parable unto certain which trusted in themselves that they were righteous, and despised others:

10   Two men went up into the temple to pray; the one a Pharisee, and the other a publican.

11   The Pharisee stood and prayed thus with himself, God, I thank thee, that I am not as other men *are,* extortioners, unjust, adulterers, or even as this publican.

12   I fast twice in the week, I give tithes of all that I possess.

13   And the publican, standing afar off, would not lift up so much as *his* eyes unto heaven, but smote upon his breast, saying, God be merciful to me a sinner.

14   I tell you, this man went down to his house justified *rather* than the other: for everyone that exalteth himself shall be abased; and he that humbleth himself shall be exalted.

This parable is especially applicable to these times, when so many are resting in their church membership as being sufficient for their salvation. Having instructed them in the necessity of much prayer to enable us to keep holy, in readiness for his coming, he shows the folly of mere ceremonial and formal praying, which many substitute for real spiritual prayer and life. While holy people have real soul communion with God, the Pharisaical substitute forms and ceremonies. The trouble with them is they are not even justified. They need to take the place of the Publican and do their first works of repentance over again.

Such people like the Pharisees trust "in themselves that they are righteous." This Pharisee was a boaster in himself. It is not wrong to make our boast in the Lord but it is decidedly so when we boast in ourselves. This parable is a rebuke to that spirit of Phariseeism that claims that the ordinances of the church and good works will of themselves make us holy.

Dr. Brown in connecting this parable with the parable of the poor widow says, of the Pharisee, "A specimen of that class, who satisfying themselves with a certain external freedom from gross offences have remained ignorant of the plague of their own hearts, and have never learned to say, deliver me from my adversary; who do not even know that they have an adversary."

The Publican was not a churchman but an outbreaking sinner. They were the tax gatherers. They were extortionate and very odious to the Jews. (See Luke 3:12 and notes there.) Notice the difference in these two men's prayers. The prayer of the Pharisee was not a real prayer. It was more an address to the Almighty. There is much of this kind of praying, especially in public, when men deliver orations and give the Lord advice *and never ask for anything*. It is insulting to Him. He stood when he prayed. There is no virtue in the posture of the body in prayers. The Jews usually stood when they prayed. (See 1 Kings 8:22; 2 Chron. 6:12; Matt. 6:5; Mark 11:25) although in times of great distress or emotion, they knelt. (See Dan 6:10; 2 Chron. 6:13; Acts 9:40; 20, 36 and 21:15.)

This Pharisee like other proud, supercilious men divided the whole world into two classes. The first class was himself. The second the rest of the world. There was nothing too good for him to say about himself and nothing too bad for him to say about others. His boasting was negative and positive. He boasted first of what he did *not* do. He boasted secondly of what he *did* do.

He had a right to thank God for what he did not do; which was wrong. God had perhaps given him a better opportunity in life than many sinners, who had not his education, training, surroundings or disposition. He did wrong in boasting that he **was** better than others. Here is the seed of fanaticism. If he had real heart holiness, he would not have thought of comparing himself with others. Fanaticism springs from a pride that considers itself superior to others, that says my idea, my life, theology and ideas. Whenever we meet the wild eyed, long-haired, harsh spirited fanatic, we will find this pride of opinion and fancied superiority at the foundation of all this fanaticism.

There are people whose chief hopes of heaven are not that they come up to what God requires, but that they are better than other people. They are great in the matter of confessing, not their own, but other people's sins. They are like a Catholic priest. They want other people to confess to them.

He gives a list of the sins of other people—injustice, extortion and adultery. He only speaks of outward sins. He says nothing about inward sin and sins—malice, envy, jealousy, hate, pride, etc. He like many modern religionists does not reguard the truth, that God not only requires outward righteousness but inward holiness. The same disregard of holiness in religion exists in the ecclesiastical world today. God not merely demands inward holiness but he puts the emphasis upon it, and not an outward righteousness, for if we are holy within we shall be righteous without.

He boasted of what he did. Notice he uses the perpendicular, first, personal pronoun five times. The law only required fasting once a year (Lev. 16:29) but he declared he did it over a hundred times a year. He not only did his duty, but thought he did more, and was entitled to extra credit; even put the Lord in debt to himself.

He gave tithes (a tenth) of his income to religious purposes. In this respect he did better than many professing Christians of today.

But the publican stood afar off—no doubt back by the door, through humility. Perhaps an unwritten law of the Pharisees would keep him from coming near the altar of prayer. He stood with downcast eyes, because of his sorrow for sin, and smote upon his breast as if he would punish his guilty heart, and cried, "God be merciful to me, a sinner." His prayer was for mercy. Literally it was "God be propitiated." This Greek word translated "have mercy" is used in only one other place in the New Testament. (Heb. 2:17.) He asked God to be propitiated and forgive him. Notice his prayer was personal. He admits his guilt. He tries to cover up nothing. He says "me, a sinner." He confessed his sins. The Pharisee said nothing about his own sins.

He "went down to his house justified." The temple was on rising ground. He went *down* to his house. Peter and John went *up* to the temple to pray. (Acts 3:1.) He "went—justified." People could be justified by confessing and forsaking their sins under the Old Dispensation. Justification and forgiveness are the same thing virtually.

Men get what they want most. The Pharisees wanted the praises of men and got them. The Publican wanted the forgiveness of God and received it.

The opinion of Jesus concerning the two men is given in verse 14 thus. "Every one that exalteth himself shall be abased and he that humbleth himself shall be exalted." Here we see the character and destiny of each depicted.

So we see the church membership and religious performances of the Pharisee went for nothing.

THE FIRST DEGREE OF HOLINESS. Vs. 15-17.

15 And they brought unto him also infants, that he would touch them: but when *his* disciples saw *it* they rebuked them.

16 But Jesus called them *unto him*, and said, Suffer little children to come unto me, and forbid them not: for of such is the kingdom of God.

17 Verily I say unto you, Whosoever shall not receive the kingdom of God as a little child shall in no wise enter therein.

The first degree of the holy life is regeneration and we must have the spirit of a child or we can never fulfill the conditions necessary to enter it. Jesus here illustrates this fact in the following manner.

Some little children were brought to him, doubtless by their parents, who wished him to touch them. Doubtless they thought his touch would bring some kind of a blessing. The disciples did not even wish them to be touched by Jesus. They thought doubtless it would be beneath the dignity of so great a personage to condescend to children. Matthew says (Matt. 19:13) that those who brought them wanted Jesus to ''put his hands on them and pray.'' Doubtless he was in the midst of a discourse and the disciples thought he should not be interrupted. Jesus knew how to turn an interruption to good account. A lesson to teachers and preachers.

Mark says that Jesus was displeased at the disciples for rebuking them. He is displeased now if we hinder children from coming to him. Labor bestowed on the conversion of children as a rule is more fruitful than upon adults.

''Forbid them not.'' There are different ways by which children may be forbidden—by neglect, false teaching and evil examples, as well as by word.

''Of such is the kingdom of God.'' Children, not having reached the years of accountability are by the atonement of Jesus in the kingdom of God. They are innocent but not pure. They still have the carnal nature. If they die before coming to years of accountability God will fit them somewhere for heaven.

Then Jesus said if we do not receive the kingdom of God as a little child we cannot enter. Regeneration is the state or condition of these who enter the kingdom of heaven. We must receive it with the simplicity and humility of children. Its entrance is so lowly that we must get through the gate on our knees and lay aside all our pride and sin of every kind.

What a remarkable way of teaching! He made children examples for older people. What great religious teacher ever thought of such a thing! Usually parents have been held up as models for their children.

If we are regenerate we are babes in Christ. But we are *in* Christ even if babes, and that is a greater rank than to be strong men in the service of Satan and the world. Regeneration—the initial degree of holiness—is a great experience.

Let us therefore not sorrow over the loss of children, as do the world. They are safe in the arms of Jesus. Let us fear over our situation, lest we fail to meet them in the skies.

THE SECOND DEGREE OF HOLINESS. Vs. 18-30.

18 And a certain ruler asked him, saying, Good Master, what shall I do to inherit eternal life?

19 And Jesus said unto him, Why callest thou me good? none *is* good, save one, *that is,* God.

20 Thou knowest the commandments, Do not commit adultery, Do not kill, Do not steal, Do not bear false witness, Honour thy father and thy mother.

21 And he said, All these have I kept from my youth up.

22 Now when Jesus heard these things, he said unto him, Yet lackest thou one thing : sell all that thou hast, and distribute unto the poor, and thou shalt have treasure in heaven : and come, follow me.

23 And when he heard this, he was very sorrowful ; for he was very rich.

24 And when Jesus saw that he was very sorrowful, he said, How hardly shall they that have riches enter into the kingdom of God !

25 For it is easier for a camel to go through a needle's eye, than for a rich man to enter into the kingdom of God.

26 And they that heard *it,* said, Who then can be saved?

27 And he said, The things which are impossible with men are possible with God.

28 Then Peter said, Lo, we have left all, and followed thee.

29 And he said unto them, Verily I say unto you, There is no man that hath left house, or parents, or brethren, or wife, or children, for the kingdom of God's sake,

30 Who shall not receive manifold more in this present time, and in the world to come life everlasting.

This is complete holiness. Regeneration is holiness begun. Entire sanctification (or the second degree) is holiness complete. We now have the experience of a church member who had the experience of entire holiness presented to him, who as far as we know refused to pay the price and obtain it. This follows immediately after the illustration of the experience of the justified and regenerate as shown in the case of the children. Will Jesus say, "Of such is the kingdom of heaven" to one who is not ready to pay the price even if he had kept the commandments? No he does not say so. This young man did not have the humility and simplicity of children. He went away sorrowful for he had great possessions. Notice several things about his experience. I. *He was in justified relations with God* for: 1. He was a member of God's church. 2. He was a ruler. The Jewish ruler was the president of the ten men who had charge of the synagogue worship, in each town. He was considered the best of the ten. He corresponded to the modern minister of the Gospel. 3. This young man kept the commandments, as mentioned in verse 20.

4. We believe he had done his best up to his light thus far. And every man who does this is accepted of God. (Acts 10:34-35; Rom. 2:12, 13.) 5. Justification was granted under the Old Dispensation. (Isa. 55:7.) It was also a fact before Pentecost. (Luke 15:17 and Luke 18:14.) Men were converted under that dispensation. (Isa. 6:10.) We do not doubt that such a man was converted in our day. 6. He was anxious for more light, as is everyone who is true to present light. Mark (Ch. 10:17) says he came *running*. 7. He was bold. It was in the public highway. He did not fear to have people know that he was seeking Jesus. 8. He was humble. Mark says he "kneeled to him." He was like many in the church of today, who are doing the best they know, and yet do not find that satisfaction that their hearts crave.

II. He got new light. Everybody does who improves on the light already received. He got light on three points. 1. On the particular phase of the carnal nature most prominent in his case. It was covetousness. 2. Light on consecration. Consecration requires that all our possessions are held at the disposal of God. It is the condition of Christian Perfection. 3. He got light showing him that he must come up to the standard of Christian Perfection. Matthew says Jesus replied "If thou wilt be perfect." (Matt. 19:21.) We learn from verse 22 that he lacked only "one thing." A man who lacks only one thing would be perfect when that one lack is supplied. We learn too from this that we can not be partakers of eternal life unless we are perfect. To love God with all the heart is the substance of the Christian religion and the sum of Christian Perfection. Covetousness spoiled this, for covetousness is love of money. Had he entirely consecrated to God, he would have been entirely sanctified at once, and the love of money would have been taken from his heart. Godet says, "The perfection to which Jesus called this young man is not a law superior to the law strictly so called but the real fulfilling in opposition to that external literal fulfilling which the young man already had." A man to whom God shows the need and privilege of having inbred sin removed, who refuses, will be lost.

Jesus thus replies to his question thus, ''Why callest thou me good?'' He tests this young man's faith in him by this question. It is a challenge. It reveals whether the young man recognizes Jesus as divine. Had he so recognized him he would have said, ''Yes, but you are divine. You are more than man; hence you are good.'' In the absolute sense only God is perfectly good. But the term is applied in a limited sense to certain men, whom the Bible calls in many places ''good men.''

So Jesus told him to sell all that he had. This does not mean that it is wrong to be rich. But it is wrong to love riches. We must hold our money at the disposal of God. He wants some men to be rich like the perfect Job and Abraham. A rich consecrated man can accomplish for God what a poor man can not. God does not want the devil to wield all the money power of the world.

Jesus commanded ''Come follow me.'' This young man was evidently called to be a preacher. If he had followed Jesus then he would have had the privilege of preaching the gospel. How many have refused to preach the gospel for the same reason— love of money.

Jesus here takes the opportunity of uttering a solemn warning against the dangers of the rich, and their great difficulty in getting to heaven. The reason rich men find it so difficult to get to heaven is they are tempted to often yield to put faith in money rather than in God. How then can professed followers of Jesus be greedy for wealth, when Jesus has told us how difficult it is for the rich to enter into the kingdom of God? Entire sanctification was never more needed in any age of the world than in this money worshipping age, when there is so much wealth in the church *and the cause of God goes limping and halting for lack of money.*

Jesus said, ''It is easier for a camel to go through the eye of a needle'' than for a rich man to enter the kingdom of God. This was a proverb of the day. He means that humanly speaking it is impossible for a man who loves money to get into the kingdom.

What or who is a rich man as Jesus here intends the term? Not necessarily a man who has a good deal of money, but a man whose heart is set upon money. Quesnel says, ''A man may be rich without riches; he may leave all without having ever possessed anything. With the heart we cling to earthly possessions; by renouncing them in our heart we disengage ourselves from them. We leave them, when we cease to desire and love them, because we possess them more by desire and love than by possession itself. We properly leave or forsake anything only when we do it by the Spirit, and for the sake of Christ, and in order to follow Him; otherwise, whatever our hands let go, is retained by the desire of our hearts.'' It is hard to possess riches and not love them.

Such radical talk startled the disciples. (Jesus had a startling way of teaching.) The disciples in dismay asked, ''Who then can be saved?'' This question shows that they understood him to mean that it is impossible for a rich man to enter heaven; and as they thought every one is seeking to be rich, therefore this would cut off everybody or prevent their becoming rich.

Jesus in his reply that ''All things are possible with God'' meant to tell them that it could be done by divine power, but was impossible otherwise. He can save a rich man from sin. The power of man is useless in saving men. All things ''are possible to him that believeth''—even the cleansing of the heart from all sin.

Peter the loquacious, impulsive spokesman of the disciples here voices their self complacency. They really felt as if they were entitled to great honors in the kingdom of God for what they had done in forsaking their boats and little fishing business. If the young man now at the eleventh hour forsaking all would receive eternal life, how much more would they receive who had been with Jesus from the beginning of his ministry. So he says, ''Lo, we have left all.'' We have done it for a long time too. Matthew (19:27) adds ''What shall we have therefore.'' Jesus gives the parable of the laborers who received the penny although coming in at the eleventh hour. (See Matt. 20 as an answer to this.) He declares that those who forsake all for Jesus shall receive manifold more than they have forsaken. This refers to the reward as being received in this life for he says (Mark 10:30) this reward is ''with persecutions.'' Such a man will get a salvation so full, rich and sustaining as to be called ''manifold more'' in spite of the persecutions. Real communion with God is so marvellous that the loss of all things else to obtain it is a low price, a trivial matter—not to be mentioned. There are the two rewards—''manifold'' here and eternal life in the world to come. Persecution is not worth mentioning if we have the real salvation. When we whine about persecution it is evident that we are not enjoying the fullness of salvation.

CRUCIFIXION, THE CENTRAL TRUTH OF CHRISTIANITY. Vs. 31-34.

31 Then he took *unto him* the twelve, and said unto them, Behold, we go up to Jerusalem, and all things that are written by the prophets concerning the Son of man shall be accomplished.
32 For he shall be delivered unto the Gentiles, and shall be mocked, and spitefully entreated, and spitted on:
33 And they shall scourge *him*, and put him to death: and the third day he shall rise again.
34 And they understood none of these things: and this saying was hid from them, neither knew they the things which were spoken.

He now begins his last journey to Jerusalem. He knew and his disciples knew it was like walking into the jaws of death. His life had already been threatened and enemies were on every hand watching his every word, and Jerusalem was full of his enemies. Mary says (Ch. 10:32) that the disciples were amazed to see him resolutely begin his journey. There was something in his aspect, attitude and actions that filled them with wonder and awe. There is a sublimity about moral courage that is godlike and inspires admiration whenever we see it. Jesus went a willing offering. He was not taken by surprise by his enemies. He had counted the cost before he started for Jerusalem. He now takes the twelve disciples aside (Mark 10:32) from the throng and tells them of his approaching sorrows, persecution, death and resurrection.

But their minds were so set on his coming in the regal splendor of the Messiah, that they failed to understand him. They were much like those religionists of today who think religion is only intended for display and is perfectly harmonious with worldly pomp and honors. The crucified life of death to sin is as little understood as the crucifixion of Jesus by these disciples at this time.

BLINDED EYES OPENED. Vs. 35-42.

35   And it came to pass, that as he was come nigh unto Jericho a certain blind man sat by the way side begging:

36   And hearing the multitude pass by, he asked what it meant.

37   And they told him, that Jesus of Nazareth passeth by.

38   And he cried, saying, Jesus, *thou* son of David, have mercy on me.

39   And they which went before rebuked him, that he should hold his peace: but he cried so much the more, *Thou* son of David, have mercy on me.

40   And Jesus stood, and commanded him to be brought unto him: and when he was come near, he asked him.

41   Saying, What wilt thou that I shall do unto thee? And he said, Lord, that I may receive my sight.

42   And Jesus said unto him, Receive thy sight: thy faith hath saved thee.

43   And immediately he received his sight, and followed him, glorifying God: and all the people, when they saw it, gave praise unto God.

Luke says (verse 35) "As he was come nigh to Jericho." Matthew says "As he was departing from Jericho." Various explanations have been made to harmonize these two statements. We like the explanation of Dr. Whedon, that there two Jerichos— an old and a new, and therefore both these statements were true. He was leaving the one and approaching the other. Jericho was fifteen miles north east of Jerusalem and seven from the Jordan. It was opposite this city that the Israelites crossed the Jordan and came into Canaan. It was directly in the way of Christ, in his last journey from Perea to Jerusalem.

A blind beggar sat by the roadside. Matthew says there were two. Mark says this man's name was Bartimeus. He was both blind and poor. In answer to his inquiry as to the crowd passing by, he was told that Jesus of Nazareth passed by. He cried "Jesus, thou Son of David." While the bystanders with eyesight, only saw "Jesus of Nazareth," this beggar without eyesight saw in him the Son of David—the Messiah. He had faith loftier than that of the more favored. How often do those whose opportunities are less, put to shame the more favored. One of the works the Jews believed the Messiah would do was the restoring of sight to the blind.

This man was so afraid that he would miss his opportunity that he cried, "Have mercy on *me.*" He made it personal. This is what we must do if we get salvation. Generalities in prayer avail nothing.

The people rebuked him for drawing the attention of Jesus to himself—a blind beggar. There will always be found people to censure and criticize those who are in earnest for salvation. There are people who care more for propriety than for the salvation of men.

But the blind beggar only cried the more. Instead of being discouraged when men try to hinder our seeking God, we ought to redouble our efforts. This was the blind man's only opportunity. It was now or never with him. Jesus would not pass that way again. Are we not all in our sins, blind beggars, whose opportunities for salvation are limited? And ought we not to be desperately in earnest in seeking salvation? This earnest cry stopped the procession because Jesus stood still and commanded the man to be brought to him. True prayer will arrest the attention of God today. He is so good and loving that he will gladly listen to the voice of distress.

"What wilt thou that I shall do for thee?" This would naturally intensify the faith of the blind man. Is not Jesus still asking every distressed soul the same question? He likes to have us make definite requests. He wants us to be definite in our asking. Rather than not hear and answer true prayer he would stop not merely a procession of people but a procession of the planets.

Jesus commanded the blind man to be brought to him. He made the bystanders who had tried to discourage the man, now bring him. He can make even hindrances become helps.

When Jesus asked him what he wanted of course he said "that I may receive my sight." Would not that be the uppermost thought! How precious is sight! Very few people however seem to realize that blindness of heart is even worse than physical blindness. If we are not saved from blindness of heart, we shall never see the King in his beauty. The worst thing about soul blindness is, it prevents many from seeing that they are blind.

Matthew says that Jesus touched his eyes (Matt. 20:34) as he said ''Receive thy sight.'' He then said ''Thy faith hath saved thee.'' It was a faith cure. The Lord ever delighted while on earth to extol faith and seemed to take special pains to commend those who exercised it. Men of faith pleased him then and please him now, for ''without faith it is impossible to please God.'' It is faith—not feeling or good works that saves.

''Immediately he received his sight.'' Faith is an instantaneous act and it brings instantaneous salvation. Soul blindness and soul defilement can be completely healed in the same instantaneous manner.

No wonder the blind man followed him glorifying God. This is the whole business of all we blind beggars who have received our spiritual sight—to follow Jesus and glorify God. And if we have been really saved we will delight to do it.

This set all the people to glorifying God. It is our privilege by praising God for what he has done thereby to start additional praise in the hearts and on the lips of others. Whoever heard of the tricks of Spiritism or the lying wonders of Christian Science to set multitudes to praising God! We ought to praise God for what he has done for others.

CHAPTER XIX.

HOLINESS SOMETIMES POPULAR.

Conversion Is Initial Holiness and Is Conditional on Abandonment
of Sin. Vs. 1-10. The Degree of Eternal Reward Is to Be
Conditioned upon Our Present Holy Works. Vs. 11-27.
Holiness Popular for a Season. Vs. 28-40. Holiness Means
Sadness in Contemplating the Hardness of the Human Heart.
Vs. 41-44. Holiness Requires a Clean Church. Vs. 45-48.

This chapter describes the most popular period in the ministry and life of Jesus. Holiness is popular until men know how
much it costs. When they see it first, they recognize its worth
and applaud. But such is the attitude of the carnal mind that
this popularity does not last long. Jesus was now received by the
richest of the Publicans then escorted by the multitudes in triumph to Jerusalem as their king. But in a few days the same
multitude were crying "Crucify him." Let us not be discouraged if popular favor towards holiness is as fickle today.

CONVERSION IS INITIAL HOLINESS AND IS CONDI-
TIONAL ON ABANDONMENT OF SIN. Vs. 1-10.

1 And *Jesus* entered and passed through Jericho.

2 And, behold, *there was* a man named Zacchæus, which was the
chief among the publicans, and he was rich.

3 And he sought to see Jesus who he was; and could not for the
press, because he was little of stature.

4 And he ran before, and climbed up into a sycomore tree to see
him: for he was to pass that *way.*

5 And when Jesus came to the place, he looked up, and saw him,
and said unto him, Zacchæus, make haste, and come down; for to day
I must abide at thy house.

6 And he made haste, and came down, and received him joyfully.

7 And when they saw *it,* they all murmured, saying, That he
was gone to be guest with a man that is a sinner.

8 And Zacchæus stood, and said unto the Lord; Behold, Lord, the half of my goods I give to the poor; and if I have taken anything from any man by false accusation, I restore *him* fourfold.

9 And Jesus said unto him, This day is salvation come to this house, forsomuch as he also is a son of Abraham.

10 For the Son of man is come to seek and to save that which was lost.

We have already spoken of the location of Jericho. (Ch. 18:35.) See notes there and also concerning the Publicans. (See Ch. 3:12.) Jesus now meets the chief publican or chief collector of customs for that district. Like all the Publicans, this man had become very rich doubtless by oppressing the Jews and extorting money from them. It was quite necessary that the traveller to Jerusalem should rest at Jericho, as the road up to Jerusalem was very rough and steep. It is an ascent of about 2,400 feet in fifteen miles.

Something more than mere curiosity prompted Zaccheus to climb the sycamore, (or Egyptian mulberry) tree. It was conviction of sin, even if he were not fully aware of his motives. God has a way of capturing wicked men. Evidently this man had been under conviction for a better life, for a long time. Still his apparent (perhaps to himself) motive was curiosity. There have been many people since then who have been drawn by curiosity to see Jesus, who have been captured by him.

Jesus had his eye on Zaccheus as truly as the latter had his eye upon Jesus. He always sees inquiring souls. Let us be encouraged, he will reveal himself to honest seekers. He knew Zaccheus by name too.

Jesus invited himself to visit Zaccheus. He is inviting himself to abide with us. It is a beautiful place when Jesus abides in a home. How sad a place is a home where there is no family religion; no altar of prayer. This is an illustration of the power of holy character to draw men to it. Zaccheus was drawn by Jesus, the embodiment of holiness, and Jesus was drawn to Zaccheus because holiness always yearns to embrace sinful men to make them good.

Zaccheus made haste and came down to meet Jesus. This was his last and great opportunity. How many have had more and better opportunities and have failed.

Zaccheus received Jesus joyfully. If we receive Jesus as joyfully to our hearts we shall receive salvation by faith, for faith is but receiving Jesus. (John 1:12.) ''Earthly goodness draws admiration to itself. The heavenly imparts itself—inspires a spirit and such preeminently was the holiness of Christ. Had some earthly great or good one come to Zaccheus' house, his feeling would have been, 'What condescension is here.' But when *he* came, whose very word and act had in it life and power. no such barren reflection was the result; but instead, the beauty of holiness had become a power within him, and a longing for self-consecration.'' (Robertson.)

Going to accept the hospitality of a sinner like Zaccheus made the multitude murmur. The publicans were such extortioners that the Jews hated them. We can therefore see that Zaccheus had many obstacles in coming to Jesus. One was the ostracism that was heaped upon them by the Jewish people generally.

The same spirit of self-righteousness is in society today—holding itself aloof from the erring and finding fault with those who seek to save them. In the world's harvest field the gentlemanly loafers resting in the shade find the most fault with the reapers in the field.

Zaccheus now stood up and spoke. He had probably now reached his house. He said, ''Lord, the half of my goods I give to the poor.'' This refers not to his past life, but to the present. He is beginning to make restitution. He goes further and says, ''If I have taken by false accusation.'' It was frequently the case that the publicans accused the Jews of having more property than they really possessed in order to make them pay more taxes. If a Jew protested they had little redress, for the Romans who ruled the country did not care. (See a hint of this in John's sermon. Luke 3:13.) There is no repentance that does not make restitution.

''I restore him fourfold.'' The Jewish law only required the restoration of the principal and one-fifth in such cases. The Roman law required fourfold. Repentance is more than shedding tears. Such is not godly sorrow unless it makes crooked things straight.

Then Jesus said, "This day is salvation come to thine house." There is such a thing as salvation, so said he who spake as never man spake. Salvation comes as soon as men turn away from sin to Jesus. This is initial holiness (or wholeness). The religion of Jesus is wholeness all the way through. It begins with a whole repentance, a whole faith, a whole regeneration, and a whole justification, and keeps on in a whole hearted service, welcoming all the light that comes. Such a person will have no difficulty in accepting the greater light of complete holiness when he sees his privilege. The trouble why many do not accept entire holiness is because they never had a whole hearted repentance and regeneration as did Zaccheus.

Zaccheus was a son of Abraham—a Jew. His name is the same as Zaccai (Ezra 2:9). But now in a deeper sense he had become a spiritual son of Abraham, (Rom. 4:12) who "believed God and it was accounted to him for righteousness."

"The Son of Man." This was a title Jesus gave himself because he was the ideal man, illustrating what Adam was in his original creation. This Man came not merely to save sinners, but to *seek* to save them. He came to seek them out for the purpose of saving them. And all his servants are to be in the same business of seeking the lost. This remark of Jesus shows that up to this time Zaccheus was lost. So Jesus here teaches that men may be in a lost condition in this world.

We are to learn from this that we are to look for conversion in unfavorable and unexpected surroundings. Here is a lesson showing that it pays to be compassionate and kind to the erring. Jericho was called the city of fragrance and the fragrance of this experience of Zaccheus still lingers about the name of that city, when other things—its gardens, groves and market places are gone.

THE DEGREE OF ETERNAL REWARD IS TO BE CONDITIONED UPON OUR PRESENT HOLY WORKS.
Vs. 11-27.

11 And as they heard these things, he added and spake a parable, because he was nigh to Jerusalem, and because they thought that the kingdom of God should immediately appear.

12 He said therefore, A certain nobleman went into a far country to receive for himself a kingdom, and to return.

13 And he called his ten servants, and delivered them ten pounds, and said unto them, Occupy till I come.

14 But his citizens hated him, and sent a message after him, saying, We will not have this *man* to reign over us.

15 And it came to pass, that when he was returned, having received the kingdom, then he commanded these servants to be called unto him, to whom he had given the money, that he might know how much every man had gained by trading.

16 Then came the first, saying, Lord, thy pound hath gained ten pounds.

17 And he said unto him, Well, thou good servant : because thou hast been faithful in a very little, have thou authority over ten cities.

18 And the second came, saying, Lord, thy pound hath gained five pounds.

19 And he said likewise to him, Be thou also over five cities.

20 And another came, saying, Lord, behold, *here is* thy pound, which I have kept laid up in a napkin :

21 For I feared thee, because thou art an austere man : thou takest up that thou layedst not down, and reapest that thou didst not sow.

22 And he saith unto him, Out of thine own mouth will I judge thee, *thou* wicked servant. Thou knewest that I was an austere man, taking up that I laid not down, and reaping that I did not sow :

23 Wherefore then gavest not thou my money into the bank, that at my coming I might have required mine own with usury?

24 And he said unto them that stood by, Take from him the pound, and give *it* to him that hath ten pounds.

25 (And they said unto him, Lord, he hath ten pounds.)

26 For I say unto you, That unto every one which hath shall be given ; and from him that hath not, even that he hath shall be taken away from him.

27 But those mine enemies, which would not that I should reign over them, bring hither, and slay *them* before me.

Jesus now utters another parable. This is not the same parable as that of the talents, (Matt. 25:14-30) although in some respects quite similar. That was given to the church to warn them to be faithful. This was given more particularly to teach them not to expect the immediate appearing of the kingdom of God. *This* parable was given when he was nigh to Jerusalem; *that* after he had entered the city.

The kingdom of God as described by Jesus is not an earthly, political kingdom as they supposed but it is spiritual. In every age there have been formalists in the church who have failed to realize the spiritual nature of true religion. It has been their weakness that they have seen nothing in religion except the spectacular and formal part.

In this parable the nobleman represents Jesus, and the far country, where he waits until the consummation of his kingdom, is heaven. It was a warning to the fickle crowd accompanying him, expecting him as a worldly Messiah, that his going away was to be immediate, so that they might not be disappointed and stumbled at his death.

The return of the nobleman represents the second coming of Jesus. Since the parable represents him as about to go away, therefore the second coming of Jesus and the siege of Jerusalem are not the same event, for Jerusalem was destroyed soon after the death of Jesus.

This nobleman delivered to each of his servants a pound apiece. In the parable of the talents, he delivered different sums according to the ability of each. A pound or *mina* was equal to from $15 to $30. He told his servants to trade with this sum. Dr. Brown says, in contrasting this parable with that of the talents in Matt. 20:14-30, ''The one illustrates equal fidelity with different degrees of advantage. The other different degrees of improvement of the same opportunities.'' The one pound given to each denotes that common salvation which all believers have alike—pardon and regeneration. The improvement of grace is very much like the improvement of money. Often when men start with the same amount of money, some become wealthy; others lose what they have. Our external wealth or poverty depends upon like improvement of the experience of regeneration. In verse 17 Jesus implies that the grace of regeneration is a *very* little. Of course he means in comparison with what we may add to it.

The citizens hated the nobleman and rebelled against him. His servants must keep on trading in the midst of the rebellion. This is the condition of the servants of God today. We are occupying or increasing our stock of grace when there is a rebellion all about us against Jesus.

Notice several lessons: 1. At the return of Jesus every man must tell concerning himself. ''We must all give an account of

ourselves at the Judgment which will occur at that day.'' He
only calls three sample cases, probably the remaining seven were
all represented in these three classes.   2. It was the nobleman's *pound*—the grace given is lent to us by God for his glory.
The pound has gained tenfold already.   Grace increases in this
world. It was an increase of the same kind. It was money added
to money. Grace is added to grace. Growth in grace does not
add any new qualities, nor subtract old ones. It is an increase
of *what we have*. Therefore we can not get rid of sin by growth
in grace.

Then Jesus said to the first ''Because thou hast been faithful
in a very little.'' Each of the two had been faithful in a *very
little* matter. One had gained more than the other because he
had better facilities or opportunities. But it was not the increase
but the faithfulness that was commended.   Our reward will be
commensurate with our ability to enjoy it.   Therefore the pos-
sessor of ten mansions in heaven will not be envied by the pos-
sessor of five, for each will be satisfied. It will require more to
satisfy some great souls than it will to satisfy others.

3. A faithful and successful *servant* becomes a *ruler*. Fidelity
in small affairs brings promotion in the kingdom of God.   And
does not real grace make us as true in little as in large affairs?
Is it not true that when God takes a faithful child of God home,
whom we think can hardly be spared, it is to give him larger
work?

4.   The man who had the five pounds did not have the opportunities of the first, but he was faithful in what he had.   We
learn here that every faithful soul will make some gain.

The man who laid his pound away in the napkin came saying
''here is thy pound.'' Hardly, for money and grace unused cor-
rode. ''The Jews had a custom which they called *possession by
a napkin* or linen cloth, which is, that when they buy or sell anything, they use a piece of cloth which they call *sudar*, the word
used in this passage; thus the parties lay hold of to ratify or confirm the bargain.'' Upon which custom as connected with these
words, Dr. Gill observes, that ''this man had made no use of his
sudar or napkin in buying or selling; he traded not at all; he
wrapped up his money in it, and both lay useless.'' He feared his

lord. He was like the man who serves God from fear of hell. It is a legal service, devoid of love. Such people declare that it is difficult to lead a Christian life. They sing "Look how we grovel here below." They say it is impossible to keep all the commandments. We can not keep from sinning. Godet says "he is a legal Christian, who has not tasted grace and knows nothing of the Gospel, but its severe morality." It represents a professed Christian, who has lost his way, because he would not go on to perfection. His sin lay not so much in doing nothing wrong as in not doing right.

Jesus said he should be "judged out of his own mouth." God will make the unfaithful servant condemn himself. His condemnation is self pronounced. Because if he knew his Lord to be an exacting man, he should have acted to please his Lord. "Give it to him that hath ten." Godet says on this, "This or that pagan population that might have been evangelized by the young Christians. who remained on the earth as the slave of selfish ease, shall be committed in the future dispensation to the devoted missionary, who has used his powers in the service of Jesus."

We have here in verse 25 an illustration of the interest the audience took in the words of Jesus. Verse 25 is the ejaculation of his hearers, who had become so interested in the story that they gave forth this ejaculation. What a fascination there was in the words of Jesus!

It is as true today as then that "unto him that hath it shall be given." He who has and keeps grace will get more, and he who hath not (increase) will lose what he has now. All we do not use, we lose. We must get more grace to keep what we have. It is greater salvation or no salvation; greater light or no light; more fruit by sanctification or no fruit. (John 15:1-2.) Money unused is not really possessed. It is of no good to us, until it is used.

The citizens who sent the message (Vs. 14) after him that they would not allow him to reign over them, he calls here his enemies. He says they shall be slain. This took place at the siege of Jerusalem and will take place at the end of the world. The result of rebellion is death.

HOLINESS POPULAR FOR A SEASON. Vs. 28-40.

28 And when he had thus spoken, he went before, ascending up to Jerusalem.

29 And it came to pass, when he was come nigh to Bethphage and Bethany, at the mount called *the mount* of Olives, he sent two of his disciples,

30 Saying, Go ye into the village over against *you;* in the which at your entering ye shall find a colt tied, whereon yet never man sat: loose him, and bring *him hither*.

31 And if any man ask you, Why do ye loose *him?* thus shall ye say unto him, Because the Lord hath need of him.

32 And they that were sent went their way, and found even as he had said unto them.

33 And as they were loosing the colt, the owners thereof said unto them, Why loose ye the colt?

34 And they said, The Lord hath need of him.

35 And they brought him to Jesus: and they cast their garments upon the colt, and they set Jesus thereon.

36 And as he went, they spread their clothes in the way.

37 And when he was come nigh, even now at the descent of the mount of Olives, the whole multitude of the disciples began to rejoice and praise God with a loud voice for all the mighty works that they had seen ;

38 Saying, Blessed *be* the King that cometh in the name of the Lord: peace in heaven, and glory in the highest.

39 And some of the Pharisees from among the multitude said unto him, Master, rebuke thy disciples.

40 And he answered and said unto them, I tell you that, if these should hold their peace, the stones would immediately cry out.

He now starts up the steep ascent from Jericho to Jerusalem, and comes first to Bethphage and Bethany, two villages east of Jerusalem. As he draws near them he sends two of his disciples ahead to provide a colt for him to ride upon into Jerusalem. This shows that the triumphal journey was no accident. He deliberately planned it. He intended to assert his kingship in this manner, riding into the royal city of his father David, after the manner of a king.

So the two disciples went as they were told and found the colt as Jesus had said. He never displayed his omniscience except on necessary or suitable occasions.

Animals previously unused were reserved by the Jews for special purposes and occasions and uses. The ass was the symbol of peace. Jesus came not on a horse, the emblem of war, but on this symbol of peace, as king of peace about to enter the capitol city of his kingdom; thus proclaiming himself Messiah in the face of his revolting subjects. But the Jews did not recognize the symbolism.

He entered Jerusalem publicly although he had for several months lived in secret retirement. His hour had now come and he did not fear to face the issue.

The disciples found the colt "as he had said." If we are obedient as they were, we will find all things as he has said. "If any man will do his will, he shall know of the doctrine."

As they led away the colt, the owners asked why they were doing it. They replied "The Lord hath need of him." In a certain sense the Lord had need of so humble an animal for his glory. In the same sense he has need of all we have—our money, time, talents, the inventions of man's ingenuity, such as the telegraph, railway, steamship, etc—for the spread of his glorious kingdom. He is coming in still greater triumph and he needs us all to help spread his kingdom. The man who owned the colt was probably a disciple of Jesus, who held his property at the Lord's disposal, as all disciples should.

And now the triumphal march begins. It had been prophecied 500 years before by Zechariah (Zech. 9:9). Matthew says it was a fulfillment of that prophecy. A very great multitude accompanied them through the city. Dean Stanley says, "Two vast streams of people met that day. The one poured out of the city (John 12:12) and, as they came through the gardens, whose clusters of palms rose on the southeastern corner of Olivet, they cut down the long branches, as was their wont at the feast of Tabernacles, and moved upward towards Bethany with shouts of welcome. From Bethany streamed forth the crowds who had assembled there the previous night. The two streams met midway. Half of the vast mass, turning around preceded; the other half followed." This whole mass advanced through the city gates praising God and shouting Hosanna, "with a loud voice." Those who do not like exhibitions of religious enthusiasm, because "it makes so much noise," should notice here that Jesus endorsed it and only Pharisees and Scribes condemned it. Anything that is commended by Jesus and condemned by Pharisees must be right. Are we rejoicing because Jesus is now on his triumphal march and will one of the days come in triumph to the New Jerusalem? Let dead men remain silent, but let those who are alive in Jesus sound forth his praises!

Verse 38 is a quotation from Psalms 118:25, 26.

Why was Jesus so popular for a short time? Because the people recognized his majesty and because of the notoriety of his wonderful miracles. People will applaud virtue when they see it, *and it costs them nothing.* Had Jesus taken the throne at once his popularity would not have waned. But his enemies seized him and the fickle people deserted him. It cost too much to stand up for him. They feared the Sanhedrim and yielded to its authority and power. He who sees holiness for the first time will admit and endorse it, until he finds it means the lone way with Jesus and persecution.

Some of the Pharisees asked Jesus to rebuke his disciples. Pharisees still oppose religious enthusiasm. Why not? They never see anything in religion to cause enthusiasm. They have nothing in their own religion worth rejoicing over.

Up to this time Jesus had discouraged demonstrations, but now he encouraged them. He thought the occasion demanded it and rather than not have this triumphal entry accompanied by proper demonstrations he declared enthusiasm would have been wrung out of the very stones of the street. It shows how important in the history of redemption was this demonstration. We believe these shouting people were the very 3,000 that at Pentecost cried ''What shall we do?'' (Acts 2:37.)

HOLINESS MEANS SADNESS IN CONTEMPLATING THE HARDNESS OF THE HUMAN HEART. Vs. 4-44.

41 And when he was come near, he beheld the city, and wept over it.

42 Saying, If thou hadst known, even thou, at least in this thy day, the things *which belong* unto thy peace! but now they are hid from thine eyes.

43 For the days shall come upon thee, that thine enemies shall cast a trench about thee, and compass thee round, and keep thee in on every side.

44 And shall lay thee even with the ground, and thy children within thee; and they shall not leave in thee one stone upon another; because thou knewest not the time of thy visitation.

What transitions there are in life—one moment rejoicing, the next sorrowing; one moment triumphing, the next mourning. This was emphatically the experience of the Son of Man—the typical man, the absolutely holy man. Truly glory and suffering go together. He stops in the midst of his triumph to weep over this hardened, doomed city, that five days later shed not a tear over his sufferings and anguish upon the cross. His pity overcame his manhood and he wept. This is one of the most pathetic passages in all literature. Sorrowing over the sins of others, the holy man feels thus, even when rejoicing over the triumph of the cross. Twice we read that Jesus wept—at the grave of Lazarus and here. His grief was not for himself but for others. He in this displayed both his divine and human natures.

"In this thy day." Had Jerusalem known its day! What was its day? The day of its gracious visitation by God's only begotten Son. It is as true today, that the sin of all sins is rejection of Jesus Christ.

Notice how clearly it is taught here that there is a limit to probation. God has fixed it. And sometimes probation ends in this life, before death, as in the case of Jerusalem. Apparently Jerusalem still had the opportunity of salvation for it was several years before the enemy destroyed it. But really probation had ended when Jesus spoke these words. They had rejected the light until now the light was removed and "the things which belonged to their peace were hid from their eyes." Men get to the place sometimes in this life when they have lost their power to repent for the Spirit has left them and probation has ended.

He now predicts the destruction of Jerusalem which took place at the hands of the Romans within fifty years. Who but Jesus would have dared predict such an event, and right in the time of his triumphant entry into the city too?

He predicts that enemies should cast a "trench" about it. The translation should be not "trench" but a "rampart." The American Revision has it a "bank." The Romans put a wooden rampart all about the city and when the Jews burnt that, they built a wall four miles in circuit in three days. This cut off all hopes of escape. Josephus, the Jewish historian describes the seige and destruction of Jerusalem exactly as Jesus prophecied. The destruction of Jerusalem was one of the saddest events in all history, and all because the proud city rejected Jesus. It is an awful sin to reject Christ. The Jews are still suffering for it.

HOLINESS REQUIRES A CLEAN CHURCH. Vs. 45-48.

45 And he went into the temple, and began to cast out them that sold therein, and them that bought;
46 Saying unto them, It is written, My house is the house of prayer: but ye have made it a den of thieves.
47 And he taught daily in the temple. But the chief priests and the scribes and the chief of the people sought to destroy him,
48 And could not find what they might do: for all the people were very attentive to hear him.

The first thing Jesus did was to go into the temple and clean it up. It was his Father's house, even if it was defiled. This was the second time that he cleansed the temple. The first time was at the beginning of his ministry (John 2:13-17). The templo bore the same relation to the land of Judea that the heart bears to the human body. It was the center of the religious life of the people. From it went forth the piety of the nation. It is so with any people, the state of the church determines the morality and well being of the nation. The temple having become corrupted, the religious life of the people was corrupt. It must be purified. He had purified it once before, but nothing in this world, whether the temple or the heart will of itself remain clean. It must be *kept* clean. "If Israel in a spirit of holiness, had joined with Jesus in this procedure, the act would cease to have a simple typical value; it would have become the real inauguration of the Messianic kingdom."

For the convenience of those Jews who lived at a distance, booths had been erected in the temple court to keep those victims for sale that were used in sacrifice. Money changers were there to change the money into the half shekel required of every Jew for the support of the temple. As the nation had become corrupt, abuses of these privileges had taken place. From being a place for the accommodation of strangers, who had come to worship, the spirit of greed and merchandise had sprung up. The religious state of a people can be told by the way they act in their house of worship. When the church becomes dead and formal, the spirit of merchandise creeps in. When churches are used to make money in, even "for the Lord" they have begun to gravitate towards the corruption of the Jews. Modern church methods of supporting the gospel by bazaars, fairs, suppers and sales, indicate a corrupt state of heart, that does not willingly and gladly give to God, but has to be coaxed by receiving something in return for the money given. It is the same spirit of merchandise that Jesus rebuked. It makes the house dedicated to the worship of God anything but "a house of prayer."

By their sharp bargains the house of God had become "a den of thieves."

All the sacrifices were vehicles of prayer beseeching the forgiveness of God for sins. Prayer is the vital part of religion. Where there is no prayer there is no religion. A true church is a house of prayer. Just as far as people use their churches for commercial purposes it will be noticed they are not people of much prayer.

Here we have three phases of the holy life of Jesus in one day —triumph, sorrow, and righteous indignation.

If Jesus called it a den of thieves where men were fleecing the people, what shall we call the modern church festival, where the most exhorbitant profits are often realized? Once more: the cleansing of the temple was a type of the cleansing of the heart from all sin. "It is a type of the cleansing of the heart, which Christ comes to do for everyone who is a temple of God, and out of which all unclean things must be driven by the power of God, before it is fit for God's indwelling." (Abbott.) "May He then come and cleanse our hearts by his spirit, that they may be holy temples for the Lord. May he purify his church and his holy ordinances, from all those practices and persons which pervert or defile them." (Scott.) As Christ symbolized his work of heart purification here, some have seen in the two cleansings of the temple symbols of the two works—regeneration and entire sanctification. Albert Barnes says, "Jesus purified the temple. It was the house of God. So our hearts should be the dwelling place of the Holy Spirit. So, also, they should be pure. All worldly cares . . . and pollution should be banished. And unless we are *pure in heart,* he will not be with us, and we shall not see his face in peace. Jesus only can purify our hearts. He does it by his blood and Spirit. Over all our sins he holds the same power as he did over the traffickers in the temple. At his rebuke they will flee and we shall be pure. If our hearts are ever purified, therefore it will be by the blood of Jesus. Nor should we wait in sin for him to do it. We should come to him and beseech him to save us from our pollution.'' The chief priests and scribes were momentarily stunned by this blow. They were baffled and retired from the contest to mature their plans and see what the morrow would bring forth. Why have church officials so often been opposed to Christ and deep spirituality? What is there in ecclesiasticism that hinders spirituality? How few can fill office even in the church and not be puffed up? Is it not especially true in the attitude of the officiary in most churches, against holiness? Do not be discouraged if church officials fight holiness. Has this not been the rule, with few exceptions in church history? Adam Clarke says ''Strange as it may appear, the priesthood in all corrupt times, has been ever the most forward to prevent a reform in the church. Is it because they were conscious that a reform would find them no better than money changers in and profaners of the house of God, and that they and their system must be overturned if the true worship of God were restored? Let him who is concerned, answer this to his conscience.''

But while the chief priests and scribes were arrayed against Jesus the common people were eager to hear him. The common people have usually less prejudice against reforms in the church than ecclesiastics have.

CHAPTER XX.

HOLINESS DEFENSIVE AND OFFENSIVE.

Holy People Must Defend the Truth. Vs. 1-40. Holy People Must Attack Error. Vs. 41-47.

We find in this chapter Jesus, defending himself and his gospel against the challenge of the chief priests, scribes and elders. He also attacks his enemies in the last seven verses of the chapter. Those who think holiness is a jelly fish affair, a sweetness that allows the truth to suffer, are mistaken. We are set for the defense of the truth and should defend it, as did Jesus. Sometimes the very best way to defend the truth is to attack error.

HOLY PEOPLE MUST DEFEND THE TRUTH. Vs. 1-40.

1 And it came to pass, *that* on one of those days, as he taught the people in the temple, and preached the gospel, the chief priests and the scribes came upon *him* with the elders,

2 And spake unto him, saying, Tell us, by what authority doest thou these things? or who is he that gave thee this authority?

3 And he answered and said unto them, I will also ask you one thing; and answer me:

4 The baptism of John, was it from heaven, or of men?

5 And they reasoned with themselves, saying, If we shall say, From heaven; he will say, Why then believed ye him not?

6 But and if we say, Of men; all the people will stone us: for they be persuaded that John was a prophet.

7 And they answered, that they could not tell whence *it was.*

8 And Jesus said unto them, Neither tell I you by what authority I do these things.

9 Then began he to speak to the people this parable; A certain man planted a vineyard, and let it forth to husbandmen, and went into a far country for a long time.

10 And at the season he sent a servant to the husbandmen, that they should give him of the fruit of the vineyard: but the husbandmen beat him, and sent *him* away empty.

11   And again he sent another servant: and they beat him also, and entreated *him* shamefully, and sent *him* away empty.

12   And again he sent a third: and they wounded him also, and cast *him* out.

13   Then said the lord of the vineyard, What shall I do? I will send my beloved son: it may be they will reverence *him* when they see him.

14   But when the husbandmen saw him, they reasoned among themselves, saying, This is the heir: come, let us kill him, that the inheritance may be our's.

15   So they cast him out of the vineyard, and killed *him*. What therefore shall the lord of the vineyard do unto them?

16   He shall come and destroy these husbandmen, and shall give the vineyard to others. And when they heard *it*, they said, God forbid.

17   And he beheld them, and said, What is this then that is written, The stone which the builders rejected, the same is become the head of the corner?

18   Whosoever shall fall upon that stone shall be broken; but on whomsoever it shall fall, it will grind him to powder.

19   And the chief priests and the scribes the same hour sought to lay hands on him; and they feared the people: for they perceived that he had spoken this parable against them.

20   And they watched *him,* and sent forth spies, which should feign themselves just men, that they might take hold of his words, that so they might deliver him unto the power and authority of the governor.

21   And they asked him, saying, Master, we know that thou sayest and teachest rightly, neither acceptest thou the person *of any,* but teachest the way of God truly:

22   Is it lawful for us to give tribute unto Cæsar, or no?

23   But he perceived their craftiness, and said unto them, Why tempt ye me?

24   Shew me a penny. Whose image and superscription hath it? They answered and said, Cæsar's.

25   And he said unto them, Render therefore unto Cæsar the things which be Cæsar's, and unto God the things which be God's.

26   And they could not take hold of his words before the people: and they marvelled at his answer, and held their peace.

27   Then came to *him* certain of the Sadducees, which deny that there is any resurrection: and they asked him,

28   Saying, Master, Moses wrote unto us, If any man's brother die, having a wife, and he die without children, that his brother should take his wife, and raise up seed unto his brother.

29   There were therefore seven brethren: and the first took a wife, and died without children.

30   And the second took her to wife, and he died childless.

31   And the third took her; and in like manner the seven also: and they left no children, and died.

32 Last of all the woman died also.

33 Therefore in the resurrection whose wife of them is she? for seven had her to wife.

34 And Jesus answering said unto them, The children of this world marry, and are given in marriage:

35 But they which shall be accounted worthy to obtain that world, and the resurrection from the dead, neither marry, nor are given in marriage:

36 Neither can they die any more: for they are equal unto the angels; and are the children of God, being the children of the resurrection.

37 Now that the dead are raised, even Moses shewed at the bush, when he calleth the Lord the God of Abraham, and the God of Isaac, and the God of Jacob.

38 For he is not a God of the dead, but of the living: for all live unto him.

39 Then certain of the scribes answering said, Master, thou hast well said.

40 And after that they durst not ask him any *question at all.*

In this section we find Jesus defending himself against three attacks of the ecclesiastics. The Jewish chief council, called the Sanhedrin, was composed of three sections. 1. The priests. 2. Expounders of the law. 3. Heads of the principal families of Israel. On one of the last days that he spent in Jerusalem, this august body of priests, scribes and elders came to frighten and overawe him with a challlenge as to his authority for cleansing the temple and teaching as he did. They could not answer his arguments or gainsay his doctrine. So they thought they could nullify his teaching by questioning his authority. Many an apparently harmless inquiry about religion is like Herod asking the wise men where Jesus was, that he might worship him, but really that he might kill him. They were seeking some evidence in order to accuse him of blasphemy. They felt that they were the leaders of religion and so demanded the reason why he interfered with their leadership of the people.

He answers them by asking them a question—"The baptism of John was it from heaven or men?" This was a question that showed the rare ability of Jesus in argument. He knew how to put his enemies in a corner. John the Baptist had testified of Jesus that he had seen the Spirit resting as a dove upon him. Now if these enemies should say that the baptism of John (his doctrine and mission) were from heaven then they endorsed Jesus, for John had endorsed him. John as a divine messenger told the truth when he said Jesus was greater than he, and was the Lamb of God that taketh away the sin of the world. In endorsing John therefore they endorsed Jesus. They were in a dilemma surely. They therefore said, We cannot tell. What poor religious leaders and expounders of the word, who could not tell in such a case. It is the business of religious leaders and teachers to be posted- on the isms, doctrines and notions of all kinds, to point out the truth and expose error. And John had preached six months and now they pretended they could not tell whether John was sent of God or not. What stupid churchmen they were, to confess their ignorance! They did not dare to tell what they believed about John. How could Jesus give credentials of authority, for which they asked, to men who had heard John and had no opinion as to his character. What good would it do to give His credentials to them? So they were foiled.

No wonder Jesus said ''Neither tell I you by what authority I do these things.'' If they were not able to form an opinion of John the Baptist's work of what use to give them the authority for that of Jesus?

He seems to have followed up this with the three parables: that of the two sons (Matt. 21:28; 32) and the marriage feast (Matt. 22:1-4) and this of the Wicked Husbandman, which we now have before us, as follows: God is represented as the owner of a vineyard. This allegory was familiar to them, as Israel is likened to a vine and a vineyard many times in the Old Testament. (See Deut. 32:32; Ps. 80:8-16; Isa. 5-17, 27:1-7; Jer. 2:21; Ezek. 15:1-6; 19:10.) This is the only figure of the Old Testament that is used in the New Testament.

Matthew says that he ''hedged it round about.'' (Matt. 21:33.) This refers to the separation of Israel from the heathen world. The country of Palestine where God let the Jews work out their destiny is somewhat remarkable. This little strip of land about 125 miles long with an average breadth of about fifty miles, not only contained the cradle of the world's Redeemer, but was the home of the most wonderful race and the birth place of the mightiest movement the world has ever known. Truly God did shut the Jews in from the outside world. On the east were the river Jordan, lake Galilee and the Dead Sea. On the south was the desert and mountainous country of Idumea, and on the west lay the Mediteranean Sea, without any good sea ports. God had arranged for Israel to live alone.

This exclusiveness of the Jews is referred to by Paul in Eph. 2:14 where he speaks of "the middle wall of partition," between the Jews and Gentiles. No church ever had a more favorable opportunity to be good.

He "let it forth to husbandmen." He put his church in charge of the Jewish ecclesiastics. The object of the planting of the vineyard was to obtain fruit—the fruit of holiness.

"Then he went into a far country." God is apparently a good ways off, because he lets people have their own way. The Jews of that day and the wicked of today act as if God were a long ways off and would never bring them to reckoning. Trench says that the confession of the Levites in Nehemiah 9:26 is an admirable commentary upon this parable.

So "at the season" when fruit of the vineyard was due, he sent his servant to receive it. Fruit is due in our cases as soon as we are in Christ. (John 15:2, 5, 8.) The servants God sends today are the Holy Spirit, the ministry, the Bible and special providences. God sent prophets to the Jews, again and again. Mark (Mark 12:3-5) shows that each servant was treated worse than the one who preceded him. If we read the Old Testament we will find that the prophets of God suffered much at the hands of the church. It has often been the case. (Jer. 44.4.) Ungodly church members are the greatest foes of true religion, on earth. "We have parable after parable, to show us the rage and enmity of the human heart against the religion of the Saviour. How can we, if faithful to his cause, expect a favorable reception from a wicked world and from ungodly professors of Christianity, when the holy prophets and the well beloved Son of God, were thus rejected with contempt, and treated with cruelty by his professed worshippers." (Scott.)

God sent his only Son, as the master of the vineyard sent his son. He did his best. He could do no more. We speak it reverently. God could do no more. If men will not be touched with the sacrifice of Jesus, nothing will move them. That is the reason that rejection of Jesus means damnation. God asks this very question in Jeremiah 5:4. ''What could have been done more to my vineyard that I have not done in it.'' God always does his best for every man.

These foolish husbandmen thought that if they killed the messenger they would escape the responsibility of not sending in the products of the vineyard. Jesus by this figure warns the Jews of the very thing they would do—crucify him. Their crime was therefore all the more heinous, because they had been warned. People are just as wicked today who attempt to dodge their responsibility by denying the deity of Jesus Christ and attempting to disprove the truths of the Christian religion. Those people who have attempted to dispose of the demands of God that they lead a holy life by getting rid of the holiness preacher are just as foolish and wicked. God will require it just the same.

''That the inheritance may be ours.'' This was the secret of their opposition. They wanted the vineyard. The Pharisees did not wish the people to follow Jesus. They wanted them to be *their* flock. It was their jealousy that led them to crucify him. Unfaithful ecclesiastics for this reason are the bitterest foes in all reforms in the church. They do not want to lose their hold on the people.

So they cast the son out of the vineyard and killed him. Not only was Jesus crucified outside of the city of Jerusalem, but he was an outcast from the church and society. Paul applies this to our case of today thus, ''Wherefore Jesus that he might sanctify the people with his own blood suffered without the gate.'' Let us go forth therefore without the camp bearing his reproach. (Heb. 12:12-13.) We must consent to be cast out by men for his sake.

Jesus then closes the parable with this question, ''What therefore shall the Lord of the vineyard do?'' For he must do something. Men must receive the deserts of their deeds.

Jesus answers his own question by saying he would destroy the husbandmen and give the vineyard to others. Forty or more years after this was spoken came the terrible punishment of the Jews in the destruction of Jerusalem, the slaughter of thousands of Jews by the Roman armies and the scattering of the survivors. From which dispersion they have never returned. The punishment of this unhappy nation is an illustration of the doom of backsliders, who reject the Son of God.

God did give the vineyard to others. We are in the Gentile epoch today (See Acts 13:46) and God is calling out a church from among the Gentile nations.

Jesus had a way of preaching that enabled his hearers to know whom he meant. His audiences see here the force of the parable and involuntarily as he pronounces the punishment of the husbandmen (whom they see to be themselves), cry out, "God forbid."

Having illustrated the doom of Judaism by a parable, he clinches the truth thus spoken by a quotation from Scripture. This is a good way to sermonize. He quotes Psalms 118:22, "The stone which the builders refused is become the head stone of the corner." He here shows that the Psalms are inspired and prophesied concerning himself. He gave a meaning to this scripture that they had not seen. The rejected stone was to be not the top stone, but the corner stone. Jesus Christ is the foundation on which are built, prophets, apostles and holy men. Since Jesus the foundation stone was rejected by the builders of the church, how can the holy men built upon him expect any better treatment? "The great corner stones in all world-famous causes have been stones which the builders rejected; that is, unpopular, unwelcome truths, unconventional but consecrated men." (Glover.) Holiness is the great corner stone of the Christian system and it meets with the same treatment that its author received.

Daniel told of the stone cut out of the mountain without hands that rolled on until it filled all the earth, crushing all before it. (Dan. 2:44.) This is evidently a reference to that idea. Trench says, "They fall upon the stone who are offended at Christ in his low estate. They on whom the stone falls are those who set themselves in self-conscious opposition against the Lord; who knowing what he is, do yet to the end oppose themselves to him and his kingdom. These shall not merely fall and be broken; for one might recover himself, though with some harm, from such a fall; but on them the stone shall fall as from heaven, and shall grind them to powder." "Yet, blessed be God, there is a remnant of such as adorn the Gospel by their holy lives; may we be found among them.'' (Scott.)

The battle between Jesus and his enemies grows more and more fierce. In every encounter they are worsted, which only makes them the more desperate. The only reason that they have for not laying hands on him at once is, they fear the people, with whom Jesus is still popular. They, who like Jesus attempt any reform in the church, must expect great opposition.

They seek every way to entrap him in order to frame an accusation against him. So they send spies to ask him if they ought to pay taxes to Caesar, the Roman emperor, who had conquered the Jews and compelled them to pay tribute money for the support of the Roman empire. The Jews all hated this tax. If he should say, Pay it, he would lose his favor with the people. If he said Refuse to pay it, they would accuse him to the Romans of teaching rebellion. There seemed no escape from the dilemma.

Any ordinary man would have been caught in the snare but not so the Son of man. By a simple, yet rational method, he solved the question. ''By this singular reply the hypocrisy and inconsistency of the question was at once exposed. The mere payment of the tribute is a secondary matter after all. The true question was, Should the Roman rule be submitted to or not? Was it, or was it not lawful to bear the foreign yoke? There was this manifest token of subjection that Roman money was circulated among them as the common and accepted coin of the realm.'' (Hanna.) When they accepted the coined money of Rome they had accepted and acknowledged the supremacy of Caesar. They owed Caesar the coin for they had accepted and used his money.

It might be well to inquire what are the things that are God's. This covers a good deal in our lives.

They were astonished at his answer and were obliged to be silent.

The infidel Sadducees now try to entrap him by a different question. The Sadducees were the infidels of that day. They denied the resurrection of the body and the existence of the spirit. (Acts 23:8.) They were like the modern Soul-Sleepers in doctrine. They put a question which they were sure would puzzle and confound him. It was this: to which of seven brothers, who had married one woman would she belong, in the resurrection state, for she had been the wife of seven.

It would be well for the materialists of today—that class that deny the existence of the soul only as it is exhibited in and by the body, to heed the answer of Jesus, "Do ye not therefore err because ye know not the Scriptures, neither the power of God?" He does not accuse them of hypocrisy as he did the Pharisees, but of error. They erred because they were in ignorance of the Scriptures and the power of God. That is the cause of the error of the Soul-Sleepers of today. Had they known the scriptures they would have seen that the doctrine of the future life of the soul is there taught. Had they known the power of God, they would have believed God could raise the dead and give a new existence in the future world; and they would have known that the resurrection life will be far above this life of births and deaths and marriage.

He gives some information of the future life. He says the saints will have an immortality like the angels in heaven, as Quesnel says very aptly, "They will have no passions there, no more occasion for food, and no more fear of dying, than pure spirits. They will have no other father but the Father of the world to come, who will restore life to the members as he has to the Head, by the eternal and immortal Spirit working in them. They will no longer have any of the life of Adam."

He says in verse 36, that they will be "equal to the angels." They will be on an equality with the holy angels. He also says they are "children of the resurrection." The God who regenerated and sanctified them will immortalize them. They will then, having passed the degrees of regeneration and entire sanctification, take the third degree—glorification.

Jesus having said this, in meeting the objection of the Sadducees against the resurrection, now brings positive prooofs of it. He proves it by showing that when God said, "I am the God of Abraham," he meant that Abraham was still alive. He could not be the God of some one, who no longer existed, but had been annihilated. He was not the God of some one who had no existence. Stier says, "If these words are to be understood in any way worthy of God, then must the fathers still exist as persons as their *names* indicate, inasmuch as he thus speaks of them.'' Thus the Sadducees were confuted. We can thus find according to Jesus, the doctrine of immortality taught in the Old Testament.

He still further adds ''for all live in Him.'' That is, all who have died are still alive in Him in another state. In His estimation the dead still exist.

Notice how reserved Jesus is in speaking of the future state. An imposter would have tried to tell us a good deal about it, as did Mohammed in the Koran. There are no ridiculous descriptions here of the future world.

A scribe who had listened to all these attempts now speaks up, out of the honesty and candor of his heart, saying, ''Master thou hast answered well.'' The Pharisees were always seeking arguments against the infidel Sadducees, especially as regards the Resurrection. Jesus evidently gives them this new one that they had never seen in the Scriptures before. So clearly does he bring it out that the Scribe in admiration forgets himself and utters these words. We learn from this the propriety and benefit of argument, if it be done in a Christ-like spirit. We shall all meet with cavillers who will seek to perplex us but we may argue if in a sweet spirit. After this they were afraid to ask him any more questions.

HOLY PEOPLE MUST ATTACK ERROR. Vs. 41-47.

41 And he said unto them, How say they that Christ is David's son?

42 And David himself saith in the book of Psalms, The Lord said unto my Lord, Sit thou on my right hand,

43 Till I make thine enemies thy footstool.

44 David therefore calleth him Lord, how is he then his son?

45 Then in the audience of all the people he said unto his disciples,

46 Beware of the scribes, which desire to walk in long robes, and love greetings in the markets, and the highest seats in the synagogues, and the chief rooms at feasts;

47 Which devour widows' houses, and for a shew make long prayers: the same shall receive greater damnation.

Jesus not only answered the arguments of his foes but attacked them with arguments that they could not answer. A false idea prevails that we must take no stand, but allow the world to have the best of the argument. This is a mistake. We are set for the defence of the truth, and one of the best methods of advancing the truth is to attack error.

So he asks them a question that sorely puzzled them. Jesus evidently asks this question to discomfit the Pharisees, in the presence of the people and weaken their authority.

"David therefore calleth him Lord." David never called Absalom, his son, Lord. Abraham never called Isaac, his son, Lord. No one of that time ever called a son, Lord. Why then did David call his descendant, Jesus, by that name? Because he was more than son. He was divine. From the divine standpoint he was David's Lord. He then quotes a prophecy from Psalm 110, which the Jews acknowledged to be a prophecy of the Messiah. "They could not answer because they would not answer, and they would not answer because they could not answer, without confessing that the Christ of the Hebrew Scriptures must needs be both God and man." (Huntingdon.)

Now that he had silenced the Scribes and Pharisees he turns to the people and follows up his advantage by telling them to beware of the scribes as much as to say, Beware of unholy ministers. Be suspicious of preachers who are self-seeking, who desire the highest places in the denomination or church. "The clergy are to be discerned (or distinguished) not so much by their apparel as by their learning; not by their habit only, but by their conversation; not by adornment of the body, but by purity of mind." (Pope Celestine in Whitby.)

CHAPTER XXI.

HOLINESS GIVES READINESS.

Only Entire Consecration Is Acceptable to God. Vs. 1-4. Holiness Makes Us Prepared for All Emergencies. Vs. 5-38.

ONLY ENTIRE CONSECRATION IS ACCEPTABLE TO GOD.
Vs. 1-4.

1 And he looked up, and saw the rich men casting their gifts into the treasury.

2 And he saw also a certain poor widow casting in thither two mites.

3 And he said, Of a truth I say unto you, that this poor widow hath cast in more than they all:

4 For all these have of their abundance cast in unto the offerings of God: but she of her penury hath cast in all the living that she had.

We have here an illustration of the fact that our consecration must be entire, no matter how little or much of this world's goods we have. Consecration is in the will—the determination of the heart.

Mark says (Ch. 12:4) that Jesus ''Beheld *how* the people cast money into the treasury.'' He still watches to see *how* (the spirit of it) we give; he is seeing the spirit with which we do everything. It was no accidental glance. The same eye that saw the woman touch the hem of his garment, that beheld Zaccheus up the tree, that penetrated the very hearts of the Pharisees, saw this woman.

''Their gifts.'' Literally, *their consecrated things*. He is watching to see whether our consecration is genuine. We can not deceive him.

He had got over his battle with the Pharisees and now sits down calmly to watch the givers into the Lord's treasury.

He saw a poor widow cast in two mites. It might seem a very

403

insignificant act but nothing is insignificant in the sight of the God that numbers the hairs of our heads. He notes the little acts, little thoughts and little words.

The mite was the smallest coin that the Jews had. Mark says (Chapter 12:42) that two mites make a farthing. It was all she had to give, but she might have kept one mite. A current idea with people when they say they give their mite is to give the least sum or coin they have. They like to tell about the Widow's Mite; but it is a misnomer. She did not give her mite. She gave her *two mites*—all she had. We ought to be as willing in heart to give our all, if God requires it, as she did in reality. This teaches that the offering of the poor, no matter however humble, ought to be given as well as the abundance of the rich. If we give a dollar for appearance-sake when we would prefer to give only half as much we will not get credit for more than half a dollar with the Lord. We are not sure that we would get credit at all, under the circumstances. Our motives must be pure or our actions will be vain. We cannot leave our money out of our consecration. The trouble is too many do that. "God will not refuse the poor offerings of the poor, but he will not accept the poor offerings of the rich." (Medley.)

Jesus said this poor widow cast more into the treasury than all the rich men who cast in their great sums. This was because of her attitude of soul towards God's cause. She gave her all. They did not. He explains what he means in verse 4. God puts all mankind on a level—the rich and poor. Adam Clarke says, "The poorest person has it in his power to make his mite acceptable to the Lord, by simplicity of intention and purity of affections, as the millions given by the affluent."

This incident teaches several things about the morality of an action. It does not depend upon noble birth or noble connections. This widow could perform as grand an action as the highest and noblest of the Pharisees, no matter if she had been of the lowest rank. Some people think the poor and lowly know but little about the exalted virtues of righteousness.

Nor does the morality of an action depend upon intellect or native genius. We have no means of knowing whether this woman had a great intellect. But she performed a great act.

Often times men of great intellect and genius are sadly little men because of the meanness of their moral purpose.

Nor does the greatness of an action depend upon wealth. She was poor. Some of the smallest souls in the world, apparently incapable of a great moral act are rolling in wealth.

The greatness of an act does not depend upon external or apparent results. Her money was not a large sum and would go but a little ways towards the expenses of the temple, but it was a great action just the same.

Let us look again at the qualities that make an action great, or in other words let us see upon what the greatness of an action depends. 1. On the intention. 2. On the spirit in which it is performed. 3. On the sacrifice required to perform it.

While the rich ought to give and ought to be encouraged to give, they ought not to be flattered lest we spoil the glory of the action and hurt them spiritually. "They ought not to be flattered into the opinion that their actions are meritorious, or that they will atone for their ungodliness and licentiousness, and prove a substitute for repentance, faith and holiness." (Scott.) "It is a poor thing when we speak of the church to let our discourse dwell upon its pomps, or revenues—for the king's daughter is all glorious within." (Henry.)

HOLINESS MAKES US PREPARED FOR ALL EMERGENCIES. Vs. 5-38.

5 And as some spake of the temple, how it was adorned with goodly stones and gifts, he said,

6 As *for* these things which ye behold, the days will come, in the which there shall not be left one stone upon another, that shall not be thrown down.

7 And they asked him, saying, Master, but when shall these things he? and what sign *will there be* when these things shall come to pass?

8 And he said, Take heed that ye be not deceived: for many shall come in my name, saying, I am *Christ;* and the time draweth near: go ye not therefore after them.

9 But when ye shall hear of wars and commotions, be not terrified: for these things must first come to pass; but the end *is* not by and by.

10 Then said he unto them, Nation shall rise against nation, and kingdom against kingdom:

11   And great earthquakes shall be in divers places, and famines, and pestilences ; and fearful sights and great signs shall there be from heaven.

12   But before all these, they shall lay their hands on you, and persecute *you,* delivering *you* up to the synagogues, and into prisons, being brought before kings and rulers for my name's sake.

13   And it shall turn to you for a testimony.

14   Settle *it* therefore in your hearts, not to meditate before what ye shall answer :

15   For I will give you a mouth and wisdom, which all your adversaries shall not be able to gainsay nor resist.

16   And ye shall be betrayed both by parents, and brothren, and kinsfolks, and friends ; and *some* of you shall they cause to be put to death.

17   And ye shall be hated of all *men* for my name's sake.

18   But there shall not an hair of your head perish.

19   In your patience possess ye your souls.

20   And when ye shall see Jerusalem compassed with armies, then know that the desolation thereof is nigh.

21   Then let them which are in Judæa flee to the mountains : and let them which are in the midst of it depart out ; and let not them that are in the countries enter thereinto.

22   For these be the days of vengeance, that all things which are written may be fulfilled.

23   But woe unto them that are with child, and to them that give suck, in those days ! for there shall be great distress in the land, and wrath upon this people.

24   And they shall fall by the dge of the sword, and shall be led away captive into all nations : and Jerusalem shall be trodden down of the Gentiles, until the times of the Gentiles be fulfilled.

25   And there shall be signs in the sun, and in the moon, and in the stars ; and upon the earth distress of nations, with perplexity ; the sea and the waves roaring ;

26   Men's hearts failing them for fear, and for looking after those things which are coming on the earth : for the powers of heaven shall be shaken.

27   And then shall they see the Son of man coming in a cloud with power and great glory.

28   And when these things begin to come to pass, then look up, and lift up your heads ; for your redemption draweth nigh.

29   And he spake to them a parable : Behold the fig tree, and all the trees ;

30   When they now shoot forth, ye see and know of your own selves that summer is now nigh at hand.

31   So likewise ye, when ye see these things come to pass, know ye that the kingdom of God is nigh at hand.

32   Verily I say unto you, This generation shall not pass away, till all be fulfilled.

33   Heaven and earth shall pass away : but my words shall not pass away.

34   And take heed to yourselves, lest at any time your hearts be overcharged with surfeiting, and drunkenness, and cares of this life, and *so* that day come upon you unawares.

35   For as a snare shall it come on all them that dwell on the face of the whole earth.

36   Watch ye therefore, and pray always, that ye may be accounted worthy to escape all these things that shall come to pass, and to stand before the Son of man.

37   And in the day time he was teaching in the temple ; and at night he went out, and abode in the mount that is called *the mount* of Olives.

38   And all the people came early in the morning to him in the temple, for to hear him.

As these and other talks of Jesus were given under the shadow of and in the outer court of the temple, which was the glory of the Jewish nation, some of his hearers wished to know his opinion of that great and magnificent building. So they spoke of the goodly stones that formed its ornamentation. They certainly were "goodly stones." Josephus says these stones were fifty feet in length and twenty-four in breadth and sixteen feet thick. It was a magnificent pile of architecture of different colored marble. But to Jesus the chief ornament of the church is not its wealth or architecture. The gems he regards are those of the heart. They had converted his Father's house into a den of thieves. It was no longer a house of prayer.

Therefore briefly he foretold the doom of that beautiful temple.

Is it not marvelous that a mere Galilean peasant should even dare if he believed it, to predict, when surrounded by bitter enemies, the destruction of that temple, the admiration and pride of the Jews? Is it not marvelous too that he should have refused to be intoxicated by the triumphal march and the adulations and praises of the people. An imposter would have taken the opportunity to praise the beauty of the temple and prophesy its future glory.

And again is it not marvelous that he should have had the foresight that led him to prophesy the destruction of this marvelous building? When the Roman general after the destruction of Jerusalem saw these huge stones upon the ground it is said that he expressed his astonishment and said a divine power must have assisted him. Truly Jesus was all he claimed to be—divine.

Jewish writers themselves acknowledge that Terentius Rufus, who was left to command the Roman army, tore up with a plough-share the foundations of the temple, thereby fulfilling the prophecy of Micah 3:12, ''Therefore shall Zion for your sake be plowed as a field, and Jerusalem shall become heaps.''

This stern prophecy uttered at such a time, when his words had been so mighty in their influence upon the multitude, forced from the disciples (Matt. 24:3) the question, ''When shall these things be?''

We must study carefully this in connection with the account of Matthew (Matt. 24.) There it says the disciples asked him three questions. 1. When these things should take place. 2. What should be the sign of his coming. 3. What should be the sign of the end of the world (or the age). If we keep in mind that his coming at the destruction of Jerusalem is a type of his coming in his grand personal appearing at the end of the age, we shall escape much confusion of thought on the subject. He now goes on as far as verse 25 to give the signs that should precede the destruction of Jerusalem. So verses 8-24 are the answer to the questions of the signs of his coming to destroy Jerusalem, through the instrumentality of the Romans.

The first sign preceding the destruction of Jerusalem was the appearance of false Messiahs. Many false Christs did come within the next forty years.

The second sign was wars and commotions. Although it was a time of universal peace when Jesus was born, yet shortly after his death the whole East was in commotion. Judea had rebelled against the Romans. The armies of Spain, Gaul, Germany, Illyricum and Syria were all marching to Italy to decide who should be the successor of Nero, to the throne of the Caesars. The phrase ''Not by and by'' is an incorrect translation. It should be ''Not immediately.''

The third sign was great earthquakes. Josephus tells us of fearful earthquakes and other fearful phenomena just as Jesus prophesied. ''Josephus furnishes the best commentary on this chapter. It is a wonderful instance of the care of Providence for the Christian church that Josephus, an eye-witness of great credit, should be preserved to transmit a collection of facts which exactly illustrate this prophecy in almost every instance.'' (Doddridge.)

It is said that among the fearful sights that were manifest about the doomed city was a comet shaped like a scimitar that hung over it for a year previous to its destruction.

He told them (verse 12) that before these earthquakes, etc., the disciples should suffer persecution. This was literally fulfilled. Their lives were one continued experience of persecution. They were imprisoned, beaten, brought before kings and councils, and many of them put to death.

He declared that these persecutions should ''turn to them for a testimony.'' The very persecution would testify that Jesus who had foretold it was a true prophet. It would prove his word true. We in our day, if persecuted because we are determined to be true to Jesus ought to rejoice too that we are proving the truth of that Scripture, ''All they that will live godly in Christ Jesus shall suffer persecution.'' Let us remember that the more the devil hates us the more the Lord loves us.

They were to fully make up their minds not to prepare any defence before hand when brought before magistrates and councils. God would give them wisdom in that hour. It is strange that some modern would-be preachers, who have no such exigency to meet should construe this to mean that preachers should make no preparation for the pulpit. It has no reference whatever to preaching, but to the defence a man makes when his life is endangered by being faithful to the cause of Jesus.

Another sign would be that even members of their own family would betray them. Carnality is so mean that it will actually trample on the most sacred relations of life in its hatred of God. Abbott says, ''This and the succeeding verses indicate four dangers which will assail the church; persecution from without, apostasy, schism and controversy within; false doctrine and worldliness, and consequent backsliding. Each of these dangers came in a small measure upon the Apostolic Church, before the destruction of Jerusalem. And in the subsequent history of the Christian church, the reader must look for a larger fulfillment.''

But he declared not a hair of their heads should be hurt. He who is true to God can not be hurt. Nothing but sin can really hurt us, even if we are burnt at the stake.

''In your patience possess ye your souls.'' This is a remarkable saying. The correct translation is, ''*In your patience ye shall win your souls.*'' How much is said in the New Testament about bearing our trials with patience; looking patiently for the coming of Jesus. The only way to win or save our own souls is by patience. We all need it, for while we do not have the extreme persecution that the disciples had, we have plenty of opportunity to have patience tried and developed.

Keeping in mind the prophecy of Jesus when the disciples saw Jerusalem surrounded by Roman armies they fled, as they knew the end was near. Early Christian writers tell us that in A. D. 66, a Roman army attacked Jerusalem and were defeated, and that the disciples within the city recognized this sign of the Lord's prophecy and fled to the neighboring district of Pella. Four years later the final siege by the Romans under Titus began, but the Lord's disciples were out of the city *and not one perished in that awful* massacre.

Truly those were ''the days of vengeance'' when God punished that haughty city through the instrumentality of the Roman army. Lange, the great German Commentator says, ''We may call to mind the expression, even of a Titus, 'That God was so angry with this people, that even he feared his wrath if he should suffer grace to be shown to the Jews,' and how he refused every mark of honor on account of the victory obtained, with the attestation that he had been only an instrument in God's hand to punish this stiff-necked nation.'' This language of this general of the Roman army, a heathen, is certainly startling.

He then refers to ancient prophecies and says the destruction of Jerusalem was the fulfillment of them. Read Lev. 26:14-23; Deut. 28:15 and Dan. 9:26-27. Still farther, read how the Apostle makes their fate a warning to those today who now neglect the Gospel. See Heb. 2:1-3.

Jesus says ''they shall fall by the edge of the sword.'' Josephus says "a million Jews perished and ninety seven thousand were carried away captive.

Jerusalem has been trodden under foot of the Gentiles until this day. The Jews have no government. The Sultan of Turkey reigns over it. And it is to be so "until the times of the Gentiles are fulfilled." We are now in the Gentile dispensation. We, Gentiles are now in our time of *probation*. Will we be found wanting as were the Jews? At the end of the Gentile dispensation comes the destruction of the world, just as the destruction of Jerusalem ended the Jewish dispensation.

With verse 25 begins another set of signs—those that will come before the Second Advent. These signs are somewhat similar and will be as real as those that preceded the fall of Jerusalem.

When these signs are manifest, then shall they see another greater sign still—the Sign of the Son of Man in the heavens, "coming in a cloud." He went away on a cloud. He is coming back on a cloud.

While the hearts of the wicked are failing them as indicated by verse 26 the righteous in that day are to lift up their heads and rejoice. If we would meet the Lord without fear and with joy we must be ready—ready all the time. Whether death comes to us before the Lord comes or the Lord comes and not death we need to be sanctified in either event, for only an entirely sanctified heart will make us ready for either.

There are many stalwart champions of the coming of Christ, whose zeal will profit them nothing because they do not believe in "the sanctification without which no man shall see the Lord," and even ridicule it as a possible experience in this life. They are the most inconsistent people in the world. Of all people in the world, advocates of the Second Advent ought to make a specialty of holiness.

Their "Redemption draweth nigh," because they have already been saved from sin, when wholly sanctified. At the advent of Jesus they will be delivered from the temptations and assaults of a wicked world and a tempting devil.

Just as when we see the fig tree shooting forth its leaves, so when we see the signs mentioned in verses 25-26 we may know the Coming of Jesus is at hand. This is however no good reason for setting the time of his coming, as so many have foolishly done.

It is uncertain what he means by "this generation." Certainly Jerusalem was destroyed before that generation of Jews passed away. If the word means more than a generation that lives forty or fifty years, then it was true. If the word in the original will bear to be translated *nation*, then it is true as regards the Second Coming also, for the Jews are still kept on the earth without king, government or country. We are inclined to believe it may be used in both senses and may apply to both events therefore.

He said his words would remain after heaven and earth had passed away. These words are more potent today than ever. He is the best quoted man that ever lived. These words concerning his coming will yet be fulfilled, however men may ridicule the idea of his coming.

Having answered their questions as regards the destruction of Jerusalem and his Second Advent, he now comes to the practical part of it in these words, "Take heed to yourselves." Jesus uses this expression in but one other place in the whole New Testament and then it was directed to his disciples. The passage is in Luke 17:3, where he bids them beware of becoming sour and having ill feeling towards those who did not treat them well. In the passage before us he warns them (and us too) of living a self pampering life, whereby our spiritual life is hindered by gluttony, intemperance and the cares of this life. In other words we are to make spiritual things of the chief importance. The soul must not be hindered in any way whether by appetite or by undue care for the things of this life. That is the way we are to live every day, waiting for the coming of Jesus. We are not only to be holy, *but we must keep our bodies under.*

We must do this because as the summons will be sudden, we may be caught as in a snare. The devil catches many people who want to be good through physical indulgence. When Jesus comes according to verse 35 the majority of mankind will not be expecting him. The rich will as a class be surfeited and the covetous will be full of care.

Against all excesses and allurements from readiness to meet Jesus, we are to *watch*. No matter to what degree of holiness we may have come, we must watch, that we may be found of him "without spot and blameless," that we may be *accounted worthy to escape these calamities*. We must not only be holy but maintain a life of holiness constantly. Paul said he and others had such an experience. (Coll. 1:12.)

Jesus filled up the time with incessant labor to the very last. This was the last week of his life. Daytimes he spent in teaching in the temple, and every night he went out and lodged at Bethany (Matt. 21:17) on the other side of the mount of Olives. Thus he finished his life as he began it (Luke 2:49) constantly about his Father's business. He began his work in the temple (Luke 2:46-49) and finished it there.

CHAPTER XXII.

TEMPTATIONS.

Temptation of Judas Iscariot. Vs. 1-6. The Lord's Supper, a Symbol of Soul-Communion with Christ. Vs. 7-23. Temptation of the Disciples. Vs. 24-30. Temptation of Peter. Vs. 31-36. Temptation of Jesus. Vs. 37-46. The World Never Crucifies Jesus Until Some of His Professed Followers Make It Possible. Vs. 47-49. Holiness Is Merciful. Vs. 50-53. Inbred Sin Tempts to Denial of Christ. Vs. 54-62. The Enmity of the Carnal Mind Against God Illustrated. Vs. 63-71.

In this chapter we have the account of the temptations of several persons.

TEMPTATION OF JUDAS ISCARIOT. Vs. 1-6.

1 Now the feast of unleavened bread drew nigh, which is called the Passover.

2 And the chief priests and scribes sought how they might kill him ; for they feared the people.

3 Then entered Satan into Judas surnamed Iscariot, being of the number of the twelve.

4 And he went his way, and communed with the chief priests and captains, how he might betray him unto them.

5 And they were glad, and covenanted to give him money.

6 And he promised, and sought opportunity to betray him unto them in the absence of the multitude.

It was now about time for the Passover or Feast of Unleavened Bread. It was called the Feast of Unleavened Bread because on the night that the Israelites left Egypt they went in such haste that they had no time to wait even for their bread to rise, but took it unyeasted or unleavened in their mixing troughs. Leaven is used throughout the Scripture (except in one place,

Lev. 23:17) as a type of corruption. Unleavened bread therefore represents purity or holiness. This feast was called the Passover because the destroying angel *passed over* the houses of the Israelites and spared the first born on that dark night when Israel left Egypt with the unleavened bread. (Exodus 12.)

The chief priests were seeking every way to destroy Jesus. Satan took advantage of this to tempt Judas. When a man is disposed to evil it is remarkable how Satan will make it convenient to do wrong. The chief priests and Satan were in hellish harmony to ruin both Jesus and Judas if possible.

It was at this juncture that Satan entered into Judas. The latter was a good example of inbred sin in a believer. His master passion was covetousness. This was the prominent phase of his carnal nature. Judas was a good man once. Jesus never would have chosen a bad man to be his disciple. He did not choose any to be his disciples until they had been saved under the ministry of John the Baptist. Judas was a preacher of the Gospel. He was one of the twelve whom Jesus chose to preach the Gospel and cast out devils. To suppose he was an unsaved man is to accuse Jesus of employing an nusaved man to preach the Gospel, which is absurd. Satan came first to his unsanctified heard with a suggestion (John 13:2) to betray his master. He was angry with Mary for ''wasting'' the precious ointment. Jesus had rebuked this criticism of Mary. Satan came when Judas was under criticism and put into his heart the thought of betraying his Master. There is nothing too mean or contemptible that the spirit of covetousness will not dare. A covetous man is a dangerous man both to himself and others. How many murders have been committed in the history of the world through love of money.

This thought, having been allowed to enter, became a fixed purpose. And now he allowed Satan himself to follow the evil thought. It is very easy for Satan to come in when we cherish devilish ideas and thoughts. An unsanctified man has Satan's property—the carnal mind in him, and it becomes easy for Satan to come to his own possessions. An unsanctified man is tempted from two sources—the carnal mind within and Satan from without. Under the circumstances it is easy for Satan to come in.

A wholly sanctified man, like Jesus has his temptations wholly from the outside. So we see from this, that Satan does possess men's hearts. And if it be true that Satan enters men's hearts —why should it be incredible that the Holy Spirit too shall dwell in men's hearts? Why should we give more credit to the powers of evil than of the powers of righteousness?

Let the covetous man remember that covetousness is abhorrent to God. It was the great enemy of Jesus while on earth and is supremely so today. Monod says, "Scarcely had Jesus commenced his work, when *covetousness* lifted itself up against him; it everywhere intruded upon his path; it disputed every step he took. It misunderstood and forsook him in the person of the rich young man; it incited his holy anger in the person of the buyers and sellers in the temple; it hated him; it railed at him; it persecuted him in the person of the Pharisees; and in the person of Judas it tithed the fruit of charity for the poor; it begrudged the honor bestowed on his burial; it betrayed him, it delivered him up, it sold him. Oh, prophetic crime, which casts a sad light upon the future of the Christ of God. This same crime of him, who for thirty pieces of silver sold the blood of the Son of God, is the same crime which will show itself most active in depriving men of the ineffable benefits of this shed blood; for covetousness will oppose equally the salvation of the individual, the fidelity of the church and the conversion of the world." Reader if you are covetous you ought to be as much alarmed (and even more) as if you had an awful black leprosy already eating out your vitals. Nothing short of the cleansing blood of Jesus can save you from this fire of hell already in your bosom. *There is no such being on earth as a stingy, penurious Christian.* It is a contradiction of terms.

And Judas bargained with enemies of Jesus, who dared not seize him in public, to show them his secret place and time of retirement, that they might take him there; and all for thirty pieces of silver—about fifteen dollars in our money. This was the price usually paid, to a master for a slave that had been slain. (Ex. 21:23.) This had been prophesied by Zechariah. (Zech. 11:12, 13.) The Christian, with inbred sin as a part of his nature, is in danger of betraying Christ to his enemies at every temptation. "A minister of the Gospel, who is a lover of money, is constantly betraying the interests of Christ. He cannot serve two masters; and while his heart is possessed with the love of self, the love of God, the zeal for perishing souls cannot dwell in him." (Adam Clarke.) Do not many today betray Christ for less than $15?

THE LORD'S SUPPER IS A SYMBOL OF SOUL-COMMUNION WITH CHRIST. Vs. 7-23.

7 Then came the day of unleavened bread, when the passover must be killed.

8 And he sent Peter and John, saying, Go and prepare us the passover, that we may eat.

9 And they said unto him, Where wilt thou that we prepare?

10 And he said unto them, Behold, when ye are entered into the city, there shall a man meet you, bearing a pitcher of water; follow him into the house where he entereth in.

11 And ye shall say unto the goodman of the house, The Master saith unto thee, Where is the guestchamber, where I shall eat the passover with my disciples?

12 And he shall shew you a large upper room furnished: there make ready.

13 And they went, and found as he had said unto them: and they made ready the passover.

14 And when the hour was come, he sat down, and the twelve apostles with him.

15 And he said unto them, With desire I have desired to eat this passover with you before I suffer:

16 For I say unto you, I will not any more eat thereof, until it is fulfilled in the kingdom of God.

17 And he took the cup, and gave thanks, and said, Take this, and divide it among yourselves:

18 For I say unto you, I will not drink of the fruit of the vine, until the kingdom of God shall come.

19 And he took bread, and gave thanks, and brake it, saying, This is my body which is given for you: this do in remembrance of me.

20 Likewise also the cup after supper, saying, This cup is the new testament in my blood, which is shed for you.

21 But, behold, the hand of him that betrayeth me is with me on the table.

22 And truly the Son of man goeth, as it was determined: but woe unto that man by whom he is betrayed!

23 And they began to enquire among themselves, which of them it was that should do this thing.

Then came the 14th day of the month Nisan, the day when the preparation began for the Passover week. As Jesus had sent the two disciples for the colt upon which he should ride through the city, so now, he sends Peter and John to prepare the Passover, directing them to a man whom they should find bearing a pitcher of water. They were to follow him into a house. Doubtless this method was taken to prevent the enemies of Christ knowing where they were to eat the Passover. The man would find a large upper chamber furnished. The disciples found it as Jesus had said. It was usually woman's work to carry water. It was therefore such a singular thing to see a man carrying water that they would be sure and follow the right man.

It was customary to rent rooms to strangers, who came to Jerusalem to celebrate the Passover.

Have you a guest chamber in your heart for the Lord and you to commune? Our hearts should be as willingly offered as was this guest chamber. "I have desired to eat this passover with you." Notwithstanding he knew that it was to be a preparation for his approaching agony and death, yet he gladly welcomed it.

Jesus will eat the Passover with us now, if we sincerely look to him in partaking of the Lord's Supper—renouncing our sins and praying that his precious blood may cleanse us from all sin. Every time that we partake of the Lord's Supper, we ought to be so completely given up to the will of God, as to be ready for our Gethsemane or Calvary.

The great central fact of his ministry he states in these words, "Before I suffer." It was not his example or words but his sacrifice that is celebrated in the Lord's Supper. It is a constant remembrance of the suffering of Jesus.

He said he would no more partake of the Passover until it was fulfilled in the kingdom of heaven. By this we see that the Lord's Supper is symbolical. It symbolized the heavenly feast of the Marriage Supper of the Lamb. Jesus is getting that feast ready and is getting a holy people ready for it.

"He took the cup." There were two cups—one at the beginning and one at the close of the supper. (See verse 20.) This taking of the cup was the abrogation of the Passover and the inauguration of the new rite—The Lord's Supper. This was the point of transition between the two.

When Jesus took the bread and said "This is my body" he meant, it symbolizes my body. Just as when Daniel said to Nebuchadnezzar concerning the image he saw in his dream, "Thou art the head of gold." He meant that the head of gold symbolized the king. So here he means, This represents or symbolizes my body. The name over a man's store or on the door plate is not the man, but represents the man.

Jesus wished to be remembered by his disciples in all ages. So he institutes this rite and said, "This do in remembrance of me." The most fitting way to celebrate it is to pray that all the fruits of his suffering and death may be realized in our lives, and receive him by faith that we may feed upon him spiritually and be cleansed from all sin by his precious blood.

"The New Testament." The word Testament means covenant or will. He now makes the New Testament or Covenant and ratifies and seals it with his blood. It is a covenant that God makes for Jesus's sake to write his law on our hearts and thereby make us holy. (Jeremiah 31:33-34 and Heb. 10:14-17.) The blood of Jesus was the seal (like the seal to a legal document), of the new covenant; just as the wine of the Lord's Supper was the symbol of the blood of Jesus, just so the Lord's Supper is a symbol of the Marriage Supper of the Lamb, and not that supper itself. This is an explanation of this symbolical language. How absurd the Romish pretensions that the priest transforms the bread and wine into the real body and blood of Jesus.

Although the great crime of Judas was turned into a great blessing to mankind, yet this did not lessen the guilt of Judas. The motive makes an action good or bad, not its results. Woe to Judas although God turned his crime into a blessing to mankind.

TEMPTATION OF THE DISCIPLES. Vs. 24-30.

24 And there was also a strife among them, which of them should be accounted the greatest.

25 And he said unto them, The kings of the Gentiles exercise lordship over them ; and they that exercise authority upon them are called benefactors.

26 But ye *shall* not *be* so : but he that is greatest among you, let him be as the younger ; and he that is chief, as he that doth serve.

27 For whether *is* greater, he that sitteth at meat, or he that serveth? *is* not he that sitteth at meat? but I am among you as he that serveth.

28 Ye are they which have continued with me in my temptations.

29 And I appoint unto you a kingdom, as my Father hath appointed unto me;

30 That ye may eat and drink at my table in my kingdom, and sit on thrones judging the twelve tribes of Israel.

We have already seen that the backsliding of Judas was the development of inbred sin. We now have another manifestation of inbred sin in the remaining eleven disciples.

Around this first communion table there actually arose a strife among the disciples as to their individual rights. Inbred sin or carnality is such an impudent principle that it has no regard for times, places or persons. It will manifest itself in the most sacred places. We see it cropping out here in unhallowed ambition. Would that this were the last time it had thus manifested itself in the church and ministry in the unhallowed ambition of clerical politics. Two years' training and that too under the instruction of Jesus, had not in the least either exterminated or subjected "the old man" who "is not subject to the law of God neither indeed can be." During this period, they had not outgrown inbred sin, nor educated, nor evoluted it out. Nor would it have been removed by growth or development if they had lived a thousand years. How great their need of the exterminating, purifying fires of Pentecost!

In this quarrel for place; this desire to be the chief of the college of Apostles, Jesus would surely have named Peter as the leader, if he had intended him to be the first Pope.

He reasoned with his unsanctified disciples to show them that they were acting just like the unsanctified world. They were coming down to the level of those who were not friends or acquaintances of Jesus. *Inbred sin makes Christians who have not been wholly sanctified act like the unsaved world,* because when they give way to it, they backslide. He reasons with them by contrasting what the world do, with what the disciples of Jesus should do. He tells them that the titles and honors given to kings and great ones in the world are usually given by dependents and flatterers to curry faver. But this should not be the conduct of the children of God. What are titles and honors and fame to a true child of God. Yet how pitiful is the scramble for place and position among eccleciastics in the church of God! Alas! How much need there is of the work of holiness in the church. "Of how little avail has this condemnation of 'lordship' and vain titles been against the vanity of Christian ecclesiastics." (Brown.)

He utters one of his startling truths in his frequent mode of paradox thus, "He that is greatest among you, let him be as the younger." In the kingdom of God the humblest are the greatest. It takes perfect love to be able to arrive at such a state of humility. The spirit of selfseeking and desire to rule found among some professors of holiness shows they are mistaken in their profession.

We must be lowly and humble here. Why should we care for place and honor? Has he not *appointed for us a kingdom?* This far transcends all the places and positions for which the world are striving. These apostles had been with him in his temptations, and the future would be their full recompense. This kingdom to which they were appointed was the inner spiritual kingdom of righteousness, peace and joy in the Holy Ghost. Alexander says, "His great central conception of the kingdom of God, a kingdom based upon truth, administered by moral influences, pervaded by love, and holiness and joy, and open to all of whatever class or clime, is a conception as magnificent as it is original."

He promised some kind of exaltation in the future world, which it is impossible for us to understand. He calls it sitting on thrones judging the twelve tribes of Israel. We may not have the same degree of exaltation that the disciples will have in the future kingdom, but if true to God we will share all the glory of which we are capable.

TEMPTATION OF PETER. Vs. 31-36.

31 And the Lord said, Simon, Simon, behold, Satan hath desired *to have* you, that he may sift *you* as wheat:

32 But I have prayed for thee, that thy faith fail not: and when thou art converted, strengthen thy brethren.

33 And he said unto him, Lord, I am ready to go with thee, both into prison, and to death.

34 And he said, I tell thee, Peter, the cock shall not crow this day, before that thou shalt thrice deny that thou knowest me.

35 And he said unto them, When I sent you without purse, and scrip, and shoes, lacked ye any thing? And they said, Nothing.

36 Then he said unto them, But now, he that hath a purse, let him take *it,* and likewise *his* scrip; and he that hath no sword, let him sell his garment, and buy one.

He then turned to Peter and called him twice by the name, Simon, he bore before he called him to follow him, as notwithstanding his spiritual insight on account of which he had called him, Peter, the rock (Matt. 16:13-20) inbred sin within him made him yet too much "of the earth, earthy."

"Satan hath desired to have you that he might sift you as wheat." An old writer has noted the difference between the testing of Christ and that of Satan. Christ has his fan in his hand to winnow away the chaff and leave the good wheat (Chapter 3:17), while Satan wants to put us through his sieve, sifting out the good and leaving the bad. Let us be sure and have Jesus use his winnowing fan, removing the carnal nature and then we will be doubly strong to resist the sifting process of Satan.

But Jesus offered the comforting word, that he had prayed for Peter. Let us remember in every trial that Jesus, our Great High Priest is in heaven praying for us, and hence we need not fail, for strength will be given us, as *much as we need.*

He prayed that Peter's faith might not fail. If faith does not fail, we can be assured of victory. It is not a question whether emotions or feelings survive or fail. The question is does our faith keep bright, for victory comes through faith. (1 John 5:4, 5.) It is impossible to be defeated while we maintain our faith.

"When thou art converted." This is an important passage, because it is the only passage that the opponents of holiness bring against the fact that the disciples were regenerated before Pentecost. The Scriptures teach that these disciples were regenerated men; hence they were candidates for the richer, fuller blessing of Pentecost. On this passage we remark, 1. The Calvinistic commentators generally agree that Peter had been regenerated but that he fell away to some extent this time, but not entirely.   2. The Arminian writers substantially agree that he apostatized from his experience of regeneration.   3. The term convert means simply to *turn about*. It may be used to denote the turning about of a backslider like Peter to be reclaimed, as well as the turning about of a sinner to be saved. Jesus as much as said to Peter ''Your vain-glorious confidence will cause you to backslide, but when you are turned back—recovered, your special mission will be to strengthen the brethren, and help them to keep from backsliding.

But Peter speaks up very confidently saying that he was ready to go to prison and die with Jesus. We must make some allowance or at least extend our charity, to Peter. The Christian faith was so new that there had been very few severe tests as yet put upon the disciples.

Self confidence is the result of indwelling sin. This is one of the characteristics of the unsanctified Christian. He is apt to feel confidence in his own power of overcoming temptation and think that he can do it himself. God blesses him richly in the beginning of his experience, and he has the idea that the blessing will carry him right along, without special reliance upon God. No man, who has not been wholly sanctified, ought to be too confident: and no man who has been wholly sanctified ought to be too sure that he will be victorious. No experience will carry us along of itself. We must every day feel our helplessness so much, that we shall lean heavily on Jesus.

After Pentecost we have a new Peter. He was restored at the Sea of Galilee (John 21) and had his heart purified at Pentecost (Acts 15:9). By being sanctified wholly, as he was at Pentecost, we lessen the possibilities of our backsliding.

In verse 34 Jesus uses the name Peter instead of Simon as in verse 31. Peter means rock. Jesus seems to speak ironically to this his over-confident follower. As much as to say ''I tell thee *rock* man, that thou wilt betray me three times today.''

He now refers the disciples to the time when he sent them out to preach (Chapter 9:1-3). He sent them out to live by faith alone, for their support, but now he changes his plan for them. (Vs. 36.) Hitherto they had a comparatively easy time. Now they must enter the arena of debate and contest for the faith. They must henceforth be engaged in warfare against sin. He who has no sword must have one, even if he has to part with some of his clothing to buy it. We must understand him as speaking figuratively when he says "Sell your garments and buy a sword." As much as to say prepare for the contest. The contest is more than the fight of carnal warfare. It was to be the great battle between sin and holiness. The Revised Version has it thus, "He that hath no wallet, let him sell his cloak and buy a sword." It is as much as to say let the Christian ministry make proper preparation for their great work of combating sin. We are certain we are right in saying the buying of the sword is a figure or symbol of the spiritual warfare in which they were to engage for in verses 50-51 he forbade Peter using the literal sword. Godet says, "It is clear that in the mind of him, who said, 'I send you forth *as lambs* among wolves' this weapon represents the power of holiness in conflict with the sin of the world—that sword of the spirit, spoken of by Paul (Eph. 6:17)." As this passage comes in connection with Peter's temptation, it would seem to teach that we are to wage aggressive warfare against a tempting devil, as the best method of resisting and overcoming temptation.

TEMPTATION OF JESUS. Vs. 37-46.

37 For I say unto you, that this that is written must yet be accomplished in me, And he was reckoned among the transgressors : for the things concerning me have an end.

38 And they said, Lord, behold, here *are* two swords. And he said unto them, It is enough.

39 And he came out, and went, as he was wont, to the mount of Olives ; and his disciples also followed him.

40 And when he was at the place, he said unto them, Pray that ye enter not into temptation.

41 And he was withdrawn from them about a stone's cast, and kneeled down, and prayed,

42 Saying, Father, if thou be willing, remove this cup from me : nevertheless not my will, but thine, be done.

43 And there appeared an angel unto him from heaven, strengthening him.

44 And being in an agony he prayed more earnestly : and his sweat was as it were great drops of blood falling down to the ground.

45 And when he rose up from prayer, and was come to his disciples, he found them sleeping for sorrow.

46 And he said unto them, Why sleep ye? rise and pray, lest ye enter into temptation.

We now come to the second great temptation of Jesus. He had been tempted and defeated Satan in the Wilderness (Chapter 4:1-13). Satan had left him for a season. He does that after a defeat very often. But now he comes back to the attack in a more subtle form doubtless. He does that often, when the great crises and tests of our lives come, one complication of the matter is the advantage Satan takes of the hour to tempt us to give up principle and duty. He told his disciples (Vs. 37) that the prophesy of Isa. 53:12 concerning him must be fulfilled. This prophesy was that he should be numbered with transgressors. This was not merely fulfilled when he hung between the thieves, but also that very night, when the mob led by temple officers came out against him as if he had been a thief. According to his usual custom he went that night to the mount of Olives to pray. Our Christ had a regular place and time to pray. Have we? It was this mountain, a mile from the city. If he needed to pray surely we do.

Before he prayed he charged his disciples to pray for themselves that they enter not into temptation. This was the same prayer that he had recommended in Chapter 11, verse 4. The word temptation here properly means testing. (See our notes on verses 31-36). He knew what sore temptation means. We can not understand this mystery—how he could be tempted. In fact we cannot fully explain how we are tempted ourselves.

About a stone's throw from the disciples, he knelt and prayed the Father to remove this cup from him. He took the cup of wrath that we might have the opportunity to take the cup of salvation. "It seems to be an allusion to a very ancient method of punishing criminals. A cup of poison was put into their hands and they were compelled to drink it. Socrates was killed thus, being obliged by the magistrates of Athens to drink a cup of the juice of the hemlock. To death by poison, there seems to be an allusion in Hebrews 2:9. Jesus Christ by the 'grace of God tasted death for every man.' The whole world is here represented as standing guilty and condemned before the tribunal of God; into every man's hand the deadly cup is put, and he is required to drink of the poison—Jesus enters, takes every man's cup out of his hand, drinks off the poison, and thus tastes or suffers death, which every man otherwise, must have undergone." (Adam Clarke.)

But he could say notwithstanding he was drinking the cup of condemnation of a last world, "Not my will but thine." This is the model of true prayer. Prayer has two answers—direct and indirect. The direct answer is when we receive the thing for which we asked. The indirect answer is that reflex influence in our own hearts which we feel as we are able to sincerely say, "Thy will O God! be done." The latter is an answer and a blessing to us, even if we did not receive anything in direct answer.

As he prayed there appeared an angel to give his human nature strength in this great trouble. It was the divine will that he drink the cup. He must drink it. Hebrews 5:7-8 tells us why he was heard, "Who in the days of his flesh, when he had offered up prayers and supplications with strong cries and tears unto him, that was able to save from death, and was heard in that he feared; though he were a Son, yet learned he obedience by the things that he suffered." It is vain for us to attempt to understand how so great agony of soul could come to him, for two reasons. 1. We can never understand the union of the human and the divine in the Lord Jesus. We can not understand the union of soul and body in our own makeup, and how can we understand this greater union. 2. No one can understand any other's sorrow unless they have passed through similar experiences. We will never be called to bear the sins of the world as did he, how then can we understand this experience of Jesus! The curse of sin was on him for the time being. It teaches us that sin is an awful thing; its punishment dreadful, and the malignity of Satan to which he was now subject, most horrible.

In his awful agony he *prayed more earnestly;* no longer to be saved from the cup. He now had victory over that temptation, but he now prayed for grace and strength to bear the agony.

So great was his mental agony that the blood was pressed through the pores of his skin. Similar instances are recorded by the medical profession. Luke, the writer, being a physician, would naturally mention this. Had it not been for divine assistance, he evidently would have died under the pressure, which wrung out of him the bloody sweat. "It was just shuddering nature and indomitable will struggling together. But again the cry, if it must be, *thy will be done*, and all is over. 'The bitterness of death is past.' He had anticipated and rehearsed his final contest and won the victory—now on the theatre of an invincible will, as then, on the arena of the cross. 'I will suffer' is the grand result of Gethsemane. 'It is finished' is the shout that bursts from the cross. The will without the deed had been all in vain; but the work was consummated, when he carried the now manifested will into the palpable deed 'By the which will we are sanctified through the offering of the body of Jesus once for all.'" (Brown.)

The apostle Paul teaches that the crucifixion of Jesus is the symbol of the crucifixion of the carnal nature. Then Gethsemane must represent the death struggle that comes before crucifixion of sin.

When he returned to his disciples he found them asleep. Eight of them were near the entrance to the garden of Gethsemane and three were the distance of a stone's throw from him. Luke says they were sleeping for sorrow. They sympathized with his distress as far as they could understand and appreciate it. Sleep does not conquer sorrow; it will come again. Jesus conquered sorrow by prayer. This is the very thing to do in the sorrows of life—pray.

He asked them "Why sleep ye?" Matthew says he asked this question when he came to them the second time. He came three times and found them asleep. Too often the church has been found asleep when the Lord needed them and they could have assisted his cause.

THE WORLD NEVER CRUCIFIES JESUS UNTIL SOME OF HIS PROFESSED FOLLOWERS MAKE IT POSSIBLE.
Vs. 47-49.

47 And while he yet spake, behold a multitude, and he that was called Judas, one of the twelve, went before them, and drew near unto Jesus to kiss him.

48 But Jesus said unto him, Judas, betrayest thou the Son of man with a kiss?

49 When they which were about him saw what would follow, they said unto him, Lord, shall we smite with the sword?

And now the depths of the hellish character of the carnal mind display themselves in the conduct of Judas and the enemies of the gentle, harmless Jesus.

Judas knew where he was accustomed to retire for secret prayer and deliberately planned to interrupt his communion with the Father. Judas in the employ of the chief priests and scribes comes to him, with a mob composed of Roman soldiers and a large company of people, who had been stirred up by the elders. This mob carried swords, staves, lanterns and torches.

The baseness of the betrayal by Judas is intensified by a kiss that Judas gives his master. By a symbol of love he commits the foulest crime.

One of the disciples asks Jesus for permission to fight, saying shall we fight with the sword? They had two swords. (Vs. 38.) But Jesus forbade it. The great weapons of the cause of God are not sword or spear or musket. They are spiritual weapons. Jesus never had an army like the great leaders of the world. But he has accomplished more than they. The church of God does not depend upon carnal weapons for its conquests. Jesus illustrated his teaching of non-resistance that he gave in the sermon on the mount. (See Matt. 26:52.)

It is true today that the world could never crucify Jesus if his followers were all true. Infidels and skeptics are not the most deadly foes of the cause of God. The worst enemies of Christ are those who profess to be his followers, but who are really of and with the world.

HOLINESS IS MERCIFUL. Vs. 50-53.

50 And one of them smote the servant of the high priest, and cut off his right ear.

51 And Jesus answered and said, Suffer ye thus far. And he touched his ear, and healed him.

52 Then Jesus said unto the chief priests, and captains of the temple, and the elders, which were come to him, Be ye come out, as against a thief, with swords and staves?

53   When I was daily with you in the temple, ye stretched forth no hands against me: but this is your hour, and the power of darkness.

The impetuous Peter (John 18:10) does not wait for the reply to the question in verse 49 but draws the sword and smites a servant of the high priest. But in fighting with the sword, instead of accomplishing some thing he really gives way to the devil. It is not always those who are the most demonstrative that are the most spiritual.

But Jesus in his hour of apparent weakness, showed forth his power by healing the servant of the high priest who had been smitten by Peter. Here was a miracle of power and mercy blended. Jesus reached his hand and touched him. Thus the last act of the hands of Jesus before they were bound was one of mercy. This is the only case on record where he cured a wound, although he healed all sorts of diseases. Holy people, like Jesus are full of mercy even towards enemies.

Jesus then said to the soldiers, "Suffer thus far." It was an apology for the violence of Peter, and a plea for permission to touch and heal the wound. He performed the miracle to shield Peter as well as to show mercy.

But he stops to reason with chief priests and captains. He shows them how wickedly and unreasonably they are acting. In addition to the violence of their actions they were grossly insulting. They came against him as they would against the most hardened criminal. Jesus felt the insult. Perfect love is not an opiate that benumbs us, so we do not have any feelings, or recognize an insult. But it saves us from all vindictiveness, or desire to retaliate.

This was their hour—their short hour of apparent triumph, but simply because he had permitted it, that he might offer himself a sacrifice for the sins of the world.

It was the hour of the power of darkness. The darkness of the night was a fitting symbol of the blackness of the deed. The triumphing of the wicked is short, and can not be permanent. Inbred sin in the heart of a disciple (Judas) was in league with the powers of darkness. Unsanctified Christian, inbred sin in your heart is in league with Satan.

INBRED SIN TEMPTS TO DENIAL OF CHRIST. Vs. 54-62.

54   Then took they him, and led *him,* and brought him into the high priest's house. And Peter followed afar off.

55   And when they had kindled a fire in the midst of the hall, and were set down together, Peter sat down among them.

56   But a certain maid beheld him as he sat by the fire, and earnestly looked upon him, and said, This man was also with him.

57   And he denied him, saying, Woman, I know him not.

58   And after a little while another saw him, and said, Thou art also of them. And Peter said, Man, I am not.

59   And about the space of one hour after another confidently affirmed, saying, Of a truth this *fellow* also was with him : for he is a Galilæan.

60   And Peter said, Man, I know not what thou sayest. And immediately, while he yet spake, the cock crew.
cock crow, thou shalt deny me thrice.

62   And Peter went out, and wept bitterly.

63   And the men that held Jesus mocked him and smote *him.*

64   And when they had blindfolded him, they struck him on the face, and asked him, saying, Prophesy, who is it that smote thee?

65   And many other things blasphemously spake they against him.

66   And as soon as it was day, the elders of the people and the chief priests and the scribes came together, and led him into their council, saying,

67   Art thou the Christ? tell us. And he said unto them, If I tell you, ye will not believe :

68   And if I also ask *you,* ye will not answer me, nor let *me* go.

69   Hereafter shall the Son of man sit on the right hand of the power of God.

70   Then said they all, Art thou then the Son of God? And he said unto them, Ye say that I am.

71   And they said, What need we any further witness? for we ourselves have heard of his own mouth.

Then they siezed Jesus and took him to the house of the high priest. John tells us (John 18:13) that they led him first to Annas, then to Caiphas, the high priest. Annas and Caiphas are both called the high priest. (Luke 3:2.) The reason for this is that Annas had been high priest, but had been removed from office by the Romans and his son-in-law had been appointed in his stead. The Jews considered Annas, the real high priest; hence we see why both are mentioned.

Peter followed the band afar off, as they went to the palace of the high priest. Had he been bolder he might have had the honor of suffering martyrdom with his Master. There are some things to be said in favor of Peter. He followed his Master, even if it was afar off. The others forsook him and fled. Had Peter however been more bold he would never have yielded to temptation. Indecision often makes temptation possible. Let us be decided in our confession of Christ, and we shall escape one class of temptations, and lessen the force of others. The night was cold and a fire was kindled in the hall (or court) of the Palace. Eastern houses were built so as to enclose a hollow square or court in the center, open to the sky. Such a house was like a big wall with rooms in it, built around a garden. Peter sat in this open enclosure and while warming himself at the enemy's fire, could hear some of the proceedings of the trial, which was in one of the rooms opening out into the court.

Inbred sin (or carnality) that made Judas a traitor, tempted Peter to become a coward and led him to deny his Master. Peter was naturally bold and strong, but he was here vanquished by a little servant girl. Anyone before whom we shrink in giving our testimony really vanquishes us. And so when the girl accused him of being the disciple of Jesus, he not only surrendered but also lied, saying of Jesus, ''I know him not.''

It is our privilege to know Jesus today and there are many who profess to know him among his friends, who act when among enemies as if they never knew or even heard of him.

When Peter had denied him the third time, the cock crowed, the Lord turned and looked on Peter. He *said* nothing. What volumes of compassion and love were in that look. It showed how well the Lord knew *him*, although he had just denied knowing the Lord. It is better to have the Lord look upon us even in sorrow than not look at all. From that look heaven and earth shall flee away (Rev. 20:11). Are we so saved that we can abide that piercing look?

Then Peter went out into the night with a broken heart. There is still more to be said in favor of Peter. His conscience was not seared like that of Judas. Peter went out under miserable self-condemnation, but not like Judas in remorse and despair. The case of Peter was not hopeless, for he still loved Jesus. It has been beautifully said of Peter. He went out to ''meet the morning dawn.'' Farrar says, ''Innocence had left him, his 'younger brother' the angel of Repentance.''

Then the men that held Jesus began to smite him on the face, and insult him with jeers and taunts. What an awful thing sin is! How cruel! Ought we not to hate it as the principle that took the life of the Son of God? Ought we not to allow our Redeemer to save us from sin?

As soon as the day dawned. The council came together to try Jesus. It probably convened in the temple (Matt. 27:5). They were in a great hurry to convict him, thus to meet so early.

They began with inquisition, asking him ''If he was the Christ,'' (Revised Version). This question was not asked until they had failed to convict him by false witnesses. (Matt. 27:5.) It was contrary to Jewish law to condemn a man upon his own testimony. Jesus shows this attempted injustice by saying ''If I tell you, ye will not believe, and if I also ask you, ye will not answer me nor let me go.'' The last four words are omitted in the Revised Version. He tells them in these words that they would not answer his cross questioning but expected him to answer theirs. He however replies to their question, ''Art thou the Christ,'' by saying, ''Hereafter (*from henceforth*, Rev. Ver.) ye shall see the Son of Man sit on the right hand of the power of God.'' He had been styling himself the Son of Man ever since his public ministry began. What a wonderful prophecy to make of himself in his present condition that he should sit on the right hand of God. To sit upon the right hand of the power of God was considered by the Jews a certain indication of the Messiah.

They asked him again if he is the Messiah and he replies ''Thou hast said.'' This was an idiom among the Jews, meaning ''Thou hast told the truth.''

''As the Passion advances, its amazing contrasts grow in affecting interest. The Deliverer in bonds; the Judge attainted; the Prince of Glory scorned; the Holy One condemned for sin; the Son of God, a blasphemer; the Resurrection and Life sentenced to die. The Eternal High Priest is condemned by the priest of a year.'' (Stier.)

Since Jesus was unjustly judged and condemned to die, why should we expect any better treatment from an apostate church?

CHAPTER XXIII.

CRUCIFIXION MAKES HOLY DYING.

The World Would Better Respect Holiness but for the Accusation of an Apostate Church. Vs. 1-24. The World Never Crucifies Christ until Encouragement Is Given by an Apostate Church. Vs. 25-38. Christ Our Example of Holy Living and Dying. Vs. 39-46. Holy Living and Dying Affect the Unsaved World. Vs. 47-49. God Has Some Salt in Every Corrupt Church. Vs. 50-56.

THE WORLD WOULD BETTER RESPECT HOLINESS BUT FOR THE ACCUSATION OF AN APOSTATE CHURCH.
Vs. 1-24.

1 And the whole multitude of them arose, and led him unto Pilate.

2 And they began to accuse him, saying, we found this *fellow* perverting the nation, and forbidding to give tribute to Cæsar, saying that he himself is Christ, a King.

3 And Pilate asked him, saying, Art thou the King of the Jews? And he answered him and said, Thou sayest *it*.

4 Then said Pilate to the chief priests and *to* the people, I find no fault in this man.

5 And they were the more fierce, saying, He stirreth up the people, teaching throughout all Jewry, beginning from Galilee to this place.

6 When Pilate heard of Galilee, he asked whether the man were a Galilæan.

7 And as soon as he knew that he belonged unto Herod's jurisdiction, he sent him to Herod, who himself also was at Jerusalem at that time.

8 And when Herod saw Jesus, he was exceeding glad: for he was desirous to see him of a long *season*, because he had heard many things of him; and he hoped to have seen some miracle done by him.

9 Then he questioned with him in many words; but he answered him nothing.

10 And the chief priests and scribes stood and vehemently accused him.

11 And Herod with his men of war set him at nought, and mocked *him,* and arrayed him in a gorgeous robe, and sent him again to Pilate.

12 And the same day Pilate and Herod were made friends together : for before they were at enmity between themselves.

13 And Pilate, when he had called together the chief priests **and** the rulers and the people,

14 Said unto them, Ye have brought this man unto me, as one that perverteth the people : and, behold, I, having examined *him* before you, have found no fault in this man touching those things whereof ye accuse him :

15 No, nor yet Herod : for I sent you to him ; and, lo, nothing worthy of death is done unto him.

16 I will therefore chastise him, and release *him.*

17 (For of necessity he must release one unto them at the feast.)

18 And they cried out all at once, saying, Away with this *man,* and release unto us Barabbas :

19 (Who for a certain sedition made in the city, and for murder, was cast into prison.)

20 Pilate therefore, willing to release Jesus, spake again to them.

21 But they cried, saying, Crucify *him,* crucify him.

22 And he said unto them the third time, Why, what evil hath he done? I have found no cause of death in him : I will therefore chastise him, and let *him* go.

23 And they were instant with loud voices, requiring that he might be crucified. And the voices of them and of the chief priests prevailed.

24 And Pilate gave sentence that it should be as they required.

Then the whole multitude (the chief priests, elders, scribes and the whole council). (Mark 15:1), led Jesus to Pilate, the Roman governor. The latter had his headquarters at Cæsarea but came up to Jerusalem at the time of the Passover, to keep order, as the Jews were hard to govern at that time. It was the most unfortunate trip Pilate ever made. The Jews could not put Jesus to death except by permission of Pilate. They seemed to think that by going *en masse* to Pilate they would overawe him, as he saw the numbers and dignity of the chief Jewish functionaries.

When they arrived before Pilate they made an entirely different charge from what they had been making in their own council. (Luke 22:67-74.) They made three false charges. 1. That he had perverted the nation. 2. He had forbidden to pay tribute to Cæsar. 3. He had proclaimed himself king. Thus they themselves acknowledged the power of the Galilean peasant. How could a mere unlettered peasant be able to do such great things and exert such an influence! Thus the very accusations of his enemies show him to be more than an ordinary character.

Then Pilate asks "Art thou the king of the Jews?" He said that he was. The gospel of the kingdom is the key to the ministry of Jesus. He was the ruler of a spiritual kingdom—the only spiritual kingdom. When he explained what he meant (John 18:36) Pilate had nothing to say against him, but said honestly "I find no fault in him." And no one yet has ever been able to find any fault in him, and the keenest minds of twenty centuries have been examining him. We have a perfect Saviour. The world often forms a better estimate of holiness than an apostate church. They say If I were going to be a Christian, I would want a religion that would save me through and through.

When Pilate said "I find no fault in the man," it only made them more determined and blood thirsty. Scott says, "No prudence, nor harmlessness, in word or deed, can secure a man from their enmity and slander; yet our unexceptional conduct may drive them into such egregious absurdities and palpable falsehoods as shall serve to expose their malignity."

In their fierceness they accuse him of stirring up the people throughout Jewry (Judea) and Galilee. When Pilate heard the name of Galilee, he asked if Jesus was a Galilean. And when he heard that he was, he thought he could get out of his dilemma by sending him to Herod. He and Herod were not on good terms and he thought it would be a stroke of policy to put the responsibility upon Herod, who was already hated by the people for the death of John the Baptist. Herod was in Jerusalem at this very time.

When Herod saw Jesus he was very glad for he had desired for a long time to see Jesus, as he wanted to see him perform a miracle. He did not desire to see him because of any desire to hear the truth or to reform his own life. Let those people remember, who are desiring miraculous manifestations, when they are publicly seeking religion, that they are actuated by the same motives in seeking Christ that influenced Herod. People may want to see Jesus from very unworthy motives.

Herod in vain asked him many questions. Jesus replied not a word. He had called Herod a fox, and seemed to have such a contempt for him that he did not reply. He had something to say to the Sanhedrim and Pilate, but not a word for Herod.

Herod showed the meanness of his little soul by causing Jesus to be arrayed in mock kingly majesty, while his men of war mocked him. He sent him back in a gorgeous robe to Pilate, to show that he made light of his pretentions of being a king. Jesus was the jest of these wicked men.

It is wonderful how men, who hate each other like Herod and Pilate will lay aside their enmity to fight against the things of God. It is evident that Herod was much pleased with Pilate for sending Jesus to him.

Again Pilate tells the Jews that he has no fault to find with Jesus, and adds that Herod also had found no fault with him. And yet the leaders of his own church condemned him when Pilate would have let him go.

Pilate said he would chastise him and let him go. He wanted to release him to satisfy his own conscience. He wanted to chastise him to please the Jews and high priests. So he had really decided against Jesus, after saying he found no fault with him. This was the beginning of Pilate's crime in the matter. The sharp eyed Jews saw that Pilate had weakened in ordering him to be scourged, and they followed up their advantage. If he had stood firm, on the ground that Jesus was innocent, he might have saved himself eternal regret. Let us beware of the first concessions to evil. It is hard to get back when once started down hill.

Verse 17 says Pilate had to release some one at the feast of the Passover. This was a custom. He wanted to release Jesus. They wanted him to release Barabbas.

So they all cried out for the release of Barabbas (Matt. 27:20). Barabbas was guilty of the very crime of which they accused Jesus. When churchmen persecute the truth, they are very inconsistent.

Pilate now makes another attempt to release Jesus, but now they are even more clamorous, and cry for his crucifixion. "It is the first time the word 'crucify' has been named in Pilate's hearing, the first time they tell him articulately what it is, that they desire to have done with Jesus. Crucify him—give up to that most ignominious of all deaths this meek and gentle man, who, he is sure has done no wrong; whom he sees well enough, that the chief priests seek to get rid of, from some religious antipathy, that they have taken against him: can the people mean it? Why, what evil hath he done?'' (Hanna.)

Barabbas was a bold leader of a fierce outbreak against the Roman government. They tried to have it appear that the guilt of Jesus was more than that of this desperate man. Pilate knew better, for had Jesus been that kind of a character he certainly would have known of it. What will we do with Jesus? Will we choose him or Barabbas today? Quesnel says, ''What will we do with Jesus, if we make him not our Mediator, our Saviour, our life, our refuge in all our evils, and the object of our adoration, love and confidence; since God has made him our wisdom, righteousness, sanctification, and redemption.''

Crucifixion had been introduced into Jerusalem by the Romans. It was not a Jewish punishment. But they hated Jesus so much that they did not hesitate to demand for him a mode of death that would have aroused their indignation had it been inflicted on any other Jew. When at the downfall of Jerusalem, the Romans crucified the Jews by the thousands they began to comprehend what it meant to have this cruel punishment carried on in their midst. They were terribly punished.

So Pilate granted their request. It was easier for him to grant their request and condemn one man, than to run the risk of offending hundreds, for he did not know what this furious crowd might do.

THE WORLD NEVER CRUCIFIES CHRIST UNTIL ENCOURAGEMENT IS GIVEN BY AN APOSTATE CHURCH.
Vs. 25-38.

25 And he released unto them him that for sedition and murder was cast into prison, whom they had desired; but he delivered Jesus to their will.

26 And as they led him away, they laid hold upon one Simon, a Cyrenian, coming out of the country, and on him they laid the cross, that he might bear *it* after Jesus.

27 And there followed him a great company of people, and of women, which also bewailed and lamented him.

28 But Jesus turning unto them said, Daughters of Jerusalem, weep not for me, but weep for yourselves, and for your children.

29 For, behold, the days are coming, in which they shall say, Blessed *are* the barren, and the wombs that never bare, and the paps which never gave suck.

30 Then shall they begin to say to the mountains, Fall on us; and to the hills, Cover us.

31 For if they do these things in a green tree, what shall be done in the dry?

32 And there were also two other, malefactors, led with him to be put to death.

33 And when they were come to the place, which is called Calvary, there they crucified him, and the malefactors, one on the right hand, and the other on the left.

34 Then said Jesus, Father, forgive them; for they know not what they do. And they parted his raiment and cast lots.

35 And the people stood beholding. And the rulers also with them derided *him*, saying, He saved others; let him save himself, if he be Christ, the chosen of God.

36 And the soldiers also mocked him, coming to him, and offering him vinegar,

37 And saying, If thou be the king of the Jews, save thyself.

38 And a superscription also was written over him in letters of Greek, and Latin, and Hebrew, THIS IS THE KING OF THE JEWS.

So the self seeking, cowardly Pilate yielded to the demands of a corrupt ecclesiasticism. Divine vengeance has been upon the Jewish nation ever since. They took the responsibility, calling down a curse upon themselves, as they cried "His blood be upon us and our children." (Matt. 27:25.) "They put Jesus to death, when the nation was assembled to celebrate the Passover; and when the nation too was assembled to celebrate the Passover, Titus shut them up within the walls of Jerusalem. The rejection of the true Messiah was their crime; and the following of false Messiahs to their destruction was their punishment. They preferred a robber and a murderer to Jesus, whom they crucified between two thieves; and they themselves were afterwards infested with bands of thieves and robbers. They put Jesus to death lest the Romans should come and take away their place and nation; and the Romans did come and take away their place and nation. They crucified Jesus before the walls of Jerusalem; and before the walls of Jerusalem they themselves were crucified, in such numbers that it is said room was wanting for the crosses and crosses for the bodies." (Bishop Newton.)

And then they led him away, outside the city walls, to be crucified. Outside the city amid the reproaches of the people he went to an ignominious death. The apostle in Hebrews uses this as an illustration, saying we are to go forth without the camp bearing reproaches, because we profess to have been sanctified by the efficacy of his blood. He died out there to sanctify us (Heb. 13:12) and we are to be willing to endure the reproaches of those who consider the sanctification for which he died as ignominious, as was his crucifixion. We must be willing to accept the same place in the estimation of men that our Lord had, if we would receive the full salvation for which he died. Besser in his book *Christ the Light and Life of the World* says "The epistle to the the Hebrews (13:12) teaches us that in his being led forth out of the city that he might sanctify the people with his own blood, he was set forth as the sin-offering, in whom the Old Testament types had been fulfilled" (Lev. 4:12; 16:27). If we are not willing to go to him without the camp—to be ostracised if need be, he can not consistently sanctify us.

It was customary to require the condemned man to carry his own cross to the place of punishment. The disgrace of bearing the cross in public was part of the punishment. But Jesus on account of the awful struggles of the past night and the abuse he had already received was too weak to carry his cross and so they impressed one Simone of Cyrene to carry it.

But all were not hard hearted. Thank God there was a company of women, in the throng that followed him, who bitterly bewailed his sad fate. Doubtless he had healed some of them or their friends. Jesus was touched by this expression of grief and stopped to console them. He did not reject their expressions of pity. It stirs a deeper sympathy in his own heart. How thoughtful he was of others in his own distress. It was just like him. He healed Malchus, whom Peter had smitten. He committed his weeping mother to John's care, while hanging on the cross and stopped in his dying agonies to save the thief.

He might well tell them to weep for themselves. The glory of Israel, as a nation had departed, never to return for thousands of years. God had rejected this people hitherto so highly favored. Defeated, persecuted, the Jew was to wander an outcast on the earth without a king, priest, temple or country.

In verse 29 he refers to the awful horrors of the siege of Jerusalem, so soon to come upon them. The destruction of Jerusalem was to be an illustration of the destruction of the world, when men should call on the rocks and mountains to fall upon them. He quotes from Hosea 10:8, "And they shall say to the mountains, Cover us: and to the hills fall on us."

Then he shows the reason why they should weep for themselves thus, "If they do these things in a green tree, what shall be done in the dry." If the Romans would punish an innocent inoffensive man, like himself, what would they do to the haughty, rebellious nation they had on their hands. Jesus like a green tree was not fuel suited for the destructive fire of wrath. But the Jewish nation was a dry tree just suited to call forth the destructive fire of the Roman wrath. He did nothing to call forth the wrath of the Romans. They would provoke it.

"When they came to the place called Calvary." The Revised Version translated it "The place called a skull." It was so called because it was in shape like a skull. Calvaria in Latin means a skull. On this spot smooth and slightly elevated like a human skull, they enacted the tragedy of all tragedies, since the world began.

Having nailed him to the cross, they raised it and thrust it into a hole in the ground. This would dislocate the joints of his limbs. Thus would he fulfill the prophecy of the Messiah by the Psalmist, "All my bones are out of joint." (Ps. 22:14.) In this excruciatingly painful position he hung for six hours.

They placed his cross between the crosses of two crucified thieves; thus indicating that they considered him the worst of the three. Hellish malice pursued him clear to the mouth of the grave. O what an awful thing is sin!

The love of Jesus that had healed Malchus (Ch. 22:51), and consoled the weeping women (Vs. 28) now poured itself out in prayer for the forgiveness of his murderers. All the plea he could make was that his murderers did not comprehend the far reaching nature of their sin. What sinner ever does? But he is no less guilty, for the heinousness of sin is in the motive of disobedience. (See Acts 2:38, 39 and 3:19.)

The picture of the awful nature of sin grows darker. Their

hellish malignity prompts them to taunt the meek, inoffensive sufferer in the midst of his awful agony. It was the challenge of hell thrust in the face of the Almighty. It was insolent defiance of God. The rulers stood in the presence of God and the assembled people and dared to say, "He saved others, let him save himself, if he be the Christ." He might have come down from the cross and have proved himself the Messiah. But what would have become of us, if he had? He was willing to give up his rights and be treated with contempt that we might be saved. These enemies unconsciously told the truth. He could not save himself, if he saved us. What was meant as a stigma is his real glory—the glory of being our Saviour.

The rough Roman, heathen soldiers joined in the derision. Here we have Jew, Gentile, churchmen and heathen all taunting one suffering man. Of what is not the human heart capable!

Then their spite reaches the farthest limit as they write and place above his head in sarcasm the sentence *This is the King of the Jews.* So his enemies told the truth although in sarcasm, for the Gospel of the Kingdom was the key to his ministry and it was published upon his cross.

John tells us (Ch. 19:20) that this sentence was written in the three languages—Greek, Latin and Hebrew. These were the chief languages of the earth.

The chief priests wished the writing changed. They did not like the reflection on themselves that they had crucified their own king. But Pilate had yielded them all he would and it had to stand there condemning them.

CHRIST OUR EXAMPLE OF HOLY LIVING AND DYING.
Vs. 39-46.

39 And one of the malefactors which were hanged railed on him, saying, If thou be Christ, save thyself and us.

40 But the other answering rebuked him, saying, Dost not thou fear God, seeing thou art in the same condemnation?

41 And we indeed justly; for we receive the due reward of our deeds: but this man hath done nothing amiss.

42 And he said unto Jesus, Lord, remember me when thou comest into thy kingdom.

43 And Jesus said unto him, Verily I say unto thee, To day shalt thou be with me in paradise.

44 And it was about the sixth hour, and there was a darkness over all the earth until the ninth hour.

45 And the sun was darkened, and the veil of the temple was rent in the midst.

46 And when Jesus had cried with a loud voice, he said, Father, into thy hands I commend my spirit: and having said thus, he gave up the ghost.

The cross divides the world since that day. On the one side hung the penitent on the other side the inpenitent thief. "There is every likelihood that the two malefactors crucified with Jesus belonged to the band of Barabbas. For good or evil they knew something about the Christ, the taunt uttered by the one expresses this no less than the prayer of the other. Barabbas, as we have seen, had been cast into prison "with them that had made insurrection with him." Two of the chief of these Pilate may have been well pleased to send to execution at this time." (Trench.) We are all either on the impenitent or penitent side of the cross.

The impetitent thief assumes or tries to, that Jesus is a malefactor like himself as he says "Save thyself and *us*." To try to drag Christ into the same class with them, was too much for the other thief to endure and he rebukes him. He protests against his blasphemy. More than that, he becomes an evangelist seeking to turn the hardened wretch to repentance.

This thief shows his penitence and confesses it saying, "We indeed justly." He acknowledged his sins, and that he is being justly punished. Again he also shows faith. He says, "Lord remember me when thou comest into thy kingdom." There was a faith found here, that this abused, insulted and tormented sufferer was the king of a kingdom. He saw something that the leaders of the church and all the people did not see, viz: that this was indeed a king.

His prayer was a short one. It contained only a few words. But it was an effectual prayer. Thank God it does not require long prayers to bring salvation. This man had no time to offer a long prayer. He was right on the borders of the other world.

Ritualism is not necessary to salvation. He had no use for a prayer book. It does not require a beautiful elaborate prayer to bring salvation.

He did not get saved by culture, evolution, growth or development. He had no time for any of these. Therefore those do not save us.

Now was he saved by looking to Jesus as his example. Some tell us that Jesus is only an example and we must pattern after him. If this had been required this man's case was hopeless. He could not follow Jesus's example.

He was not saved by his good works. He could not build churches, or give money to endow colleges, or feed the hungry. He was helpless. His hands and feet were nailed to the cross. He could do nothing but pray, confess and believe.

We have here the instance of one who had few advantages. He was not a theologian or a scholar.

Again we see here an instance of a person in a very unlikely place, finding salvation. The men in the places favorable to salvation, the religionists who read the Bible and had all the advantages of religion missed salvation and this man found it. He saw divinity in Jesus. They did not. ''There were many to call Jesus Lord when he arose triumphant from the tomb; there is but one to call him Lord as he hangs dying on the cross.'' Mark Hopkins says, ''The thief on the cross was wholly a Christian. Christ was to him all, the all and in all, for salvation. He had gone up to no earthly temple, had offered no bullock, had confessed his sins to no robed priest; but as the Jews of old, bitten by the serpents, had turned their eyes upon the brazen serpent lifted up and had been healed, so had he turned his eyes upon the Son of Man lifted up and had been saved—saved by him only. He had found the Messiah, him who was at once the victim and the priest, the Lamb of God slain from the foundation of the world and the great High Priest who was to pass into the heavens.''

The thief got saved without going to church or to an altar. We do not say this because we do not believe in going to church or to the altar, but because there are people who seem to think they can get saved nowhere else, and must wait until they have favorable surroundings.

We see how God saves people right in the midst of a conflict. The contest here was that this sufferer was a king and had a kingdom. Right at the time the chief men of the kingdom did not stop to argue against it, but treated it as a jest and ridiculed it, here was a man who dared assert it and get saved by the King. We have often noticed that God vindicated the truth by saving souls right in a time when the enemy is trying to prove there is no such thing as salvation. We have seen souls seek and obtain entire sanctification right when ecclesiastics were fighting it and saying there is no such experience.

See the marvelous answer to the thief's prayer. He only asked to be remembered in his future glory: he got more than he asked. He got *companionship* with the Lord in Glory that very day. Notice the thief believed in a future life for he knew he and Jesus would very soon die. He was thinking of future blessedness when he made the petition.

This text upsets the doctrine of the soul-sleepers. So, to save their theology they say a comma should be inserted after the word, *today.* There is no warrant for it in any of the Greek manuscripts. The Authorized Version, the Revised Version and the American Version have no comma. Thus we see the best scholarship of the world make no such punctuation. And those who claim it are doing it *to bolster up a theory.* They have no authority or proof to bring. It would make Jesus use superfluous words, *which he never did.* Dean Alford, the best New Testament scholar in his generation, says of it, "Considering not only that it violates common sense, but destroys our Lord's meaning, it is surely something worse than silly."

We learn here that there is a conscious state after death—a state intermediate between death and the Judgment Day, when the righteous will enter partially upon their reward and the wicked partially upon their punishment.

Thus was the Redeemer's triumph just beginning as he was dying. It began by snatching in dying sinner from the jaws of Hell, just ready to close upon him. In his death he began to capture sinners from the hand of Satan.

There is no ground for thinking we may defer salvation to the dying hour because of this instance. Who knows that this sinner ever had the opportunity of salvation clearly presented before? There is one other passage—"The eleventh hour"—sometimes quoted to sustain procrastination to a death bed. If we refer to that passage (Matt. 20:16) we shall find that those engaged at the eleventh hour never had a previous opportunity. Only one case of deathbed salvation is mentioned in the Bible and that was not on a death bed but a cross. This one instànce is mentioned to show that "While none need despair of salvation, none need presume to divine mercy to allow them to go on in their sins."

During the last six hours of the lingering agony of Jesus a preternatural darkness overspread all nature. The sun refused to shine. This was not an ordinary eclipse for eclipses of the sun do not take place at the full of the moon. The Passover was held at the full of the moon, and Jesus was crucified at the time of the Passover. The darkening of the sun symbolized the temporary eclipse of Jesus, the Sun of Righteousness.

The veil of the temple, that great fabric that hid the inner part of the temple from the worshippers into which only the eye of the priest was allowed to rest, was rent into two parts, and for the first time everybody could look within, because the Old Testament economy was at an end. It meant that we no longer need human priests to enter the Holy of Holies for us. Jesus the Great High Priest has entered heaven for us once for all. (Heb. 9:28.) We may now have "boldness to enter into the holiest" experience on earth and into heaven itself. "The rending of the veil typified that the veil, that shut out the vision of holiness from the hearts of the people, had been taken away (2 Cor. 3:14-16), and the way into the holy place, the state of holiness and the place of holiness was now open." (Pelonbet.) Matthew says the veil was rent from top to bottom. If it had been rent from bottom to top it might have been claimed that it was rent by man. The power that rent it was from above. It was divine power. Dr. Brown says, "Before this it was death to go into the Holy of Holies; now it is death to stay out."

The ninth hour came (3 o'clock P. M.) the light of the sun returned, as the sufferer cried with a loud voice "Father into thy hands I commend my spirit" and yielded up his spirit. His death was a voluntary yielding up of life. May we so resign ourselves to God, both in life and death. "As 'God spared not his own, but delivered him up for us all,' how shall we not, with him 'freely give us all things?' Hereby we know his love for sinful men; may we then prove our love to him by crucifying our lusts, and resigning our dearest earthly comforts, at his word for his glory, or in submission to his province.'' (Scott.)

HOLY LIVING AND DYING AFFECT THE UNSAVED WORLD. Vs. 47-49.

47 Now when the centurion saw what was done, he glorified God, saying, Certainly this was a righteous man.

48 And all the people that came together to that sight, beholding the things which were done, smote their breasts, and returned.

49 And all his acquaintance, and the women that followed him from Galilee, stood afar off, beholding these things.

When the Roman centurion who had charge of the soldiers saw all this display of divine power and the gentleness and resignation of Jesus he praised God and said, ''Truly this was the Son of God.'' Here we have the testimony of an impartial witness to the wonderful character of Jesus. ''The cross is early giving tokens of its power. It lays hold of the dying thief, and opens to him the gates of paradise. It lays hold of this centurion and works in him a faith which, let us hope, deepened into a trust in Jesus as his Saviour. From such unlikely quarters came the two testimonials borne to the Lord's divinity in the same day.'' (Hanna.)

What an extraordinary grouping of characters there was about Christ during his passion: haughty Pharisees, rulers of the church, penitent and impenitent thieves, a released prisoner, dying men, frightened disciples, a traitorous disciple, a cowardly disciple, timid disciples—Nicodemus and Joseph becoming bold,—a jeering multitude, heathen soldiers, a Roman governor, an apostate king, compassionate women, a sorrowing mother and an astonished people. The cross affects every station in life, every grade of character, and is the true standpoint from which to study character. The cross is the only hope of the whole world.

GOD HAS SOME SALT IN EVERY CORRUPT CHURCH. Vs. 50-56.

50 And, behold, *there was* a man named Joseph, a counsellor; *and he was* a good man, and a just:

51 (The same had not consented to the counsel and deed of

them;) *he was* of Arimathæa, a city of the Jews: who also himself waited for the kingdom of God.

52 This *man* went unto Pilate, and begged the body of Jesus.

53 And he took it down, and wrapped it in linen, and laid it in a sepulchre that was hewn in stone, wherein never man before was laid.

54 And that day was the preparation, and the sabbath drew on.

55 And the women also, which came with him from Galilee, followed after, and beheld the sepulchre, and how his body was laid.

56 And they returned, and prepared spices and ointments; and rested the sabbath day according to the commandment.

God would not allow the precious body of Jesus to be buried with paupers in the potter's field. That body was forever hallowed by having been the temple of divinity. And now resurrected and glorified it is in heaven. So he had raised up a man of wealth to care for this precious temple of his body.

So when even was come, Joseph of Arimathea, a wealthy man, and one of the council, who was secretly a disciple of Jesus, came to Pilate, with Nicodemus and begged the body and laid it in a new tomb, having wrapped it in the most costly linen. When Jesus was born, wise men from the East came bringing costly presents, which enabled his parents, Joseph and Mary, to bear the expense of living in Egypt to which they were obliged to flee. So now God raises up another Joseph to give him an appropriate burial. God is looking after human affairs. He makes the wealth of the world contribute to his cause.

Likewise there were women who came and watched the burial. They were Mary Magdalene and the other Mary. (Mark 15:47.)

CHAPTER XXIV.

HOLINESS IS THE RESURRECTION LIFE.

Holiness Typified in the Resurrection of Jesus. Vs. 1-12. Much Knowledge of Scripture Does Not Always Mean Much Spiritual Light. Vs. 13-35. True Testimony to the Resurrection Is Helped by the Presence of Jesus. Vs. 36-44. There May Be Much Insight into Scripture Given by Jesus, before Pentecost. Vs. 45-48. The attitude of the Believer— Tarrying for the Gift of the Holy Ghost. Vs. 49. Jesus Worshipped before Pentecost. Vs. 50-53.

HOLINESS TYPIFIED IN THE RESURRECTION OF JESUS.
Vs. 1-12.

1 Now upon the first *day* of the week, very early in the morning, they came unto the sepulchre, bringing the spices which they had prepared, and certain *others* with them.

2 And they found the stone rolled away from the sepulchre.

3 And they entered in, and found not the body of the Lord Jesus.

4 And it came to pass, as they were much perplexed thereabout, behold, two men stood by them in shining garments:

5 And as they were afraid, and bowed down *their* faces to the earth, they said unto them, Why seek ye the living among the dead?

6 He is not here, but is risen: remember how he spake unto you when he was yet in Galilee,

7 Saying, The Son of man must be delivered into the hands of sinful men, and be crucified, and the third day rise again.

8 And they remembered his words,

9 And returned from the sepulchre, and told all these things unto the eleven, and to all the rest.

10 It was Mary Magdalene, and Joanna, and Mary *the mother* of James, and other *women that were* with them, which told these things unto the apostles.

11 And their words seemed to them as idle tales, and they believed them not.

12 Then arose Peter, and ran unto the sepulchre; and stooping down, he beheld the linen clothes laid by themselves, and departed, wondering in himself at that which was come to pass.

Just as the resurrection is the chief miracle of Christianity and the keystone of the arch, so is holiness the central doctrine of Christianity and is typified by the resurrection of Jesus. This is the type that Paul uses. He speaks of being crucified with Christ and also of having risen with him (Coll. 3:1), to live an entirely new life—the life of holiness. The old man crucified and dead, then the new life of holiness begins. We are now to be as free from sin as Jesus was from his former life before his crucifixion.

On the first day of the week, having lain in the grave three days, Jesus arose from the dead. He left the company of the dead to dwell among the living. If we die with him to sin (die to sin as he died for it) we shall live with him having our fruit unto holiness (Rom. 6:6-10). By rising on the first day of the week, he forever hallowed that day. Henceforth it was known as the Lord's Day. On this day, therefore, instead of Saturday, henceforth the church of the Pentecost met to worship him. The Resurrection of Jesus was the great fact around which the faith of the early church rallied. Belief in it became one of the great tests of discipleship. (Rom. 10:9.) It being the great fact, the day on which it occurred became the great day of Christianity. It was more henceforth than the celebration of the rest of God the Creator. It also celebrated the vindication and triumph of God the Saviour, in his work of saving men, which is greater than the work of creation. So the apostles and the early church, who got their religion from the apostles, observed the first instead of the seventh day.

"On Sunday he chose to rise from the dead, because on this day began the creation of the world, with the calling into being the creation of light; the light, which was the life of the created world, was to have *one* birthday, with the light which was the life of the restored world. Sunday was the day of Christ's resurrection, is the *Lord's Day* (Rev. 1:11); this day has been set apart by the church, gathered through the preaching of the resurrection, as the day of their services of divine worship." (Besser.)

The love of the women, Mary Magdelene, Mary the mother of

James and Joses (Matt. 27:56), Salome, mother of James and John, and Joanna, wife of Chuza (Chapter 8:3) came to complete the partial anointing made by Nicodemus (John 19:39, 40), having purchased spices for that purpose. (Mark 16:1.) No task is too great or hardship too severe for love. Love comes early and stays late.

They found the stone rolled away. Matthew and Mark tell us that there was a great earthquake and that the angel of the Lord had descended from heaven and rolled away the stone that closed the mouth of the tomb. This took place before the women arrived. They had been saying, ''Who shall roll us away the stone?'' (Mark 16:3.) They find on their arrival that the great obstacle of getting to Jesus was gone. To seekers of Christ there are apparently obstacles but if the seeker is in earnest the obstacles will vanish.

Matthew tells us they went into the tomb by invitation of the angel, but the body was gone, which gave them great perplexity. Had they remembered his words concerning the resurrection they would have been spared a good deal of anxiety. Many Christians are full of anxiety, often for the same reason—they forget and fail to believe the words of Jesus.

Two men in shining garments stood before them. From John's account these were evidently angels. These angels asked them why they sought the living Christ among the dead of the tomb. We may well ask ourselves the same question, when our friends die. Why should we look upon them as inhabitants of the cemetery? They are not with the dead, but among the living.

''He is not here.'' O blessed comforting words, to his churches in all ages. The grave could not hold him. He has arisen and thus stamped the Christian system with divinity. He is not in the grave, hence immortality is proved. He is not in the tomb and therefore those who sleep in him shall also be delivered from the grave. Hallelujah!

The angels bid them remember how Jesus had spoken to them (these same women) of his resurrection while in Galilee. (Luke 8:3.) Then they remembered that Jesus had spoken of his resurrection.

The women then returned from the sepulchre and went and

told the eleven disciples of the great fact of his resurrection. Thus women became the first heralds or preachers of the resurrection. If she was fit to tell the story then, why not now; who shall forbid woman preaching the Gospel?

The disciples would not believe these humble women. Their words seemed as idle tales. There are people today who will not accept the humble testimony of God's little ones, as they testify of the resurrection power of Holy Spirit, as manifest in the hearts of believers. It is just as difficult to make some who claim to believe in Jesus believe in his complete saving power, as it was to convince these disciples. Inbred sin in disciples hinders faith and these disciples still had inbred sin in them. "Even when a measure of grace is found, how unbelieving are men on some occasions! Not only in those things that are contrary to their prejudices, but in those also that are above their experience or expectation: these however surely attested, seem to be idle tales and they believe them not! Yet a diligent inquiry will gradually led to a more clear perception of spiritual things." (Scott.)

Peter, foremost to act, immediately started on a run for the sepulchre and saw the linen clothes lying there, and then *departed to his house.* (Revised Version.)

MUCH KNOWLEDGE OF SCRIPTURE DOES NOT ALWAYS MEAN MUCH SPIRITUAL LIGHT. Vs. 13-35.

13 And, behold, two of them went that same day to a village called Emmaus, which was from Jerusalem *about* threescore furlongs.

14 And they talked together of all these things which had happened.

15 And it came to pass, that, while they communed *together* and reasoned, Jesus himself drew near, and went with them.

16 But their eyes were holden that they should not know him.

17 And he said unto them, What manner of communications *are* these that ye have one to another, as ye walk, and are sad?

18 And the one of them, whose name was Cleopas, answering said unto him, Art thou only a stranger in Jerusalem, and hast not known the things which are come to pass there in these days?

19 And he said unto them, What things? And they said unto him, Concerning Jesus of Nazareth, which was a prophet mighty in deed and word before God and all the people:

20 And how the chief priests and our rulers delivered him to be condemned to death, and have crucified him.

21 But we trusted that it had been he which should have redeemed Israel ; and beside all this, to day is the third day since these
things were done.

22 Yea, and certain women also of our company made us astonished, which were early at the sepulchre ;

23 And when they found not his body, they came, saying, that
they had also seen a vision of angels, which said that he was alive.

24 And certain of them which were with us went to the sepulchre, and found it even so as the women had said : but him they saw
not.

25 Then he said unto them, O fools, and slow of heart to believe
all that the prophets have spoken :

26 Ought not Christ to have suffered these things, and to enter
into his glory ?

27 And beginning at Moses and all the prophets, he expounded
unto them in all the scriptures the things concerning himself.

28 And they drew nigh unto the village, whither they went : and
he made as though he would have gone further.

29 But they constrained him, saying, Abide with us : for it is
toward evening, and the day is far spent. And he went in to tarry
with them.

30 And it came to pass, as he sat at meat with them, he took
bread, and blessed it, and brake, and gave to them.

31 And their eyes were opened, and they knew him ; and he
vanished out of their sight.

32 And they said one to another, Did not our heart burn within
us, while he talked with us by the way, and while he opened to us the
scriptures?

33 And they rose up the same hour, and returned to Jerusalem,
and found the eleven gathered together, and them that were with
them,

34 Saying, The Lord is risen indeed, and hath appeared to Simon.

35 And they told what things were done in the way, and how he
was known of them in breaking of bread.

The Jews knew the Old Testament very well, as far as the outward letter was concerned. But here were two, like many professed Christians of today, who failed to see the spiritual things
of the Bible.

The same day two of the disciples of Jesus were walking on
the road to Emmaus, a village seven and a half miles from Jerusalem. It was a walk of about two hours. The name of one of
them was Cleopas (Vs. 18). This was doubtless Alpheus—one
of the twelve. The two words mean the same in the Hebrew.
The other is supposed to be St. Luke.

They were talking of the things that had happened that day—the astonishing reports concerning the resurrection of Jesus. They were doubtless reasoning as to the probability of the resurrection of Jesus.

Luke says ''their eyes were holden.'' Mark says he ''appeared to them in another form.'' The latter statement is true because their ''eyes were holden.'' These men were not hypocrites. Their downcast looks showed their deep sorrow. A soul that has once been acquainted with Jesus, and has lost that fellowship is sorrowful.

Jesus drew them out by skillful questionings to tell what was in their hearts. He knew, but he wanted to make them tell it. They replied to his questioning, ''Art thou only a stranger?'' As much as to say that no one could live in Jerusalem during the previous few days and not know what the great sensation of the hour was—the crucifixion, the earthquake and the veiling of the sun.

Another question, What things made them tell the thoughts of their hearts, he did not need to know, but he wanted them to state their own case and see the discouragement in their own hearts. This is one of the blessings of prayer as we tell Jesus our troubles today. It reveals our inner self to us, and thus prayer becomes a heart searching as well as helping to a direct blessing. This passage shows the need of the Holy Spirit, the other Comforter that Jesus had promised. Bereft of the presence of Jesus and without the Holy Spirit discouragement had come to them and will come upon the church. This passage teaches us how necessary the resurrection was to establish the doctrine of the deity of Jesus in the minds of his own disciples. They only looked upon him at this time as a man, for they said he was ''a prophet mighty in deed and word.'' (Vs. 19.)

They had hoped he was the Messiah and their hopes had been blasted. We see therefore how necessary the proof of his resurrection was to their establishment in the faith.

Jesus was the only one before the crucifixion that believed in his resurrection. Although he had told it to his disciples many times they did not believe it. How wonderful were his confident predictions of his rising from the dead. ''He was never disappointed, from the first to the last moment of his course. Without a single complete example of success while he lived, amid constant discouragement and apparent discomfiture, he calmly believed in the omnipotence of spiritual truth and in the divinity of his own mission.'' (Young.)

He calls them ''fools.'' This is an unfortunate translation. It should be ''Inconsiderate ones.''

''Slow of heart to believe.'' This is a very important passage, as it locates saving faith in the heart, instead of the head. The unsanctified disciple is slow to believe the deep things of God because of indwelling sin. It is very hard to get preconceived religious nations out of people's minds. They had their preconceived notions of how the Messiah should come and hence the crucifixion was a stumbling block to them. Slowness of heart caused by indwelling sin is a fruitful source of prejudice.

He then opened the Scriptures to them as they had never seen them before, and showed them that the very things they stumbled over, as regards the sufferings and death of Jesus, were the proofs of his Messiahship. Instead of stumbling over them, they ought to be encouraged by them.

So he began at Moses. The first five books of the Old Testament were written by Moses. The author of the Scriptures himself sets us the example of using them to carry conviction. He gives us authority for believing in the inspiration of the Pentateuch or first five books of Moses, for that was what was meant by ''Moses'' in that day. He also endorses all the books of the prophets of the Old Testament as well as all the rest of the Old Testament. Doubtless he began with the first promise uttered in Eden, that the seed of the woman should bruise the serpent's head, and showed that all the types and sacrifices, and all the prophecies revealed himself.

Let no man say because he can not see holiness in the Bible, therefore it is not there. The Jews as a rule knew Scripture better than we, but they did not see Jesus at all, in it. We have to be in harmony with the author of the Scriptures to rightly understand it. Jesus said the Holy Spirit should take the things of Christ and show them unto us. Verbal knowledge of the Bible amounts to but little without the aid of the Spirit.

Hanna says, "To accompany two such humble men, and spend so much of one of his Sabbaths in instructing them out of the Scriptures, the divine Redeemer, thought not a task too lowly. By devoting so much of that first Christian Sabbath to it, has he not left behind him a pattern of what all true and faithful exposition of the Scriptures ought to be, even the unfolding of the things touching a once crucified, but now exalted Saviour; and has he not dignified, by himself engaging in it, the work of one man's trying, at any time and in any way, to lead another to the knowledge of the truth as it is in Jesus?"

When they came to Emmaus he was going right on in his journey if they had not entreated him to stay. He was not intending to deceive them. He would have gone straight on. He will not stay either then or now where he is not wanted. They liked the light he had given them so well that they wanted more. Godet says, "Every gift of god is an invitation to claim a greater. Grace for grace. (John 1:16.) But most men stop very quickly in this way, and thus they never reach the full blessing."

They constrained him "to stay and lodge with them." If we have had intercourse with Jesus and like his company, he will, on invitation consent to abide with us. When we see those who profess to have found him and to have tasted of his love, and yet do not desire a more intimate acquaintance with him, we suspect they never really got acquainted with him at the start. It was only a profession. Those who know him want to know him better. He promises to take up his abode with certain people. (John 14:23.) The celebrated hymn, "Abide with me, fast falls the eventide," seems to be based on this scene.

As they sat at the table he took bread and thus acted as Master of the feast. He will come in and sup with us if we will let him. (Rev. 3:20.)

He blessed the bread. It was not a Sacrament, nor the Lord's Supper. The use of this passage to substantiate the false claim of the Roman Catholic church that only the bread is to be given to the laity, in the Lord's Supper, shows how hard up they are for proof texts.

As he broke the bread, their eyes "were opened." That is, they recognized him. He led them gently on until he could reveal himself to them. See how he adapted himself gradually to their understanding. He first enlightened them, then warmed their hearts, then he appeared to them.

Then he vanished from their sight. This shows that his body now had new qualities, since he had arisen. It shows that the resurrection body is different from the natural body; now it was known to them only when he revealed himself. The first thing they spoke of when he vanished was their experience. They said, ''Did not our hearts burn within us as he talked with us?'' He had been showing them his life as taught in the Scriptures. It is a common experience today whenever the friends of Jesus hear the record of their Master's life, death and work, to feel the heart burn. Give us more of the preaching of Christ. No other thing can so rejoice the heart. Jesus is present when the Scripture is opened. If the world understood this, they would cease to wonder why we go to hear the Gospel. Blessed is the man who has this kind of heartburn!

This revelation was too great for them to keep still about it. They started off that very night to tell the news to the oher disciples. They did not propose to ''live it and say nothing about it.'' Acquaintance with Jesus is too big a secret to keep. One of the proofs that we have met Christ is an eagerness to tell it.

TRUE TESTIMONY TO THE RESURRECTION IS HELPED BY THE PRESENCE OF JESUS. Vs. 36-44.

36 And as they thus spake, Jesus himself stood in the midst of them, and saith unto them, Peace *be* unto you.

37 But they were terrified and affrighted, and supposed that they had seen a spirit.

38 And he said unto them, Why are ye troubled? and why do thoughts arise in your hearts?

39 Behold my hands and my feet, that it is I myself: handle me, and see; for a spirit hath not flesh and bones, as ye see me have.

40 And when he had thus spoken, he shewed them *his* hands and *his* feet.

41 And while they yet believed not for joy, and wondered, he said unto them, Have ye here any meat?

42 And they gave him a piece of a broiled fish, and of an honeycomb.

43 And he took *it* and did eat before them.

44 And he said unto them, These *are* the words which I **spake** unto you, while I was yet with you, that all things must be fulfilled, which were written in the law of Moses, and *in* the prophets, and *in* the psalms, concerning me.

As the two began to tell the story of their meeting with Jesus he appeared to confirm their testimony. His appearance frightened them. They were afraid of their best friend and thought they had seen a ghost. He asked them why they were troubled. The Lord deigns to reason with his disciples in order to dispel their fears. If we are true in testimony, of what we know of Jesus, he will help our testimony among the unbelieving.

Jesus now gives the unbelieving disciples evidence of his identity by showing the scars of the nails in his hands and feet and of the spear in his side. He had the scars even in his resurrected body. He thus qualified them to be witnesses to the fact of his resurrection in their future preaching. He tells them that a spirit hath not flesh and bones. Thus he teaches that there are two natures in man—the spirit and the body.

There are some things in this world almost too good to be true. So we sometimes think. The disciples could not for a while believe for joy. It is so in the matter of full salvation from sin. Some think it too good to be true. But it is just like God, to give his children good things.

So he took food and ate it to show that he was in the body and not a spirit only. According to this the resurrection body may be fed. Their slowness of belief is one of the evidences that relieved the account of suspicion of fraud.

He then endorses the Old Testament (Vs. 44) which so many modern critics censure. We prefer the opinion of Jesus to all the adverse scholars of the world.

THRE MAY BE MUCH INSIGHT INTO THE SCRIPTURES BEFORE PENTECOST. Vs. 45-48.

45 Then opened he their understanding, that they might understand the scriptures,

46 And said unto them, Thus it is written, and thus it behoved Christ to suffer, and to rise from the dead the third day:

47 And that repentance and remission of sins should be preached in his name among all nations, beginning at Jerusalem.
48 And ye are witnesses of these things.

Jesus had opened the understanding of the two, on the way to Emmaus, and now he opens the understanding of the whole of the eleven, that they might understand the Scriptures. So we see that they had spiritual enlightenment before they had their Pentecost. Let no one say that these men were unsaved who were enlightened in the Scriptures as none of the unsaved world about them knew or could know. He shows them from the Old Testament that it was necessary that Christ should suffer and be raised from the dead. Modern Jews can not see it even now, because the veil is over their hearts. (2 Cor. 3:15.) But these disciples had had the veil removed. Their understandings were opened. It shows the great fact that divine power has immediate access to the human heart. Let us all pray that He open our understanding also that we may have a clean insight into the Scriptures. Without it the Bible is a sealed book and all our understanding of its morals, history, literature and geography avails nothing.

He says, too, that repentance and remission of sins follow (as the logical result of preaching the crucifixion and resurrection). Vs. 47.) As sure as he died, there is no virtue in his atonement unless we turn away from our sins by repentance. And if we truly repent, remission (forgiveness and sanctification) of sins will follow. But there is no forgiveness unless we do heartily repent. Adam Clarke thus defines the term *remission*, ''Everything that relates to the destruction of the power, the pardoning of the guilt, and the purification of the heart from the very nature of sin.''

This glorious gospel of repentance and remission was to be preached to all nations beginning at Jerusalem. And so it was. The guilty men who were the murderers of Jesus were to be given the first opportunity of salvation. Amazing grace and mercy!

They were to go forth not as orators, statesmen, philosophers or scholars, but as witnesses of the fact that he rose from the dead and can open the understanding; that he forgives sins and cleanses the heart from all unrighteousness. And that is the sole business as the successors of the apostles—to witness to the same.

THE ATTITUDE OF THE BELIEVER TARRYING FOR THE GIFT OF THE HOLY GHOST. Vs. 49.

49 And, behold, I send the promise of my Father upon you: but tarry ye in the city of Jerusalem, until ye be endued with power from on high.

What was ''the promise of the Father?'' Why was it so called? It was the gift of the Holy Spirit in his cleansing power, as he came into their hearts to abide. The Old Dispensation was preeminently the dispensation of the Father—the first person of the Trinity. In that dispensation God the Father was promising this gift. He says, ''I will pour water upon him that is thirsty and floods upon the dry ground: . . . I will pour my spirit upon thine offspring.'' (Isa. 44:3.) Through the prophet Joel, God had also said, ''I will pour out my spirit upon all flesh,'' and again, ''And also upon my servants and upon the handmaidens in those days will pour out my spirit.'' (Joel 2:28-29.) Luke the writer also wrote the Acts of the Apostles and in Acts 1:4 he adds the phrase ''Which ye have heard of me.'' That is, Jesus had been telling them of the promise of the Father while he was with them before his crucifixion. He had told them of the gift of the Holy Spirit. We do not know how often he had told them. We suppose all such instances are not recorded. But we have several definite instances. In Luke 11:13 he had told them, ''If ye being evil know how to give good gifts unto your children, how much more shall your Heavenly Father give the Holy Spirit to them that ask Him.'' He had said on the last day of the feast, ''If any man thirst let him come unto me and drink. He that believeth on me, as the Scripture hath said, out of his belly shall flow rivers of living water.'' The Apostle John writing of this, years afterwards thus comments, ''But this spake he of the Spirit, which they that believe on him should receive: for the Holy Ghost was not yet given.'' On the night of his betrayal his last words were as to what the Holy Spirit would be to them—the Comforter and Guide. (John 13th to 16th chapters.) And now he had been crucified and had arisen from the tomb and yet, the promise of the Father had not been fulfilled. When that Spirit should come, they would be entirely sanctified and thus empowered for their life work, Adam Clarke says, ''The energy of the Holy Ghost was to be communicated to them for three particular purposes. 1. That he might be in them a sanctifying Comforter. 2. That their preaching might be accompanied by his demonstration and power to the hearts of the hearers. 3. That they might be able to work miracles to confirm their pretensions to a divine mission.'' So when the Spirit came on the day of Pentecost, Peter said, ''This is that which was spoken by the prophet' Joel.'' In other words, this was the promise of the Father, given in the Old Dispensation and now fulfilled. (See also Acts 2:33.)

Their only business now was to tarry until the gift was received. And that is our business. We have no other business on earth until we have received the same promised gift, for God says we may have it (Acts 2:39.) How did they tarry? Not in sloth, or indifference, or affiliation with the world, but they went to public worship in the temple (Luke 24:53) and spent the remaining time for ten days in prayer (Acts 1:13) in an upper room. We must continue in definite prayer for the blessing and he has told us (Luke 11:9) in regard to this very matter that if we ask we shall receive. Have you yet made ''tarrying'' a business? It might seem time wasted with such a commission before them to go into all the world, but it would be time wasted if they had not tarried. And so is it with us. It is time wasted to go to the work of God until we are endued with Holy Ghost power. He calls it here ''being endued (clothed) with power from on high.'' It comes from on high. When this power came Peter said (Acts 2:33) that Jesus shed forth this power after he went to heaven. (Acts 2:33.)

JESUS WORSHIPPED BEFORE PENTECOST.   Vs. 50-53.

50 And he led them out as far as to Bethany, and he lifted up his hands, and blessed them.

51 And it came to pass, while he blessed them, he was parted from them, and carried up into heaven.

52 And they worshipped him, and returned to Jerusalem with great joy:

53 And were continually in the temple, praising and blessing God. A-men.

So he led the disciples out, away from Jerusalem to Bethany, which was near by, for his farewell. His last act was to lift up his hands and bless them. He vanished from their sight in the act and posture of blessing them. We love to think of him as, last seen, blessing his disciples, and love to think that he is still keeping it up. He is still desirous to bless all who will be his true disciples. The dispensation of the Father ended in a curse (Malachi 4:6) because of a broken law. The dispensation of the Son ends in a blessing. What unutterable love and wealth of affection must have been in that last look of Jesus!

He went away. It was better he said for them and us too. And he is coming again in the same manner as he went. As he was blessing them, the laws of gravitation were reversed. The influence of earth no longer pulled him to itself, but the influence of heaven did. If we die before he comes, the same celestial influence will draw our spirits to himself and heaven. If we are alive when he comes soul and body will be carried up. Paul said ''to depart'' was to be with Christ. Godet says, ''The assimilation of the faithful to his Son, God accomplished by means of two things, which are the necessary complement of the gospel history: Pentecost whereby the Lord's moral being becomes that of the believer; and the Parousia (personal advent of our Lord), whereby the external condition of the sanctified believer is raised to the same elevation as that of our glorified Lord. First, holiness, then glory for the body, as for the head: the baptism of Jesus which becomes ours by Pentecost; the ascension of Jesus which becomes ours by the Parousia.'' Thank God we have not a dead Christ. He ever liveth, Mark says, he went to heaven and ''sat on the right hand of God.'' He is there now interceding for a lost world, and he wants us to join him in praying it home to God.

''They worshipped him.'' These men could not have been sinners, thus to worship Jesus. But they were continually in the temple, worshipping him. Of course they were in the temple only during the hours of prayer. This was their custom. (See Acts 3:1.) How unscriptural and ridiculous the notion that such worshippers and friends of Jesus were unsaved and unregenerate at this time.

They worshipped him. Our Unitarian friends think it idolatry to worship Jesus. Then these disciples were idolaters. How ridiculous the thought!

Then they returned to Jerusalem with great joy. What! Great joy when Jesus their best friend had left them? Yes because he had blessed them. The real blessing had entered their souls. He who has Jesus bless him has great joy. He who has not this joy is unblessed by Jesus. Did Jesus bless a lot of sinners and as the result give them great joy? By no means. They were not sinners. Let those who say it blush for shame. Jesus never blesses sinners with great joy. They joyed in the present blessing and at the thought of his coming again. Do we for the same reason rejoice?

So they were in the temple continually praying, waiting for the Holy Ghost. Scott says, "They abode together at Jerusalem waiting and praying for the Spirit of Power, truth and holiness." Let us remember that as the Old Testament pointed to, and prepared for, and culminated in the preparation for the coming of Jesus, so the four gospels point to and culminate in the coming of the Holy Ghost, in whose dispensation we now live. And God forbid that we should live in the dispensation and not have Him, the blessed Spirit, in his fullness in our herts. *Amen.*